UNLIKELY COLLABORATION

GENDER AND CULTURE SERIES

GENDER AND CULTURE

A SERIES OF COLUMBIA UNIVERSITY PRESS

Nancy K. Miller and Victoria Rosner, Series Editors

Carolyn G. Heilbrun (1926–2003) and
  Nancy K. Miller, Founding Editors

UNLIKELY COLLABORATION

GERTRUDE STEIN,

BERNARD FAŸ, AND

THE VICHY DILEMMA

BARBARA WILL

Columbia University Press ■ *New York*

COLUMBIA UNIVERSITY PRESS

Publishers Since 1893

New York   Chichester, West Sussex

Copyright © 2011 Columbia University Press

All rights reserved

Library of Congress Cataloging-in-Publication Data

Will, Barbara

Unlikely collaboration : Gertrude Stein, Bernard Faÿ, and
    the Vichy dilemma / Barbara Will.

    p. cm. — (Gender and culture)

Includes bibliographical references and index.

ISBN 978-0-231-15262-4 (cloth : acid-free paper) —

ISBN 978-0-231-52641-8 (e-book)

1. Stein, Gertrude, 1874–1946—Friends and associates. 2. Faÿ,
    Bernard, 1893-— Friends and associates. 3. Politics and
    literature—France—History—20th century. 4. France—
    Intellectual life—20th century. I. Title. II. Series.

PS3537.T323Z927   2011

818'.5209—dc22

[B]   2011013191

Columbia University Press books are printed on permanent
    and durable acid-free paper.

This book is printed on paper with recycled content.

Printed in the United States of America

Designed by Lisa Hamm

c 10 9 8 7 6 5 4 3 2

FOR MICHAEL

Verweile doch

CONTENTS

ABBREVIATIONS

ABT Gertrude Stein, *The Autobiography of Alice B. Toklas* (New York: Harcourt, Brace, and Co., 1933)

AE Bernard Faÿ, with Avery Claflin, *The American Experiment* (New York: Harcourt, Brace, and Co., 1929)

BN Bibliothèque Nationale

BW Gertrude Stein, *Brewsie and Willie*, in *Gertrude Stein: Writings 1932–1946* (New York: The Library of America, 1998)

CDJC Centre de Documentation Juive Contemporaine

D D'I *Dossier d'instruction for Bernard Faÿ*, in the Cour de justice du département de la Seine, Paris Archives Nationales, AN Z/6/288-292

EA Gertrude Stein, *Everybody's Autobiography* (New York: Vintage, 1973)

FAF Bernard Faÿ, "The Course of French-American Friendship," *The Yale Review* 18 (Spring 1929)

FIA Gertrude Stein, *Four in America* (New Haven, Conn.: Yale University Press, 1947)

FVJ Bernard Faÿ, *Faites vos jeux* (Paris: Grasset, 1927)

GHA Gertrude Stein, *The Geographical History of America or the Relation of Human Nature to the Human Mind* (Baltimore, Md.: The Johns Hopkins University Press, 1995)

GTF Bernard Faÿ, *La guerre des trois fous: Hitler-Staline-Roosevelt* (Paris: Perrin, 1968)

GW Bernard Faÿ, *George Washington: Republican Aristocrat* (Boston: Houghton Mifflin, 1931)

H   Bernard Faÿ, "Harvard 1920," *The Harvard Graduate's Magazine* 28 (June 1920)

JGR   Lucien Sabah, *Journal de Gueydan "de" Roussel* (Paris: Klincksieck, 2000)

JP   Bernard Faÿ, "La joie et les plaisirs aux Etats-Unis," *Revue de Paris* (July 1, 1925)

LP   Bernard Faÿ, *Les précieux* (Paris: Perrin, 1966)

MOA   Gertrude Stein, *The Making of Americans: Being a History of a Family's Progress* (Normal, Ill.: Dalkey Archive Press, 1995)

MR   Gertrude Stein, *Mrs. Reynolds* (Los Angeles: Sun & Moon Press, 1995)

PF   Gertrude Stein, *Paris France* (New York: Liveright, 1970)

PSS   Transcript of Faÿ's trial: "Le Procès Sociétés Secrètes," Paris Archives Nationales, AN 334/AP/22

RF   Bernard Faÿ, *Revolution and Freemasonry, 1680–1800* (Boston: Little, Brown and Co., 1935)

RSFA   Bernard Faÿ, *The Revolutionary Spirit in France and America* (New York: Harcourt, Brace and Co., 1927)

W   Gertrude Stein, *Wars I Have Seen* (London: Batsford, 1945)

WL   Gertrude Stein, "The Winner Loses: A Picture of Occupied France," in *How Writing Is Written: Volume II of The Previously Uncollected Writings of Gertrude Stein*, ed. Robert Bartlett Haas (Los Angeles: Black Sparrow Press, 1974)

ILLUSTRATIONS

PREFACE

T HE GENESIS of this book lies in a few yellowing manuscript notebooks tucked away in the Beinecke Rare Book and Manuscript Library at Yale University. Their pages are filled with Gertrude Stein's slanted, notoriously bad handwriting and with manifold corrections in the tiny, precise script of Alice Toklas. Deciphering the writing is hard enough: no one who has ever read a Stein manuscript has found it an enjoyable task. But reading these notebooks is nothing compared with trying to comprehend them. For what they contain are 180 translated pages of the speeches of Philippe Pétain, the head of the Nazi-occupied Vichy regime in France during World War II. They are evidence of a propaganda project in support of Vichy France that Stein began in 1941, one she hoped somehow to sell to a skeptical American public.

What was Gertrude Stein doing translating the speeches of Pétain into English? The unlikelihood of this project was clear to me from the start. Stein, a Jewish American experimental writer and famous patron of modernist art, seemed the least likely person to write propaganda in support of an authoritarian regime. The considerable reputation she currently enjoys as an intellectual and artistic iconoclast was almost impossible to reconcile with the image of Stein as a Vichy-regime propagandist. This project began, then, with a central mystery. And the mystery only deepened when, following the lead of others, I found myself looking more closely at Stein's friendship with the man who may have drawn her into the orbit of Vichy, a Frenchman named Bernard Faÿ. Described by Alice Toklas as Stein's "dearest friend during her life," Faÿ was a striking figure. A writer, translator, historian, and art patron, Faÿ was also the

1926 - 46

first professor of American studies in France as well as the youngest person ever elected to the elite Collège de France. He would also become one of the central figures in Pétain's Vichy regime, a role that would eventually land him in prison. If Gertrude Stein was an unlikely propagandist for this regime, so, it appears, was the scholar and aesthete Bernard Faÿ.

Yet as I researched their friendship, I became increasingly aware of shared affinities and trajectories. I began to understand not only why these two individuals would have been drawn toward supporting the Vichy regime but also how their relationship with one another over the course of many years nurtured and refined their political beliefs. The story behind Gertrude Stein's translation of Pétain's speeches, I realized, could only be told through her relationship with Bernard Faÿ.

This book centers on the years that Stein and Faÿ led intersecting lives: from 1926, when the two first met, to 1946, the year Stein died and Faÿ was sentenced to life in prison for collaboration with the Nazis. It also touches on the postwar fate of Bernard Faÿ, after his dramatic escape from prison in 1951. The historical focus is therefore on the troublesome interwar era, a period that, in the case of the better-known Gertrude Stein, has received less critical attention than her early life. This is also a period that alters our understanding of Stein's early years. For if before World War I Stein fits easily into the narrative of modernist writer and innovator—a narrative that she herself, as we will see, helped to shape—Stein's life and writing during the 1920s, 1930s, and 1940s is less artistically unified and certainly more politically problematic. Coming to terms with the difficulties and complexities of Stein's later years allows for a perspective on this writer and her period that has remained, up to now, largely unseen. Viewing these years through the prism of her friendship with Bernard Faÿ throws into relief the centrality of their friendship to the difficult and complex choices she made.

Although Stein is the better-known figure in this story, Bernard Faÿ is far from a secondary character. Now largely erased from history, Faÿ in his time was considered the unofficial ambassador of France to the New World. He hobnobbed with everybody who was anybody, from avant-garde artists to diplomats to American and French heads of state. Both ambitious and talented, Faÿ had a stunning career in front of him when he came up against the moment of Vichy. Six years later, he would be condemned to national degradation by a French criminal court. In a life marked by idealism, commitment, and hope as well as by narrow-mindedness, fear, and often deadly compromise, Bernard Faÿ is as complex and interesting a figure as Gertrude Stein.

This book contributes to an emerging body of work that attempts to resituate Bernard Faÿ in twentieth-century American and French history.

While the book concentrates on Stein and Faÿ's relationship, it also sees these figures as case studies for larger concerns: about the course of transatlantic politics during the twenties and thirties; about the place of America in the Vichy imagination; about the historical imagination behind the critique of "modernity"; and, crucially, about the intersection of modernism and fascism. The recent controversies surrounding the wartime writings of Paul de Man, Martin Heidegger, Ezra Pound, and Louis-Ferdinand Céline, among others, have forced us to rethink the intersection between modernist writers and intellectuals and fascist ideology, tracing the possible trajectories and openings that enable fascist or profascist "ideals" to exist on a continuum with early twentieth-century aesthetic and intellectual modernism. But so far no scholar has truly mined the archives to raise similar questions about the Stein-Faÿ collaboration and the texts it produced. What I discovered constitutes the body of this work.

In the process of researching and writing the book, I also came to realize that raising such questions means taking great care with what I call the "gray zone" of life in France during World War II. Collaboration is a serious charge, but it belongs to a black-and-white world. It is a term that tends to obscure subtle differences in the ways that people in France interacted with their Nazi occupiers—from conditional cooperation to *attentiste* accommodation to enthusiastic commitment to outright resistance. This book attempts to keep alive the seriousness of the charge of collaboration while acknowledging the shadings around this charge. While I argue that both individuals are "unlikely collaborators" in different ways, they were also "unlike" one another in the degree and ultimate outcome of their support for the Vichy regime. Determining the level of commitment as well as differences of thought and action between these two individuals caught in the mazelike situation of wartime France is one of my central concerns. While Stein's belief in Vichy and Pétain was both real and heartfelt, and while she used her considerable reputation to try to publicize this belief, Bernard Faÿ was for most of the war an active, enthusiastic, and engaged collaborator at the heart of the Vichy regime. His wartime writings and actions directly oppressed his fellow Frenchmen. His own passage from respected historian and literate patron of the arts to Vichy ideologue was itself unlikely enough, but compared to Stein, Faÿ was a very different kind of animal. And Faÿ's fall from the heights of personal success to national degradation was something that Gertrude Stein would never live to experience. While both Stein and Faÿ responded to the dilemma of Vichy—its promises and perils—in compromising ways, only Bernard Faÿ felt the long-term effects of his wartime actions. If there is any tragic figure in this story, it is surely he.

ACKNOWLEDGMENTS

THIS BOOK has benefitted from the vast generosity and support of many institutions, foundations, and individuals. I am grateful above all to Dartmouth College for providing me with the time and resources to pursue this project, and to my colleagues in the English, History, and French departments for their knowledge, interest, and encouragement. External financial support from the National Endowment for the Humanities and the American Philosophical Society allowed for generous research leave. A Frederick Burkhardt fellowship from the American Council of Learned Societies gave time and funding at the crucial moment following my tenure appointment. Residential fellowships at the National Humanities Center in North Carolina and at the Camargo Foundation in Cassis, France, allowed me to begin and end this book in beautiful and stimulating environments, surrounded by accomplished and supportive colleagues.

I am also grateful for the generosity of many individuals over the course of this project. Alice Kaplan, Michael Moon, and Maria DiBattista went beyond professional duty in supporting this book from beginning to end and in providing me with models of innovative and ethical scholarly inquiry. My debt to the three of you is enormous. Other individuals who contributed time, interest, references, and support for this project include Diane Afoumado, Karren Alenier, Mark Antliff, Jeremy Bigwood, Colleen Boggs, Niall Bond, Edward Burns, Carmen Callil, Michael Carpenter, Jane Carroll, Kate Conley, Jonathan Crewe, Robert Dundas, Tami Fay, Gretchen Holbrook Gerzina, Charles Glackin, John Harvey, Amy Hollywood, Marie-Geneviève Iselin, Daniel Laskin, Anne-

Marie Levine, Klaus Milich, Robert Nutt, Alex Erik Pfingsttag, Francis Python, Charles Robertson, Werner Sollors, Orin Starn, Andrea Tarnowski, Hugo Vickers, James West, Melissa Zeiger, and my extraordinary research assistant Kathy Casey. Profound thanks to all of you. Vincent Faÿ generously shared documents and reminiscences related to his uncle. Caroline Piketty and Martine de Boisdeffre at the National Archives in Paris and Marie-Odile Germain at the Bibliothèque Nationale were helpful in securing documents and permissions. Particular acknowledgment is due to Nancy Miller and Victoria Rosner and to my editor, Jennifer Crewe, for bringing this book to press. I am also grateful to Catharine Stimpson, Robert Paxton, and my other reviewers at Columbia University Press for their cogent suggestions for revising the manuscript. In the end stages of the book, Asya Graf and Robert Fellman provided gracious assistance. Finally, a special thanks to my friend and colleague Brenda Silver, who effortlessly sustained this project on countless levels over the course of many years.

A special thanks is also due to the truly exceptional staff at Dartmouth's Baker-Berry Library, for whom no research question was too daunting, no foreign library too inaccessible: Laura Braunstein, Reinhart Sonnenburg, Hazen Allen, and, above all, Miguel Valladares. I am also indebted to Betsy Dain and Eliza Robertson, the librarians at the National Humanities Center.

Ultimate thanks go to my family, who accompanied me throughout the research and writing of this book and who provided the support that enabled me to finish it: William, Jamie, Nick, and Heather Ermarth; Alex and Judy Will; Elizabeth Lyding Will; and Michael Ermarth, who was with me every step of the way and to whom this book is gratefully dedicated.

The author acknowledges permission from the following to reprint material under their control: Stanford G. Gann Jr., literary executor of the Gertrude Stein Estate, for Stein material; Vincent Faÿ, executor of the Bernard Faÿ Estate, for Faÿ material; Fred Dennis, executor of the Sylvia Beach Estate, for Beach material; the Archives of the Collège de France; the Harry Ransom Humanities Research Center, for material in the Stein collection; and the Yale Collection of American Literature, Beinecke Rare Book and Manuscript Library, Yale University, for material from the Gertrude Stein and Alice B. Toklas papers. The author has, in spite of all actions taken, not been able to trace the origin of some of the images. Should the rightful claimants recognize themselves in these photographs they may contact the publisher.

UNLIKELY COLLABORATION

PART I

STEIN, FAŸ, AND THE MAKING OF A FRIENDSHIP

ENDINGS AND BEGINNINGS
(1918–1930)

CHAPTER ONE

THERE WERE two things that Gertrude Stein and Bernard Faÿ had in common when they met in 1926: both had received Medals of Honor for their participation in World War I, and both were admirers of Philippe Pétain, the French general who had cut short the German offensive at Verdun in 1916 and had come to represent, for Stein, Faÿ, and many others, the triumph of French fortitude and resilience over German aggression.

Forty years old at the start of the war, Gertrude Stein had at first been slow to express interest in aiding the Allied effort. When war broke out in the summer of 1914, she and her companion, Alice Toklas, were in England visiting the philosopher Alfred North Whitehead and his wife. Shocked and frightened by the sudden—and to them, incomprehensible—onset of hostilities, the two women returned briefly to Paris to pack up their belongings before leaving again for a year's sojourn in peaceful, remote Mallorca. There Stein attempted to recapture the stability of what she called "daily living," but news from the front continued to reach her—and worry her. In a poem from 1915, Stein reflects on a general feeling: "it is terrible the way the war does not finish."[1] And in a number of other works from this period, Stein weaves the theme of war into her experimental texts, suggesting a growing concern with the continuing conflict abroad that even the pleasures of writing could not allay.

In 1916, as the battle raged fiercely at Verdun, Stein and Toklas decided to make their way back to Paris and "to get into the war."[2] Joining the American Fund for the French Wounded, a volunteer organization devoted to emergency hospital service, they spent the next two years delivering supplies, relaying messages, and distributing comfort bags to French soldiers. In a Ford truck named Auntie they ministered to suffering troops in Perpignan, Nîmes, and war-ravaged Alsace. As the war dragged on and France became a "restless and disturbed world" (*ABT* 179), the two American women gamely volunteered their service to anyone they encountered: refugees, AWOL American soldiers, the homeless and destitute. Helping those wounded, displaced, or traumatized by the war stimulated and energized Stein and Toklas, but it was the particular mixture of support for their beleaguered France and American nationalist pride that propelled them tirelessly onward. With the armistice signaling the end of the war, both were rewarded for their efforts with the French Medaille de la Reconnaisance for outstanding service to the country, Toklas receiving a particular commendation. But their ultimate reward, according to Stein, was watching "everybody except the germans" march underneath the Arc de Triomphe in December 1918 and then suddenly realizing that "peace was upon us" (*ABT* 236).[3]

FIGURE 1.1 Gertrude Stein and Alice Toklas, with "Auntie," during World War I.

Bernard Faÿ was part of the crowd in Paris that day, although it is likely that he did not march in the victory procession. Stricken with severe polio as a young child, he walked slowly and with difficulty as an adult and tended to avoid situations that emphasized his disability. Nevertheless, he had been active in the Red Cross and ambulance corps of the recent war and was a decorated veteran of both the Belgian campaign and of the battle of Verdun. Watching the march of the Allied troops, he would have felt pride not only for his fellow Frenchmen but also for the American regiment whose place at the head of the procession was indicative of their newly important global status.[4] Faÿ, who had dreamed of attending Harvard College since he was seven years old, had always been fascinated by America and Americans. But it was while fighting in the presence of American volunteers at Verdun that his dream of a people "made of joys, of confidence, and of universal ambition" became "incurable."[5] From that moment until late in his life, America would retain a special status in Faÿ's imagination, guiding and transforming his thoughts, ambitions, and desires. France remained always for Faÿ the source of both

FIGURE 1.2 Bernard Faÿ, in uniform, at Verdun during World War I.

SOURCE: COPYRIGHT VINCENT FAÿ.

culture and civilization, but America would become his "passion": an idea, and a world, saturated with emotional, intellectual, and erotic feeling. The "warm embrace" of Franco-American conciliation would be welcomed by Faÿ in 1918, but like Stein he would also contrast this friendship with the feeling toward the defeated Germans, "blamed and mistrusted by everyone."[6]

Faÿ had lost two brothers and many friends to the war and had almost been killed by the Germans on the battlefield of Verdun. He was saved in part by the military strategy of the Verdun generals, including Philippe Pétain, who would subsequently become a warm personal friend.[7] Some thirty-seven years his junior, Faÿ admired Pétain not only for his military success but also for his conservatism and traditionalism. Honored for his defensive stance at Verdun, Pétain throughout his life understood his role as one of protecting, shielding, defending; his conservatism was bred in the bone.[8] Like Faÿ, Pétain came from a family that aligned itself clearly with one side of the "two Frances": Catholic and royalist rather than secular and Republican, opposed, above all, to the French Revolution and its liberal democratic legacy. For both men, the French Revolution represented what Faÿ called an "engine of destruction," laying waste to the values, habits, principles, and "human types" of the ancien régime.[9] Far from ameliorating the excesses of prerevolutionary France, the French Revolution had in fact robbed France of its *spirit*: a complex term signifying a range of moral, juridical, religious, and even racial characteristics. It was this spirit of France that seemed to be at stake in Verdun, itself the site of a ninth-century treaty that gave to France its modern geographical borders. In his guise as the Victor of Verdun, Pétain became not only a war hero for France as a whole but also a potent symbol of the past for individuals, like Bernard Faÿ, who were deeply suspicious of modern, post-Enlightenment notions of "progress."

For Gertrude Stein as well, Philippe Pétain embodied resiliency and courage, honor and sobriety. In his defense of Verdun, Pétain represented above all the will to "peace"—a term, like "daily living," that resonated for Stein with an entire worldview. "Peace" implied balance, equilibrium, and stasis; a sense of order; a commitment to tradition and habit, to what needed to be defended and preserved in the face of change, upheaval and revolution. "Peace," "daily living," "habit," and "tradition" were terms that Stein would begin to use with increasing frequency after World War I and in contexts that often illuminated her reactionary political views. In *Paris France*, a book she published the day France fell to the Germans in 1940, Stein argued that peace, habit, and tradition were the requisite conditions for creative freedom, the backdrop, support, and foil against which "the art and literature of the twentieth century" could emerge.[10] A few pages after, Stein makes her point more generally: "I cannot write too much upon how necessary it is to be completely conservative that is particularly traditional in order to be free" (*PF* 38). Freedom and excitement in the artistic realm can easily coexist with conservatism in the political realm. Several months later, Stein would unreservedly praise Philippe Pétain for allowing the French "to make France itself again."[11] When in June 1940 Pétain signed an armistice with Hitler that for the next four years turned France into a virtual puppet government of the Nazi regime, Stein noted briskly that Pétain had "achieved a miracle."[12] The Victor of Verdun had once again brought peace to her beloved France.

▣ ▣ ▣

In the way they lived through, responded to, and attempted to understand the period between the end of the First World War and the beginning of the Second, Gertrude Stein and Bernard Faÿ are fascinating witnesses to their era. Through their involvement with the literary and artistic avant-garde, they participated in one of the most creative and dynamic moments in recent cultural history. But Faÿ and Stein were also actively, intellectually engaged with the political and social upheavals of the interwar period. In the wake of World War I, both sought to come to grips in their writing with the enormous cultural, geopolitical, and transnational changes around them; both were committed observers of the moment. And in the anxious period building up to World War II, both forged connections between the aesthetic and the political, seeking a similar course in navigating these uncertain times.

Looking back at their world, we can see it as a time of endings: of death (more than eight million killed; an entire generation of young men wiped out), of world-shattering destruction (Europe permanently altered, the "civilized" West imploded), and of the final toppling of the ancien régime ("sultans, pashas, emperors, and dukes reduced to impotence").[13] The winners of World War I understood that their victory was a relative phenomenon and that the ground they stood on would never be as firm or stable as it had been; the losers simply hoped to avoid social anarchy. In the two decades that followed the signing of the Armistice in November 1918, up to the commencement of the German offensive in September of 1939, the shell-shocked peoples of Europe put a further nail in the coffin of the old world by turning against the liberal democratic institutions and universalist values that were presumed to have contributed directly to war and social decay. Over the course of this epoch, a series of competing political ideologies—fascism, communism, and various communitarian third ways—emerged as possible successors to the dying system of liberalism. Each of these ideologies, as Mark Mazower writes, "saw itself destined to remake society, the continent and the world in a New Order for mankind."[14] None would firmly supersede its rivals until fascism finally asserted its dark force over the continent.

But the interwar period was also a time of beginnings, especially on the other side of the Atlantic, and especially for "the only victor of the war," the United States.[15] American militarism had been on display during World War I, and its Wilsonian vision dominated the subsequent peace process. But as America consolidated its control over much of Europe's war debt, its power, its ideologies, and its values became inescapable. This was a technological and economic superpower that threatened to transform European culture through the soft seductions of "modernization" rather than through brute intervention. For Stein, this new American presence was, at least during the 1920s, the source of reassurance in an otherwise "restless and disturbed world" (*ABT* 234). Yet for most Europeans, the spectacle of American mass modernization during the 1920s and of American mass economic depression during the 1930s remained striking and worrisome during the interwar period. "The masses" became synonymous in European intellectual circles with what the French historian Georges Duhamel called the "American menace."[16] Only a few European commentators, Bernard Faÿ among them, were able to see the United States as a site of positive potential during the 1930s, and by the end of this decade, Faÿ, too, feared that America was sinking into materialism, cultural brutishness, and, worst of all, communism.[17]

Torn between endings and beginnings, between a sense that something foundational to the old world had been lost and a feeling that something uncertain or menacing was to come, many in the interwar period—including Gertrude Stein and Bernard Faÿ—found hope in a set of fairly standard romantic myths or ideals. These included the myth of the Hero (Philippe Pétain) and the visionary ideal of the Nation (America or France). What made these romantic tropes contemporary was the fact that they arose from one of the most devastating experiences in world history—total war—and that, as a result of this war, they lived on in a form that was inextricable from exclusion, segregation, and violence. Indeed, despite the profound desire during the interwar period for a lasting international peace, most people affected by the war were haunted by the idea of violence. William Pfaff writes that people in the interwar period "thought chiefly in terms of catastrophe—of the violent breakdown of the civilization they had known, but also of a violent historical renewal."[18] Out of this space of violent instability, nationalism quickly took root. Gertrude Stein, often flamboyant in her expressions of patriotism during the 1930s and 1940s, was not immune from nationalist tendencies. At her most extreme, as we shall see, she legitimated violence as a necessary means to a nationalist end.[19] In less inflamed moments during the 1930s, she would express a basic nationalist credo: "every nation has a way of being of being that nation that makes it that nation," she writes in 1935. Or again in 1945: "Germans are as they are and French and Greeks and Chinamen and Japs."[20] A nation's "being," its essence—its "bottom nature," to use another Steinian term—must be respected and defended, else it leads to "real catastrophe. That is what happened in France first with Napoleon and then with Louis Napoleon. That is what happened in America first with Theodore Roosevelt then with Franklin Roosevelt."[21]

By 1935, Gertrude Stein was convinced that the Roosevelts, and especially FDR, had led the United States into a "real catastrophe," transforming America's past strengths into a present crisis similar to that of modern-day France. Roosevelt and his French counterpart Léon Blum were both pushing their countries along a slippery slope toward a soulless and debased form of social organization that hewed dangerously to the political Left. What was needed to arrest this decline, to avoid more "real catastrophe," was a new form of national awakening: "We are there where we have to fight a spiritual pioneer fight," Stein wrote in a 1945 address to Americans, "and dont [sic] think that communism or socialism will save you, you just have to find a new way."[22] Ten years earlier, in 1936, Stein had pointed the finger more directly at FDR and his policies in a series of articles she wrote for the *Saturday Evening Post*, describing the New Deal as profligate and paternalistic.[23] Her readers, evidently, were not pleased. But Stein still sensed that hers was the way forward: "the young ones said I was reactionary and they said how could I be who had always been so well ahead of every one and I myself was not and am not certain that I am not again well ahead as ahead as I ever have been."[24]

However elliptical and eccentric, Stein's political rhetoric during the 1930s and 1940s was inseparable from the feeling—shared with Faÿ and many of their contemporaries—that the societies they lived in, knew of, and wrote about were limping along in an advanced state of political and social decay. In France, home to both Stein and Faÿ during the interwar period, *decadence* had long been a defining catchphrase for the modern era; during the 1930s, it became a cultural fixation. Agreement about decadence was widespread, if not a sense of where the blame for decadence lay. According to Charles Maurras, founder of the Action Française and the spiritual leader of the French Right, modern decadence sprang from the so-called ideals enshrined by the

Enlightenment and the French Revolution—liberalism, egalitarianism, secularism—and by the democratic and parliamentary institutions to which these ideals had given rise. The glorious France of the ancien régime seemed to have devolved into a fractious and complex modern present; in the wake of the French Revolution, Maurras wrote, "everything has grown weak."[25] Four linked forces in particular defined what Maurras would call "anti-France": "les juifs, les franc-maçons, les Protestants, et les métèques" (Jews, Freemasons, Protestants, and foreigners).[26] Maurras's views on culture and politics would have an enormous influence on the generation of French writers with which Bernard Faÿ and other of Stein's French friends identified themselves. Faÿ, a personal friend of Maurras, would attempt to disseminate Maurrassian ideas during his many visits to the United States over the course of the interwar period.[27] And even Stein seemed to be parroting Maurras when she decried the laziness of the unemployed ("you can never get anyone to do any work") and railed against American "organization" (the antithesis of "individual liberty") in the *Saturday Evening Post* articles.[28]

But the critique leveled against modern decadence in the interwar period was by no means limited to thinkers, like the French Maurrassians, on the political Right. While France remained a liberal democracy during the interwar period, its administration changed thirty-five times in the years between 1924 and the installation of Pétain's Vichy regime in 1940. In the midst of this rampant political instability, both the Right—Maurrassians, monarchists, Catholics, conservatives, traditionalists—and the Left—socialists and communists—as well as the radicals and nonconformists in between—found common ground in the general sense that modern political and economic institutions were heading toward disaster. During these "hollow years," to borrow Eugen Weber's phrase, odd alliances were formed. Catholic traditionalists joined with Left activists to form "nonconformist" movements. Former socialists, fearing the doctrinal rigidity of the communist party, aligned themselves with the nascent movement of fascism. And iconoclastic members of the Parisian avant-garde—many of them expatriates, like Stein herself—found themselves seduced by, and in some cases enthusiastically supportive of, authoritarian political regimes. These unlikely collaborations can tell us much about the turmoil and confusion of political and social life during the interwar period.

⊞ ⊞ ⊞

This book emerged out of a sense of uncertainty as to how to understand the years that Gertrude Stein spent in Vichy, France, from 1940 through 1944.

My previous book on Stein and modernism had ended with the period of the 1930s, at the moment when Stein achieved public success as a result of *The Autobiography of Alice B. Toklas*. This achievement seemed to be the defining feature of Stein's late life and work; at the time, little was known of her experience in Europe during World War II outside of Stein's own retrospective account in a book published in 1945, *Wars I Have Seen*. There, Stein can be seen saying complimentary things about Philippe Pétain, the Vichy head of state, and referring to a web of protection surrounding her during the war. But for most of her critics, these elliptical comments in *Wars* were ignored in favor of a more general reading that focused on the heroic personal qualities that enabled Stein to survive the period unscathed.[29]

Then, in 1996, an American graduate student named Wanda Van Dusen began raising uncomfortable questions about an unfinished manuscript that few knew about and no one had really confronted: a project started by Stein during the war to translate into English the speeches of Philippe Pétain. The same year, a more scholarly account of the Pétain translation project also appeared, buried in the back of Edward M. Burns and Ulla E. Dydo's book *The Letters of Gertrude Stein and Thornton Wilder*. Both accounts acknowledged that Gertrude Stein was indeed a *Pétainiste*: a supporter of Philippe Pétain's National Revolution, which promoted a politics of French collaboration with the Nazis. But Burns and Dydo also tied Stein's translation project to the mediating influence of Bernard Faÿ, a French scholar and close friend of both Stein and Pétain. Faÿ, it turns out, spent the war years working in the service of the Nazis: identifying, exposing, and persecuting hundreds of French Freemasons.[30]

Since my own previous work on Stein had focused almost exclusively on her aesthetics, I found my interest suddenly piqued—and troubled—by these revelations about her politics. First, I felt I needed to know more about the mysterious Bernard Faÿ. Described by Alice Toklas as Stein's "dearest friend during her life," Faÿ until recently rarely figured even in biographies of Stein.[31] In France, his name has largely been forgotten—or repressed. A 2009 biography in French by the scholar Antoine Compagnon, *Le cas Bernard Faÿ: du Collège de France à l'indignité nationale*, has paved the way toward resituating this complex man within French intellectual life during the interwar period. Still, much remains unclear about his relationship to Stein before and during the war. Yet according to Burns and Dydo, Stein could not have undertaken the translation project and would not have survived the war without his intervention. Who was Bernard Faÿ, and how could he have performed such widely divergent roles: scholar, academic, Americanophile, high modernist aesthete, Gestapo agent?[32]

Reflecting on the complexities of Faÿ's world brought me back to the question of Gertrude Stein's own Pétainism: her support for, indeed collusion with, an authoritarian regime. Was Stein indeed a "conservative fascist," as sources on the Internet claim, or were her allegiances less clear-cut, perhaps more conflicted and ambiguous? Given the generally positive reputation Stein currently enjoys, it was simply hard to believe the accusations that now circulate widely. We want our good writers to have good politics.[33] For most contemporary readers, in fact, Gertrude Stein is an unquestionably progressive writer: the originator, in works such as *Three Lives* (1904–1906), *Tender Buttons* (1913), and *The Making of Americans* (1903–1912), of a radically antiauthoritarian, antipatriarchal poetics and a key precursor to both deconstructionist theory and postmodernist writing. Currently undergoing a critical renaissance, Stein's work has recently been the source of great scholarly interest: thirty books and almost seventy dissertations in the last fifteen years alone. In film, contemporary music, and digital media, Stein's work has been celebrated for its decentering, destabilizing use of language, its attention to everyday life, and its dialogic appeal to the audience.[34] Stein has also been embraced by the field of queer studies and by the homosexual community in general, which see in her experimental writing an expressive poetics of lesbian-feminist identity.[35] In light of her elevated status both in the university and in the public at large, those who learn of Stein's Pétain translation project find it not only disturbing but also unfathomable. Some who have addressed its place in Stein's oeuvre have tended to see it as an act of survival on the part of a sixty-six-year-old Jewish American woman unwilling to leave the country she had lived in for over forty years.[36] Others—for example Janet Malcolm, in her recent book about Stein's war years, *Two Lives*—simply cannot make sense of Stein's "perverse" translation project. Malcolm cedes all interpretation of the issue to Burns and Dydo, who themselves admit that "what [Stein] understood about Faÿ and how she saw the situation remains a troublesome puzzle."[37]

In my own early work on Gertrude Stein, I had been similarly taken with what I perceived as the deeply radical nature of her writing, its ability to elicit an absolutely unprecedented reading experience that in its open-endedness could never be fully contained or completed.[38] While acknowledging the hermetic and even narcissistic aspects of her work, I paid little attention to how this hermeticism might be entwined with a particular or specific political vision. What, I might have asked, could Stein's political views of the 1930s and 1940s possibly have to do with her earlier radical experiments in writing?

Indeed, the very work for which Stein is best known—her uniformly experimental writing from *Three Lives* (1906) to *The Autobiography of Alice B. Toklas*

(1933)—is significant precisely because it appears so profoundly dissociated from time and place, from an author and her "views." To this extent, Stein's experimental writing also seems open to the reader in the radically democratic way that Roland Barthes discusses in his famous essay "The Death of the Author."[39] Almost more than any other writer in the English language, the Steinian experimental text seems to exemplify Barthes's description of modern writing: "No one, no 'person,' says it: its source, its voice, is not the true place of the writing, which is reading."[40] For those willing to read such a text—a text notably free of any guiding authorial presence—the experience can be both disconcerting and liberating. Yet it is precisely this freedom that makes it difficult to grasp how such a text could ever be seen as inscribing a particular political position beyond a progressive one of exposing the reader to new modes of reading.[41] It is even harder to see how such a text might be seen to be anticipating, *precisely* in its literary experimentation, the reactionary political views that Stein overtly expresses in her later writings of the 1930s and 1940s.

Still, if Stein's great accomplishment has been to teach us to read in a new way, the premises and principles that inform this teaching are not necessarily unassailable. Indeed, questioning the premises and principles of modernism, or at least producing a revisionary account of their value, has become an important recent critical trend. This has occurred in the wake of empirical evidence showing that many of the most creative, original, and experimental male writers of the modernist period—including Ezra Pound, W. B. Yeats, Louis-Ferdinand Céline, Wyndham Lewis, Ernst Jünger, Filippo Marinetti, Gottfried Benn, and T. S. Eliot, alongside important twentieth-century philosophers such as Martin Heidegger, Paul de Man, Carl Schmitt, and Maurice Blanchot—were all supporters of fascist, profascist, or authoritarian regimes during the 1930s and 1940s. More recent criticism has also shown the points of convergence between fascist ideologies and regimes and female modernists.[42] Ever since the late 1980s, when it was revealed that the deconstructionist critic Paul de Man had written more than two hundred articles for a pro-Nazi publication during World War II, much attention has been paid to this alliance between modernist art and philosophy in its most seemingly progressive or avant-garde form and the eventual support for a politics of illiberal reaction.[43] Why, asks one critic, would modernists "make a home or niche for themselves within fascism"?[44]

Given the complexity and variety of both artistic modernism and political fascism, as well as the rich and continuous debate that has swirled around their relation since the 1930s, it is impossible here to do full justice to this question.[45] Moreover, the case of Gertrude Stein is quite particular. Stein could not be further in artistic temperament or political enthusiasms from a Futurist fascist like Marinetti, nor was she driven by the racist fervor of other fascist modernists like Pound or Céline. Her case seems to fall under the rubric of "reactionary modernism"—an affiliation that Stein herself captures when she states that being "well ahead of every one" may not be antithetical to being "reactionary."

"Reactionary modernism" is a concept that seems to hold in suspension contradictory tendencies: a "paradox," according to Jeffrey Herf in his book of the same name. Herf, who limits himself to the German context, argues that Nazism was at once a primitivist and irrationalist movement directed toward the recovery of some primordial past *and* a movement of technological modernization with an affirmative attitude toward the future.[46] The Nazis envisioned a future in which technological progress could be harnessed to an authoritarian cultural revolution that would offer a third way "beyond" capitalism and communism. They were reactionaries in that "they were cultural revolutionaries seeking to restore instinct and to reverse degeneration due to an excess of civilization." Yet they were modernists both in their embrace of technology and in their affinities with artistic and cultural modernism, particularly the idea "of the free creative spirit at war with the bourgeoisie"—a spirit "who refuses to accept any limits."[47]

Roger Griffin's recent monumental study, *Modernism and Fascism: The Sense of a New Beginning Under Mussolini and Hitler*, goes further than Herf in underscoring how deep this reactionary strain ran through certain artistic and intellectual modernisms, which in their rejection of modernity for an alternative social and political future found ready agreement with fascist regimes. "The condition of modernity generated myriad countervailing bids by artists and non-artists not just to find ways of expressing the decadence of modernity, but to assert a higher vision of reality, to make contact with deeper, eternal 'truths'—or even to inaugurate an entirely new epoch."[48] What Griffin terms "the sense of a new beginning under Mussolini and Hitler"—and I might add, under Philippe Pétain—was precisely this anticipation of a *future* that was also a *return* to something lost or hidden under what he calls "the decadence of modernity." The "reactionary" aspect in this idea of modernism was thus always in tension with its "progressive" anticipations: the urge "to make contact with deeper, eternal 'truths'" had to be balanced with "the pursuit of the regeneration of history and the inauguration of a new era."[49]

Such a double-edged vision parallels Stein's own ideas, expressed in the 1930s and 1940s, of a "new era" in both France and America that would arrest the soul-sucking march of modern life and return its citizens to a lost, vital, eighteenth-century pioneering spirit. This was an era, again, that Stein readily associated with Philippe Pétain and his National Revolution, with his calls for a return to a "spirit of sacrifice" in the place of a "spirit of jouissance."[50] Unlike Herf's Nazis, technological progress did not seem to play a role in Stein's Pétainism or in Pétain's own political platform. If anything, Stein idealized the life of farmers and the rural working class, and this, too, drew her to Pétain's static agrarianism. Yet like the reactionary modernists of Herf's study, Stein also felt the strong pull of a future-oriented movement that promised "a radical reversal of the process of degeneration . . . threatening the nation's body and soul."[51] Having spent years coming to terms with the idea that she was a "genius," Stein also believed deeply in the value of the "free creative spirit . . . without limits" who might lead his or her nation into this brave new era.

This book is an attempt to chart the course of Stein's views over the interwar period as they dovetailed with those of her friend and collaborator, Bernard Faÿ. The unlikelihood of these shared views has to do in part with the assumption that reactionary thinking would hold little attraction for progressive modernist intellectuals and artists. But this in turn leads us back the question raised above, a question that continues to trouble many of Stein's most ardent and enthusiastic readers. Even if we acknowledge Stein's politically reactionary leanings of the 1930s and 1940s, in what sense were these views related to her highly experimental writing of the 1910s and 1920s? To what extent were these leanings nurtured by her early modernist premises and principles? Simply put, was Stein a reactionary modernist from the outset, or did she only become one later in her life?

We can answer this question not by searching for political ideas in Stein's experimental writing—writing, again, that abstains from "ideas" and "views"—but rather by looking at the principles that guided her through her creative development, especially during the first and most radically heterogeneous decade of her writing: from *The Making of Americans* to *Tender Buttons* (1902 to 1912). Some of these principles are to be found in the text that accompanied Stein on her creative journey during this period: a book called *Sex and Character*, by the Austrian philosopher Otto Weininger. A strange blend of philosophy and hack science, *Sex and Character* presents itself as a typology of humanity based on racial, gendered, and sexual categories of identity, the varieties of which are seen to lie on a spectrum defined by two polar opposites or ideal forms: the Woman/Jew and the Man/Genius. Described by Gerald Steig as "the psychological-metaphysical prelude for National Socialism, including its variants,"[52] *Sex and Character* was widely read from the moment of its publication in 1903 up to and through World War II; the Nazis found it a "racist classic."[53] Infusing its treatise on type and transcendence with large doses of anti-Semitism and misogyny, the text was even cited by Hitler for the self-overcoming of the author himself, a Jew who converted to Protestantism before killing himself and who thus became, in the words of Hitler's mentor Dietrich Eckart, "the only decent Jew."[54]

Gertrude Stein, who read Weininger during the critical period of 1907 and 1908, produced a capacious human typology of her own in the wake of her reading, an effort that would be sketched out in her most important early text, *The Making of Americans*. As Alice Toklas notes, Stein expressed a "mad enthusiasm" for Weininger, whom she thought "the only modern whose theory stood up and was really consistent."[55] Stein also, as we shall see, used Weininger to justify her own sense of herself as a creative genius, and this self-typing would, in turn, have multiple radiating effects on the complex changes and developments of her writing style. I have argued elsewhere that the implications of this apparently enthusiastic reading of Weininger on the new experimental direction in Stein's writing, as well as on the determination of her own "type," were enormous.[56] The question confronting us here is what role, if any, Stein's reading of Weininger had on her later attraction to the figure of Philippe Pétain and to the authoritarian ideology of the Vichy regime.

In Griffin's terms, it would be specious to argue for any "*direct* lineage" between the Stein who read Weininger and the Stein who supported Pétain.[57] Nevertheless, we could posit a connection between the definition of genius that Weininger offered Stein as the type that transcends all types—a definition, again, that had a significant effect on the development of Stein's experimental aesthetic—and her attraction to an authoritarian dictator like Pétain.[58] Weininger didn't turn Stein into a Pétainist, but he gave her the terms and the framework for her discovery of genius and her sense of the importance of subjective transcendence: two realizations that lie behind both her formalist experiments in writing *and* her support for Pétain. In Philippe Pétain, Gertrude Stein saw someone who seemed to embody the imaginative and subjective reach of the high modernist writer or artist, but with real-world, transformative power. In his words and in his symbolic presence, Pétain reminded Stein of her own efforts in language to transcend and transform the public sphere. As Pétain called upon his countrymen to return to the earth ("la terre"), Stein saw herself returning Americans to the "earthy" value of words.[59] What she saw in the emerging regime of Philippe Pétain was reform, heroism, national redemption, religious piety, traditionalism, and—perhaps above all—an aesthetic sensibility not entirely alien to her own.[60]

A similar connection between Stein's early experiments in writing and her later political views can be traced through another central principle behind her creative development: the idea of the aesthetic breakthrough. Stein wrote famously in 1933 that her short story "Melanctha" (1905–1906) was "the first definite step away from the nineteenth century and into the twentieth century in literature" (*ABT* 66). We will see later how important this calculus of century identity was to Stein's Pétainism in the late 1930s and 1940s. But equally important here is Stein's reference to her writing as "the first definite step away" from something obsolete and toward something aesthetically unprecedented, an idea that courses through her popular autobiographies of the 1930s but that is also evident during the period from 1906 to 1912 *as* she was making this step.

The example here is what Stein called "the beginning, really the beginning of modern writing": *The Making of Americans*, her 925-page "record" of this early period's changes.[61] Feeling herself on the verge of something that had never before been attempted, of a radically new form of writing, Stein begins the book first as a fairly conventional story of an immigrant American family, and then, after reading Weininger, as an attempted typology of "everyone who ever is or was or will be living."[62] This second, gargantuan task becomes the catalyst for deep creative questioning, "a melancholy feeling in some that there is not a complete history of every one in some one" (*MOA* 330). The notes she kept during this attenuated compositional process are full of worry ("Trouble with writing book. . . . When sufficiently comprehensive lacks imaginative content").[63] Nevertheless, by the end of the ten-year process of struggling and writing, Stein had achieved her breakthrough. "I . . . am the original wise one," she writes triumphantly, while also lamenting the fact that "perhaps sometime I will be sad again about not any one ever having the understanding of being in men and women that I am having" (*MOA* 708).

What Herf calls "the free creative spirit at war with the bourgeoisie who refuses to accept any limits" is powerfully captured in Stein's sense of her unprecedented (and lonely) endeavor in *The Making of Americans*. Unlike the "pack of stupid fools" Stein excoriates in her notes to the project, her effort to "go on writing, and not for myself and not for any other one but because it is a thing I certainly can be earnestly doing" is not only unique but unreproducible.[64] Soon, through this process, Stein would begin to realize that she was a genius: "Slowly and in a way it was not astonishing but slowly I was knowing that I was a genius," she writes in an account of this period (*EA* 76). While recognizing that the new aesthetic standard she has set for herself demands ever-new breakthroughs—"beginning again and again" becomes her modernist mantra—she nevertheless embraces this standard as the necessary work of the truly original genius.

To be sure, the idea of the breakthrough—of "the first definite step away" from something older or outmoded or artistically stale—was not just Gertrude Stein's own aesthetic concern, the driving force behind her writing. It defines the self-identity of the avant-garde; it is the raison d'être for artistic and literary modernism.[65] As Herf and Griffin argue, it also defines how various fascist or profascist movements perceived and justified their political agendas: the "sense of a new beginning," the break with modernity, with decadence, with the outmoded, stale, and corrupt system of liberal democracy as well as with the perceived alternative to liberalism, communism. Like the avant-garde, who imagined their work to be inherently revolutionary,[66] fascist movements saw themselves in the vanguard of a future-oriented world-political organization; like the avant-garde, fascists saw themselves as "the beginning, really the beginning" of something new after almost two centuries of decadence that had followed the French and the American Revolutions. The fascists thus shared a core vocabulary with avant-garde artists and writers of the early twentieth century that allowed for certain affinities to be claimed, at certain moments and by certain individuals.[67] While it is surely possible to overstate this commonality of views, words, and impulses, the harder question is to ask precisely how, in the case of particular modernists, this commonality turns into a convergence.[68]

In the case of Stein, it is important to underscore that her politics of the 1930s and 1940s were not the express outgrowth of the thinking that inspired her early experiments in literature: her "mad enthusiasm" for Weininger and her commitment to breakthroughs and "new beginnings." Both of these commitments, we might say, form part of the background that she brought with her into the turbulent decades between the First and Second World Wars. Nor did her extraliterary views remain static and unchanging over the course of her life. Again, one of the points of this study is to argue that Stein's political views became ever more reactionary during the period of her collaboration with Bernard Faÿ. At the same time, it would be a mistake to simply dissociate Stein's early "progressive" experimental writing from her later "reactionary" politics, in the desire to excuse or compartmentalize. The tendencies that drew Gertrude Stein toward both Bernard Faÿ and Philippe Pétain, we could say, were always there.

◻ ◻ ◻

Unlike some of her modernist contemporaries, Gertrude Stein never attended a fascist rally, was never an official functionary of any fascist organization, and was almost never celebrated in the fascist or profascist press.[69] Of course, not many Jews were. And this, above all else, seems to make Stein's Pétain-ism even more troubling than the more rabid support for fascist regimes of her contemporaries such as Pound, Céline, and Heidegger. For it is not the outspokenness of Stein's commitment to Philippe Pétain's Vichy regime that matters but the very fact that she willingly sought to produce *any* propaganda in support of this regime that shocks us to this day. One can hear this shock in Picasso's voice in a conversation reported by James Lord: "Gertrude was a real fascist. She always had a weakness for Franco. Imagine! For Pétain, too. You know she wrote speeches for Pétain. Can you imagine it? An American, a Jewess, what's more."[70]

I have laid out some of the sources of Stein's commitment to Pétain: in a world where so much had been lost and where so much seemed uncertain, in a world deemed simply "decadent," almost any action could be justified in the name of an ideal, however violent and exclusionary. Time and again, how-ever, the scapegoating for the problems of the day turned upon a single pre-sumed source: the Jews. In Europe, and to a certain extent in America, doing something about "the Jewish question" in the interwar period became synony-mous with positive, progressive national change. In 1900, in the wake of the Dreyfus affair, the Action Française endorsed the idea that "anti-Semitism is essential to any truly French action"; after World War I, this view would move from the fringe to the center.[71] As Zeev Sternhell has proven, modern French nationalism became inextricable from anti-Semitism: "The nationalists saw anti-Semitism as a common denominator that could serve as a platform for a mass movement against liberal democracy and bourgeois society. The further step of concluding that anti-Semitism permitted nationalism to appear as the doctrine of national consensus was easy to take, and taken soon enough."[72] As the interwar period progressed, the romantic ideal of a renewed nationalism became increasingly tied to a violent anti-Semitism.

In 1925, the first fascist movement in France was formed, the Faisceau. Although this movement was to founder three years later in the face of tem-porary improvement in French social and economic conditions, it laid the groundwork for what Sternhell calls "a revolution of the spirit and the will, of manners and morals."[73] Unlike their anti-Dreyfusard predecessors, the Fais-ceau did not have an explicitly anti-Semitic agenda: for much of the 1920s, overt anti-Semitism remained unfashionable. Yet the Faisceau "constituted an ideological and organizational link" between prewar anti-Dreyfusism and the more virulent anti-Semitism of the Right in the 1930s.[74] The main journal of the Faisceau, *Le Nouveau Siècle*, was careful to recycle the stereotypes of an earlier era through an appeal to French national pride, making invidious distinctions between bad "foreign" and good "French" Jews. Yet while "foreign" Jews were explicitly marked out as disruptive to national unity, the Faisceau often insinuated that decadence in fact lay with assimilated Jews, whose ability to blend into their environments threatened any easy demarcations between natives and foreigners. According to Georges Valois, the leader of the Faisceau, the Jews had "used the powers of Gold to dissolve their host nations" and "sought to destroy that concrete and territorial French patriotism that would exclude them."[75] In the space of several years, Valois's cautious ideas about the Jews as anathema to "French patriotism" would become more crudely repeated: the Jews as a whole were eternal outsiders and degenerate foreign bodies in the midst of the national community.

One of the most difficult questions of this book is whether the Jewish Gertrude Stein could have herself contributed to this scapegoating of the Jews. Several issues are troubling, not the least her various comments, both public and private, that seem to justify authoritarianism in the 1930s, including—as we will see—the actions of Hitler. There is her friendship with figures on the French Right and with radical Catholic reformers calling for a new French "order," perhaps most importantly Bernard Faÿ. And then of course there is her support of Pétain and the propaganda she wrote for the Vichy regime. On the other hand, being Jewish was never a public affiliation that Gertrude Stein made much of, especially after she moved to Paris in 1903 and took up the mantle of modernist innovator and artistic genius. In fact, Stein's embrace of modernism seemed to require the suppression of her ethnic origins, much as the characters in the first sections of *The Making of Americans* "wash away" their immigrant characteristics and patterns of speech in order to become Americans.[76] That Stein connected modernism with Americanism made imperative her assimilationist position. Even in her earliest writings, in the college essays she wrote at Radcliffe, Stein had already understood Jewishness as something encompassed by and necessarily subordinate to a larger sense of belonging—for example, with the nation.

"The Modern Jew Who Has Given Up the Faith of His Fathers Can Reasonably and Consistently Believe in Isolation," an essay Stein wrote for a college composition class in 1896, argues that Jewish "race-feeling" must not get in the way of being a "true and loyal American." Jewishness, she suggests, should be a "private concern" dissociated from the public sphere of "modern national identity." It is a "feeling of kinsfolk and does not in any sense clash with the loyalty of a man to his nation."[77] Several years later, in 1903, Stein began her "breakthrough" novel, *The Making of Americans*, with the premise that American identity requires the removal of ethnic or other differentiating traits. In the early sections of the novel that deal with successive generations of Jewish immigrants, the process of assimilation—the process by which Jewishness is erased from her characters—is also the process that nationalizes them, "making" them into Americans. Stein herself seemed to take this process to heart while she was writing and revising the novel: in each successive draft Jewish names are cut out, substituted by nonethnic descriptors. By the time she finished the work in 1912, the immigrant story had morphed into a present-tense exploration of the author's "being" as she struggles to create a capacious typology of humanity. For many years thereafter, as her biographer Richard Bridgman notes, "her references to Judaism were infrequent."[78]

Telling the story of her family's assimilation into American society gave Stein her voice as a modernist writer. By writing through and beyond this story, by taking "the first definite step away" from previous generations, Stein discovered a voice that could lay claim to being absolutely new, unmarked by the past and its determinants. Stein's critics have long been intrigued by the meaning of this discovery. Linda Wagner-Martin argues that "The modernist writer aimed to be universal, above political alliances, washed clean in the purity of serious and innovative aesthetics, and Gertrude certainly wanted to play that game well."[79] Yet playing that game well was not without its costs, as another critic, Priscilla Wald, has suggested. Wald refers to Stein's "fear of self-loss" that attends cultural and narrative assimilation.[80] As Stein writes the story of Jewish assimilation, she begins to question the norms that this story relies upon: the "middle-class" habits toward which Jewish and other immigrants strive, as well as the grammatical norms of English that represent successful linguistic assimilation. The text's development from a "realist" to a "modernist" narrative, marked by the breakdown of plot, the uncertainty of the narrative voice, and the repetition of whole sections of text, "shows what has been suppressed and repressed" by the process of assimilation: the "untold stories" of immigrants who have been unable or unwilling to fully adapt to their new environment.[81] Americans may be "made," but the process of making requires a "self-loss" and "self-fragmentation" embedded in the new modernist form of the text.

In the end, however, it would be misleading to claim that Stein's erasure of her Jewishness and emergence as a modernist writer were *not* liberating for her. For it was through the "breakthrough" of *The Making of Americans*, as we have seen, that Stein discovered that she was a genius. This, in turn, would have lasting implications for her writing and for her sense of self as exceptional, as existing beyond conventional expectations and assumptions.

For Stein, being a genius justified her aesthetic drive, her physical and social displacement and eccentricity, and her homosexuality. And as her notebooks to *The Making of Americans* make clear, it also served to trump any identification with Jewishness. Despite a long tradition linking Jews with genius, Stein remained remarkably wary of this connection. Again, her "mad enthusiasm" for Otto Weininger's *Sex and Character* may have had something to do with this wariness. Weininger, who argued against the premise of "Jewish genius" as a contradiction in terms, claimed that Jewishness was antithetical to transcendence and that it tended inevitably toward a "constant close relation with the lower life."[82] Importantly for Stein, Weininger also uncoupled Jewishness as a "tendency of mind" from individual character, suggesting that one could be a Jew but not be "Jewish." Hence Weininger proved crucial for Stein not just in giving her the terms to lay claim to her own genius but also in helping her sever her outward ties to Jewishness, femininity, and the norms of heterosexuality.[83]

The Making of Americans was not the only modernist text to emerge out of Stein's displacement of the Jewish theme. Another breakthrough text, the short story "Melanctha," had its first incarnation as an autobiographical novella with a Jewish protagonist, entitled *Q.E.D.* When Stein undertook to write "the first definite step away from the nineteenth century and into the twentieth century in literature," she transformed her autobiographical Jewish lesbian story *Q.E.D.* into the narrative of an African American woman named Melanctha. While the black and heterosexual Melanctha retains certain identifiably "Jewish" traits—most notably, she is described throughout as a "wanderer"—her racial and cultural difference obscures the ethnic origins of the story. As with *The Making of Americans*, Jewishness, here, becomes one of the key points of origin for modernism *and* what needs to be abandoned or obscured in order for the modernist text to be written.[84]

Yet Stein's lifelong refusal of outward identification with Jewishness had an interesting twist. In 1907, just after the stylistic breakthroughs of "Melanctha" and as Stein was beginning to use a Weininger-esque vocabulary in new drafts of *The Making of Americans*, she met her future companion, Alice Babette Toklas. A San Francisco native from a middle-class Jewish background, Toklas, like Stein, preferred to identify with an assimilationist American narrative: she once responded tersely to a question about her Jewishness by saying that she and Stein "represented America."[85] Yet personal notes shared between Stein and Toklas throughout the 1910s and 1920s tell a story of intimacy experienced in part through Jewish identification. Stein refers to Toklas affectionately as "my little Jew" and "my little Hebrew" and to herself and Toklas as "baby and its Jew." Given the importance of Toklas to Stein's life and writing, including her role in supporting the experimental direction of this writing, it is significant that Jewishness became part of the currency through which the two women related. The repression of Jewishness at the source of Stein's modernism seems to return in intimate moments with Toklas as a form of transgressive identification. This return enables an erotic role playing that courses through Stein's creative life, however much her sense of herself as a writer may have prohibited this identification.[86]

Yet this "return" of Jewish identification can be glimpsed almost exclusively in the private notes shared by Stein and Toklas during their daily life. In the work that Stein meant to present to the public, she returned explicitly to the issue of Jewishness only rarely after 1910. In the wake of World War I, during the nationalist fervor of the Versailles negotiations, Stein made passing references to Jews and Jewishness, often in terms of the efforts on behalf of the Zionist delegation to Versailles to carve out a Jewish homeland in Palestine. She directly comments on this movement in a 1920 text, "The Reverie of the Zionist." Here, Stein rejects the idea that Zionism can speak in the name of all Jews, suggesting in fact that Jews are "anywhere . . . and everywhere," their presence producing a "wealth of imagery." She implies that Zionism obscures the more authentic emotional relationship of a person to his or her country: "Judaism should be a question of religion. . . . Race is disgusting if you don't love your country," she writes. Recalling her argument in "The Modern Jew," Stein here compartmentalizes Jewishness, limiting it to a religious practice ("Judaism") and arguing against essentializing claims to racial unity as the ground for national identification. She also proposes "love," not race or religion, as the truest measure of national belonging. While "Reverie" does not deny the existence or the creative power of Jewish figures or traditions—Jews are indeed "anywhere and everywhere," like the Old Testament figure of Shem who appears at the end—the text rests on the point that one "belongs" only to the place where one feels a deep-seated collective love.[87]

Ten years later, this kind of rhetoric would begin to have troubling resonances. While Stein in a text like "The Reverie of the Zionist" points toward a compromise between national solidarity and Jewish particularity, other writers and politicians at the time were beginning to use similar terms to stress the dissociation between Jewish and national identity. For the French Faisceau, Jews were the "symbol and cause" of decadence; many of their followers in the 1930s "insisted that Jews, by their very nature, could not be assimilated."[88] While Stein was talking about the primary importance of "lov[ing] your country," right-wing nationalists were using the same terms to stress the difference between natives and "foreigners." Stein's point that "Race is disgusting if you don't love your country" would seem to open the door for the argument that racialist or racist thinking is acceptable if you *do* love your country. And as the more optimistic decade of the 1920s turned into the hollow years of the 1930s, Stein's own rhetoric, informed by her personal sense of distance from Jewish concerns, would begin to harden. She began to refer to "the Jews" as a discrete and disruptive social entity, often seeming to exclude herself from the category. And she began to essentialize her ideas both of the nation, as having a specific and unchanging "way of being," and of national belonging as a pre-rogative of natives—not something to which immigrants or foreigners could easily aspire.

Furthermore, it was during this period that Gertrude Stein became close friends with Bernard Faÿ.

▣ ▣ ▣

Although Stein and Faÿ shared much in common, their first encounter was not particularly auspicious. According to an outside observer, Stein "was only mildly interested" in Bernard Faÿ, and Faÿ "was frightened of her."[89] In 1924, Stein had already consolidated her reputation as an avant-garde celebrity and was somewhat jaded by the stream of deferential young men who appeared at her salon. Faÿ, just back from teaching stints at Columbia, Kenyon College, and the University of Iowa, with a master's degree in modern languages from Harvard and a tenured professorship at the University of Clermont-Ferrand, was more of a scholar than many of Stein's admirers. But he had moved in avant-garde circles while in America, and on his return to Paris in the early 1920s he was drawn to the American expatriate community that flourished there. He soon made friends with many of Stein's followers: writers such as Sherwood Anderson and Scott Fitzgerald, musicians such as Virgil Thomson and Aaron Copland, painters such as Picasso and Jo Davidson. Still, with his combination of bourgeois manners, self-control, and evident ambition, Faÿ initially failed to impress in the uninhibited and experimental scene around Stein. It didn't help that Ernest Hemingway, jealous and possessive of Stein's attention, referred dismissively to Faÿ as "Bernard Fairy."[90]

It would take another few years before Faÿ would be able to move into the inner circle of Stein's group of friends. Hemingway, perceived by Toklas as a threat to her union with Stein, was banished from the ménage in 1924.[91] Anderson retreated to America, where, like Fitzgerald, he began a long descent into alcoholism. In their place, a different set of artists, writers, and assorted hangers-on began to converge on Stein's salon: women such as Janet Flanner, Bryher, and Natalie Barney; men such as Faÿ, Virgil Thomson, Carl Van Vechten, Hart Crane, Paul Bowles, Aaron Copeland, Georges Hugnet, Francis Rose, the artist Pavel Tchelitchew and his partner Charles Henri Ford, and the surrealist writer René Crevel, who "talked with a pronounced lisp."[92] Almost all of these "disciples"—Carl Van Vechten's word[93]—were homosexual or bisexual, and the electric atmosphere of the salon reflected this new orientation. At its core was a deep affection and indeed reverence for Gertrude Stein, a respect for her domestic partnership with Toklas, and an eagerness to partake in the substitute family that this partnership represented. But Stein's disciples were also invested in the queer kind of "aura" she generated. By the late 1920s, according to one biographer, Stein's "feeling in the salon . . . was that people came to hear her and so she needed to perform."[94] Whereas for Hemingway and Fitzgerald, Stein had primarily played the role of mentor and career facilitator, for Faÿ and his gay cohorts, Stein was a combination of mother, saint, star, and diva: an icon of triumphant self-sufficiency, a survivor of ridicule and disdain, and a consummate, electric performer. Her estranged brother Leo recalls the glamour enveloping Stein during this period: the *frisson* of her persona, her nicknames like "The Presence" or "Le Stein."[95] Many compared her to Saint Theresa, the protagonist of Stein's most famous opera, *Four Saints in Three Acts*, who joyously and unapologetically proclaims her eccentricity and exceptionality. Within the context of this late 1920s salon, gayness—or what Bernard Faÿ called "joy"—was a mantle to be worn without shame. Faÿ referred to Stein as Saint Gertrude and to her salon as "the chapel of Our Lady." He wrote: "Only the joy of existing and acting possessed her, guided her, and led her to dominate her entourage." She was "molded out of gaiety." She taught of "la joie de vivre."[96]

Yet for Bernard Faÿ, Gertrude Stein's allure was a complicated thing. When Faÿ recalls being "frightened" of Stein at their first meeting, it was not just her reputation and domineering personality that struck him. It was also what she represented to his own self-identity, as well as the tensions and desires that her presence evoked.

Bernard Marie Louis Emmanuel Faÿ was a curious individual of complex personal and political sympathies. Born on April 3, 1893, to a family of the Parisian *haute bourgeoisie*, the son of a lawyer father and of an "ultra-Catholic" mother,[97] Bernard Faÿ had every privilege of his class: education, culture, money—if not the aristocratic lineage he so deeply admired throughout his life. By his own admission he was a dreamy child and a loner, made more so by a debilitating bout with childhood polio that left him with a pronounced limp.[98] Confined to his bed from the ages of five to thirteen, Faÿ passed the time being read to and reading widely in French literature, an activity that would shape his scholarly tendencies and have a lasting effect on his aesthetic sensibility. Returning to school with a disability, he developed a defensive verbal wit that served him well in the classroom and earned him the respect of his peers. Childhood trauma was soon followed by academic and personal success: an "Agrégé" in letters at the unusually young age of twenty-one; a Croix de Guerre for his work with the French Red Cross in Verdun in 1917; a Victor Chapman scholarship to Harvard in 1919; a master of arts in modern languages from Harvard in 1920. After Faÿ received his doctorate from the Sorbonne in 1925, his thesis was honored with the inaugural bestowal of the Jusserand Medal from the American Historical Association for the best work on intellectual relations between the United States and Europe. It was also the runner-up for the Pulitzer Prize in history. A transatlantic network of colleagues and friends helped certify his early reputation as one of the foremost writers on American culture in France; soon, he was being asked to teach and to give honorary lectures at elite institutions throughout the United States.[99] His connections with the avant-garde Parisian musical group known as Les Six and, through his artist brother Emmanuel, to the New York visual arts scene endeared him to cosmopolites on both sides of the Atlantic, as did his friendship with both Proust and Gide.[100] By the time he met Gertrude Stein, at the age of thirty-one, Bernard Faÿ was not only a rising academic star but well positioned to impress her with his sophistication, learning, taste, and ambition.

Yet Faÿ also had other affinities that Stein may have found innately appealing. Raised in a conservative Catholic and Royalist family, Faÿ had continued to align himself with dominant currents in the French Catholic Right during his adulthood. While his aesthete friends were Proustians, his political acquaintances during the interwar period included Charles Maurras, Philippe Pétain, Maurice Barrès, Robert Brasillach, Abel Bonnard, and a host of others who would eventually become Vichy insiders. Over the course of the 1930s, Faÿ would become identified both with Maurras and his Action Française and with more militant or extreme right-wing organizations such as the Croix de Feu and the Rassemblement National Pour la Reconstruction de la France. He would eventually become one of the few establishment intellectuals during the war to actively collaborate with the Nazi occupiers.

Faÿ's intellectual ties to the French Right had been fostered by his scholarly work, first at Harvard and then in a quick succession of published volumes, on the topic of Freemasonry: a particularly charged issue in France. In the popular imagination, Freemasonry was associated with secularism, democracy, and revolutionary ideals; in the 1930s, these characteristics were inextricably linked to decadence and to the Jews. Faÿ described Freemasonry as "the most efficient social power of the civilized world" and as the central force that had given rise to the French Revolution. But Faÿ also warned against the "hidden" dangers of this power. For Faÿ, French Freemasonry—with its secret rituals involving death and resurrection, its mysticism, and its "indigestible phraseology"— represented a kind of shadow version of Catholicism, albeit one without any redeeming "refinement."[101] "A monstrous parasite, Freemasonry has grown larger out of our debasement," Faÿ writes.[102] As his scholarly criticism became sharper over the course of the 1930s, Faÿ began to align his critique of Freemasonry with more general critiques of French social decline and with militant forces calling for a violent overthrow of the Third Republic. With the installation of the Vichy regime in 1940, Faÿ finally was allowed to put his ideas into action as director of the covert Vichy agency involved in the pursuit and exposure of French Freemasons. There, as we shall see in chapter 5, Faÿ's obsessions turned toxic.

But the vehemence and sordid outcome of Faÿ's anti-Masonic crusade is only part of his—and our—story. Like Gertrude Stein, Faÿ led a double life, one framed by his sense of connection to two cultures: France and America. As the first professor of American civilization in France and the first to hold the chair in that field at the prestigious Collège de France, Faÿ began his career less as a scholar of Freemasonry itself than as a comparative historian of the French and American revolutions, within which Freemasonry had played an important role. In his Harvard thesis on the subject, Faÿ had in fact emphasized the salutary aspects of the American branch of Freemasonry, describing the lodges as "cradles of the spirit of independence" and showing in his analysis of Benjamin Franklin how much "Freemasonry envisaged the reform of society by means of enlightenment and philosophic benevolence."[103] In America, it seemed, Freemasonry could flourish without having the deleterious effects that it had on French culture, because America valued intrinsically the "didactic and utilitarian" qualities of Masonic thought. Simply put, Freemasonry "worked" in America because of the nation's essential character—something about which Faÿ, like Stein, considered himself to be an excellent judge. Americans were ambitious and passionate, optimistic and impulsive. They "adored" ideas but did not take them too seriously; their dearest values were freedom and materialism; they were profoundly conformist (JP 156–157). Unlike the French, with their clericalism and traditionalism, Americans fully and unproblematically embraced any "fever of newness" (RSFA 3). America, being a young country, always looked to the future, and appreciated

Freemasonry's investment in progress. Within the context of American culture Freemasonry was clearly not a threat, since this culture was itself unanchored to any spiritual force or dogma, such as the Catholic Church, which might resist secular Masonic "enlightenment." America, Faÿ writes in his Harvard thesis, represented to Europeans like himself "a benign, chimeric and innocuous dream" (*RSFA* 474).[104]

For most of his own life, in fact, Faÿ idealized America as a place of unorthodox desires and enlightened if secular politics, an anti-France that held all the attractions and dangers of the mythic Other. "Joy" was the word Faÿ consistently used to describe America: its optimism, its idealism, its futurity. And until he began to sour on America and its politics in the late 1930s, Faÿ also consistently—even obsessively—linked American "joy" to erotic vitality. In a 1925 essay, "La joie et les plaisirs aux Etats-Unis," Faÿ notes how "the joy of the body, the most honorable and fecund joy of all, reign[s] in America" (JP 154). Elsewhere he writes that Americans' bodies, "developed without brutality, have taught them only joy" (H 590). It was to America where Faÿ first went in pursuit of his dream, nurtured in youthful fantasies, of attending Harvard College. His earliest and most revealing essay, "Harvard 1920," written during his graduate years, locates the origin of his interest in American joy in a personal awakening. On first hearing of America at the age of seven, Faÿ asked himself: "Shall I ever be a man in body, or will my life remain forever shut up in my thought?" This cryptic question seemed to be answered for Faÿ by his experience in World War I. As Stein herself would write about him in 1937, "Bernard Faÿ was a French college professor only like so many Frenchmen the contact with Americans during the war made the romance for them" (*EA* 103). Faÿ's romance began when he caught sight of an American soldier in 1917 during the war. "His supple body, his unskillful and graceful movements, then his glance and his slow words mingled with smiles and pride attracted me. I saw him in the midst of dangers. I saw him in the midst of pleasures. I saw him abandoned and sought for. I studied him with passion" (H 588).[105] After the war, enrolling as a graduate student at Harvard, Faÿ was able to pursue ever more passionate "studying" of American men, and to refine his original assessment of their type as "beautiful. These young men have ordinarily great supple bodies, without faults and without vices, qualified to give them all the pleasures which the air, the water, the land and movement can offer, and to serve their race" (H 590). Later, in "Protestant America" (1928), Faÿ writes of America that one "cannot conceive of what physical and sexual excitement is caused by the close proximity of white, yellow, and black races." In general, for Americans, "it seems that everything is done to encourage them to enjoy their bodies as much and as freely as possible."[106]

In its charged blend of sexual, national, and racial desire, Faÿ's rhetoric about Americans in these passages and in many others is both excessive and veiled. The American bodies that he studies are "beautiful," "great," "without faults and without vices." Their presence produces inconceivable "excitement." At the same time, Faÿ remains vague about what he means by becoming "a man in body" simply by finding himself in the presence of Americans. We are reminded of the mute yearnings of Nick Carraway in F. Scott Fitzgerald's novel *The Great Gatsby* as he watches the "gorgeous" Gatsby from afar, or of Gatsby himself, gazing out across Long Island Sound at the mythic green light on Daisy's dock. The parallels between Faÿ's Harvard essay (1920) and *The Great Gatsby* (1924) are in fact remarkably suggestive. In discussing his time at Harvard, Faÿ writes that it "made my dream incurable," as though the American Dream were a sickness or a terminal, "incurable" disease—an awareness that strikes the Yale-educated Nick Carraway as well after Gatsby's death. The precise subtext of this "sickness" would only be revealed in Faÿ's case some twenty-five years later, in a deposition written by the French authorities for Faÿ's 1946 trial for collaboration with the Nazis. Among the items seized in his home, the authorities write, was a document describing his "intimate relations with a certain number of [male] American students while he was a lecturer in the United States" and including prayers to God to excuse "ces amours impures." Like Nick Carraway, like Gatsby, Faÿ's American dream was inseparable from forbidden and impure love.

And when Faÿ's dream slipped away, as it did over the course of the 1930s, it would be replaced by a new fanaticism about the need for social and political "purification" in the face of modern "decadence." The words of Nick Carraway perfectly capture this moment, when idealism turns into militaristic moralism. After abandoning his dream—the dream represented by Gatsby, by New York, and by the frenetic world of the 1920s—Nick writes prophetically, "I wanted the world to be in uniform and at a sort of moral attention forever; I wanted no more riotous excursions with privileged glimpses into the human heart."[107]

□ □ □

Within Faÿ's rich fantasy about Americans, Gertrude Stein was a cipher for conflicting desires and prohibitions. Associated in his mind with joy, Stein manifested the best traits of the Americans whom Faÿ "studied" while at Harvard. Yet as an American woman, Stein could seemingly never be the true object of Faÿ's desire. In fact, writing about Stein's "joie de vivre" many years after her death, Faÿ remarks that it was never "skewed by sensuality." Rather,

Stein taught of joy "straightforwardly, in a direct manner." In this essay, as elsewhere, Faÿ takes pains to emphasize that Stein's joy is inseparable from her relationship to language: a means of confronting the world through words that was refreshingly affirmative: "it was stylish to balk at the real, to find it so full of defects, of disadvantages, of stench that one couldn't resign oneself to love it. Gertrude rejoiced in living, in seeing life and in feeling that one was living." Contrasting Stein to the "sensual" homosexual writer André Gide, Faÿ remarks on the "purity" of Stein's language, which allowed her to approach reality in a way uncorrupted by "la volupté" (*LP* 139–140).

Yet at other moments, Faÿ's description of Stein's "joy" seems charged with an erotic feeling similar to that found in his other writings on American men. In his essay on Harvard, Faÿ had emphasized how much the attractiveness of the male Harvard student depended upon "honesty, patience, and tolerance" that produced a "noble and masterful air" (H 589–590). He echoes this description in his discussions of Gertrude Stein's "directness" and frankness, her ability to allow "the pleasure of affirming oneself in front of someone who appreciated one's affirmations" (*LP* 139). Another gay disciple, Virgil Thomson, would make a similar point when discussing how he and Stein got along "like Harvard men."[108] In both Faÿ's and Thomson's accounts, Stein's joie de vivre is alluring precisely because it reminds them of the collegial and homoerotic bonhomie of the Ivy League campus. It is significant that Faÿ often referred to Stein's voice when discussing her use of language, noting how it spoke "of joy, of health, of voluntary and spontaneous gaiety" (*LP* 138). As the physical vehicle for Stein's words, her voice seemed to embody her "gaiety" and "joy." Talking with Stein provided a way of rediscovering, through transgression and displacement, the excitement of forbidden desire. Faÿ even claims that it was an eagerness to speak with Stein that led him to master the English language. Far from avoiding the erotic, spoken exchanges with Stein were exciting precisely because they mimicked the "joy" of pivotal male homosexual experiences.

The erotic currents that flowed between Stein and Faÿ were subtle, fluid, and complex. Limited to the realm of language or conversation, these currents remained subterranean and largely unconscious. And for Faÿ, at least, any desire toward Stein was framed by the effort to negate what he took to be his own sexual impurity. As a figure for gaiety and joy, Stein represented homosexuality in its most positive, affirmative mode—a trait that made her a magnet for gay men and women. But as someone who, for Faÿ at least, seemed to avoid being "skewed by sensuality," Stein also represented a wholesome, desexualized *alternative* to "impure" homosexuality (as the comparison to Gide makes clear). "You are the *only* poet alive," he writes to her in 1930, "who makes me feel a healthy pleasure and a joyous excitement."[109] In a review of *The Autobiography of Alice B. Toklas* (1933), Faÿ again characterizes her as a "healthy woman of genius."[110] Seeing Stein as "healthy" rather than decadent seems to have enabled Faÿ to project a powerful new kind of fantasy onto her: "Saint Gertrude." Transforming Stein into a Christian saint, Faÿ made her into a source of forgiveness and absolution, a desexualized force of spiritual health and healing. Stein was both the diva-saint who drew gay men into her orbit and the mother-confessor who allowed her disciples to wash away their own "disgusts and angers" (*LP* 169). "I allowed myself to be swept up into her whirlpool," Faÿ writes, "as one allows oneself to be carried away by the waters of a bubbling fountain of youth" (*LP* 139).

Of course, Faÿ's fantasy of Saint Gertrude served another function: it allowed him to reconcile any concerns he might have had about Stein's Jewish origins. Faÿ was careful never to articulate these concerns to Stein directly, and their correspondence from the 1920s and 1930s makes no mention of the Jewish question. But in other contexts, as we shall see, Faÿ parroted the anti-Semitic rhetoric of the French Right, particularly where it could be expediently linked to a "Masonic conspiracy" that was leading France to ruin. In writing of Stein after her death, Faÿ makes it clear that her Jewishness was never a neutral issue for him. Although he refers positively to Stein's "Jewish blood," linking it to the glories of Rome and to Old Testament prophets, his comments objectify in the guise of praise; there is nothing of Stein that is unmarked by her Jewishness (*LP* 147). Eventually, Faÿ would resolve the "problem" of Stein's Jewishness with a remarkable postmortem coup: converting Alice B. Toklas to Christianity, on the grounds that as a Christian Toklas was more likely to meet Stein in heaven than as a Jew. In the 1920s, however, Faÿ dealt with Stein's Jewishness through another kind of coup, imaginatively transforming her into a Christian saint.

Curiously, Faÿ appears to have been aided in this effort by Stein herself. In 1926—the year she met Faÿ—Stein was deeply engrossed in her own imaginative exploration of saints and sainthood. She had recently written a number of texts dealing either directly or obliquely with the theme ("Saints and Singing," "A Saint in Seven," "Talks to Saints or Stories of Saint Remy"). Richard Bridgman suggests that this new interest was stimulated by Stein's experience around nuns during a hospital stay in 1921; Ulla Dydo links it to Stein's sojourn in Saint-Rémy and to her romantic memories of Spain during her Mallorca period.[111] Whatever the cause, saints began appearing regularly in Stein's writing during the 1920s, and they would eventually form the basis for one of her best-known works, *Four Saints in Three Acts* (1927). Stein would continue writing and thinking about saints for the rest of her life. She would ultimately rely on the prophecies of the seventh-century Saint Odile and the nineteenth-century Cure d'Ars to make sense of the defeat of France by the Germans and the subsequent installation of the Vichy regime in 1940.

Stein's saints are always iconic figures, eternally present and invested with deep creative and generative powers. They are associated in her mind with singing, with performance, and more generally with artistry and the artist: in *The Autobiography of Alice B. Toklas*, she links saints to the "individual force" of "actual creation" (*ABT* 280).[112] Over the course of the 1920s and 1930s, saints would join a list of other iconic figures in Stein's imaginative pantheon— geniuses, generals, celebrities, prophets, heroes, and dictators—all synonymous with the figure of the artist and thus with Stein herself. But saints in particular fascinated Stein and seemed to mirror her own sense of self. As she writes in "Talks to Saints": "I am said to resemble them and they are said to resemble them and they are said to resemble me."[113]

There is nothing overtly ecclesiastical about Stein's saints, and, indeed, their religious aspect might seem almost beside the point. Stein uses the term "saint" in a loose way to refer equally to canonized figures (St. Teresa of Avila, St. Michael the Archangel, St. Ignatius of Loyola, St. Paul), to fictional beings (St. Settlement, St. Plan), to friends and family (St. Sarah, St. Michael), as well as to herself. What these figures share in Stein's writing is a dimension of difference from others, of separateness and distinction, "beyond the functions of history, memory, and identity."[114] As such, saints appear in Stein's work like static figures in a tableau, or like the elements of a still-life painting, or like actors on a stage, for it was also her interest in plays, opera, and performance that initially led Stein to saints. As she writes in *Everybody's Autobiography* (1937), "A saint a real saint never does anything, a martyr does something but a really good saint does nothing," a statement she would also make about her own genius: "It takes a lot of time to be a genius, you have to sit around so much doing nothing, really doing nothing" (*EA* 109, 70). As Melissa R. Jones writes: "Saints personify that deceptive stillness of internal action in which 'nothing really moves but things are there.'"[115] Since they live in a continuous present and embody the fullness of being, saints, like geniuses, are not exactly performers, but they are often featured in a performative context with its own rituals, practices, and beliefs. It is worth remembering that Stein's interest in saints coincided with her own emergence as gay salon hostess, where she presided over an ongoing spectacle of drama and gossip, all the while enjoying a campy kind of deification of her own. Welcoming her gay male disciples by posing herself performatively underneath the famous portrait of her by Picasso, Stein seemed to mimic Saint Theresa in *Four Saints in Three Acts*: "All to come and go to stand up to kneel and to be around."[116]

But if Stein's interest in saints and sainthood was less religious than it was aesthetic or performative, the Catholic faith was also not irrelevant to Stein— especially during a period when she was disavowing, in "The Reverie of the Zionist," the claims of a politicized world Jewry. While Stein's opinions on the topic of religion during the 1920s were clear—"I am really not all that concerned about it," she told her friend Samuel Steward—her growing fascination with Catholicism suggests a more ambivalent, complex attitude toward matters of faith.[117] One could even argue that Stein appears publicly to have embraced Catholicism, its rituals, and its icons *in place of* embracing Judaism—as a way of displacing her anxieties over her own Jewishness. We have already seen how Stein displaced the Jewish theme in her early works such as *The Making of Americans* and "Melanctha." In 1927, Stein surely had "Melanctha" in mind when she wrote the libretto for *Four Saints in Three Acts* and when she agreed with Virgil Thomson to cast African Americans in the roles of the saints for the American performance of the opera. Stein explicitly refers to the Catholic saints she writes about as wanderers, invested with deep creative and generative powers, unfixed by semantic or narrative structures; they are, as Melanctha's lover Jeff said about her, "too many" for the form that would attempt to portray, represent, or embody them.[118] Yet at no point in her career does Stein ever acknowledge the Jewish Ur-text, or the figure of the wandering Jew, that lies behind the "Melanctha"-*Four Saints* lineage. The obscuring of the Jewish theme also works to Stein's benefit in her effort in *Four Saints* and elsewhere to imagine her own creative genius as saintly. Perhaps most importantly, identifying herself with Catholic sainthood at a moment in which Jews, as one of the forefathers of French anti-Semitism wrote, represented a "slide toward decadence" was not without its importance for Stein.[119] At the end of the 1920s, and as her friendship with Bernard Faÿ deepened, Stein seemed to grasp the expediency of a positive attitude toward Catholicism.[120]

In his retrospective account of their relationship, Faÿ states that Stein's "curiosity" about Catholicism was sparked by their mutual conversations during long walks through the French countryside. "She loved to speak with me about God," Faÿ writes, and while Stein always prefaced their discussions by remarks about her Jewish background, she also to Faÿ manifested a clear "taste" (*goût*) for Catholic culture and the various forms of Christian devotion (*LP* 141). What Faÿ fails to mention is that Stein's interest in Catholicism was not simply intellectual. As the 1920s turned into the 1930s, whatever distance Stein may have felt from organized religion generally was gradually replaced by an appreciation for the political critique of the French Third Republic emerging from Catholic intellectuals on the Right. Faÿ was one of these figures, but there were others among Stein's friends who would become key players in the Catholic movements calling for French national renewal: men such as Henri Daniel-Rops and Anatole de Monzie, both of whom would support the National Revolution of Philippe Pétain. These "political Catholics," many of them, like Faÿ, former followers of Charles Maurras, were drawn to authoritarianism and its fascist permutations as the only alternative to the decadent Third Republic and as the only counterweight to the perceived threat of international communism. Their influence lies behind Stein's remarkable claim from 1937, reported by Steward, that "Catholicism" represented the only possible future for France.[121] By the late 1930s, Stein, like many others, would begin to voice support for what she called the "Catholic solution" to France's social and political woes. What remains at issue is whether she understood, and even embraced, the connection between this solution and the eventual regime of Philippe Pétain.

⊡ ⊡ ⊡

There was one final characteristic that Gertrude Stein and Bernard Faÿ had in common, and that made them, for a time, true equals: both were expert at controlling and manipulating the people around them. Both "collected" friends and disciples like fine paintings or *objets d'art*, cultivating and discarding acquaintances throughout their respective lives with alacrity and sometimes cruelty. Both were savvy critics of interpersonal relationships, and both enjoyed and encouraged social intrigue. By the time they met in the mid-1920s, both had also developed a sophisticated way of protecting themselves from the needs and demands of others.

As a "disciple," Faÿ was at first clearly the less dominant figure in the relationship with Stein, but this too gave him a certain amount of latitude to charm, flatter, and manipulate. While he initially claimed to be "frightened" of Stein, he was also calculating about winning her favor. In fact, by the mid-1920s, Faÿ was in the process of developing a social *modus vivendi* that would serve him well in his career up to World War II. As his contemporary Bravig Imbs writes, Faÿ was "coldly analytical and calculating in his friendships." Imbs recounts a telling conversation he once had with Faÿ about friendship: "'It's simple,' [Faÿ] said, 'first you choose the people you want ultimately for your friends, then you choose those who are the friends of theirs. You begin with the latter, of course, and as soon as they have introduced you to their friends, you drop them. Just make a new list every year and drop people as fast as you acquire more important friends."[122] Although Faÿ never wholly dropped Virgil Thomson, the "less important" friend who may have originally introduced him to Stein, he did manage to arrange a tighter and more lasting collaboration with Stein than Thomson ever did.[123] In his memoirs, Faÿ claimed that Stein quickly became for him "a need," leaving unstated the degree to which his "necessity" for her had to do with her greater authority at a moment when Faÿ was cultivating his career (*LP* 140).

Like Faÿ, Stein too saw friendship as a process of selection and rejection inextricable from an arc of power. In her first literary works, "Fernhurst," *Q.E.D.* and *Three Lives*, Stein had explored her particular sense of human relationships as sites of struggle, competition, and hierarchy. Writing about friendship in *Three Lives*, Stein described its blossoming, its fading, its shifts, and its lulls as degrees on a subtle spectrum of mutual influence and manipulation, more complex than familial relationships and certainly less predictable, supportive, or lasting. While families required accommodation, friendship for Stein was in the end about what she called "winning"—or losing. Much of Stein's understanding in this matter had to do with her own formative experiences at college when, as an "obstreperous and bossy" undergraduate,[124] Stein took it upon herself to understand and describe the essential character—or what she called "bottom nature"—of those around her, her close associates as well as Harvard students as a whole. One college acquaintance recalls that "friendship" with Stein seemed to take the form of a psychology experiment: Stein would listen intently during a conversation until she had figured out the "bottom nature" of her companion. "I've got you!" she would then triumphantly announce. Needless to say, Stein's will to power and dominance required that her acquaintances remain submissive "losers" in the game of friendship.

From the outset, Stein would use her discoveries about her friends' bottom natures as fodder for her writing. She would easily dash off a literary portrait of an acquaintance with little apparent preparation. Her "research" appears in *portraits* *Q.E.D.*, in *The Making of Americans*, and in the portraits that she began doing of friends and family around 1908. In later years, Stein would confess that her study of bottom natures offered her the ability to know, control, and hence rid herself of any dependence upon those whom she was portraying:

> there has to come a moment when I know all I can know about anyone and I know it all at once and then I try to put it down to put down on paper all that I know of anyone their ways the sound of their voice the accent of their voice their other movements their character all what they do . . . because after

anybody has become very well known to me I have tried to make a portrait of them well I might almost say in order to get rid of them inside in me. Otherwise I would have got too full up inside me with what I had inside me of anyone.[125]

Stein describes the buildup to the writing of portraiture as a process of being engorged by the presence of another; the act of writing then becomes a way of ejecting this presence from her system. This is a strikingly abject image and one that speaks to Stein's lifelong attraction to the dynamic of sadomasochism. Doing portraits becomes a way of asserting dominance over others, of "winning"—although submitting or "losing," as Alice Toklas and eventually Bernard Faÿ recognized, could also develop into a form of power over Stein.

Several years after they met, in 1929, Stein sent Faÿ a note together with a literary portrait she had just written entitled "Bernard Faÿ." The note reads: "My dear Faÿ, Here is a portrait of you that I have just done, I do hope you will like it, do write and tell me that you do, I made it out of grammar and I am very pleased with it."[126] Stein's "pleasure" seems related to her ability to achieve what she calls "a very detailed action upon the parts of a sentence": nouns, prepositions, adverbs, and, in particular, the articles "a" and "the."[127] Stein was intrigued by the unusual pronunciation of Faÿ's name (Fae-ï), and she uses this pronunciation to explore differing permutations of "a" and "the" as well as to create a sort of alphabet of parts of speech ("A is an article. / The is an article. / A and the. Thank you.").[128] The text also apparently refers to a debate that Stein had with Faÿ in the late 1920s over the relative merit of nouns, with Faÿ "for" nouns and Stein "against" ("What is a noun. Favored. A noun can be best. Why does he like it as he does.").[129] But Stein may also have been pleased with "Bernard Faÿ" because the portrait seemed to capture the essence of Faÿ's nature and in so doing seemed able to "get rid of [him] inside in me."

"Bernard Faÿ" reveals what Stein thought of Faÿ at the beginning of their friendship. The image on the cover of the "Bernard Faÿ" draft notebook—a picture of a Spanish bullfighter who looks remarkably like Faÿ and a printed description of the "Toréador Espagnol"—is clearly meant to be representative and associates Faÿ with vigor, courage, and a "quickness to anger and to joy [gaité]." The portrait itself reiterates these qualities, referring to patience, amiability, deliberation, prudence, to "zeal," to "delight," and to the "relief" of "sense." Faÿ is "careful" and "sure." According to her own theory of portraiture, these qualities represent "all [Stein] can know" about Faÿ: her best efforts at grasping him, dominating him, pinning down his bottom nature. She ends with a penultimate sentence that cryptically affirms her control: "The own owned own owner."[130]

But there was much more to Faÿ's character that this portrait does not acknowledge, including Faÿ's ongoing and subtle manipulation of Stein herself. As Stein would discover over the course of the next fifteen years, it was not so easy either to own Bernard Faÿ or to rid herself of her dependency on him. Although she didn't realize it when they first met, Stein's friendship with Faÿ would soon become a determining factor in her life.

TRANSATLANTIC CROSSINGS, TRANSLATIONAL POLITICS (1930–1935)

CHAPTER TWO

T HE FRIENDSHIP between Gertrude Stein and Bernard Faÿ emerged at a moment when "friendship" was suddenly an au courant term, especially in political circles. In the decade following World War I and among the survivors of that event aptly characterized by Stein as a "lost generation," all effort was geared toward the avoidance of conflict, the settling of old disputes, and the pursuit of peace. Yet the war and its immediate aftermath had permanently altered the nature of international relations. Peace was an uncertain and provisional, if desperately desired, condition; violence, so much a part of life in the trenches, simmered beneath the surface calm; deep grievances continued to be felt by both the "victors" and "losers" of the recent conflict; and all around, as Marc Ferro has written, was an "uneasy atmosphere."[1] In this tense environment, the slippery and deceptively innocuous term "friendship" came to stand in for the complex dance of the world's major powers as they sought to navigate the relationships of their new world and to avoid a repetition of their immediate past.

Among the pacts and treaties of friendship signed during the 1920s were the following: Russia's Treaty of Friendship with Afghanistan in 1921; Italy's Treaty of Friendship with the Kingdom of the Serbs, Croats, and Slovenes in 1924; and, in 1926 alone, Romania's Treaty of Friendship with France and with Italy, Greece's Friendship Treaty with Poland, Spain's Treaty of Friendship with Italy, Italy's Friendship Treaty with

Yemen, and the Treaty of Neutrality and Friendship between Germany and the Soviet Union. Two years later, in 1928, one of the most unusual of these friendship pacts was signed between France and the United States: the Treaty of Paris, also known as the Kellogg-Briand Peace Pact, which effectively declared war between France and America to be illegal. This treaty could be seen as the gold standard for international friendship pacts—some thirteen other nations signed it in 1929, including England, Germany, Italy, and Japan—were it not almost immediately violated by Japan's invasion of Manchuria in 1931.

Indeed, Kellogg-Briand was to have virtually no effect on the subsequent buildup of European hostilities over the course of the 1930s. In a sense, the failure of Kellogg-Briand, including its "appallingly naïve"[2] provision outlawing war, seemed to signal the end of the postwar political fixation on international friendship: after 1929, in the wake of the American stock-market crash, deepening economic crises in Europe, and the rise to power of the Nazis in Germany, signing friendship pacts no longer seemed like the right political game to play. Where once "friendship" had sounded more diplomatically palatable, and indeed hopeful, than the militaristic term "alliance"—a term that resonated with the tortured associations of World War I—as the war receded from memory and as new geopolitical concerns arose, "friends" once again began to seem less important than political "allies" or even "collaborators." When one spoke of "friendship" in the 1930s, as did the German political theorist and Nazi sympathizer Carl Schmitt in *The Concept of the Political* (1932), one meant a political ally willing to defend to the death a community or a way of life: the existential antithesis of "the enemy."[3] The darkness of Schmitt's vision perfectly matched the mood of the thirties, where "friendship" had now become overtly tied to the workings of power.

But even in the 1920s, friendship as a political ideal was far from a neutral or unmarked state of relations. While statesmen such as Aristide Briand and Frank Kellogg made eloquent pronouncements affirming the "spirit of justice and humanity [that] has never ceased to unite our two countries,"[4] their co-authored Pact of Perpetual Friendship concealed a far less harmonious relationship between the United States and France. For France, gripped by mounting security concerns, the continuing crisis of war debts, and a weakened economy, the friendship pact with America meant a potentially vital safeguard for its future. Yet although France recognized and indeed deferred to America's new political and economic hegemony in the 1920s, this era was also characterized by virulent anti-Americanism on the part of the French public. Books with titles like *The American Cancer* and *America: The Menace* became bestsellers in France at this time; French intellectuals earned their stripes on the strength of their anti-Americanism.[5] Americans, for their part, had grown increasingly cynical toward international disputes in the wake of World War I and were swayed by the controversial idea that their French and British "allies" had duped them into the war. Ill feeling toward the French in particular was sustained by France's inability and ultimate refusal to fully repay their $21 billion dollar war debt. These feelings contributed to a mood of deepening isolationism and pacifism, which paradoxically fueled popular support for the Kellogg-Briand Pact outlawing war. Yet the true source of this support by the American public was hardly a desire to affirm "perpetual friendship" with France. Rather, what the United States wished above all was not to be drawn again into a destructive and protracted war with duplicitous European powers.

Poised precariously in the midst of this shifting and uncertain world, the French "America expert" Bernard Faÿ seemed to sound the complexities of Franco-American relations in two writings from 1929. "The Course of French-American Friendship," an essay Faÿ wrote for the *Yale Review*, echoes the rhetoric of the Kellogg-Briand Pact by arguing that rapprochement between the two nations is worth pursuing, because France and America have historically shared "a legend of friendship . . . with the benign face of Franklin, the dignified figure of Washington, the youthful La Fayette as illustrations."[6] Drawing heavily on his master's thesis at Harvard, published in 1925 in Paris as "L'esprit revolutionnaire en France et aux États-Unis à la fin du XVIIIème siècle," Faÿ discusses the "revolutionary spirit" that thrived on both sides of the Atlantic between 1770 and 1800 and that produced a "friendship of ideas" between France and America. This shared historical experience had in turn informed a complementary appreciation on both sides, with Americans "enjoying France as the place which was most unlike their home" and the French accepting America "as a nation that had none of the typical shortcomings of Europe" (FAF 440). In the present "era of bad feeling," Faÿ writes, such complementarity has been lost, yet for reasons having to do with postwar misunderstandings rather than deep differences of opinion and outlook.[7] In the end, Faÿ writes, the friendship between France and America "cannot be set down in dollars and francs . . . because there is no vital conflict of interest between the two nations, and also because the people of perception in each nation can find true pleasure in sharing the life of the other." Faÿ even trumps his contemporary Aristide Briand, suggesting that Franco-American friendship "is on a higher plane than conventional 'good will' and formal 'pacts.' It is friendship in its finest meaning" (FAF 455).

Yet a more instrumental idea of friendship underlies Faÿ's other major text on Franco-American relations from 1929, *The American Experiment*.[8] In this book, Faÿ acknowledges the "warm, rich, generous, sturdy pulse of life" (*AE* 7) that a Frenchman finds in America, yet he devotes little space in his analysis to the "legend of friendship" shared between France and the United States, nor does he make much of the "spirit of justice and humanity" that has historically united French and American citizens. *The American Experiment*, as its title suggests, centers around an invidious comparison between America's victorious "experiment" with democracy and France's unfortunate one. Faÿ's goal is to show France what it must do in order to maintain or recover its position as America's political equal, in order to "turn towards America without fear or jealousy. Then only will the two continents arrive at a true friendship, born of mutual appreciation and respect for each other's qualities" (*AE* 263–264). "True friendship" here has little to do with "true pleasure in sharing the life of the other," nor is it linked to some indefinable attraction. It is something that takes place between two dominant powers who share "mutual appreciation and respect for each other's qualities," who balance each other's extent and mode of power. This definition recalls Faÿ's framing of personal friendship as a game of power and calculation (friends, we are reminded, are those whom you "drop . . . as fast as you acquire more important friends"). What matters in the game of friendship is not fellow feeling but one's relative power vis-à-vis the position of the other.

The American Experiment conveys a much greater depth of anxiety about the state of world affairs than does "The Course of French-American Friendship." While the latter essay paints a rosy picture of two great nations celebrating a shared humanist legacy, the former book refers to "tired and bleeding Europe," with its postwar "fatalistic acceptance of the worst disasters"—a marked contrast to America's "new world power—sinewy, youthful and generous" (*AE* 6–7). The joy and vitality that elsewhere Faÿ finds so seductive about Americans here underscores France's own lack of vitality, its degeneracy, and this in turn feeds into France's bitterness, resentment, and dislike of the United States. "A hateful fear of the United States is spreading and may eventually submerge all other feelings," he writes (*AE* 6). Yet unlike so many of his French contemporaries, Faÿ does not place the blame for this fear on the United States, nor does he see America as an "abomination" (the title of another popular French anti-American tract from 1930, Kadmi-Cohen's *L'abomination américaine*). His position on the United States is, and remains, dialectical. While Faÿ agrees with Kadmi-Cohen and others that a new kind of threat lies beneath those "sinewy, youthful" American bodies Faÿ so admires—the threat of "imperialistic temptations which will be difficult indeed to resist" (*AE* 257)—Faÿ is also quick to point out that it is *France* who must change its ways, who must work to acquire America as its "more important friend." Only in this way will France once again be a player on the world stage.

What is it, for Bernard Faÿ, that France must learn from its American ally at the end of the 1920s? As he ponders this question in *The American Experiment*, Faÿ begins to outline the first dimensions of a new blueprint for French society, one that would eventually, over the course of the following decade, align his work precisely with the French and European Right.

In the first place, while both France and America profess a constitutional commitment to moral, civic, and democratic liberties, the effect of this commitment has been different in each society. Returning to the moment of the French and American revolutions, Faÿ argues that while both were waged in the name of certain ideals—liberty, equality, and democracy—the French Revolution had ultimately devolved into a catastrophic parody of social renovation. The vital spirit that had led French citizens to overthrow the bonds of tradition in the name of democratic human rights had produced a disastrous vacuum in leadership and power. Like his spiritual father Charles Maurras, Faÿ felt that the rejection of the two major sources of authority in French society, the Catholic Church and the monarchy, had had shattering effects on social order and stability. Far from redressing inequalities and bettering the lives of "the humblest," the French Revolution had done the work "of leveling and obliterating, of destroying the great and reducing the strong and active" (*AE* 253). "Democracy" had worked only to place everyone on the same debased level, favoring the "turbulent, envious, and mostly powerless elements" in society (*AE* 42). Moreover, the vacuum in leadership opened up by revolutionary events had been filled, clandestinely, by a cabal of shadowy figures who secretly directed society to their own ends—a subject that would increasingly preoccupy Faÿ as he turned his attention to the "problem" of French Freemasonry.

In comparison, America's revolutionary experiment had produced far different results. While America's "revolutionary spirit" had likewise worked to overthrow certain traditional structures of social order (in the case of America, British colonial rule), the new ideal of democracy in America never came to signify a total capitulation to "the masses," as it did in France. Rather— and here Faÿ departs from almost every other French commentator of the day—America appeared to have escaped the problem of mass rule in large part because the framers of America's revolution and constitution were themselves an elite and hence committed to a system that would reflect and support their interests.[9] While the French revolutionaries looked for a radical restructuring of prerevolutionary, eighteenth-century society, America's "republican aristocrats"—"men of means or of exceptional intellectual capacities" such as

Washington, Jefferson, and Franklin—shared none of the French revolution-ary antipathy toward the elites of the ancien régime. In a formulation that is more than simply historical, Faÿ writes that the American revolutionaries were profoundly "eighteenth century" in character. Their revolutionary spirit was the result of anti-British feeling rather than antimonarchical fervor. Their actions aimed not to dismantle the aristocracy in favor of a democracy of "the common people" but to create a democracy "of the strong." To this extent, Faÿ argues, America neither was nor is a democracy in the French sense—neither in its political structure nor in its ideology of individual achievement.

Faÿ cites two aspects of American society that radically challenge French democratic ideals. The first is America's federalist political structure based in a constitutional division of powers, what Faÿ calls "truly an eighteenth-century masterpiece" (*AE* 44). Federalism preserves the autonomy of the local and the individual, again preventing the popular voice from achieving dominance. Unlike French democracy, which "always obliged [the individual] to yield or conform to the will of the majority" (*AE* 11), American federalism works according to compromise rather than majority rule. "Democracy," Faÿ writes, "was made to serve here . . . the American Nation was built not on a theory of majority rule, or obedience to higher authority, but on one of the harmonious interworking of separate interests" (*AE* 10). This heterogeneity, built into the American system, has required Americans to act with "prudence, compromise and moderation" in their political deliberations, while allowing the elites to maintain their positions of authority in the executive branch, on the Supreme Court, and in the judiciary. On yet another level, Faÿ writes, Americans, unlike the French, have always disdained truly democratic or communitarian ideologies. Although Americans express a great deal of public conformity— "Clothes, pleasures, attitudes, styles, opinions, momentary preoccupations, belong to all, and are adopted or rejected by all" (*AE* 132)—within themselves, Americans are each individual strivers, each dreaming of a way to break free from the pack. Blessed with enormous natural resources and prodigious geo-graphical space, America has been able to sustain its central ideology of indi-vidual achievement and call it "democratic." But, in fact, in this "land of strong and ambitious men," democracy is less important than the "tendency to avoid strict limits and to seek a constantly enlarging scope" (*AE* 50, 155).

In his final chapter, "The Lesson of America," Faÿ articulates a set of pre-scriptions that merge his ideas about America with the prevailing concerns of the French Right, particularly those Maurrassian factions committed to a restoration of the monarchy and those nonconformist groups working toward a European "new order."[10] America's "lesson," Faÿ writes, is one alien to the democratic and parliamentary traditions of postrevolutionary France; it is a lesson of federalism and authoritarianism undiluted by the false claims of democratic egalitarianism: "Europe might derive salutary results from a sincere trial of federalism, from organized collaboration aiming at the reconciliation of conflicting interests, from obligatory arbitration, and from a resolve to suppress, once and for all, the political considerations born of the French Revolution."[11] The Maurrassian rhetoric in this passage—"suppressing the French Revolution" (that is, rejecting the specious doctrine of parliamentary democracy), deferring to "obligatory arbitration" (that is, vesting authority in a higher power such as a monarch or dictator)—here merge with an account of America in which such "ideals" were once omnipotent. Like his friend and eventual Vichyite Pierre Drieu la Rochelle, who wrote in 1922 that "we must create a United States of Europe, because it is the only way of defending Europe against itself and against other human groups,"[12] Faÿ saw America as the model for a new order in Europe, an order that would transcend and reverse two centuries of democratic rule through reasserting its united supremacy and power to defend itself against "other [non-European] human groups."

Of course, this argument was a double-edged sword. If America was the model for a new pan-European empire, then it also represented a threat to this New Europe: one version of the "non-European human group" beating down the gates of European civilization.[13] This, as we have seen, was the argument of most French intellectuals of the day, including Drieu himself, for whom *américanisation* was synonymous with a creeping, miasmic cultural and social abomination. Nevertheless, "the United States of Europe" remained for Drieu and others a powerful structural model for a new and eventually fascist Europe, speaking to the deep relevance of such a model in transatlantic relations.[14]

Faÿ's sense of America as an example and a threat, as a friend and a competitor, was more historical than that of his contemporaries. For Faÿ, it is *eighteenth-century* America that remains the model and exemplar for present-day Europe; it is eighteenth-century America whose "harmonious unity" offers the best prototype for a new federal European Order: "The federalism which rendered such great aid to the youthful United States would now be of invaluable assistance to the ravaged continent of Europe," he writes. "It would teach the nations that their interests in common are not the least important. . . . It would impress the voter with the fact that, after all, his ballot is a very small thing and that his opinion is generally quite negligible. . . . [It would allow for] the principle of authority, conferred upon one leader, who alone should discern what is useful" (*AE* 259, 262).

The alternative to this admittedly undemocratic eighteenth-century ideal, Faÿ writes, is a dismal one for both America and Europe:

> In our complicated world of today no one save economists and bankers has the right to speak unequivocally and to make demands. There is no aristocracy in the true sense of the word, except for a number of Jews, whose international situation and technical knowledge place them apart. The fate of nations, in the final analysis, is decided in the private offices of business men, who alone may dictate and alter conditions. This is a cruel, derisive and ludicrous fact.
>
> (AE 262)

Faÿ's indictment of the "world of today" here encompasses both America and Europe, each representing a corrupt system of governance dominated by the interests of an illegitimate, shadowy elite. Unlike the legitimate elite— the Anglo-Saxon "aristocracy" in America and the monarchy and Church in France—the "economists and bankers" who dominate the current scene do so only with an eye to their own transnational and economic self-interest and at the expense of the national good. Hence America's lesson—and one that present-day America itself need also learn—is one rooted in the past, in a youthful prerevolutionary world organized around community, work, and authority. This is a lesson, Faÿ writes, that teaches its observers to be wary of the claims of the present, which are after all only a screen behind which reside the *real* power brokers—"Jews and businessmen"—and their corrupt, self-serving interests.

In a remarkable short story he wrote two years before *The American Experiment,* "La Manille aux Enchères" (1927), Faÿ creates an allegory in which the forces of good, embodied in a young Christian man, square off against the forces of evil, represented by an "old, dirty . . . Jew."[15] On a crowded New York City subway, an unnamed protagonist finds himself squeezed between a supple and beautiful young man, "surrounded by a halo of joy," and a menacing elderly Jewish man, delusional and violent, who presses a gun into the side of the protagonist and threatens to kill him. The story ends without resolution, but the symbolism could not be thicker: will the protagonist be saved by the Jesus figure on his left or murdered by the Judas figure on his right? What adds interest to this turgid melodrama is the American context: to the protagonist, his beautiful friend (simply referred to in the text as "Mon Ami") represents the real citizen of this nation, its finest type, "one [of the crowd] and nevertheless hardly like them" (*FVJ* 25), marked by the quality that most frequently appears in Faÿ's descriptions about Americans: "joy." This is someone who "in his perfection embodied a hundred generations of thought" and who speaks always "of the future." He is also quite clearly racially marked by his "Anglo-Saxonism"—a term that Faÿ, in *The American Experiment*, links to "a natural pride and distinction."[16] Yet this Ur-American, princely, godly, and racially pure, exists always in tension with his evil Jewish counterpart: "one of those German Jews, recently arrived even though they had actually been here for about fifty years, greedy, jealous, avid." Which force will conquer him, the protagonist wonders, as he contemplates the inevitable end of his journey. The stakes of this cultural card game ("la manille aux enchères") could not be higher.

The impetus behind this and other texts that Faÿ wrote in the late 1920s was not simply to idealize "aristocratic," Anglo-Saxon, and Christian America, with its "splendid race of men" (*AE* 50) and its "eighteenth-century" values. It was also to sound the warning about the forces within both America and Europe that threatened this ideal type: corrupt democratic and individualist ideas, popular sovereignty, false universalism, and the Semitic gods of a new economic religion, "priests [who] are alone invested with the right of pronouncing oracles and enforcing them" (*AE* 262–263).

⊞ ⊞ ⊞

In the late 1930s, several years after Bernard Faÿ presented eighteenth-century America as a model for present-day Europe, Gertrude Stein too saw in the not-so-distant future a resurgence of "eighteenth-century" feeling:

> perhaps the twenty-first century like the eighteenth-century will be a nice time when everybody forgets to be a father or to have been one. The Jews and they come into this because they are very much given to having a father and to being one and they are very much given not to want a father and not to have one, and they are an epitome of all this that is happening the concentration of fathering to the perhaps there not being one.
>
> (*EA* 142)

This passage corresponds to Faÿ's vision of a renewed future born from the resurrection of "eighteenth-century" values, associated with Stein as a time "when everybody forgets to be a father or to have been one." But it is not just "fathers" who are to be purged from this future/past; chillingly, the sentence also seems to be anticipating a moment where both "fathering" and "the Jews" may end up "not being one." Written in 1937, a year before the Nazi pogrom known as *Kristallnacht*, Stein's comments are eerily prophetic. But they are also disturbing, perhaps above all in objectifying "the Jews" as a discrete social entity—as though Stein herself were somehow excluded from this entity. This would not be the only moment in the 1930s when Stein would distance herself from Jews and Jewishness.[17] Ambiguous to the extreme, Stein's comments here are only unequivocal in her rather banal description of the eighteenth century: "a nice time."

Like Faÿ, Stein's interest in the eighteenth century was lifelong, and has usually been noted in light of her aesthetic appreciation for eighteenth-century English novelists such as Defoe and Sterne. But while Stein claimed that "[i]t is nice thinking how different each century is and the reason why," her comparative thinking on this subject was far from anodyne.[18] Indeed, by the 1930s, Stein's references to "the eighteenth-century" had a distinctly polemical cast, functioning invariably through contrast with the modern epoch of "organization" and self-enslavement in which "everybody wanted to be organized and the more they were organized the more everybody liked the slavery of being in an organization."[19] Like several of her American contemporaries, Stein fetishized the historical eighteenth century as the high point of a kind of authentic American populism as well as the pinnacle of classical economic liberalism. Looking back nostalgically to prerevolutionary America and to the rugged masculine individualism of Thomas Jefferson's idealized yeoman farmers,[20] Stein and other early twentieth-century American intellectuals—including William Carlos Williams, John Dos Passos, Edgar Lee Masters, and John Dewey—insistently contrasted this lost epoch with an urbanized, effeminate, industrialized, and capitalistic modernity.[21] It would not seem much of a stretch to translate this nostalgia for prerevolutionary America and corresponding critique of modernity into contemporary European profascist terms.

The most visible proponent of this kind of translational thinking was of course Ezra Pound, who famously wrote that American civilization began in 1760 and ended in 1830 and who infamously perceived a renascence of old American values in the surging movements of European fascism.[22] In his 1933 tract *Jefferson and/or Mussolini*, Pound portrayed Italian fascism as a neo-Jeffersonianism—incorrectly, to be sure, given the utter discrepancy between Jefferson's myth of personal autonomy and Mussolini's ideology of self-sacrifice to the State. Nevertheless, *Jefferson and/or Mussolini* perfectly exemplifies how a fascination with prerevolutionary America overlapped with—even inspired—a militant commitment to European fascism in the 1930s, both signifying a potent form of antimodern and anticapitalist reaction. Pound's idealized eighteenth century was less a historical epoch than an ideological

foil against which to contrast all the evils of the modern world: industrialization, mass production, bureaucratization, and, above all, finance capitalism
or "usury"—Pound's central term to describe an economic system organized
around debt and interest and dominated by "eastern Jews" and "Wall St. swin-
dlers."[23] Pound became the shrillest critic of this system created by "Jews and
businessmen," but he was not alone; as Alec Marsh notes, Pound's stance was
"largely consistent with American Populist prejudices" as well as with profascist ideologies during the 1930s.[24] Thrown into relief by Pound's more extremist views, Gertrude Stein's political and "historical" pronouncements about the
eighteenth century take on new meaning.

While critics have long underscored and praised Stein's populist convictions, emphasized repeatedly by Stein herself throughout the 1930s, few have
paid attention to the kind of populist prejudices that would align Stein with
a figure like Pound and with his political sympathies. Although Stein, to her
credit, found little to like in Pound himself—she refers to him caustically in
The Autobiography of Alice B. Toklas as a "village explainer"—her politics over
the course of the 1930s began to resemble quite closely the profascist populist
Jeffersonianism that lay behind Pound's tedious "explanations." While Stein
had an instinctive dislike of pontification and felt that explanation or "eluci-
dation" could never be a straightforward literalistic process, she was remarkably insistent over the course of the 1930s on reiterating a basic hypothesis:
"the beginning of the eighteenth century went in for freedom and ended with
the beginning of the nineteenth century that went in for organization"; "The
beginning of the eighteenth century, after everything had been under feudal
and religious domination, was full of a desire for individual liberty and they
went at it until they thought they had it . . . so there they were and everybody
was free and then that went on to Lincoln"; "The eighteenth century began
the passion for individual freedom, the end of the nineteenth century by con-
ceiving organization began the beginning of a passion for being enslaved not
so much for enslaving but for being enslaved."[25] As these passages suggest,
"the eighteenth century" is for Stein both an idealized and mythified historical
epoch and a means for invidious comparison with "the nineteenth century,"
insistently portrayed in her writing as a moment of decline, loss, fragmenta-
tion, and petit bourgeois values.[26] Perhaps Stein's most interesting claim, and
one we will return to in chapter 4, is that which links the nineteenth century
to an impoverishment of the English language and linguistic experimentation:
"And now came the nineteenth century and a great many things were gone,"
she writes in "What Is English Literature" (1934), "[t]hat the words were there
by themselves simply was gone. That the words were livelily chosen to be next

one to the other was gone. . . . And the clarity of something having completion that too was gone completely gone."[27]

Loss and dissolution characterize the modern fall from an eighteenth-century apex, but again, Stein's "eighteenth-century" always contains a surplus value not fully reducible to a historical or temporal economy. What matters for Stein is that the "eighteenth-century" may, and perhaps already is, on its way back; that the future—or the present occupied by an avant-garde—may emerge as a return to the past, now fully realized as the solution to, rather than the precedent for, nineteenth-century decadence. Stein's "historical" think-ing in these matters is unorthodox yet not unfamiliar to a postmodern age. In refusing to imagine the past as something passed, as "an objective reality that could be grasped and contained," Stein portrays a past always available to the interpreter as part of a living present and potential future.[28] For Stein, the past is not something that ends but is something open-ended, on hand, and ready for appropriation and mobilization to new ends. In her writings of the 1930s, Stein repeatedly moves from speculative musings on historical continuity and disjunction to prescriptive accounts of the need for present and future change. And while her "political" thinking, like her "historical" think-ing, is often eccentric—at times seeming to be uttered on a whim—it becomes sharper and more argumentative as the 1930s wear on. It is indeed at this point where Stein's rhetoric begins to dovetail with emerging reactionary discourses of the French Right, including those of Maréchal Pétain's National Revolution, which promised to redress the "corrupting" influence of the French Revolu-tion and its ideals of "*liberté, égalité, fraternité*," and return France to its core values of "*famille, travail, patrie*" (family, work, fatherland).

Philippe Pétain's France, his "imaginary community" (to borrow Benedict Anderson's phrase), was constructed around the mythic ideal of the French peasantry: those "left behind" by urbanization, industrialization, internation-alism, and nineteenth-century progressivism.[29] The future on which he staked his National Revolution was a regressive one, based on a return to the past that was also a rewriting of all the "democratic decadence" that had come after this past.[30] For a reactionary modernist such as Gertrude Stein, Pétain's ide-als resonated deeply with her sense of the necessary backward direction in which both France and America needed to go. This helps explain, at least par-tially, why Stein so often referred to the twentieth century as an old century and to America as "the oldest country in the world," since only in the twenti-eth century could the values and glories of the American eighteenth century come to fruition—at least by those moderns willing to fight, retrogressively, what she called "a spiritual pioneer fight."[31] In fact, Stein came to realize, it was

Pétain who, as a neo-American founding father (a comparison, as we shall see, that she makes explicit in her Vichy propaganda), would return America to its promise and lost potential. "The trouble is, Americans aren't land-crazy any more," she writes. "That's what the pioneers were, land-crazy, and that's what all Frenchmen are and always have been, because they know that owning a place of your own is what gives you independence and lets you stand on your own feet, and no body is rich unless he owns his own soil."[32] Pétain, who promoted his Vichy revolution through propagandistic images of iconic peasants tilling a field, represented for Stein a return to eighteenth-century values embodied in French peasants and American pioneers alike. It was, therefore, absolutely crucial that Pétain's version of a "spiritual pioneer fight" be yoked to the revolutionary projects of American moderns, like Stein herself, who wished to see in the twentieth century the fulfillment of a lost eighteenth-century promise.

▣ ▣ ▣

Bernard Faÿ and Gertrude Stein made varying use of "the eighteenth century" as a galvanizing phrase to forward their own political and ideological agendas: the former, through systematic historical accounts of the period as a lost epoch of advanced culture; the latter, through ruminations on a rather unusual convergence of literary and economic decadence. On another level, though, both also yearned to experience firsthand this bygone epoch—to truly relive the past as part of a living present. Each seems to have enjoyed ancien régime role playing: Stein, channeling Benjamin Franklin at Faÿ's social teas;[33] Faÿ, playing the lord of the manor in his country home in the Loire valley and occasionally affecting eighteenth-century dress in his breeches and gaiters. Their friendship was "contentedly cemented" (Stein's phrase)[34] in the late 1920s through an important gesture on the part of Faÿ that finally enabled Stein to acquire her own piece of prerevolutionary property, in the form of a Louis XV–era chateau located in the Bugey region of southeastern France. This was the region immortalized by the eighteenth-century gourmet Brillat-Savarin in his *Physiology of Taste*: "a charming countryside with high mountains, hills, rivers, limpid brooks, waterfalls, chasms."[35] During repeated trips with Toklas to the Bugey over the course of the late 1920s, Stein herself came to see this region as the epitome of *la France profonde*: that mythic, rural heart of France untouched by modernity and its problems.[36] Settling there in 1929, in the small picturesque hamlet of Bilignin, Stein believed she had found "the house of our dreams"; Toklas referred to it as "better than our dreams."[37] Visiting them

FIGURE 2.1 Gertrude Stein and Bernard Faÿ at Stein's home in Bilignin, France (1937).

there in 1930, Faÿ felt that he was in "Arcadia." He was particularly impressed, he wrote, by the spoken language of the locals: "charming, careful, almost too literary, in the manner of the eighteenth century."[38]

Yet all three may have felt a twinge of remorse even in the midst of their ancien régime paradise. Along with Georges Maratier, another French friend of Stein, Faÿ had been instrumental in helping Stein secure the lease on the house in Bilignin, in the township of Belley. When Stein wrote Faÿ, "I like writing to you from here [Bilignin] because it was here that our friendship really began," she makes reference to this help and, crucially for the years to come, locates the source of their friendship in contractual affairs.[39] Stein had reason to be grateful to Faÿ and Maratier, because at the time she decided she would take the house, even buying furniture in anticipation of the move, she needed first to deal with the fact that the property was already occupied. The renter, a French lieutenant named Ferdinand Bonhomme stationed in Belley, clearly had no inkling of the problem his presence created for Stein, nor, as he was on the verge of retirement from the army, had he any intention of leaving his peaceful corner of France. Undeterred, Stein devised a plan to have the lieutenant removed from the scene by having him promoted to captain and then, because there could not be more than one captain in the Belley regiment, having him dispatched elsewhere.

In an undated note in the hand of Alice B. Toklas, found in the Georges Maratier archives, several key details are provided about the forty-three-year-old Bonhomme: "3 citations . . . 2 fois blessé . . . Legion d'honneur."[40] This bravery on the field proved of little use in the face of Stein and her friends, who eventually arranged for Bonhomme to be transferred to Morocco, making the house available for them to lease. "May the Good Lord . . . reward him," Toklas remarked, apparently sharing with Stein only minor guilt about this happy turn of events.[41] The two women quickly settled into provincial life, enjoying both the chateau and the land around it, which enabled Toklas to pursue her own version of eighteenth-century homesteading—gardening.

Yet when new concerns arose about Lieutenant Bonhomme, who inconveniently longed to return to the Bilignin chateau, Stein knew just whom to turn to. "The house is ours for this year," she writes to Faÿ in an undated note from the early 1930s,

> and all that is now necessary is that our lieutenant who is now a captain, does not come back to Belley on his return to France in July. He has now no longer a lease but an engagement by the year and so as soon as he takes up his residence in a logement elsewhere in France the owner of the property can give

us a lease. Now if it is possible to do anything about it will you. The enclosed paper gives the information. The regiment he is in now, the regiment that he is *not* to be versed in, because that is the one that has a battalion in Belley, preferably also not in Bourg en Bresse, because that is too near, but a good distance off and in an entirely different regiment and not a temporary but a permanent situation. There are we bothering you a lot. But you will forgive us, I know.[42]

This letter is remarkably revealing not only about Stein's sense of her own power and influence but also about the nature of the relationship between Stein and Faÿ from the early 1930s on. Most striking here is the imperious way Stein dispatches with the threat of the "lieutenant who is now a captain" by plotting out in detail the terms of his *logement* (residence) in France and the confidence with which she arrogates to herself the power to make this kind of decision.[43] A similar sense of entitlement inheres in her manipulation of Bonhomme's own professional title ("our lieutenant who is now a captain")—a real-life example of what Stein will do to Ulysses Grant, Wilbur Wright, Henry James, and George Washington in her contemporaneous text *Four in America*. Stein's playful alteration of the lives of these historical figures—"if Henry James were a general," etc.—becomes more insidious in the case of Lieutenant Bonhomme, whose career is here considered a relatively trivial issue in light of the more "serious" matter of securing a long-term property lease. In fact, "trivial" and "serious" in this entire episode seem strikingly inverted, a charge that would also be leveled at Stein by critics of her wartime activities and writings.

Stein's letter reflects a deep assurance, even arrogance, in addressing Faÿ and enlisting his assistance. Never one to follow the conventional rules of punctuation, Stein's lack of a question mark following her basic request to Faÿ ("Now if it is possible to do anything about it will you") seems at first glance a typically Steinian gesture. Yet without a question mark, Stein's "request" reads more like a direct command, leaving Faÿ little room to decline. Stein's peremptory tone is somewhat sweetened by the end of her note ("There are we bothering you a lot. But you will forgive us, I know"), but here, too, Stein, in her apologetic cajoling, creates a manipulative dynamic that makes it impossible for Faÿ to resist her.

It is useful to focus on the two rhetorical modes of Stein's letter to Faÿ because they point to the complex nature of their developing personal relationship in the early 1930s. On the one hand, we see Stein in a familiar guise toward a younger disciple: domineering, peremptory, somewhat dismissive, assured that Faÿ's full commitment is to affirm and support her trajectory as a writer of genius—whether this involves praising her work or securing a house in which to write. During this period, while Faÿ was developing and broadening his career as a historian and critic of America, he was also aiding Stein's own in numerous ways: reviewing and promoting her writing in various publications in America and France, advising Stein on publication details, helping to prepare an official bibliography of her work, and, most importantly, serving as a French translator for texts such as "Melanctha," *The Making of Americans*, and *The Autobiography of Alice B. Toklas*.[44] In 1934, William Aspinwall Bradley, Stein's American editor, referred to Faÿ as Stein's "official translator" (*traducteur attitré*), a title that subordinates Faÿ and belies his arguably greater intellectual reputation in America at this time.[45]

Faÿ himself, during the early 1930s, seemed only too willing to play for Stein the role of handmaiden, admirer, and booster of her genius. A typical letter from 1931 has Faÿ writing Stein that "your friendship and intimacy has changed for me the reality of my life—I don't have so much to give—my only real quality in the intellectual field being that I am a thirsty beggar." Stein responds: "I always did say an artist does like appreciation and yours is appreciation and how."[46] In essays that Faÿ wrote about Stein's work in 1930 and 1933, he called her "the most powerful American writer of today" and "the only Anglo-Saxon writer of today who has the same sense of the modern as do we French."[47] In his translations of Stein's work, Faÿ remained a faithful amanuensis, transforming the rough linguistic contours of a work such as *The Making of Americans* into something elegant and rather conventional. By contrast, an earlier French translator of *Making*, Georges Hugnet, who had sought to reproduce what he called the "freshness" and "awkwardness" of Stein's language, was eventually dismissed by Stein over a precise dispute regarding the relative powers of creator and translator.[48] The diplomatic and savvy Faÿ sidestepped all such disputes, never demanding that Stein treat him as a writer of equal talent and expressive capacity. Unlike most of Stein's other disciples, Faÿ remained in Stein's good graces throughout this period of social turmoil; alone among Stein and Toklas's friends, Faÿ vacationed at the Bilignin chateau twice during the summer of 1932.

Yet during this same period, the balance of power in Stein and Faÿ's relationship was shifting subtly but irrevocably. While Faÿ was aiding Stein in legal and literary matters, he was also collaborating with and indeed influencing Stein with his own intellectual and political views. No critic or biographer has yet adequately acknowledged the remarkable convergence between the writings of Stein and Faÿ in the early 1930s.[49] During this time, both write substantial pieces on George Washington, Faÿ's preceding Stein's by a year; both write on the idea of history and historical methodology; both publish critiques of Franklin Roosevelt based upon his economic policy and "seductive" character—

Stein's in the form of a public letter to Faÿ. While it is hard to determine the exact lines of influence in this mutual production, it is clear that their growing friendship brings to the fore latent interests of each. Continuing to compose eclectically and experimentally, Stein from 1930 on nevertheless reveals a new fascination with both early American history and the prerevolutionary French aristocracy, in texts such as "The Pilgrims. Thoughts About Master Pieces"; "Louis XI and Madame Giraud"; "Say It with Flowers," set in the time of Louis XI; and "Scenery and George Washington," which became a part of the "George Washington" section of *Four in America*. Faÿ, already a prolific writer on Franco-American history, begins to follow Stein's theoretical interest in what she calls "Messages from History": imaginative ways of understanding the past that bring it into the living present and make it available for the future.

In the early 1930s, both seemed to feel, as Stein put it, that "we do amuse ourselves with ourselves and each other and it is rather nice."[50]

🖫 🖫 🖫

Faÿ's biography of Washington, published in 1931 as *George Washington: Republican Aristocrat* and in French as *George Washington: Gentilhomme*, was read and edited by Stein in manuscript; she deemed it "xtraordinarily compact clear and powerful" despite some reservations about its form.[51] As a biography, *George Washington* is rich in detail and colorful anecdotes; in it, Faÿ hones the elegant, somewhat facile style that will characterize his writing from that point forward. A year earlier, Faÿ had written a lengthy, heavy, complex biography of Benjamin Franklin, a figure who would continue to preoccupy him throughout the next decade; the Washington biography, by comparison, is lighter, more inviting, and more pointed. Faÿ himself described it as "small, but decent. Not too dull. Not too bold."[52] It was, as Stein noted, destined to become a bestseller in America.

The central point of *George Washington* becomes clear in Faÿ's final chapter, "George Washington, the Father of His Country." In the preceding chapters, Faÿ's silent, inarticulate General Washington had been presented as a heroic but uncertain figure, one who struggled to reconcile his aristocratic "sense of taste for authority" with the democratic "phraseology" he felt compelled to utter in an atmosphere of revolutionary populism. While Washington "had publicly recognized the people as supreme in authority . . . he knew that as masters, they were lazy, unfaithful, and forgetful, very little aware of their real interests." In the final chapter, the newly elected President Washington emerges as the creator and "father" of a new national narrative, one in which his own strong presence plays a central role. In this narrative, Washington—"so little a democrat"—presents himself as the expression and offshoot of the people, as the mythical center of a democratic republic. Yet Washington's "genius" is to merge this democratic narrative with a "practical aristocracy": a federal system dominated and guided by a strong, landowning elite that nevertheless claims to represent the citizenry at large. Washington thus achieves a spectacular balancing act, presenting himself as a man of the people while maintaining the spirit of aristocratic rule; he is a public-relations expert, "the first of the great modern politicians who had an infallible instinct for public opinion" (*GW* 235, 273).

Here Faÿ returns to the same ideological ground he covered in his 1929 book *The American Experiment*. The lesson to be learned from eighteenth-century America's experiment with democracy is that democracy in its pure form cannot thrive: that universal suffrage leads inevitably to mob rule. The only way to reign in the mob is to vest power in a functional aristocracy—however much this aristocracy clothes itself in populist garb. This is the inherent truth about his country that Washington understood, digested, and ultimately manipulated to his own glorious ends; this, Faÿ writes, sets Washington apart as one of the heroes of his time and "as one of the leaders of mankind" (*GW* xvi).[53]

A year after Faÿ wrote *George Washington: Republican Aristocrat*, Stein produced her own account of George Washington, first in a shortened version in the journal *Hound and Horn* and later in an extensive "biography" she wrote as part of *Four in America*. Stein had conceived *Four in America*—which echoed both the title and the subject of her 1927 opera "Four Saints in Three Acts"— as an exploration of American "greatness" through the lives of four exemplary figures.[54] But Stein had long been fascinated by the greatness of Washington in particular. As early as *The Making of Americans*, she had evoked Washington in the character of George Dehning, who "bade fair to do credit to his christening" by being "not foreign in his washing. Oh no, he was really an american" (*MOA* 15), and in the late 1920s Washington had again appeared briefly "on horseback" in her experimental text "Finally George: A Vocabulary of Thinking."[55] Both of these references are interesting: the former, in connecting Washington to personal hygiene (a particular obsession of Stein)[56] and to a fully assimilated "really" American character—the counterpart to the old-world Jewish family that Stein eventually writes out of her narrative; the latter, in presenting Washington mounted on horseback, above the fray—an image that would be repeated in her later 1941 portrait of General Philippe Pétain, whom she explicitly compares to Washington.

In the elliptical, fragmentary "George Washington" section of *Four in America*, Stein creates a textual collage of references from her own and other writings about Washington as well as many other subjects. As one example, notable again because she will repeat it verbatim in her 1941 portrait of Pétain, Stein refers to Washington as "first in peace first in war and first in the hearts of his country men"—a phrase lifted directly from General Henry Lee's famous "Funeral Oration on the Death of George Washington" (1799). Stein borrows other phrases and insights from extratextual sources in this section, even inserting large sections of her own previous writing into "George Washington."[57] But her "borrowing" from Faÿ's *George Washington: Republican Aristocrat* is perhaps more essential than that from any other source. Like Faÿ's, Stein's Washington is a "leader of mankind" and "the father of his country"; he is, she writes, the creator of "the novel the great American novel."[58] While Faÿ refers to Washington as "the prototype whom millions of human beings have tried to imitate since his time" (*GW* xv), Stein attributes the power of creation and naming to Washington, who "wrote what he saw and . . . saw what he said" (*FIA* 168). For both writers, Washington is a generative and original figure, the creator of the story that becomes *the* story of America; for Stein, moreover, Washington is a crucial prototype of her own original American genius.[59]

But Stein also refers to the text she has written as an "index" ("This is a narrative as an index" [*FIA* 201])—a curious statement, given the resistance this text poses to clear or certain signification. To what larger meaning or context is Stein's "George Washington" pointing? One possibility lies in a digression in the midst of the text, where an initial critique of Washington's nemesis, Alexander Hamilton, is transformed into a sudden attack on "the Democratic party," including Grover Cleveland, Woodrow Wilson, and Franklin Roosevelt. Stein here refers disparagingly to the "seductive" and demagogic nature of this party and anticipates its future demise, because "anything that is seductive does not go on again. Not again" (*FIA* 175). In 1934, this entire passage from the "George Washington" section of *Four in America* would be repeated word for word in a public letter Stein writes to Bernard Faÿ, printed in the *Kansas City Star*.[60]

Now the interconnections between Faÿ's and Stein's work on Washington become quite suggestive. For Faÿ, Washington is an historical figure, yet one whose aristocratic leadership provides insight into the pitfalls of contemporary democracy. He is both a figure from the past and a vital example to a Franco-American present in deep decline. For Stein, too, Washington's story—the one he writes and the one she tells—serves as an "index" to a decadent present, one dominated by "seduction" rather than authority. Stein's fascination with Washington as a figure of cleanliness and honesty, and as a "real . . . american," serves as a jumping-off point for her critique of the "dirty" seductiveness of contemporary politicians such as Wilson and Roosevelt. Later, she would add to this critique by describing FDR as "foreign" to America; like the unwashed immigrants in *The Making of Americans*, the Roosevelt family "were American but really they are not American."[61]

There is more than just a coincidence of theme and perspective in Stein and Faÿ's mutual representations of Washington during this period. As the appropriations and resonances of Stein's text suggest, her sense of Washington and of eighteenth-century American history is embedded in an ongoing and productive dialogue with Faÿ of what she would call in a 1932 letter "conversation and advice."[62] In particular, the uses to which history can be put serves as a growing point of intellectual connection between the two writers during this time. Both compose significant treatises on the nature and value of historical inquiry in the early 1930s, and both suggest that their dialogue with each other is part of their thinking on the subject. Moving beyond the specific focus on the eighteenth century, both begin to raise large questions about temporality, continuity, and reading the past in light of the present and future.

Faÿ's essay "An Invitation to American Historians," published in *Harper's* in 1932, interrogates the need for contemporary historians to disengage the past from the present, to treat the past as something of "no further concern" rather than as an indicator "of the most characteristic actions of the imperishable human spirit." In calling for a new attitude toward historical inquiry, and particularly toward archival work, Faÿ advocates treating material from the past in a spirit of "intelligence," "psychological insight," and with "a well-developed artistic sense," rather than examining it "as a geologist treats a stone." According to John L. Harvey, Faÿ felt that historical writing needed "to be conceived as an art and to be guided by an aesthetic instinct that touche[s] on actual human mentalities, as interpreted through current-day sensibilities."[63] The thrust of Faÿ's criticism is here directed specifically at European armchair historians of America, who produce "scientific" analyses without any real experience or study of the country they consider; it is, as well, an attack against the "reductionist" nature of Marxist historical materialism. Most of all, though, this essay underscores the activism of Faÿ's historical scholarship. Faÿ's appeal to a "living history" characterized by insight and "instinct" rather than dry "accuracy" reflects his abiding interest in becoming above all a critic and molder of present-day opinion. In a prophetic statement about his own future career, Faÿ writes that historians who "can accurately define the dreams, the desires, the purposes, and the triumphs of their country . . . will promptly become leaders and will win followers."[64]

Written in late 1930, Stein's *History or Messages from History* seems patently unconcerned with the issue of historical accuracy, but like Faÿ's text it asks a larger question about the meaning and availability of the past for the present and future. The semantic difference between "history" and "messages from history" underlies this question. While the term "history" connotes objectivity, fact, and what Stein calls "spectacular consistency," "messages from history" foregrounds mediation and the subjective acts of interpretation and narration.[65] In this spectacularly *in*consistent text, where signifiers and sentences announce themselves with no seeming connection to what comes before or after, Stein seems to be emphasizing the primacy of interpretation above all else. If "history" is not an objective and consistent science but a series of cryptic "messages," then the contemporary interpreter who must read these messages and deliver their meaning becomes paramount. Picking up on Stein's emerging interest in prophecy, *History or Messages from History* suggests that the ability to make sense of temporal change lies in the ability to read signs—and out of this process to bring meaning to the seemingly random text or event.

For both Faÿ and Stein, then, historical thinking always comes back to the perspective of the thinker, and to bring up the past is necessarily to comment upon the present and the future. Meeting on this common ground, their discussions in the early 1930s invariably swung from meditations on the eighteenth century and on nationalism and national identity to discussions of contemporary politics and to the course of Franco-American affairs to come. Yet in their sense of themselves as historical interpreters *and* leaders, Gertrude Stein and Bernard Faÿ also fed their mutual belief in their own personal importance; each attributed to the other the power not only to interpret and understand but to influence the events around them. Returning to the past in order to imagine a new future, Stein and Faÿ found in each other mutual attitudes and mutual ambitions. In the conclusion to one of her many letters to Faÿ at this time, Stein writes, "we have it the real are you and I and the best of greatness and friendship always Gertrude Stein."[66]

▣ ▣ ▣

For Stein, this belief in her own greatness was confirmed by the major publishing success of *The Autobiography of Alice B. Toklas* in 1933, an event that catapulted her into the ranks of American celebrityhood and finally brought her the glory she had awaited for so long. Appearing on the cover of *Time* magazine on September 11, 1933, Stein appeared to have really made it. Although this sudden success was not without its anxieties for Stein, it also gave birth to a new public persona and voice—one newly empowered to make political pronouncements about the state of current affairs. In the wake of the *Autobiography*, politics enters into Stein's writing as never before, even popping up in

FIGURE 2.2 Gertrude Stein on the cover of *Time* magazine (1933).

her most relentlessly experimental texts of the late 1930s. And for the first time in her life, Stein—with Faÿ's encouragement—started imagining that what she wrote could have an effect on the political situation around her.

Faÿ, for his part, was also coming into his own. In February 1932, he achieved in France what in America would be the equivalent of an endowed research professorship at an Ivy League university. After a decade teaching at the relatively obscure University of Clermont-Ferrand, Faÿ finally won the inaugural chair in American civilization at the elite Collège de France, in Paris. He was the youngest person to hold a chair in the history of the Collège.[67] This honor would have an enormous effect on Faÿ's career and on his subsequent intellectual and political trajectory.

Few people outside France are aware of the Collège de France and its significant role in French society. A peculiarly French institution located in the heart of Paris—on the same street as the Sorbonne—and made up of renowned academics from all branches of the scholarly world, the Collège has no students and does not award academic degrees. The duties of its members, who have included many of the leading lights in modern French intellectual life—the historian Jules Michelet, the philosophers Ernst Renan and Henri Bergson, the anthropologist Claude Lévi-Strauss and the poststructuralist critics Roland Barthes and Michel Foucault—are limited to a series of general lectures, free and open to the public. These lectures tend to be hugely popular and overcrowded affairs, speaking both to the intellectual appetites of the French public and to the particular crossover skills of French professors. It is at the Collège where, to this day, the quintessentially French figure of the "public intellectual" is on visible display.

As one critic has noted, those who win chairs at the Collège de France tend to be *mondains* or worldly thinkers rather than dry academicians, "'arbiters of the *goût public*' shaping the intellectual outlook and sensibility of their times."[68] For Bernard Faÿ, with his successful career on both sides of the Atlantic as an historian and a journalist, and with his ambitions to "lead" public opinion rather than merely reflect it, a chair at the Collège was the achievement of a lifetime. It was also hard won, since appointment to the Collège was itself a deeply political event.

Faÿ's major competitor for the chair in American civilization was the French historian and economist André Siegfried, still known today for his trenchant and pessimistic writings on America in the first decades of the twentieth century. A generation older than Faÿ, Siegfried by the 1920s had become an "unavoidable reference" in any discussion of American culture, and his book *America Comes of Age* (1927) was deemed "essential reading for at least two generations."[69] A knowledgeable commentator and frequent visitor to the States, Siegfried was far from the type of "armchair historian" whom Faÿ derided in 1932; nevertheless, like most of his French contemporaries, Siegfried took a critical and almost wholly undialectical view of America's rise to power, linking it inexorably to modern decadence in general and European degeneration in particular. His writings rehearsed the standard anti-American line, but with the pretensions of a scientist armed with statistics and demographics. And his conclusions invariably flattered his native audience, even while prophesying a bleak future for Europe. Americans were materialistic, acquisitive, and solely production oriented; they were "cog[s] in the immense machine"; they had no qualms about "sacrificing certain rights of the individual, rights which we

FIGURE 2.3 Courtyard and main building of the Collège de France, Paris.

SOURCE: AUTHOR

in the Old World regard as among the most precious victories of civilization." In a marked departure from Faÿ, Siegfried notes bitterly that America's biggest flaw is its lack of both an aristocratic and an artistic sense: "The material advance is immeasurable in comparison with the Old World, but from the point of view of individual refinement and art, the sacrifice is real indeed."[70]

With the popular appeal of his sweeping anti-American polemic joined to a firm academic reputation as a professor at the École Libre des Sciences Politiques, the fifty-seven-year-old Siegfried was a formidable opponent for Bernard Faÿ. His appointment at this most prestigious of French institutions would have affirmed the legitimacy of the French anti-Americanist stance at the moment when "American civilization" was becoming a legitimate field of study. But Faÿ, who referred to his maneuvers toward the Collège as his "electoral campaign," was no political naïf. With an unerring sense of the larger stakes involved in this appointment, Faÿ enlisted the conservative French prime minister, André Tardieu, to support his candidacy. In addition to having been praised by Faÿ in print at the expense of Siegfried, Tardieu had two other reasons to be sympathetic toward Faÿ's candidacy.[71] The first was his generally positive stance toward the United States, which differentiated him starkly from the mass of his contemporaries but which endeared him to American allies (Ambassador Bullitt referred to him as one of a handful of "intelligent" French politicians).[72] It was Tardieu who succeeded Aristide Briand as prime minister in 1929 and who at that point echoed many of Briand's diplomatic views.[73] Having at one point been a professor at Harvard before launching his political career, Tardieu also shared with Faÿ a similar academic background and appreciation for what he referred to in the same breath as both the "price-less friendship" and the "wealth of friendship" between France and America.[74]

Like Faÿ, moreover, Tardieu hewed to the political Right, and while never an extremist, Tardieu shared with Faÿ a skepticism and eventually a deep dis-trust of parliamentary and democratic institutions.[75] In this, as with Faÿ, his antipathy toward the socialist and communist Left fed into his pro-American stance. In his idealization of American efficiency and prosperity, Tardieu sharply diverged from those, like Siegfried, who warned of the "sacrifice" of the individual that such prosperity entailed. For Tardieu, such a sacrifice was already being accomplished within faux-democratic "representative" institu-tions dominated by an entrenched and self-interested elite. By contrast, again like Faÿ, Tardieu found the American governmental system to be a markedly better alternative to French parliamentary democracy. Moreover, with Soviet Russia dictating from afar the agitation of the French Left, the only alternative for France in the early 1930s, Tardieu felt, appeared to be an alignment with the United States. Whatever the conservative Tardieu thought of Bernard Faÿ, therefore, it was manifestly true, as Faÿ himself noted in a letter to Stein, that he "positively hate[d]" the moderate, anti-American Siegfried, and for this reason alone would have supported his opponent.[76]

Faÿ was assiduous in courting Tardieu, but he found real emotional sup-port for his maneuvers in Gertrude Stein. Stein appears to have followed and advised Faÿ in this affair every step of the way, from the first moment of his nomination in 1929 to his victory in February 1932. Ulla Dydo notes that Stein "interpreted and advised [Faÿ] with relish, for her years of observing the workings of power in human beings had sharpened her judgment," but even more, Stein's "relish" for Faÿ's ambitions reflected her own sense of the mutual greatness that she and Faÿ shared, as well as the glory that they so evidently deserved.[77] Stein was thus a useful and supportive resource for Faÿ in guid-ing him through developments at the Collège, but she also seemed to adopt his cause as her own. In a piece Stein wrote during this period, "Lynn and the Collège de France," she describes Faÿ as "Beatrice Glory," a characteriza-tion that "echoes her hope for her own 'success with glory.'"[78] When Faÿ first learned of his nomination, Stein proposed a scheme to yoke his writing to hers, an idea that eventuated in the preface Faÿ wrote for the French translation of *The Making of Americans*. And when Faÿ learned of setbacks to his nomination and declared to Stein that "maybe I was never meant to become an official," Stein sought to lift his spirits by sending him "affectionate hopes, for the destruction of all the enemies."[79] Finally, after Faÿ had beat out Siegfried for the chair, Stein confronted an acquaintance who was skeptical about the outcome by pronouncing that "Siegfried was admirably suited not for the Collège de France but for the Haute Ecole"—an assessment based on questionable insight but passionate commitment.[80]

Stein's investment in Faÿ's success was palpable and complex. Certainly, one cannot underestimate the degree to which Stein herself was craving the kind of public validation given Faÿ by the appointment at the Collège. This was true especially in the period just before Stein wrote the *Autobiography*, when she was facing a continued lack of recognition after a twenty-plus-year engagement with literary experimentalism. From her 1926 lectures at Oxford and Cambridge to the Plain Edition venture—an effort to self-publish her writing—to a series of aggressive pitches to Anglo-American editors and publishers including Ellery Sedgwick and Bennett Cerf, Stein had spent much of the 1920s searching for a wide audience for her work. At the same moment, younger disciples such as Scott Fitzgerald and Sherwood Anderson were beginning to be recognized, and a rival contemporary, James Joyce, had seen his modernist *Ulysses* sell out in the first several weeks of its publication. When Hemingway produced a series of best-selling novels in the late 1920s (*The Sun Also Rises*, 1926; *A Farewell to Arms*, 1929), Stein found her comparable lack of recognition to be especially wrenching. In her 1931 poem "Winning His Way. A Narrative Poem of Poetry," Stein writes suggestively: "The name. Which is destined. To fame. / Is. My name. And so. They thank me. Sometime."[81]

Yet "sometime" needed to arrive on Stein's own terms, the terms of a self-proclaimed genius. Such were not necessarily the terms of the rest of humanity. Above all else, Stein saw herself as an artist, a "*femme de lettres*,"[82] and never what she disparagingly referred to as an "employed type" who, she told Faÿ, "have only one concern: to take on the habits imposed on them by their milieu or their job and to guard them until their death."[83] In her sense of herself as a genius breaking through encrusted habits of thought and writing, Stein, like other high modernists, placed a premium on being revolutionary, a "spiritual pioneer," "ostracized . . . with God," as the modernist writer Mina Loy wrote in her poem "Apology of Genius." However conservative her politics and however bourgeois her daily life, Stein always perceived that her writing made her a critical outsider and a "singular" individual. And although she was soon to capitulate to public tastes with *The Autobiography of Alice B. Toklas*, Stein to the end of her life saw her writing not in instrumental terms but as a "daily miracle."

It is not surprising, therefore, that while Stein greeted Faÿ's success at the Collège with excitement, she also made it clear that for persons of "greatness"—as opposed to mere "employees"—institutional validation was not an end in itself. "Do get into the academy," she writes Faÿ after his Collège win, "get into everything and then afterwards be as naughty as you can that will be nice."[84] Faÿ was more than willing to heed Stein's advice, if only because like Stein he too had a particular ego investment in both queerness and privilege; like Stein, Faÿ wanted to be publicly accepted, even celebrated, for his exceptionality. In fact, his maneuvers to get into the Collège aside, Faÿ seemed to have no particular institutional affiliation, seeing institutions rather as stepping stones on the way to a brilliant career—as sites of prestige and power to conquer, control, and transcend. As such, Faÿ was consummately political, or, as he preferred to put it, "free." Musing on his career and his temperament in a 1930 letter to Stein, Faÿ wrote: "Maybe no job would be better. . . . After all, I love freedom."[85]

For the next eight years, up to the outbreak of World War II, the Collège would prove perfectly suited to Faÿ's purposes. The freedom he sought in the early 1930s was above all the freedom to pursue and publicize ideas that could not be readily accommodated by secular democratic educational institutions. First and foremost, there was his critique of the Third Republic in France, his loathing of individualism and democracy, and his deep monarchist leanings. Then there was his positive attitude toward American-style federalism, a possible model for a new European order. Finally, there was his growing fixation on the dangers of contemporary Freemasonry, which he perceived as a shady nexus of anti-Catholic influence. With the Collège de France's commitment to not interfering with the work of its professors, Faÿ had at last found a venue to disseminate openly these "naughty" ideas.[86] In this, Gertrude Stein understandingly spurred him on.

☐ ☐ ☐

In *The American Experiment*, Faÿ had talked about "true" friendship between nations as one "without fear or jealousy" born of "mutual appreciation and respect for each other's qualities." Such an ideal was, of course, contingent upon a balance of power, with no elements on either side feeling superior or subordinate to the other. In the early 1930s, such an ideal comes closest to describing *not* the relationship between America and France—which at this time was in fact marked by tension and mistrust, by mutual recriminations and failed diplomacy—but between the American Gertrude Stein and the French Bernard Faÿ. Together, the two formed a harmonious convergence of interests, one marked by mutual affirmation and a deep belief in the correctness of their shared vision.

This is confirmed by an account of Gertrude Stein and Bernard Faÿ's friendship during this period by a friend of both. In 1934, James Laughlin, the founder of the publishing house New Directions, was a frequent visitor to Stein's country house, and he described the scene with an appreciative eye: "Evenings at Bilignin were spent in conversation, which meant a monologue from Miss Stein. . . . [But when] Bernard Faÿ came down for weekends from Paris there really was conversation. The two old friends knew each other so well they could play off each other's interests and eccentricities. It was like hearing a duet, and Alice and I just listened."[87]

Laughlin's description is Steinian in its differentiation between "conversation" and "real . . . conversation"—the latter being of crucial import to Stein, who throughout her career would talk about her work in terms of an ideal exchange of "talking and listening" between self and other.[88] Most critics have tended to describe Alice Toklas as Stein's ideal interlocutor, as the companion whose support and admiration for Stein's work facilitated her move into experimental writing in the early years of the twentieth century. Yet Laughlin's description of the Stein-Faÿ "conversation" suggests a different kind of dynamic from that between Stein and Toklas. The image of Laughlin and Toklas "just listen[ing]" while Stein and Faÿ "play[ed] off each other" reconfigures Stein's cherished notion of "talking and listening" to emphasize a conversation (or "play") among equals performed for the benefit of a silent audience of "listeners." The Stein-Faÿ exchange was, Laughlin states, a performative duet: a lively, sympathetic banter in which each side complemented and heightened the other, as well as a performance among raconteurs used to the spotlight.

Sixty years old in 1934, Stein was still the respected *grande dame* to the forty-one-year-old Faÿ, and in their correspondence Faÿ continued to defer to Stein and her abilities. Even in 1935, when Stein dedicated her book *Lectures in America* to him, she emphasized the passivity of his role: "To Bernard, who comfortingly and encouragingly was listening as these were being written."[89] Yet over the course of the early 1930s, Faÿ was increasingly becoming much more than a "comforting and encouraging listener" to Stein and was coming into his own as a "talker" and performer. In Stein's own mind, this shift really began with the public lectures Faÿ gave to inaugurate his appointment to the Collège de France.

In a letter she wrote to Faÿ in 1933 after hearing one of these lectures, it is Stein, rather than Faÿ, who occupies the subordinate position in the relationship:

> *My dear Bernard,*
>
> *When I got home just a little tired I realized fully how moved and passionately interested I had been. It was an extraordinary experience. I was living in you and living in the thing and for once in my life almost not living in myself. A strange and very moving xperience and giving me quite a new point of view toward life. Thanks a thousand times for that and all. I am beginning to write the confessions of the writer of the autobiography of Alice B. Toklas and there will be much to confess but this is a new way to confess, listening to you to-day gave me distinctly a new way to confess, contact with your mind is comforting and stimulating, and nothing is more deeply satisfying to me than that. We do mean a great deal to each other.*
>
> *Always, Gtde.*[90]

The framing of this letter in terms of climax and release—Stein describes being "moved and passionately interested" to the point of "almost not living in myself," only to find herself "just a little tired" afterward—reminds us of Stein's early erotic exchanges with Toklas, as do the cryptic and encoded phrases "contact with your mind" and "we do mean a great deal to each other." The epistolary style here is more than a little reminiscent of sentimental Victorian exchanges between female friends, a genre that Stein herself experimented with in her early lesbian novella *Q.E.D.*[91] In her letter to Faÿ, Stein, like a lover, presents herself as a supplicant and pupil to her beloved: it is Faÿ who gives Stein "a new way to confess" as well as "quite a new point of view toward life." The intimacy and vulnerability of Stein's position is as touching as that of Adele, the protagonist of *Q.E.D.*, when she implores Helen, her indifferent beloved, that "I could undertake to be an efficient pupil if it were possible to find an efficient teacher."[92] Flushed with the excitement of giving in to a more powerful master, Stein, like Adele, constructs a fantasy of "contact" with Faÿ that revolves around her capitulation to his "new point of view toward life."

What Faÿ reveals, of course, is how to give an effective public lecture: a lesson that will sustain Stein during her lecture tour of America in 1934 and 1935. Ironically, Stein's capitulation to Faÿ's "lesson" will enable her to find her own public voice as a lecturer. Yet Stein's note makes it very clear who is the teacher in this pedagogical scene and who the pupil. In fact, this remarkable letter describes one of the only moments in Stein's entire oeuvre in which she presents herself not as a talker or creator of works of genius, nor as an interlocutor in an exchange among equals, but simply and fully as a listener.

Listening to Faÿ may also have allowed Stein to fully embrace—and openly announce—her latent political leanings. As Laughlin noted in his description of the Stein-Faÿ exchange, the talk did not limit itself to aesthetic matters and to gossip:

> An exchange I heard one night troubled me. . . . They got on the subject of Hitler, speaking of him as a great man, one perhaps to be compared with Napoleon. I was stunned. Hitler's persecution of the Jews was well publicized in France by that time, and Miss Stein was a Jew. Faÿ, in his turn, had nearly gotten himself killed fighting the Germans in World War I. I couldn't forget that strange exchange.[93]

For Laughlin, it was strange, disconcerting, and altogether unlikely to hear the two friends talk of Hitler's greatness. But for Stein, at least, conversing with Bernard Faÿ could be a seductive and liberating thing. In a letter from the early 1930s, she writes perhaps her most significant sentence about their friendship: "and of course I see politics but from one angle which is yours."[94]

MOVING RIGHTWARD
(1935–1940)

CHAPTER THREE

I N MAY 1934, six years after the ill-fated Kellogg-Briand
Peace Pact, Gertrude Stein had something new to say
about the idea of international peace: "Hitler should have
received the Nobel Peace Prize . . . because he is removing all elements
of contest and of struggle from Germany. By driving out the Jews and
the democratic and Left elements, he is driving out everything that
conduces to activity. That means peace."[1] Delivered bluntly in an interview with the *New York Times Magazine*, Stein's comments remain
unexplained, unapologetic, and elliptical. At the time, and for years
afterward, these comments have troubled, baffled, and divided Stein's
readers. On the one hand, they seem to confirm the surprised observations of Jay Laughlin during the same period: that for Stein, as for
Bernard Faÿ, Hitler had the features and the promise of a "great man."
Yet for many of Stein's defenders, the comments about Hitler are clearly
ironic and provocative: "a point of black humor" that is, and has been,
"easily misread" by literalistic readers.[2]

Stein probably wanted her audience to respond in both ways. Her
"political" pronouncements of the 1930s often verge on the outrageous,
deliberately scandalizing her listeners in order to shock them out of
their habitual ways of thinking and responding. As with the rest of her
writing, Stein sought in her political statements to speak against the
grain, to break through clichés, and to undercut ideological pieties.
Yet there is also a strong element of conviction and intentionality in

what Stein says in such pronouncements, as though she requires—indeed demands—that her words be taken literally. Long used to being perceived, and dismissed, as a modernist eccentric by mainstream audiences, Stein expresses her political views in the 1930s with something approaching exasperation, as though she had simply gotten tired of having to explain or excuse herself and so defuse the force of her beliefs. Lansing Warren, Stein's interviewer for the *New York Times Magazine* article, talks about the "irrefutable terseness" of her statements; another interviewer, Helen Buchalter, notes that "her speech is not only lucid, but vigorous, pointed, aggressive—and often, pontifical."[3] To these interviewers during her American lecture tour of 1934 and 1935, Stein is bewildering precisely because her political "pontifications" are *not* clearly ironic but apparently deeply felt.

In part defensively opinionated, in part provocative and playful, Stein's shifting stance in her political statements speaks to the ambivalence of a high modernist writer newly thrust into the public eye. Having spent the first sixty years of her life in pursuit of an elusive fame, Stein's sudden celebrity after the success of *The Autobiography of Alice B. Toklas* was at last undeniable proof of her greatness. Yet it seems to have induced not only an injurious writer's block but also a degree of disbelief and indeed resentment at the very audience that celebrated her. Gone were the days in which aesthetic matters could, as she wrote in the early 1900s, "become the whole of me."[4] Suddenly, the pressures of what she called "the outside," placing new demands on her ability to talk and listen, would preoccupy and hinder Stein. In a crucial and as yet unacknowledged way, this ambivalence about her own celebrity during the 1930s seems to have been related for Stein to the issue of Jews and Jewishness.

At the close of World War II, reflecting back on Nazi persecution of the Jews, Stein writes:

> Publicity, that is what we hear them say publicity, and is not that the real meaning of persecution, publicity, it is not nearly as complicated as it seems. There always has been a great passion for publicity in the world the very greatest passion for publicity, and those who succeed best, who have the best instincts for publicity, do have a great tendency to be persecuted that is natural enough, and here I think is the real basis of the persecution of the chosen people.
>
> (W 108)

This passage appears in *Wars I Have Seen*, a late work that portrays the experience of World War II from the perspective of a valiant and optimistic survivor of its many atrocities and deprivations. In it, Stein clearly identifies herself with Jews as the victims of German resentment, fear, and envy, and despite a residual (and disturbing) Pétainism, there is no question that Stein sees herself on the side of "the chosen people." Nor would there be, given the harrowing experiences that she details throughout this book. But what is interesting about this passage in *Wars* is the way Stein explains anti-Semitism as the effect of Jewish success in "publicity": a point she insists is "not nearly as complicated as it seems" but one that has particularly complex resonances for her own personal history.

Publicity was indeed something that Stein thought about, yearned for, and pursued in the interwar period; the triumph of *The Autobiography of Alice B. Toklas* was plotted and planned. Looking back on this period in *Everybody's Autobiography* (1937), Stein wrote poignantly that "one does not, no one does not in one's heart believe in mute inglorious Miltons. If one has succeeded in doing anything one is certain that anybody who really has it in them to really do anything will really do that thing. Anyway I have done something and anyway I did write The Autobiography of Alice B. Toklas" (*EA* 9). Stein implies that the success of the *Autobiography* was the proof that she had it in her "to really do anything"; it finally confirmed her abilities for a skeptical public. Yet in retrospect, Stein also worried about what this success really meant, not least in the face of those modernist peers and critics who wrote of the *Autobiography* that it represented a "final capitulation to a Barnumesque publicity."[5] As the 1930s proceeded, fame or "publicity" would be associated for Stein with a kind of discomfiting pleasure, one contingent not upon personal fulfillment but upon the approval of others.

At its worst, publicity had the capacity to rob Stein of "peace," a term that resonated for her with the habitual experience of daily life "where nothing much changes as one is very busy, just writing and eating and sleeping and walking and talking."[6] Stein was a great believer in the stabilizing and rejuvenating powers of habit or routine, especially for the artist; "peace" was the term that invariably described this routine. And it is here where Stein's "Nobel Peace Prize" comments about Hitler and the Jews take on a deeper meaning. What years later would become a point of ethnic pride—the fact that "the chosen people" display the "best instincts for publicity"—is in 1934 a more fraught issue associated with creative disconnection and self-alienation. In her comments about Hitler, Stein seems to be translating her own experience with the *Autobiography* into the realm of international politics, linking "the Jews" and their "activity" with everything that threatens "peace." While it is precisely "activity" that brought Stein the international fame she desired, it is this supposedly Jewish aspect of her own character that seems to have deprived Stein of the peaceful context so necessary to true artistic creation. Wanting publicity enough to sacrifice her "inside" to it, Stein ends up by lashing out at these own "best instincts" after comprehending what they have cost her.

Stein's comments about Hitler are therefore more than merely provocative. They mirror a personal crisis in which "activity" and "instincts for publicity"—directly associated in the Nobel Prize interview and *Wars I Have Seen* with Jews/"the chosen people"—are pitted against the fruitful but unremarkable "peace" of daily life. This opposition allows Stein to frame Hitler's violent actions as a legitimate national expression of the desire for "peace." Most ominously, this opposition would seem to inform Stein's decision to stay in France during World War II, a France newly purged of Jewish presence.[7] Yet Stein would also resist this opposition, again revealing a deep ambivalence about the issue of Jewishness during the turbulent years of the 1930s. In a curious passage from the beginning of *Everybody's Autobiography*, Stein rehabilitates the idea of "activity" as a positive thing associated explicitly with "peace" as well as with success. She writes: "and anyway the Oriental . . . is invading the Western world. It is the peaceful penetration that is important not wars" (*EA* 10). Wishful thinking, perhaps, since it was precisely this perceived "peaceful penetration" of the Jewish "Orient" into Europe that would be used to justify the Nazi war machine. Indeed, Stein's idea of "peaceful Oriental penetration" would be echoed precisely by anti-Semitic rhetoric about shadowy Jewish conspiracies taking over the Western world, as in Hitler's own repeated references in *Mein Kampf* to the Jewish "parasite . . . [who] keeps spreading as soon as a favorable medium invites him."[8] Yet in the passage from *Everybody's Autobiography*, "peaceful Oriental penetration" is actually associated with the positive quality and activity of creative genius. To be "Oriental" in the twentieth century is to be at the forefront of culture, in a way that Europe alone, Stein claims, has ceased to be. Hence, "Einstein was the creative philosophic mind of the century and I have been the creative literary mind of the century also with the Oriental mixing with the European" (*EA* 21–22).

To be Jewish—or rather "Oriental"[9]—is therefore a mark of distinction and superiority in twentieth-century Europe. It is the powerful yet peaceful activity of Orientals rather than brutal world wars, Stein claims, that will have the most influence on the future direction of European culture. This is a sentiment utterly at odds with Stein's Hitler comments, where "peace" is something hard-won only through the exclusion of Jews and their Left or democratic counterparts. It concurs with Stein's oft-repeated dislike of Germans "all having the same point of view."[10] Again, the disparity between these two contemporaneous perspectives speaks to the troubled and overdetermined nature of Jewish identity for Gertrude Stein in the 1930s. Yet her ambivalence would play right into the hands of those for whom the "Jewish question" was becoming a mercilessly straightforward matter.

▣ ▣ ▣

Bernard Faÿ was one of those who grasped the fluidity of Stein's affiliation with Jewishness during this period. For it was Faÿ who would take the audacious step of featuring Stein in the pages of the notoriously anti-Semitic journal *Je Suis Partout* in 1935.

Published between 1930 and 1944, *Je Suis Partout* was one of the main organs of the French extreme Right, staffed from the outset by followers of Charles Maurras. As the 1930s went on, most of these young Maurrassians—including Robert Brasillach, Lucien Rebatet, and Pierre-Antoine Cousteau (brother of the famous oceanographer Jacques Cousteau)—broke with Maurras's anti-German stance in order to embrace a "hardcore pro-Nazi" viewpoint.[11] The journal that they founded served as the perfect vehicle for their views. Caustic, aggressive, fervently anticommunist and pro-German, *Je Suis Partout* by the mid-1930s was also "openly and deliberately" anti-Semitic.[12] Alice Kaplan has described it as "the leading proponent of fascism and anti-Semitism in France."[13] Its anti-Semitic tone took on a feverish pitch during the Vichy regime, when it engaged in open denunciation of Jewish citizens, often publishing pseudonyms and the exact location of hiding places.[14]

In 1934, Faÿ contributed the first of some twenty articles to *Je Suis Partout*. "Salzbourg d'été" was a light satire of the idle summer pleasures of the Austrians in the face of mounting pan-European tensions. It revealed little of the political posturing that dominated the pages of the journal. But several months later, in January 1935, Faÿ wrote a different kind of essay, a feature article on Gertrude Stein. Appearing in the midst of Stein's lecture tour of the United States, "L'apothéose de Gertrude Stein" (The Apotheosis of Gertrude Stein) describes the "enchantment" and "joy" of Stein's American audiences in the face of her "mysterious language of infinite repetitions, of distant innuendos, of daring associations."[15] It was the kind of thing that Faÿ had written about Stein before, in his preface to the French translation of *The Making of Americans*. And it was the kind of thing that he would write again later in 1935, in an essay for the *Revue de Paris* called "Gertrude Stein, Poète de l'Amerique," where Stein is presented as the only writer to give true expression to the popular voice of the American people.[16]

But in *Je Suis Partout*, Faÿ's point would get sharper yet. "The triumph of Gertrude Stein is a national and nationalist triumph," he writes, insistently locating Stein's American reception in a discourse of nationalism. As opposed to the school of American naturalism—"proletarian art"—which cares more for "democratic ideas" and "social life" than for "artistic forms," Stein seeks not to critique and denounce but to celebrate and underscore the beauty of American life and American language. Stein's is "the triumph of american America over antiamerican America," Faÿ announces, setting her off against leftist "antiamerican" writers such as Theodore Dreiser, Sinclair Lewis, or Upton Sinclair. Like Emile Zola, who "knew nothing of contemporary poetry and applied himself to proving the innocence of Dreyfus," the crime of Dreiser and company is to use literature as socialist agitprop rather than as a means of celebrating and glorifying the nation. Their overtly political writings ignore the degree to which true art, art of the "spirit" and of "beauty," always precedes and transcends politics. This awareness is something that Gertrude Stein, alone among all her American contemporaries, has achieved.

However flattering to Stein, this was still a curious argument to be making in the pages of *Je Suis Partout*. No journal of the day could be less "aestheticist" or more conscious of the ties between literary or artistic expression and politics. None was more aware of the politics of promoting one aesthetic form over another. Yet the journal's disdain for "proletarian" art and its embrace of a high modernist like Stein suggests a specific way of thinking about the intersection of art and politics. For Robert Brasillach, Faÿ's friend and the editor-in-chief of *Je Suis Partout* after 1937, the most valuable literature was a "unified" literature: a "complex totality" created out of a violent "fusion of different forces" that in turn provided a model for a vibrant, unified nation.[17] Literature was not meant to reflect politics so much as inspire it through its presentation of a totalized universe, which would return to its readers "the identity of a people rooted in the land, tradition, and authentic national values." As the critic David Carroll understands Brasillach's "literary fascism," literature is valuable in terms of "how it relates to tradition and the past; and more specifically, how it relates to and exploits the resources of the national language and culture to reawaken the creativity and 'genius' inherent in them."[18]

Faÿ's representation of Gertrude Stein in *Je Suis Partout* seems to locate her within this "genre" of literary fascism. Stein's writing is "triumphant," because it allows for "a sort of reconciliation of America with itself." With her "joy" in the English language and her Whitmanesque love of American culture, Stein renders for her audience "the movement, the strangeness, the rapidity, the quickness, the passion of all these beings." Her love for this culture and its language is "contagious." As she brings Americans back to themselves, as she awakens in them their own "genius," they in turn respond to her as would a mass audience to its fascist leader. Faÿ notes that during her lecture tour Stein was received "like Mussolini when he is greeting a fascist crowd." Several years later, on the eve of World War II, Faÿ would again refer to Gertrude Stein as among a handful of "exceptional" writers shoring up American culture in the face of its corrupt democratic "standardization," whose "imperial, genial, and sovereign" style "might one day conquer the nation."[19]

Since the beginning of their friendship, Stein and Faÿ had supported each other in the sense of their own "greatness" and in the conviction that greatness was in some essential way expressed in leadership. Suddenly, in the pages of *Je Suis Partout*, Stein's "greatness" is portrayed as that of a fascist leader, and her "triumph" is like that of a Mussolini: the meaning and sense of belonging she brings to her people. Faÿ obviously intended this representation to prevail over the more problematic aspect of Stein's Jewishness for the *Je Suis Partout* audience, which by the late 1930s would be expecting the journal to espouse an uncompromisingly anti-Semitic line.

▣ ▣ ▣

From Saint Gertrude to Il Duce: through such projections did the Stein-Faÿ relationship develop. Moreover, Stein's transformation in Faÿ's eyes reveals much about the shift in his own personal perspective from the 1920s to the 1930s and about the larger cultural shifts during this period of enormous intellectual and social turmoil. Faÿ's particular trajectory—from historian and professor of American culture to right-wing critic and, eventually, Vichy ideologue—was by no means unusual during the course of these "hollow years." For Faÿ, as for so many others, the 1930s was a decade of disillusionment and reaction as well as radical politicization. It was a moment when complaint and criticism seemed more virulent and pointed than in previous epochs, more apt to lead to revolutionary action and, eventually, to violence.

Historians have long seen the 1930s in France as a period of crisis linked to national and international upheavals—from France's steadily worsening economic depression, to the continuing instability and corruption of its ever-changing government, to the terrifying rise of Hitler's Germany on its borders. Yet these events do not in themselves explain why the politicization of so many people in France took the pessimistic and deeply polarized form that it did in the interwar period. A majority of the French population during the 1930s, as Eugen Weber has shown, considered their epoch to be one of decadence. But similar moments of social instability in the past had not produced quite the degree of critique or the same investment in radical solutions as were generated during the interwar period. Why, Weber asks, should the interwar period in France, and the 1930s in particular, feel "so much more like decadence?"[20]

The answer to this question is embedded in the trauma of World War I, an event so shattering that its afterlife continued to be felt for decades to come. It was Freud who would define the modern notion of "trauma" in the wake of World War I, commenting on the "dark and dismal" feelings of war survivors as a way of grasping a more general constitutional human condition. The Great War enabled Freud to study systematically not only the experience of trauma and subsequent efforts at repression but also the inevitable return of these repressed experiences in the thoughts and actions of war survivors and of subsequent generations. By the 1930s, World War I was nearly a generation past but remained both everywhere and nowhere, from wounded veterans in the streets to the unhealed bereavement of the thousands of civilians who had lost loved ones. It was the source of painful remembrance and repression and displacement, giving rise to positions as varied as pacifism, defeatism, denial, and vengeance. Its long-term presence continued to be felt as much in the idealism of Aristide Briand's various peace pacts during the 1920s as in the refusal by France to respond to Hitler's remilitarization of the Rhineland in 1936. One could rightly argue that there was little in the period leading up to World War II that was not marked traumatically by the experience of the Great War or by the visible—or missing—remnants of the war generation.

Yet, as Weber notes, the trauma of World War I would have been less ambivalent to the French population, and perhaps less painful and persistent, "if the nation had been more clearly one."[21] In fact, the so-called two Frances— democratic, secular, and republican France on the one hand and Catholic, monarchical, and traditionalist France on the other—had been at odds since the time of the French Revolution, a moment when "Left" and "Right" were for the first time defined as literal seating arrangements in the Chamber of Deputies. Yet in the wake of World War I, and particularly in the 1930s, the sense of shared patrimony that held the two Frances together seemed increasingly fragile, increasingly uncertain. Earlier moments of similar social tension, such as the Dreyfus affair at the turn of the twentieth century, had also been characterized by deep-seated political rifts. One of the key figures to emerge from the Dreyfus affair, Charles Maurras, warned that France had become "feeble" and that "the future belonged to men of action"; intellectuals needed to act, not simply think—a point that would galvanize his Action Française followers for decades to come.[22] Nevertheless, Maurrassians tended to remain armchair warriors: for all their antirepublican rhetoric, there was little real blood on their hands. It would not be until the 1930s—and, specifically, until the events of February 1934—that the struggle between the two Frances would turn deadly.

In late 1933—as Gertrude Stein was receiving the first news of the success of *The Autobiography of Alice B. Toklas* in America and as Faÿ was basking in his Collège de France appointment and other academic honors[23]—the discontent and instability of the postwar era at last erupted in France in a significant way. The beginnings lay in a seemingly minor French political scandal involving a Jewish embezzler named Serge Stavisky, who was accused of perpetrating a financial pyramid scheme in the southwestern city of Bayonne. As it happened, Stavisky had friends in high places, and his fraud scheme was soon discovered to have stretched far into the inner recesses of the French government. When on January 8, 1934, Stavisky was found dead—suspected of committing "suicide by persuasion"[24]—his death unleashed a financial and political storm of enormous magnitude. By January 30, the entire cabinet of the center-left premier Camille Chautemps had resigned. A week later, on the evening of February 6, 1934, right-wing antiparliamentary groups took advantage of the political crisis to stage a bloody public demonstration. This motley crew of right-wing royalists, veterans, intellectuals, and street thugs found a common voice that night in their effort to storm the Parliament building. Fifteen people were killed and at least 1,500 injured, most of them Action Française members. The next day, the fragile new government of Edouard Daladier would be forced to resign. With the "victims of February 6, 1934" turned into right-wing martyrs and the political Left in shambles, this episode would become the Dreyfus affair of its day, a turning point in the mutual antagonism of the two Frances. As Faÿ himself wrote in 1934, "The 6th of February has been in fact a revolution from which I don't expect that parliamentary government can ever recover. But what is going to take its place is very difficult to guess."[25]

Stavisky himself was an unremarkable figure—a small-time confidence man and swindler—although some in France, Gertrude Stein among them, saw him as the political mastermind behind the rise to power of Léon Blum and the Popular Front.[26] In any event, what mattered about Stavisky was the controversy he generated. Like the Dreyfus affair, *l'affaire Stavisky* brought to the surface all of the simmering resentments of the French Right. With his shadowy ties to the world of finance capitalism and his Russian-Jewish background, Stavisky represented everything that the anti-Semitic, profascist, and monarchist leagues of the 1920s and 1930s reviled. Jewish, wealthy, and suspiciously well connected, Stavisky embodied "corruption" for the Right, and in the tense atmosphere of the 1930s, this corruption was quickly seen to be part of a sweeping conspiracy. The codeword for this conspiracy was "Freemasonry" or "Judeo-Freemasonry": a dark underground brotherhood that secretly ran French society, a network known only to initiates and their families. As even the mainstream press reporting on the events of 1933 and 1934 repeatedly noted, several of the members of the Chautemps government involved in the scandal, including Camille Chautemps himself, shared a secret affiliation that now seemed tainted with the corrupt practices of Stavisky: they were all Freemasons. "Masonic crooks," cried *Action Française* on February 6, 1934: "enough of this putrid regime!"[27]

In the wake of the Stavisky affair, French Freemasons—alongside and often in tandem with Jews and communists—would be targeted by the Right as never before. And this in turn would create a significant change in the fortunes of the man who was quickly becoming known as the foremost critic of Freemasonry in France: Bernard Faÿ.

. ▣ ▣ ▣

What exactly was this Masonic "brotherhood" that so rankled the sensibilities of a man like Bernard Faÿ? For rankle, it did: over the course of some twenty-five years, from his master's thesis at Harvard to his final efforts on behalf of the Vichy regime to expose what he called "the nefarious influence" of Freemasonry, Faÿ relentlessly questioned the meaning, purpose, and ultimately the very existence of the organization.[28] Many of his Vichy colleagues, fervent ideologues themselves, went so far as to call Faÿ's interest in Freemasonry obsessive. Yet few would resist him when this obsession turned into a witch hunt.

To most Americans, Freemasonry is a mysterious yet relatively innocuous organization, associated with the Founding Fathers, local orphanages, and the symbols on our dollar bills.[29] As in France, Freemasonry has played a significant role in defining and shaping the American public sphere and has been at the center of many of our nation's most transformative events, starting with the American Revolution. It has, as well, included among its members a number of political leaders, including Presidents George Washington, Andrew Jackson, James Buchanan, Teddy and Franklin Roosevelt, Harry Truman, Lyndon Johnson, and Gerald Ford. Yet the ties between political power and the Masonic brotherhood in America are not self-evident, despite the insistence of a handful of conspiracy theorists. While America is home to nearly half the world's Freemasons, their presence is of little concern to the mainstream

American public.[30] Today, indeed, the organization has a largely philanthropic air about it, closer to the Rotary Club or even a college fraternity than to the Trilateral Commission.

The case is rather different in France. French anti-Masonic rhetoric can be found all over the Web, in print media, and in the passing comments of people on the street. Paranoia seems to attend any discussion of the brotherhood in France, both outside and within the organization. This is largely the result of Freemasonry's antagonistic relationship with the Catholic Church, itself an institution that wields enormous social power in France. In a predominantly Catholic country, Freemasonry rankles: with its unholy alliance of mysticism and rationalism it has, from the Protestant Reformation onward, been characterized as performing the devil's work. It has become inseparable from debates over the French Revolution, an event that for many permanently shredded the fabric of traditional, monarchic, Catholic French society, leaving it soulless and falsely egalitarian. Relatedly, anti-Masonic thinkers have tended to see the brotherhood in apocalyptic and eschatological terms, as a secret force bent on secularizing and eventually dominating the world. A series of modern scandals, including the infamous "Affaire des Fiches" of 1904–1905, in which Masonic elements within the French War Ministry were shown to have discriminated against Catholic army officers seeking promotion, has only intensified the distrust. While recent revelations of internal dissension, financial mismanagement, and petty competition within the French organization have worked to debunk the myth of Masonic unity, it is still generally assumed that Masonic brothers protect their secrets—rituals, symbols, handshakes, and, most importantly, secret political networks—above all else. It is this close connection between Masonry and secrecy that has most fueled the anti-Masonic crusade, lending both the brotherhood and its critics a delusional quality steeped in hallucinatory visions of power and veiled ambition run amok.[31]

For Bernard Faÿ, Freemasonry provided the material for his ideological and vocational "development" as a writer, from scholar to journalist, from academic historian to full-blown political polemicist. This development was inseparable from an increasingly paranoid worldview, from an insistent effort to read events and symbols in terms of a total system: the Masonic New World Order. On a psychological level, Faÿ's paranoia about Freemasonry seemed to spring from deep and persistent sources. The psychoanalyst Jacques Lacan has argued for the fundamental place of paranoia in the constitution of the subject, with paranoia serving as a link back to the experience of primary trauma through imaginary delusion and hallucination. Paranoia represents a "loss of trust in the capacity of the Symbolic Order to represent things"—thrusting the subject back into a primary, presymbolic unknown.[32] For Faÿ, the primary trauma was undoubtedly located in a family scene in which Catholic piety dictated the very horizon of what could possibly be thought, said, or done. In such a scene, Freemasonry and the challenge it posed to Catholic hierarchy and dogma would represent an alternative world so dangerous and threatening as to be self-shattering. Faÿ's paranoid response to Freemasonry, like his comparable tortured relationship to his own homosexuality, thus restaged a moment in his past defined by both possibility and prohibition, a moment that became reimagined and reinterpreted through increasingly totalized visions of future catastrophe.[33]

This might explain the complexity of Faÿ's portrayal of Freemasonry in numerous articles of the 1920s and 1930s as well as the significant interpretive shift in this portrayal in his most developed work on the subject, *Revolution and Freemasonry, 1680–1800* (1935). As a culmination of several previous studies, including his master's thesis on the French and American revolutions, biographies of Washington and Franklin, and a 1933 book on Franklin D. Roosevelt (*Roosevelt and His America*), *Revolution and Freemasonry* does not so much break new ground as alter the terrain in evident ways. With this book, in fact, Bernard Faÿ abandons his role as academic historian and emerges as a full-blown ideologue of the Right.

In his early studies, Freemasonry is portrayed as a powerful and transformative force in both France and America and as the stimulus for both the American and French revolutionary wars. Faÿ makes note of Masonic achievements, including a philanthropic and open-minded worldview that directly fed into Enlightenment notions of democracy and equality, as well as its necessary reformation of corruption within the Church and the monarchy. His discussion of eighteenth-century Masonic activity and of its links to an "Anglo-Saxon" rationalist worldview remains largely *sui generis*. As with Faÿ's portrayal of America in *The American Experiment* (1929), these early writings leave unresolved the question of Freemasonry's ultimate influence on the course of contemporary events and are typically couched in the neutral and objective rhetoric of the academic historian focused on the distant past. They are closer to the writings of a "geologist treat[ing] a stone" than to the "living" history that Faÿ would increasingly advocate. This is not yet the work of a polemicist drawing the past into a critique of the present.[34]

Five years later, in *Revolution and Freemasonry*, a new strain of paranoia has entered into Faÿ's writing. From the book's title to its bibliography, Faÿ abandons the nuance of his previous works in order to drive home two basic points: that Freemasonry was the principal agent behind the French and

American revolutions and that these Masonic-driven revolutions are the cause of present-day social degeneration. In France in particular, Faÿ argues, Freemasons used an activating ideal like democracy to gain support for eighteenth-century revolutionary events, but the subsequent destruction of traditional social and religious institutions had been catastrophic for French society in the nineteenth and twentieth centuries. Committed to effecting an "equal footing" among social classes by dissolving social and political hierarchies, the Masonic-driven French and American revolutions only served to impoverish the lives of the masses while secretly consolidating power among the Masonic ranks. Indeed, Freemasonry's interest in cloaking its own will to power within eighteenth-century revolutionary rhetoric is the book's most tendentious claim. By "preparing" and "achieving" the French and American revolutions, Freemasons transformed the modern world. Yet ultimately their efforts served only to exchange an older, traditional, hierarchical social system for another, more modern, but much more secret and sinister one.

Secrecy is a central idea to this analysis, as it allows Faÿ to interrogate the transparency of "Masonic" words such as *democracy, progress,* and *rationality*. Behind these eighteenth-century terms and beneath the Enlightenment itself, Faÿ claims, lies a shadow world of power, ambition, and craven desires on the part of an insidious Masonic elite. What Faÿ hopes to do in *Revolution and Freemasonry* is to bring the "shadows" in this supposedly "enlightened" discourse of Freemasonry to light and to expose the problematic continuity of this discourse within present-day liberal and parliamentary politics. As he writes in his chapter "Lights and Shadows of Freemasonry," for all its stated commitment to enlightened and rational discourse, the Masonic brotherhood was in fact a "shadow elite" and Masonic Enlightenment humanism a "shadow religion" (*RF* 117–174). Beyond all else, Faÿ argues, Freemasonry was and continues to be essentially a counter-Catholicism, using the mystical rituals of the Catholic Church—including a mock crucifixion and mock resurrection as part of the central Masonic rite—within an organization outwardly opposed to religious belief. With its internal hierarchies and mystical rituals, Freemasonry simply inverted the order of the Catholic Church, providing a similar sense of place, belonging, and spiritual fulfillment as Catholicism while claiming to be modern, rational, democratic and secular. Outwardly antagonistic toward hierarchies and doctrinal thought, Freemasonry cultivated its own aura of mystery that did not so much challenge traditional institutions and hierarchies as reinstate them in a secular guise. This was and is the hidden truth of Freemasonry. "With a great scorn for dogmas, a complete independence of kings and religions—wrapped in its mystery, which shone around it like a black and luminous cloud—Freemasonry had the supreme dexterity to replace a mysterious Divinity by a divine mystery" (*RF* 317), Faÿ writes in the concluding sentence of his book.

Revolution and Freemasonry, unlike Faÿ's earlier writings on the subject, purports to rip the veils off Freemasonry, which itself claimed to enlighten, rationalize, and liberalize societies stuck in social and religious feudalism. One of the ironies of the book is that it proceeds through a form of dialectical argumentation not unlike that practiced by the early free-thinking Masons themselves, exposing the truisms of Masonic belief to be precisely the opposite of what they claim. For Faÿ, secularism is really a debased religion, the Enlightenment was a movement of impious darkness and secrecy, democratic or parliamentary government is really a corrupt cabal, and what we call progress is in fact decadence. Yet Faÿ himself clearly sees his own critique of Freemasonry in *Revolution and Freemasonry* to be enlightening and progressive: his work is no longer simply an academic exercise but a polemical tract placing him in the forefront of an activist French Right calling for a wholesale revolution in French society in the latter half of the 1930s. Like others on the Right, Faÿ had come to feel that something radical needed to be done to arrest the decadence of the French Third Republic. But he also believed that he alone had discovered the reason for the sickness at the heart of French society. In Faÿ's mind, French decline in the 1930s was the fault of the Masonic New World Order. For others, it was the fault of the Jews, or of "Anglo-Saxons," or of communism, or—increasingly, as the 1930s came to a close—of some combination of the above.

Indeed, with paranoia at its core, political critique in the 1930s was by definition unbounded and excessive, and discourse against the Masons almost invariably slipped into a discourse against "Judeo-Freemasonry" or "Judeo-communist-Freemasonry" or "Judeo-Anglo-American-Freemasonry."[35] As Faÿ became more and more haunted by the specter of Freemasonry, he joined forces with a broad coalition of others on the French Right whose grievances found expression in a transposable constellation of global adversaries: Freemasons, Jews, communists, liberals, Anglo-Saxons, and foreigners in general (with the possible exception of Germans). As the 1930s came to a close, Faÿ devoted prodigious energy in his journalism, lectures, and right-wing underground activities to spread the news of the multipronged menace facing France. Throughout this period, Faÿ signed his name to pamphlets denouncing Freemasonry, the Jews, the Popular Front, liberalism, parliamentarianism, and the "Crusade of Democracies" (*Croisade des Democraties*).[36] In the pages of right-wing journals such as *Je Suis Partout*, the Maurrassian *La Revue Universelle*, the monarchist *Courrier Royal*, and the protocollaborationist *Deutsch-Fran-zösische Monatshefte / Cahiers franco-allemands*, Faÿ developed his argument that Freemasonry was just one—if the most significant—element in a larger nefarious network of forces threatening the tradition and spiritual integrity of France.[37] He would continue this discussion in his contributions to the Nazi-financed French newspaper *La Gerbe*.[38]

Ironically, Faÿ's own paranoia about Freemasonry and its secrets would eventually lead him into a dark and sinister realm of secrecy, deception, and even death. In the end, the greatest irony of all was that the "Masonic sickness" Faÿ hoped to eradicate would emerge in a dark and shadowy form in Faÿ's own paranoid anti-Masonic crusade.

❏ ❏ ❏

Not surprisingly, *Revolution and Freemasonry* consolidated Faÿ's reputation as a political journalist, man of letters, and leading intellectual on the Right. Published in the wake of the Stavisky scandal and at the very moment in which members of the French Chamber of Deputies and Senate formed an "Inter-parliamentary Group of Action Against Freemasonry," Faÿ's book was per-ceived as timely, courageous, and galvanizing.[39] For *Je Suis Partout*, among other critics, this "quick and dense, alert and profound" book proved defini-tively how much Freemasonry had acted as a "dissolvent" toward "the catholic and monarchic civilization of old France" and established Faÿ as a formidable defender of that civilization.[40] Suddenly, Faÿ found himself very much on the right side of French history, in the several senses of that word: within the space of the next few years, anti-Freemasonry would "ascend to the highest level within the moral genealogy of the contemporary right."[41]

Nevertheless, critics in America were less persuaded by Faÿ's effort to describe the defining role played by Freemasonry in the modern world and, particularly, in the origins of the American and French revolutions.[42] For Henry Steele Commager, *Revolution and Freemasonry* was a "fascinating piece of historical sophistry," one that pushed its "large thesis" despite all facts to the contrary and that blithely resolved problems of causality that had per-plexed historians for decades. Commager noted ironically that had the great nineteenth-century historian George Trevelyan known of Faÿ's thesis about Masonic influence on the course of history, "he might have saved himself the labor of six volumes."[43] And writing in the *American Sociological Review*, Vin-cent Scramuzza disputed Faÿ's claim that "Freemasonry has become the most efficient social power of the civilized world." Rather, it was a hyperbolic effort to "catch the ear of the groundlings in present-day France" by "whisper[ing] mysteriously about 'the Masonic Menace.'"[44]

In fact, *Revolution and Freemasonry* represented more than just a shift in Faÿ's position from historian to ideologue. It also represented something of a turning point in Faÿ's personal love affair with the United States. Since 1920, Faÿ had written appreciatively of "the American character," with its simple pleasures and unbounded capacity for "joy." He had described the American "experiment" as "the only dream of the eighteenth century that has come true"—a characterization that had enormous historical and political resonance for him.[45] He had discussed Franco-American friendship in glowing, if anxious, terms and had praised America for its federalist structure, expansionist impulse, and "harmonious unity." At the high point of his outreach toward Franco-American conciliation, he had helped to found a short-lived historical journal, *The Franco-American Review*.[46] And in early 1935, he had written a private note to Stein that seemed to capture the sum of both his and her own feelings up to that point: "I can't be surprised that you are in love with your country," he wrote, "I am myself and I have been for over 18 years. It's the most thrilling and vital country on earth."[47]

Yet after 1935, Faÿ's writings on America grew increasingly skeptical, critical, and eventually embittered. As one Vichy acquaintance put it, Faÿ's feelings toward America in the late 1930s and 1940s were those of a jilted lover ("d'amoureux déçu").[48] In *Revolution and Freemasonry*, only thirty-four of the book's 349 pages are devoted to the American Revolution, with the bulk of the critique directed toward the "disaster" of 1789 in France. Yet the argument portrays Freemasonry as somehow integral to the very existence of the United States while remaining "entirely unnatural to France."[49] As Faÿ's paranoia about the Masonic menace grew, so too did his criticism of the Masonic elements within American culture, particularly the shadowy Anglo-Saxon connection between America and Great Britain, the spiritual home of Freemasonry. By the late 1930s, Faÿ's love affair with America and its promise had almost entirely dissipated. In his writings, his hopes now centered on the more radical political model of a federalist Europe dominated by Nazi Germany. And in 1938, the American universities he had once been welcomed into shut their doors to him, citing his overtly pro-German stance and his numerous propaganda pieces on Franco-German rapprochement.[50]

If there was anything that crystallized Faÿ's changing attitude toward America over the course of the 1930s, it was his growing dislike of the Freemason Franklin D. Roosevelt. In *Roosevelt and His America*, published in 1933 in both France and America, Faÿ stresses above all FDR's seductive and "charming" character—something that Stein would also make much of. For Faÿ, Roosevelt's "seduction" and "subtlety" explains why the American public is willing to place its trust in him in the midst of the greatest economic depression the country had ever seen. Like George Washington, Faÿ's Roosevelt is an Anglo-Saxon demagogue, leading his people out of their historical crisis by sheer force of will and hope for the future, by his "energy and initiative" and "freedom from all formulas and methods."[51] For the most part, this is a favorable representation, one that presents Roosevelt as an ideal: "a wise and firm man, who in trying to remedy the evils [does] not destroy the whole fabric."[52] The book emphasizes Roosevelt's ability "to rule rather than to dictate" and praises his qualities of leadership in terms that mirror Faÿ's own self-serving vision of "greatness" in his 1932 essay "An Invitation to American Historians."[53] There is also an interesting indication that Bernard Faÿ, himself a polio survivor, sympathized with Roosevelt's physical disability, which is presented as the cause for FDR's "exacting intelligence" and deep powers of perception and understanding.[54]

Yet there are also indications of unease in this early portrayal. Faÿ acknowledges that Roosevelt's "Anglo-Saxon" background, like that of his spiritual predecessor George Washington, links him to both Freemasonry and the Jews. He argues that like the Freemasons (who directed Roosevelt's "Anglo-Saxon" undergraduate education at Harvard and whose group Roosevelt eventually joined), Roosevelt has a strong will to power and desire to dominate his social and political context. Like the Jews (with whom FDR honed his skills as a law student at Columbia), Roosevelt has a "sense of money, of the economy, and of finance."[55] These are the skills that inform Roosevelt's Hundred Days Recovery program in 1933, but they are also for Faÿ potentially dangerous attributes. Again like Washington, Roosevelt is an "aristocrat" whose patrician bearing is complexly tied to both his "Masonic" and "Jewish" sides. Faÿ's technique is not to impugn directly but to taint through inference, as when he notes that Roosevelt's commitment to action and manipulation over ideas or doctrine "is his great strength or his secret weakness."[56] Yet in 1933, Faÿ leaves unresolved the question of Roosevelt's ultimate impact on American history.

Several years later, in the wake of *Revolution and Freemasonry*, Faÿ's critique is much sharper, his inferences more developed, and his paranoia more pronounced. While Faÿ's American publications continued to express moderate opinions, in the pages of *Je Suis Partout* Faÿ makes clearer his growing animus toward Roosevelt. Roosevelt is "supple" and "adroit," but also "cunning" (*malin*).[57] His Anglo-Saxonism is a source of both aristocratic strength and threat. He is the "spiritual cousin of M. Blum"—a pointed dig by association with the leader of the hated Popular Front government.[58] Roosevelt's power also links him, confusingly in Faÿ's mind, to both fascism and communism. By taking America off the gold standard, regulating the banking industry, and instituting the reforms of the New Deal, Roosevelt had created a "peaceful and popular dictatorship" with seemingly limitless power. One could indeed "compare him to Mussolini, to Hitler."[59] Like his European fascist counterparts, and like his eighteenth-century forebears, Roosevelt wants to effect a "revolution" in the very fabric of American society. But because of the influence of "socialist" and "extremist" elements in Roosevelt's cabinet, this revolution may turn out to be more like Stalin's than Hitler's. Faced with a "communist" Roosevelt, Faÿ ultimately lines up against him.

By 1938, Faÿ—who had since become *Je Suis Partout*'s chief American correspondent—was espousing the journal's party line. Increasingly open to the ideologies of Nazism and Adolf Hitler, *Je Suis Partout* had hardened its criticism of the Jews and other perceived social outcasts. Faÿ's writing quickly took up this line. An article in April 1938 on the American economic crisis blamed the Depression on the recent immigration of "Jewish intellectuals and extremists" who had brought "social disarray" to the country.[60] In February 1939, Faÿ again argued that "the presence of Jews in contact with blacks creates an explosive mixture" in America, one especially dangerous in the parts of the country where Jews "amass themselves." He continues: "Their quickness of spirit, their ability to work, their intellectual audacity and the grudges that they hold from centuries of a wandering life, of suffering, and of persecution, lead them to take a position as champions of all international ideas and of all the causes of social reform.... The Jewish problem is thus in the United States of a physical, commercial, and moral nature."[61] Two weeks later, Faÿ would connect this "Jewish" reformist spirit to Freemasonry, its democratic ideals, and its "deformation of Christianity."[62] The specter of Roosevelt, himself a Freemason with many Jewish advisors in his cabinet, would seem to lie behind this dark assessment.

By the end of the 1930s, Roosevelt—and America itself—had become a "catastrophe" for Bernard Faÿ.[63] In his 1939 book *Civilisation américaine*—the only of his major works of the 1930s not to be translated into English—Faÿ sees Roosevelt as part of "three centuries of collective errors" that have led America to the disastrous point of the 1930s.[64] With its blind belief in rational, scientific, and technological progress, America had sacrificed its energies to an illusion and been dominated by secular, rational, and "Jewish" thought rather than by sublime Christian faith. As with Europe, the only hope for America lay in acknowledging the failure of its revolutionary Enlightenment ideals and in creating a significant new future, one of "fields and trees, of fresh mornings and sunsets, of houses and a few cathedrals, and here and there a few skyscrapers."[65] This final, somewhat bizarre vision closes Faÿ's 1939 book on American civilization. What place could a few skyscrapers have in Faÿ's fantasy of the traditional French countryside? In fact, this utopian vision of the future is significant because it parallels dominant strains in fascist thought of the same period, ideals that combined primitivist reaction with technological progressivism. Skyscrapers, like trains that run on time, were not incompatible with fascism's goals but could actually be yoked into a retrogressive vision of a premodern, traditional world. For Faÿ and others, "a few skyscrapers" served as an urbane, vital, and virile backdrop to the more crucial and primal image of a timeless, preindustrial France. Technology had made American modernity catastrophic; fascist Europe would use technology but not be overpowered by it. Such would be the image that Faÿ would continue to fight for in his writings in support of the New European Order dominated by Germany.

Gertrude Stein would offer her own contemporaneous version of this vision in the "love letter to France" that she wrote in 1939, *Paris France*. This text is famous for Stein's initial argument that Paris provided the context or backdrop to the emergence of modernism: "that is what made Paris and France the natural background of the art and literature of the twentieth century. Their tradition kept them from changing and yet they naturally saw things as they were, and accepted life as it is" (*PF* 17). France, in short, was the timeless and unchanging stage upon which the more exciting and vital pageant of modernism unfolded. Yet by the end of the book, Stein has arrived at almost the opposite conclusion: that the "twentieth century," including "exciting" modern art and literature, was and is the necessary background to the emergence of a renewed yet traditional France. She writes of the modernist period as an "adolescent" period "of fashion without style, of systems with disorder, of reforming everybody which is persecution, and of violence without hope" (*PF* 119). And she writes of the decline of this adolescent period as a "process of civilising," one natural and necessary to the reemergence of tradition and order as stabilizing social forces. In the end, the "adolescent," revolutionary period of modernism had become a passing phase on the way back to the "civilized" world of traditional France. On the eve of the Vichy regime, Stein, like Faÿ was more than ready to throw her "modernism" behind the forces of tradition and national renewal.

▣ ▣ ▣

If Faÿ's anti-Semitic remarks in *Je Suis Partout* and elsewhere make it hard to understand how he could have remained such close friends with Gertrude

Stein during this turbulent time, two short sentences in the February 1939 *Je Suis Partout* article provide an answer. "Anyway," Faÿ writes, in the midst of describing the supposed Jewish problem in America, "the American Jew is not an homogenous type. Certain Jews have been there since the eighteenth century and constitute an aristocracy, others established themselves only in the current of the nineteenth century, but have succeeded economically and are truly nationalized."[66] Faÿ might well be describing the Jewish "types" in Stein's early novel *The Making of Americans*, whose gradual Americanization signals the loss of any distinguishing, and hence problematic, Jewish traits. Or he might be describing Gertrude Stein herself, with her own sense of connection to prerevolutionary, eighteenth-century American pioneers and her own investment in being seen first and foremost as a "real" American. Indeed, it was precisely Stein's patriotic stance throughout the 1930s that seemed in Faÿ's mind to make her writing so significant to his own vision of national renewal. But it was also the critical conservatism of Stein's patriotism that appealed to Faÿ's sensibilities and that enabled him to overlook the "problem" of her Jewishness.

The 1930s was in fact a period in which Stein rediscovered America both literally and figuratively. From abroad, she had watched as *The Autobiography of Alice B. Toklas* became a bestseller and as her image was placed on the cover of *Time* magazine (see figure 2.2). She achieved enormous personal fulfillment when the opera *Four Saints in Three Acts* debuted on Broadway in February 1934 to great acclaim. And finally, after thirty-one years in exile, she decided to return to the homeland that was celebrating her. From October 1934 to May 1935, Stein undertook a cross-country American lecture tour, stopping at places arranged for in advance by Bernard Faÿ and by Faÿ's friend Marvin Chauncey Ross. She lectured in Chicago; Washington, D.C.; Connecticut; and New York; and at Columbia, Princeton, Stanford, and Amherst College. She met Charlie Chaplin, Lillian Hellman, and Dashiell Hammett at a party in Hollywood; she joined policemen on the beat in Chicago; she had tea at the White House with Eleanor Roosevelt. She shared the podium with Bernard Faÿ at the Colony Club in New York, where they "vanquished" the audience of society ladies. And she found America "beautiful, beautiful in the American way, beautiful just in this way."[67] Observing the food, the houses, the people, and the geography, Stein felt that much had changed from the time when she lived there. All the same, she writes, "America is where we had been born and had always been even though for thirty years we had not really touched it with our feet and hands" (*EA* 169). This sense of both difference and sameness in her return to her native land became a driving preoccupation of Stein in the 1930s, one that was often a source of pleasure and wonderment for her. For example, in discussing American food, Stein writes: "There are two things that are very striking when you come back. In the first place desserts have disappeared out of America and the lots of cakes. Salads fruit salads have immensely taken their place." Or again on language: "The fact that they all talk American, that strikes one as it does the American going to France that they all talk French." Observing the States after thirty years abroad, Stein was exhilarated by the fact that "it was all strange and it was all natural."[68]

But Stein was not entirely sanguine about the changes she saw in the country she returned to. Many of the pieces on America that Stein wrote during and after her lecture tour draw an invidious distinction between a vital American past and the present-day epoch of loss and national decline. In "The Capital and Capitals of the United States of America," Stein describes a country both economically and psychologically indebted to public expenditures of capital and stresses the benefits of an extended economic depression for arresting the dependency and moral "enslavement" of many American citizens. Playing on two senses of the word "capital" (state capitals and economic capital), Stein claims that Americans have traditionally preferred to have their money and their lives left alone by government, in a private realm "where nobody would notice it unless they happened to be looking for it." But this eighteenth-century Jeffersonian ideal of state minimalism and private self-interest seemed to be fading in the present-day moment of governmental regulation and the New Deal. Classical economic liberalism had faded into the decadent social liberalism of the twentieth century. She laments of Americans that "perhaps they have changed now but I hope not."[69]

In another article from this same period, "American States and Cities and How They Differ from Each Other," Stein raises an unusual question: "And going over and on all that country the presidential timber country I wondered do they want that it should be that everything should be easy or that it should not. And I still wonder about that."[70] The standout phrase here— "presidential timber"—had deep national resonance for Stein. In her 1934 public letter to Faÿ about Franklin Roosevelt, for example, Stein associates "presidential timber" with the Republican party and its potential for strong leadership (the Democrats, we will recall, did not have "presidential timber" but excelled at "seduction").[71] In a private letter to Faÿ, Stein also aligns "presidential timber" with "the real glory of our country."[72] "Presidential timber" resonates with Stein's cherished vision of the country as a land of rugged pioneers: of self-made individuals unencumbered by restrictive systems of governance, each with the "timber" (material) to become president. As she argues in her essay, "presidential timber" is antithetical to the concept of "having things easy," because only through difficulty can the strength and determination of a people emerge. Writing in 1935, Stein "wonders" whether this is still the case in America. In the country Stein returns to in 1934, "it has been thought that anybody does like things to be easy but do they. Easy things make confusion even if you let them alone."[73] Six years later, in 1940, Stein would use the same rhetoric to justify Pétain's dictatorship, praising it for challenging the "softness" and "weak vices" of the French public.

Stein's writings on America during the late 1930s show a writer torn between patriotic display and uneasy disapproval. On a psychological level, this dual reaction can be understood as a displacement of the larger anxiety Stein felt in the wake of her enormous success with *The Autobiography of Alice B. Toklas*. Finding herself suddenly the cause célèbre of the moment in a highly celebrified culture, Stein began to worry about how a person can remain herself when she is looked at from the outside by a mass audience. "When a great many hear you that is an audience and if a great many hear you what difference does it make," she asks, adding, "an audience never does prove to you that you are you."[74] The difference between two seemingly incommensurate things—self and other, inside and outside, "I" and an audience—began to fascinate and worry Stein on her lecture tour. Arriving in Times Square on the eve of this tour, Stein

> saw an electric sign moving around a building and it said Gertrude Stein has come and that was upsetting. Anybody saying how do you do to you and knowing your name may be upsetting but on the whole it is natural enough but to suddenly see your name is always upsetting. Of course it has happened to me pretty often and I like it to happen just as often but always it does give me a little shock of recognition and non-recognition.[75]

An outside audience may pave the way to external "recognition," bringing fame, riches, and public approbation, but it may also stand in the way of internal self-recognition. As Stein grappled with her desire for success, she also grappled with the self-alienation this success brought. In the wake of her lecture tour, Stein often asked herself: what is the difference between writing for onself and writing for strangers? Could she really do both, as she seemed to think early on in her career?

By the mid-1930s, Stein had come to grasp the enormous costs of her newfound celebrity. Looking back to the moment of her shift from obscure modernist writer to American best-seller, Stein writes:

When the success began and it was a success I got lost completely lost. You know the nursery rhyme, I am I because my little dog knows me. Well you see I did not know myself, I lost my personality. . . . So many people knowing me I was I no longer and for the first time since I had begun to write I could not write and what was worse I could not worry about not writing and what was also worse I began to think about how my writing would sound to others, how could I make them understand, I who had always lived within myself and my writing.[76]

Before her success, Stein was prolific and creative but unknown; after her success, she was known but "lost." Gradually, Stein was beginning to believe that this fundamental difference between writing for an audience and writing for oneself was incommensurable. Once an outside audience has gotten you in its sights, genuine creative ability dries up.

We have already seen how Stein's feelings about her own celebrity, and her future as a writer, were grafted onto the issue of Jewishness. But they were also grafted onto her understanding of America. On the one hand, America was the place that "had made me what I am." It was the source of creativity, of possibility: of her own typicality and her own uniqueness. It had given Stein "the habits and character of being American." In fact, it was "the most natural thing in the world to be an American."[77] Yet America was also the place that had separated Stein from her writing: "It always did bother me that the American public were more interested in me than in my work. And after all there is no sense in it because if it were not for my work they would not be interested in me so why should they not be more interested in my work than in me. That is one of the things one has to worry about in America" (*EA* 50).

In 1937, Stein created an explicit analogy between her own fate as a writer in the wake of celebrity and the fate of present-day America. In *The Geographical History of America or the Relation of Human Nature to the Human Mind* (1937), Stein theorized two antithetical modes of being: "human nature" and "human mind." "Human nature" refers to an exterior world of temporality, identity, and relationality, the world of audiences; "human mind" refers to an interior world of timeless creativity, entity, or being, the world of the genius writer. Her popular books, such as *The Autobiography of Alice B. Toklas* and its sequel, *Everybody's Autobiography*, as well as most of her audience writing of the 1930s, catered to "human nature"; her more experimental texts were masterpieces of the "human mind." But the same could also be said about America itself. America's "geographical history" was in fact deeply concerned with the human nature/human mind distinction and with what Stein understood to be the ongoing struggle between these two competing ways of thinking about existence.

On the one hand, America—the source of her own creative being—was associated in Stein's mind with genius and with a particular kind of experience that she called "wandering." She writes: "Can one say too often . . . that the straight lines on the map of the United States of America make wandering a mission and an everything" (*GHA* 85). "Wandering" describes an exploratory, multidirectional, and open-ended existence that Stein would often portray admiringly in the heroines of her fiction, including the Catholic saints she writes about in the 1920s and 1930s.[78] Stein also associates wandering with two of her distinctly American heroines, Melanctha (from *Three Lives*) and Ida (from *Ida*).[79] Both Melanctha and Ida are wanderers, both move freely and disinterestedly throughout their lives in a timeframe of continuous presence, and both inhabit an America whose geography is characterized by endless, abstract yet heterogeneous expanses. This America, the America of Melanctha and Ida, is a land of the human mind: of a kind of free and absolute being. Stein herself experienced this form of wandering as she traversed the country in an airplane, looking down on the abstract "straight lines" of the land that seemed so much like a cubist painting. She writes: "And think, it is very exciting but think how much America and I do think America has something to do with the human mind" (*GHA* 123).

Yet the America that Stein encounters in the 1930s is also associated with everything that denies this absolute being, this human mind: namely, "government and propaganda," as well as the self-alienating, contingent realms of "time and identity." All of these stifling worldly intrusions into the realm of genius, all of this exteriority that Stein associates with an audience, only precludes real existence, because "Human nature is not interesting." In the America that turns Stein into a celebrity, human nature seems to predominate over human mind. She notes: "Poor America is it not saying yes, is it losing the human mind to become human nature. Oh yeah" (*GHA* 125).

As the 1930s drew to a close, and as America's economic and social woes appeared ever more intractable and knotty, Stein, like Faÿ, placed the blame for modern American "decadence" on a very particular source: Franklin Delano Roosevelt and his administration.

From the start, Stein took a strong and public dislike to Roosevelt—a stance that would even bring her some unwanted attention from the FBI.[80] In her writings, Stein referred to Roosevelt as "American but really . . . not American": part of the "riff-raff" of the Democratic party.[81] Her 1934 review of Faÿ's *Roosevelt and His America*, already discussed in chapter 2 as a point of contact with Faÿ concerning the character of George Washington, allowed Stein to criticize Roosevelt's "seductiveness" as wily rather than trustworthy—an assessment that Faÿ only arrived at toward the end of the 1930s. In a series of articles on "Money" that Stein published in the *Saturday Evening Post* in 1936, she leveled her most direct attack, decrying what Roosevelt and his New Deal were doing to America's "being," particularly its "eighteenth-century" individualist ethos. With its opposition to big business and its emphasis upon taxation and on "getting rid of the rich," the New Deal had turned out to be a bum deal for everyone, since by doing away with the rich "everybody is poor." New Deal efforts to redistribute wealth, unionize workers, and address unemployment were for Stein all antithetical to the eighteenth-century Jeffersonian ideals of freedom and self-making. All were insidious forms of what she calls "organization." She laments in particular that the New Deal has encouraged in Americans "a passion for being enslaved": "the other day a very able young man, you would not have expected he would feel that way about it, wrote to me and said after all we are all glad to have Roosevelt do our thinking for us. That is the logical end of organization and that is where the world is today."[82]

For Stein, Roosevelt embodied state paternalism at its worst. She likened him to "father Mussolini and father Hitler . . . and father Stalin and father Lewis and father Blum and father Franco," adding, "Fathers are depressing. . . . The periods of the world's history that have always been most dismal ones are the ones where fathers were looming and filling up everything" (*EA* 133). Like dictators and American union organizers (John L. Lewis), Roosevelt and his French counterpart Léon Blum dominate and enslave the public with their collective systems of "organization." Their paternal influence is also more or less explicitly linked to "the Jews," whom elsewhere, we will recall, Stein had decried for their "concentration of fathering." In a slippery chain of association in *Everybody's Autobiography*, Stein condemns Roosevelt and the communists for attempting "to do away with money"; in the next paragraph, she adds "the Jews" to this list, who "being always certain that money is money finally decide and that makes a Marxian state that money is not money." If money is what differentiates humans from animals ("because if you live without money you have to do as the animals do live on what you find each day to eat"), then Roosevelt and the communists are guilty of leveling the difference between humans and animals.[83] But the worse malefactors are "the Jews," who, despite "being always certain that money is money," deliberately *decide* that "money is not money"—a claim that seems to invoke the insidious cliché of Jewish international backroom power politics allied with "a Marxian state."[84]

While critics have been eager to stress the feminist dimensions of Stein's famous attack on fathering, it is also important to read this statement in the context of its critique of the New Deal, particularly its understanding of the role of government and its intervention into what she called "the private life." With her criticism of Roosevelt's "persistence of insistence in a narrow range of ideas" and of his effort to do away with individual "thinking" in favor of public "organization," Stein soundly rejects social programs of recovery and reform (*GHA* 170). In a newspaper interview of the period, Stein even praises the slogan "every man a king" of the anti-Roosevelt presidential contender Huey Long, America's homegrown fascist (Stein notes, "It's really very good, you know . . . I'm for that").[85] Her subsequent blast in *Everybody's Autobiography* against "liberals that is intellectuals, the kind of people that believe in progress and understanding," shows the ever-hardening shift of her politics to the right (*EA* 75).

Yet there are also significant contradictions in Stein's thinking at this time. Surprisingly enough, despite her attacks on "fathering," including the paternalism of fascist dictatorship, Stein also seemed convinced that national renewal could only be achieved through the influence of a strong male authority figure. In an essay on the excesses of taxation during the New Deal, for example, she asks that "everybody who votes public money" remember "how he feels as a father of a family, when he says no, when anybody in a family wants money." Without this paternal decisionism (to borrow a term from Carl Schmitt), "there is going to be a lot of trouble and some years later everybody is going to be very unhappy."[86] In this context, fathers function as salutary forces of discipline, compelling their wayward charges to control and limit their urges.

It is for this reason that Stein advocates resisting both the false egalitarianism of liberal democracy and the collectivist specter of communism—the latter of particular concern to her. As Catharine Stimpson notes, Stein's anticommunism was acute, presumably fueled by her dislike of Léon Blum and his Popular Front government in France. Indeed, Stimpson argues, Stein's visceral fear of communism may have been *the* factor behind her support for the Vichy regime in 1940.[87] It is certainly undeniable that this fear motivated Stein's Pétainism, if only because Pétain himself made anticommunism such a vocal part of his agenda. Yet in her comments on money, Stein surprisingly suggests that it is less communism than the *lack* of an authoritarian ideology that lies behind the "decadence" of modern mass society.

A more troubling version of these comments is detailed in private letters from 1937 to her friend W. G. Rogers. Here Stein writes about the attractions of dictatorship in a mass society: "disguise it to yourself as you will the majority does want a dictator, it is natural that a majority if it has come to be made up of enormous numbers do, a big mass likes to be shoved as a whole because it feels it moves and they cannot possibly feel that they move themselves as little masses can, there you are, like it or not there we are."[88] In this chilling assessment of "the masses" as self-deluded, masochistic, and easily manipulable by elites, Stein distances herself firmly from liberal democratic platitudes about majority rule. In the place of liberal democracy, Stein argues for the power and, arguably, the rightness of authoritarian leadership. It is the dictator who gives the masses what they want, who makes them "feel . . . and move." Like the celebrity, the dictator uses his authorial voice to "shove" people. But shoving can be a good thing if it brings "peace": "[In Italy under Mussolini] they do let you work and live in the country and be peaceful . . . and nobody thinks you can live and be quiet under communism, nor under constitutional government as made today." Following this logic, fascism—and its dictatorial permutations—can be seen as the only solution, however compromised, to the political crises of the 1930s: "You see what in Europe everybody is hollering about is whether communism is not worse than fascism and here everybody thinks you have to be either red or white and I am not sure they are not right and certainly white is bad but not so bad as red."[89]

These thoughts recall the sentiments about Hitler and his achievements with "peace" that Stein shared publicly in her *New York Times* interview and privately with Bernard Faÿ. They suggest that for all her dislike of "fathering," particularly as it is seen to interfere with foundational American liberties, Stein admired the strong-arm practices of father figures—including dictators—in times of social crisis and unrest. If Roosevelt and Blum were only exacerbating the crises in their respective countries and leading their people away from peace, another "white" father figure might emerge to bring countries like America or France back to their core values. For both Stein and Faÿ, Philippe Pétain would clearly play this role for France—and perhaps for America as well.

▣ ▣ ▣

Had Gertrude Stein remained defensively patriotic about America throughout the 1930s, her relationship with Bernard Faÿ might have fallen by the wayside, torn apart by the passion of their separate ideological convictions. This, after all, was a moment in which politics was everything, when there could be "no more constructive debate between people of different political stripes. Only clashes."[90] Yet the fact that both friends experienced a deep-seated sense of disillusionment about their idealized America in the wake of the New Deal served only to consolidate their shared conservatism and mutual esteem. Upon reading *The Geographical History of America* in 1937, Faÿ gushed to Stein: "It's fascinating—and you are so wise! I agree so much with you that it is embarrassing."[91] For her part, Stein continued to accord Faÿ the privileges befitting a close friend, discussing details of her writing and publication schemes with him, as well as the possibility of yet another American lecture tour in 1939. This, despite an event that nearly derailed their friendship.

Faÿ's behind-the-scenes brokerage of Stein's American lecture tour had gone smoothly except for one episode, but it was a disastrous one—and Stein did not suffer slights easily. In Chicago, Faÿ and Marvin Chauncey Ross had worked hard to make Stein's stop on her tour a success, enlisting the support of Fanny Butcher, literary editor of the *Chicago Tribune* and president of the Chicago PEN Club, as well as Bobsy Goodspeed, a prominent society matron and arts supporter. Faÿ had even approached Butcher about the possibility of Stein receiving an honorary degree from the University of Chicago. (Butcher advised against the idea, stating that members of the faculty were already suspicious of Stein's chief supporter at the University, Robert Maynard Hutchins, for "foisting 'modernity'" on the campus.)[92] Yet this advance planning was preempted by the unexpected doings of a man named Colonel Jean-Jacques Rousseau Voorhies, a sometime friend of Faÿ and Stein hanger-on from the early 1930s. This colorful character, described by one contemporary as a "former Broadway actor, member of the Louisiana Bar, liaison officer between French and American armies during the World War, and well known figure in the publishing world," had asked Faÿ for an introduction to Stein in Paris in the summer of 1932.[93] He reappeared in Stein's life in early 1934, months before she had decided to do a lecture tour, and courted her by offering to talk about her work at the College Club in Chicago. Stein sanctioned this idea, even providing suggestions for texts to read and explicate. But later that year, when Stein began her American tour, she was horrified to discover that Voorhies was capitalizing on their acquaintance by passing himself off as her "personal representative" and "Press Agent de Luxe" in Chicago.[94] Even worse, he had arranged with two venues to charge an admission fee to the lectures she planned to give, something that Stein had explicitly prohibited. Upon her arrival in the States, Stein lost little time in dismissing Voorhies. She also made her displeasure known to Faÿ, who was mortified. He wrote her, "I am terribly sorry to have been the indirect cause of so much trouble and bother for you— and so much fatigue for Alice."[95] But neither he nor Stein had seen the last of Colonel Voorhies.

In 1936, Voorhies published a nasty two-part interview with Lucille Hecht in *Real America*, "Gertrude Stein's Magnificent Hoax: How a Party in Paris, Where the Wine Flowed Freely, Led to the Most Gigantic Practical Joke Ever Perpetrated on the American Literary Public." Among the allegations in this piece were that Stein was an alcoholic and liked to drive drunk, that *The Autobiography of Alice B. Toklas* was written at the insistence of Voorhies, and that Stein, Toklas, Voorhies, and Faÿ saw themselves as living embodiments of the Four Saints of Stein's opera. Also that Bernard Faÿ had given a diploma from the Collège de France to Stein's dog Basket—the only claim that turned out to be true. But the nastiest allegation of all was the leading one: that "Gertrude cannot write, and that none knew this better than she." Stein's "magnificent hoax," Voorhies argued, was a three-decade-long bluff that had convinced a naïve audience to see her writing as the output of a literary genius. Her lecture tour was the most audacious ruse of them all, one cooked up by Voorhies and Stein during a drunken bender. Voorhies also described Faÿ as fully in on the joke. He quotes Faÿ, the "peerless French historian," as saying that Stein "has convinced many people that her childish rambling is literature," and indeed, that it was Faÿ "who first recognized Stein as the world's greatest clown."[96]

Needless to say, both Stein and Faÿ were furious with the Voorhies depiction. For Stein, it recalled the bitterness of the blast against her published in *transition* magazine after *The Autobiography of Alice B. Toklas*. Faÿ, for his part, took it upon himself to dispatch a rejoinder to the agencies publishing Voorhies's comments, stating firmly that "there is no truth whatever in any one of these statements."[97] He also meekly approached Stein through Toklas in order to plan a counterattack.[98] Stein coldly responded by warning Faÿ never to discuss the affair in her presence.[99] But retrospectively, Faÿ claimed that the Voorhies affair had only fortified his friendship with Stein: "it made her feel more the value of our intimacy and rendered it more perceptible to me as well."[100]

The fallout from the Voorhies affair was seemingly minor. Still, Stein and Faÿ would never again be as closely in touch as they had been in the early 1930s, when "Bernard Faÿ was the one we were seeing more at that time than we were seeing any other one" (*EA* 102). Above all else, Faÿ had simply become much too busy and preoccupied to spend long hours over tea with Stein and Toklas. Now fully ensconced at the Collège de France, Faÿ had a full-time, highly visible teaching and lecturing career in Paris that required significant preparation and forethought, especially given the charged, contested nature of his courses. In 1936, Faÿ taught on the French Revolution, on Freemasonry during the French and American revolutions, and on FDR; in 1937, he taught on the revolutionary-era Freemason La Fayette, on revolutionary thought during the eighteenth century, and on the history of American journalism; in 1938, he taught again on La Fayette, now described cryptically as "champion of Franco-American liberalism," on Freemasonry in America, and on America in general; and in 1939, Faÿ lectured on Freemasonry, on American democracy, and, significantly, on the origins of Franco-American friendship. According to Faÿ himself, these courses "have a very great success [*sic*] and amuse me much but it's a ticklish subject and that requires a lot of work."[101] In the same letter to Stein, Faÿ gives a stronger indication of the polemical nature of his intellectual work: "Fun is everywhere. A silly man at the Sorbonne has been so shocked at the success of my lectures that he has started answering and criticizing them at the Sorbonne. Think of it! They are making of me a national character! I can't tell you how jammed is my lecture room and how excited people are."[102]

There was more to Faÿ's reputation during these years than his rousing lectures at the Collège. During this time, Faÿ had become an active contributor to both mainstream and extreme-right publications, *Je Suis Partout* among them. As we shall see in chapter 5, Faÿ's writings in the late 1930s increasingly involved him in underground networks working to overthrow the Third Republic in France. His trips to Spain during the Spanish Civil War and to

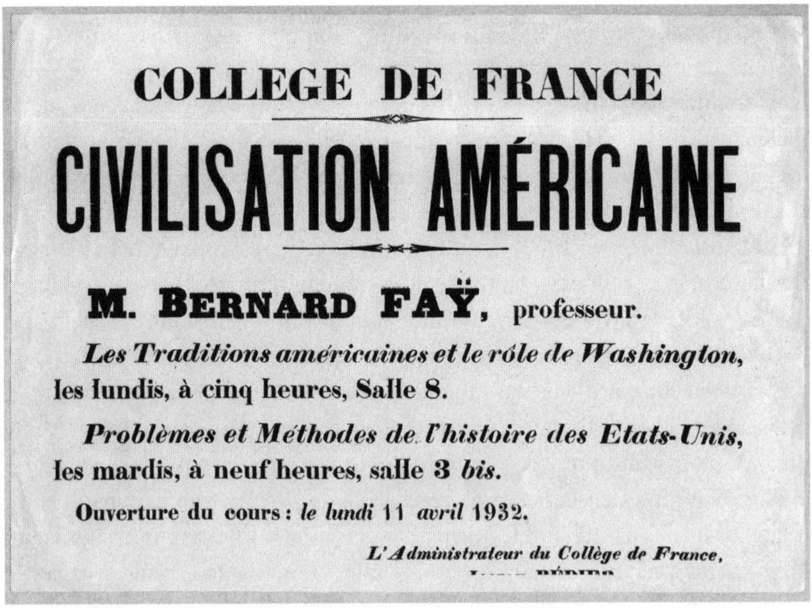

COLLEGE DE FRANCE

CIVILISATION AMÉRICAINE

M. BERNARD FAŸ, professeur.

Les Traditions américaines et le rôle de Washington, les lundis, à cinq heures, Salle 8.

Problèmes et Méthodes de l'histoire des Etats-Unis, les mardis, à neuf heures, salle 3 *bis.*

Ouverture du cours : *le lundi 11 avril 1932.*

L'Administrateur du Collège de France,

FIGURE 3.1 Advertisement for Faÿ's lecture at the Collège de France.

Berlin in 1937 allowed Faÿ to forge lasting personal contacts within a right-wing pan-European movement composed of Catholic, anti-Masonic, and anti-Semitic forces. As the 1930s drew to a close, Faÿ increasingly became known as *un homme de confiance* in French right-wing circles.

While these activities kept Faÿ from continued close contact with Stein, they did not estrange the two friends. A personal note from March 1937 by Faÿ tells of a shared evening: "Gertrude dine chez moi. Elle est tres gai. Elle me raconte qu'elle est accusée de 'fascisme' par beaucoup de gens aux États-Unis. Je lui dis que c'est aussi mon cas. Nous en rions ensemble." ("Gertrude dines at my house. She is very happy. She tells me that she has been accused of 'fascism' by many Americans. I tell her that this is also the case with me. We laugh about it together.")[103] Their shared laughter was enormously fortifying for the two friends, perhaps indicative of the distance both felt from such a charge at this moment. This may have been especially the case for Stein. While Faÿ was thriving with the confidence of a right-wing ideologue whose moment had finally arrived, Stein in the late 1930s was confronted with a series of difficult events: the death of her beloved brother Mike in 1938; the dissolution of her salon as family, friends, and fellow Americans left Europe on the eve of war; and perhaps most challenging, the failure of her publishing ventures in the late 1930s as the American public once again rejected the more experimental writing that she had hoped to hitch to the star of her celebrity.

In fact, looking back at Stein and Faÿ in the late 1930s, it is evident that the relative position of each toward the other was becoming the inverse of what it had been when the two first met. While Faÿ had once been a satellite in the orbit (or halo) of Saint Gertrude, by the end of the 1930s it was Faÿ whose career was most visibly on the rise and whose writings and lectures seemed to generate the most public interest. And while Faÿ's politics had him flourishing on the front lines of the extreme Right in France, Stein's politics had only alienated her from her American audience. After Stein's article series on "Money" appeared in 1936, she writes, "the young ones said I was reactionary and they said how could I be who had always been so well ahead of every one and I myself was not and am not certain that I am not again well ahead as ahead as I ever have been" (*EA* 311). The double negatives in this tortured construction—"I am not . . . certain that I am not again well ahead"—reveal the anxiety of Stein's response. They suggest a troubled uncertainty at being criticized by the American audience she had courted for so long. At this moment, the emotional support and political fellow-feeling of Bernard Faÿ must have seemed not only welcome but galvanizing for Gertrude Stein.

FIGURE 3.2 Stein, Toklas, and Faÿ at Bilignin (1930s).

But it was also Faÿ's energetic appraisal of the rapidly changing political scene in numerous articles he wrote during the late 1930s that continued to stimulate and attract Stein. Her deep-seated conservatism and disillusionment with the present-day course of events in both America and France were her own, but Faÿ gave her the terms, and the foci, through which to articulate her sense of these events. Her "opinions" on subjects such as Catholicism and Freemasonry during this period are awkwardly framed reiterations of Faÿ's own. Never one to think through a political argument with deeply reasoned views,

Stein in this period is clearly out of her depth and reliant on Faÿ to orient her. In a letter to Faÿ after hearing one of his lectures, Stein notes cryptically that "these kind of people are the same in all countries, as I looked at the faces around me, for once a french audience was not french but might have been anywhere, near East, Europe, South America or America. It was strange, but we will talk about that and many other things very soon I hope." In another letter to Faÿ after one of his lectures, Stein claims "that Anglosaxon men being naturally childish and emotional can naturally indulge in masonic ritual just for itself alone, but frenchmen not being naturally childish and they are not just as naturally cannot . . . and so you are completely right they should never try."[104] Such "logic" reveals, at the very least, the extent of Stein's ignorance about the darkening world around her. The most notorious instance of this is Stein's analysis of the French defeat by the Nazis in 1940, "The Winner Loses, A Picture of Occupied France."

Written for the *Atlantic Monthly*, "The Winner Loses" is, like other propaganda pieces Stein wrote for Vichy, a strained effort to appeal to an American audience using the same celebrity persona developed during her lecture tour. While the text presents itself as a casual bit of reportage about Bilignin at the start of the war, the effort comes across as painfully glib. Stein admits that during the Phoney War of 1939–1940 (when European hostilities were at a standstill following the German invasion of Poland), she relied on a book of prophecies to determine the future course of events, that she was tempted several times to flee France for America but decided not to because "it would be awfully uncomfortable and I am fussy about my food," and that she preferred gardening to listening to the radio for news of current events. Yet at the end of the essay, Stein remains fully capable of analyzing the effect of France's defeat in the spring of 1940 in glowing terms, as a salutary event. Everywhere in the French countryside around her, as people barter their livestock and fetch wood from the forests to heat their homes, Stein senses a return to good, healthy, peasant life—what she would elsewhere associate with the populist energies of the agrarian eighteenth century. "Everybody was happy, because their men were alive and a good many of them had come home," she writes, reasonably, but then: the French "feel alive and like it . . . they seem much more wide-awake than they were." After all, "they were tired of the weak vices that they were all indulging in, that if they had had an easy victory the vices would have been weaker and more of them, and now—well, now there is really something to do—they have to make France itself again and there is a future . . . and they all think that French people were getting soft, and French people should not be soft" (WL 130–132).

These comments underscore the double message of "The Winner Loses." Writing about the French defeat for the *Atlantic Monthly*, Stein is not simply trying to sell Pétain's Armistice to her fellow Americans. She is also trying to sell it as a possible model for America itself. "Perhaps everybody will find out, as the French know so well," she writes, "that the winner loses, and everybody will be, too, like the French, that is, tremendously occupied with the business of daily living, and that that will be enough" (WL 132). "Everybody" here is none other than the American people, those who can learn from what "the French know so well." The addressee of "The Winner Loses," like the addressee of the introduction to the speeches of Marechal Pétain and the addressee of the last section of her postwar text *Brewsie and Willie*, is "Americans." And the point of these writings is not so much descriptive as proscriptive. In her idealized picture of a rejuvenated French populace, we can see a reiteration of Stein's Jeffersonian vision of the pioneering American eighteenth century. In her admonition that "the business of daily living" is "enough," we can hear her appreciation of conservative and libertarian values. And in her point about the "weak vices" of the French, we can hear the echoes of her critique of Americans under the Roosevelt administration. Once strong, resilient, and independent, both societies have become soft from two centuries of letting their government "do their thinking for them." They have fallen victim to "red" propaganda that threatens to level "inevitabl[e]" distinctions between the classes.[105] Stein had been developing and refining this critique over the course of the 1930s and was convinced that only a significant change in political direction in both countries could arrest the creeping softness and weakness of liberal democracy or the more looming threat of "red" communism. When the Third Republic in France finally met its end in 1940, Stein welcomed this defeat, despite the fear and anxiety she describes in "The Winner Loses" as the Phoney War turned into a real campaign. And she welcomed this defeat because it pointed to a radically new political direction in France that might also serve as a blueprint for the United States.

"The Winner Loses" presents itself as an ironic, even light-hearted, chin-up account of stoic survival in the midst of wartime chaos. Its tone seems to have prevented many of Stein's readers from seeing, or acknowledging, the pointed political commentary that ends this piece. But the simple fact that this was a propaganda piece written by Stein in support of the Vichy regime demands that we acknowledge these comments for what they are: a troubling apologia for the emergence of this regime. "The Winner Loses" would prepare the ground for Stein's decision soon thereafter to attempt to get Pétain's speeches published into English. As an anonymous Vichy diplomat said about this essay in February 1941: "the only good [English-language] propaganda was made by Gertrude

Stein," whose "article of the Atlantic Revue [*sic*] was the best and the most appreciated . . . the very words and thoughts that would move the Yankee opinion."[106]

But to what extent was Stein simply "seeing things from Faÿ's angle" in this essay? When Stein writes that France would "win" by capitulating to Hitler, because that would force the citizenry to abandon "the weak vices that they were all indulging in," she is in fact reiterating an argument that Faÿ himself had been trumpeting since at least 1938. In an essay for the *New York Times Magazine* of May 1938, Faÿ blasts the Popular Front for "giving generous habits of laziness to the whole population"; he also notes that "good fortune may be as fatal to Hitler as ill fortune has been favorable" and "that Germany would win as long as she is weak—and lose as soon as she becomes really strong." In a lecture he gave in Québec in October 1938, Faÿ argues that France's renewal lies largely in the people's ability to "accept the discipline that they know well that they need," to be prepared to "suffer" in order to regain "their strength and their prestige." And in a series of articles Faÿ wrote for the pro-Nazi journal *La Gerbe* at the beginning of the Vichy regime, he returns again and again to the theme that "there is more of greatness . . . in the recovery of the loser than in the exaltation of the winner; the former has to surmount the destiny that weighs it down."[107]

"Losing" becomes a source of possibility for an individual who desperately desires a change in the direction of his country's future. It is also an appealing stance for a pious Catholic believing strongly in the spiritual value of suffering. But Faÿ's defeatism had a more cunning side to it as well, since the fall of France would initiate a positive change in his own fortunes, allowing him to "win" at the precise moment when his fellow French citizens were losing their lives, their land, and their identity.

Borrowing this argument from Faÿ, Stein brought her own particular spin to the idea that winning is really losing, and losing winning. And this helps to explain one of the great mysteries of Stein's late life for biographers and readers alike. Why didn't Stein leave France in the late 1930s, as she had been urged to do by friends, family, and even the United States consulate? Why did Stein, unlike so many other Jews, choose to remain in a situation that was clearly life threatening? "The Winner Loses" provides several possible answers to this conundrum. Perhaps Stein's sense of being on the cusp of a new future in France—a future that might also serve as a model for a renewed America—was what really led her to stay. Perhaps, seeing politics now largely from Faÿ's angle, Stein felt reassured that the darkening world around her would soon give way to a light-filled future. Perhaps it was inconceivable to Stein that this future, one that she had so fervently anticipated throughout the 1930s, might include the silencing of her own voice.

PART II

STEIN'S WAR

"HAVING FAITH" IN PÉTAIN (1940–1944)

CHAPTER FOUR

IT IS believed that close to forty million French people—the entire population of France—supported Philippe Pétain and his Vichy regime in the summer of 1940. When Pétain came to power on June 16, after a grim month-long struggle against German forces, in which over ninety thousand Frenchmen lost their lives, he was widely perceived as a national hero. Pétain's quick reassurances to the citizens of France that the uncertainties of the Phoney War with Germany were over, that the social and political instability of the 1930s had come to an end, and that France was on its way to recovery fell upon eager ears. The will to believe in his leadership was palpable in all corners of the population and signified an abiding desire for national healing after years of perceived decadence. In the following weeks, an armistice with Germany was signed, the parliamentary government of the Third Republic was dissolved—along with most of the French Republic's core principles—and Pétain was named chief of state of Vichy France. During this period, according to Zeev Sternhell, "France changed more radically in a few months than at any other time in its history since the summer of 1789."[1]

Even those who initially resisted an armistice with the Nazis respected the stately eighty-four-year-old Pétain, who retained a "remarkable alertness" that belied his age and physical capacities. Looking back at the widespread exhaustion and fear within French society in June 1940, it is not hard to understand why so many were drawn to Pétain's calm and authoritative presence. As historians have noted of the period just before the armistice, "the French were weary, divided, tense, devoid of all sense of adventure, and reaching out for security and comfort."[2] Although the Germans may have held as little as 10 percent of the country by the time of the armistice, the widespread perception of "inhuman" German might quickly sapped French morale and lent support to capitulation.[3] Pétain powerfully addressed his country's felt needs. When Pétain made his famous pronouncement on taking power—"I give to you the gift of my person"—he underscored the Christlike nature of his efforts.[4] Self-sacrifice would describe the tone of his administration, as it had in his days on the battlefield at Verdun. His tenacity in one of the most important battles of World War I had earned him the title "the Victor of Verdun"; his perceived courage on behalf of a defeated country in 1940 would transform him, Joan of Arc–style, into the "Savior of France." Yet although Pétain's power would be cloaked in selfless patriotism, and although Vichy ideology would advertise itself in terms of a return to traditional Catholic values, Pétain's regime was an important first: the first modern dictatorship that France had ever known.

Defeat is a complex phenomenon, one that can produce widely differing responses depending upon how the losers interpret their loss. In *The Culture of Defeat: On National Trauma, Mourning, and Recovery*, Wolfgang Schivelbusch argues that the French had developed a particular way of coming to terms with military defeat since at least the fall of Napoleon I. Gloom and anxiety about a national humiliation was invariably followed by immediate calls for renewal, for a fresh start. Schivelbusch identifies the specific French term for this process: *revanche*, understood as both revenge or retaliation and the reestablishment of social equilibrium. *Revanche* served multiple purposes: while usually directed at the external victor who had conquered France, it could also refer, as it did in 1940, to the internal social elements who had led to France's defeat. In Third Republic France, *revanche* functioned "as a political religion, foundational myth, and integrating force."[5] But even with the fall of the Third Republic in the summer of 1940, *revanche* remained a powerful and mobilizing term for the Pétain regime. André Gide would capture this idea in describing the events leading up to Vichy: "Yes, long before the war, France stank of defeat. She was already falling to pieces to such a degree that perhaps the only thing that could save her was, is perhaps, this very disaster in which to retemper her energies."[6]

Pétain immediately strove to acknowledge and interpret the defeatism of his constituents. His explanation for the fall of France seemed remarkably appropriate at the moment of France's defeat. "Too few allies, too few weapons, too few babies," he announced in June 1940, at the same moment sounding the call for a *revanchist* National Revolution.[7] Although historians now agree that the blame for France's defeat lay predominantly with military strategy, at the time of his pronouncement Pétain's words resonated.[8] Finally France could address the internal corruption that had led the nation to its unfortunate pass; finally France could recover from one hundred and fifty years of misguided parliamentary democracy. As the historian Denis Peschanski writes, "Vichy conveys, to begin with, a special idea of defeat. The ideologues of the new regime found their way again by seeking through defeat the possibility of completely remaking French society: utopia from a clean slate."[9] Attacking the now-defunct Third Republic's views on education, secularization, urbanization, women's emancipation, and parliamentary rule, Pétain and his administration proposed a wholesale "recovery plan" for the nation based on *famille, travail, patrie* (family, work, fatherland). "I invite you to an intellectual and moral renewal first of all," Pétain stated in his famous speech of June 25, 1940, justifying the armistice with Germany. And again on October 11: "We must, tragically, achieve in defeat the revolution which in victory . . . we could not even imagine."[10]

Interestingly, Pétain's idea of *revanche* was not the expected one, directed at the external enemy who had actually caused France's defeat: Germany.

FIGURE 4.1 Philippe Pétain propaganda poster.

Although suspicious of Germany from the start, Pétain, according to most of his biographers, felt that German plans for a New Europe might indeed allow France "to regain her status as a major power in Europe and the world." "Cooperation with Germany," for Pétain, "was the only possible policy."[11] It helped enormously that the armistice had appeared to guarantee France's sovereignty, and appearances at this moment were everything. It was in fact the British, not the Germans, who had decimated part of the French fleet at Mers-el-Kebir in July 1940, an event that seemed to tip the balance in favor of the Germans at this crucial moment of political leveraging. Pétain's prime minister, Pierre Laval, seized this opportunity to do everything he could to secure "sincere and unreserved cooperation" with Nazi Germany. This was sealed by the infamous handshake between Pétain and Hitler at the French town of Montoire on October 24, 1940. After this event, Pétain delivered what would in retrospect be his most damaging pronouncement: "It is with honor and in order to maintain French unity, a unity ten centuries old, in the framework of a constructive activity of the new European order, that I have today entered the way of collaboration."[12]

Hence *revanche*, for Pétain at the start of the Vichy regime, had a very particular resonance. The humiliation of the fall of France could be refigured or "spun" as an opportunity to correct the course of France's destiny, a course that had veered badly off track during the Third Republic. "Enter[ing] the way of collaboration" with the Nazis would not only offer France a new opportunity to join its past ("a unity ten centuries old") with its future ("the new European order"). It would also allow the nation to wreak revenge upon those elements that had shattered French unity into two distinct halves: left-leaning, democratic elements that could now be purged from the system.

Over the course of four years, however, Vichy policy proved to be markedly less transformative than it proclaimed itself to be in 1940. Pétain's National Revolution seemed to offer a blueprint for France's future, and many plans were laid for excising the supposed decadence and rot from French culture. But the practical implementation of this revolution was continually thwarted by internal corruption and dissension as well as by the stark demands of the German occupiers for money, food, and materiel. In fact, the very purposeful agenda of Vichy's first two years—a revolution at home and voluntary association with Hitler's Germany abroad—would produce little social change but much social unrest. When the Nazis invaded the Soviet Union in June 1941, a groundswell of communist resistance in France followed by brutal Nazi reprisals turned Vichy into a virtual police state. And when the Nazis occupied all of France in November 1942, whatever useful function the regime served had

largely dissipated. By 1943, the thrust of Pétain's 1940 agenda had been transformed into passivity and the generalized attitude of *attentisme*: "waiting."

Ironically, this later posture of Petain and his administration would serve
the postwar defense of the Vichyites: *attentisme* seemed much more justifiable after the war than the activist agenda of the National Revolution. Thus
Yves Bouthillier, Pétain's minister of finance, wrote after the war that the Vichy
regime was not a "clear, logical, and rational construction"; rather, it was driven
by the belief that "waiting, as clear-sightedly as possible, was the surest path
to safeguard the French future."[13] Or as Pétain defended himself to the French
on the eve of the Liberation in 1944: "If I could not be your sword, I tried to be
your shield."[14] And Bernard Faÿ, as we shall see, would also invoke the shield
metaphor to defend his actions retroactively in his trial for collaboration after
the war.

Yet however much these Vichy ideologues used the idea of *attentisme* as a
way of obscuring in retrospect the purposefulness of the National Revolution
between 1940 and 1942, it is also true that "waiting" characterized the stance
of certain segments of the regime from the start of the war. This could be
seen in the varying attitudes of collaborationists toward the Nazi occupiers.
While there were some in France—the so-called Paris collaborationists such
as Pierre Laval and Fernand de Brinon—who continually sought to strengthen
and affirm the unity of France and Nazi Germany, others in the regime were
more circumspect, guarded, or desultory in their posture toward the Nazis.
Defending, shielding, and waiting seem to have been from the outset of the
regime ways of dealing with the occupier and other foreign entities. And waiting could also keep alive conflicting allegiances. It could place France in a
holding pattern with uncertain antagonists like Britain. It could also justify
surprising relationships, like that between Vichy and the United States.

At once allies and adversaries, France and America performed a strained
diplomatic dance throughout the war. The United States did not sever ties with
France in June 1940, and both countries continued to maintain diplomatic
relations with the other even after America had entered the war against the
Axis powers in December 1941. Pétain, according to his confidantes, had a
"real passion" for America, stoked by his close personal ties to General John
Pershing, with whom he had fought side by side in World War I.[15] His instructions to his own representative to Washington, Gaston Henry-Haye, were suc-
cinct: "save American friendship."[16] Roosevelt, for his part, understood intrinsically the value of remaining neutral toward France, with the ultimate goal
of persuading Vichy to reenter the war against Nazi Germany. His concern
to preserve the autonomy of both the French empire and its war fleet, still

under the control of the Vichy government, was also of paramount importance. However, Roosevelt's official line was a carefully constructed humanitarian one, encouraging Americans to think of their old friends the French as wartime victims worthy of aid rather than Nazi fellow travelers. This allowed the United States to offer diplomatic recognition to Vichy and material aid to France and its colonies. Roosevelt only hoped that his neutral stance would encourage restive French elements to rebel. Well into 1941, he was assured by his ambassador to France, William Leahy, that the French "look to you as their one and only hope for release from Nazi rule."[17]

Yet Leahy also admitted to Roosevelt in November of that year that Pétain was a "feeble, frightened old man . . . controlled by a group which, probably for its own safety, is devoted to the Axis philosophy."[18] The overtly pro-German stance of Laval and other Paris collaborationists, along with events such as the Pétain-Hitler handshake at Montoire, made difficult any concrete signs of rapprochement between Pétain and the United States. Trying to play as many angles as possible while avoiding conflict, Pétain sought to steer a mediating course between America and the Nazis, hoping above all for a "compromise alliance against their real mutual danger, communism."[19] Yet his stance of *attentisme* became increasingly tenuous as the war ground on and as Vichy policy, such as it was, buckled under the sheer brutality of German demands. By the summer of 1942, several months after the Germans had reinstated Laval as prime minister, Roosevelt recalled Ambassador Leahy to Washington, leaving only an American chargé d'affaires to do business with the crumbling Vichy regime. At the same moment, Roosevelt assigned an official representative to Charles de Gaulle's Committee of National Liberation, prefiguring a crucial if still uncertain shift in support away from Pétain and toward the London-based Gaullist Free French.[20]

In the end, *attentisme* tested and eventually poisoned diplomatic negotiations between the United States and Vichy. Henry-Haye, Pétain's American ambassador, deplored his "thankless" mission to an American government increasingly suspicious of Vichy's passivity and intractability. Writing in his memoirs, *La grande eclipse franco-américaine*, Henry-Haye condemned the "tragic eclipse" of Franco-American relations as a result of American perfidy, particularly Roosevelt's decision to forsake the "authority" and "integrity" of Maréchal Pétain in favor of de Gaulle. It was America's growing belief in the "criminal compliance of the men of Vichy" with the Nazi regime that shattered whatever trust there was between French and Americans during the war.[21] Little mention is made in these memoirs of the fact that the character of Pétain and the "men of Vichy" was rather obscure to outside observers; as a diehard

Pétainiste, Henry-Haye, like many of his contemporaries, simply could not understand American suspicions of Pétain's vaunted integrity.

As Julian G. Hurstfield writes, "many of the mere functionaries of the Vichy regime would survive its demise; none of the true believers did."[22] Gaston Henry-Haye, publicly attacked in the United States as an agent, by proxy, of the Nazis and unable to secure American protection in Paris at the Liberation, defined the character of the Pétainiste true believer. His memoirs about the Vichy regime and its failed mission, published in French in 1972, are bitter and tinged with irony. But they are also remarkably germane to our story. Framed as a dialogue between himself and an anonymous close friend, a "former professor of the Collège de France, who had taught at various American universities . . . between 1920 and 1940," Henry-Haye gives an intimate portrait of Vichy and America not only from his own perspective but also from that of his "anonymous" interlocutor, Bernard Faÿ.[23]

As Faÿ feeds Henry-Haye questions about his experience as Vichy ambassador to America—questions designed to flatter and soothe Henry-Haye's bruised ego—we catch a glimpse of two elderly "true believers" rehashing the painful disappearance of their once cherished ideals of Franco-American conciliation and, above all, of Pétain's vision of a National Revolution for France. How do we explain the "inhuman feelings" of the Americans toward Vichy, Faÿ asks? They were the feelings of the "megalomaniac" Roosevelt, who "never responded to the confidence which Pétain manifested in regards to the United States," Henry-Haye answers. How did you deal with American diplomatic treachery and duplicity as Vichy ambassador, asks Faÿ? Henry-Haye: through my "oath of fidelity" to Pétain, and through my refusal to abandon "the cause of the Maréchal." "What sorrow for such a friend of America" to be treated so badly, exclaims Faÿ. "Above all a moral sorrow," responds Henry-Haye, convinced to the end of American duplicity and moral failing in its dealings with Vichy France.[24]

Faÿ's role as sounding board and confidant in Henry-Haye's memoirs is subtle but significant. Alone, Henry-Haye's reflections would have seemed the rants of an embittered old man; in chorus with Faÿ, his memoirs serve as a judgment on history. Together, the two make the case for a crucial breakdown in twentieth-century Franco-American relations as a direct result of American failure to understand the Vichy regime. Unable themselves to comprehend the American mistrust of Philippe Pétain and his ideology of *attentisme*, Faÿ and Henry-Haye present themselves only as unwitting victims of fate, once-central figures who had the bad luck to be on the losing side of history. In neither of their voices is there any sense of personal culpability for choosing to support the Vichy regime and its ideologies. As these memoirs make clear, the defeat of the Vichy regime would do little to alter the belief of both men in the "integrity" of Pétain and in the inherent value of his vision of national renewal. The price they would pay for this loyalty would be steep: postwar *dégradation nationale*, social marginalization, and, as we shall see in the case of Faÿ, exile from France.

◫ ◫ ◫

Like Gaston Henry-Haye, like Bernard Faÿ, Gertrude Stein too felt the strong pull of Pétainism. In *Wars I Have Seen*, a book she began writing in the winter of 1943, finished in 1944, and published in 1945, Stein makes it clear that even Pétain's ultimate ruin had not much changed her mind about the man. "Pétain was right to stay in France and he was right to make the armistice," she contends, explaining that "in the first place it was more comfortable for us who were here and in the second place it was an important element in the ultimate defeat of the Germans. To me it remained a miracle" (*W* 56–57). Elsewhere in *Wars* Stein seems to misread Pétain's effort to reclaim power from Laval in the fall of 1943 as a sign of his "republicanism" (that is, support for the principles of the French Republic) and portrays his actions even in 1944 as "really wonderful so simple so natural so complete and extraordinary . . . like Verdun again" (*W* 68, 114). These statements, troubling as they are, are utterly consistent with the "political" worldview that Stein adopted in the interwar period. This was a worldview that privileged above all the pleasures of daily living, peace, and "comfort," regardless of what might be lost in the bargain, and one that justified itself by turning French defeat at the hand of the Germans into a counterfactual thesis that, by losing, the French were really winning. In his 1945 review of *Wars*, the French Jewish existentialist philosopher Jean Wahl, who was interned in a French concentration camp and who escaped to America in 1942, reproached Stein for this point, describing it as "almost unbelievable in its naiveté."[25] Yet Wahl's would turn out to be largely a solitary critique.[26] Most readers of *Wars* celebrated the book for its stoic tone and had little to say about its unrepentant Pétainism, and to this day the story is praised uncritically for its courage.[27]

In fact, unlike Faÿ and Henry-Haye, Stein would emerge from the war unscathed by her support for Pétain. When the Phoney War broke out in the fall of 1939, Stein had retreated to her country house in the Bugey, the region of France where she would remain for the rest of the war. "Discovered" by American journalists at the Liberation, Stein was immediately hailed in the postwar press as a survivor and, for the two years remaining of her life, enjoyed a triumphant return of the public admiration she had experienced in America in the 1930s. In France, her rediscovery was of less public import, but then the French had other things on their mind during the period known as the *aprés-liberation* (Summer 1944–January 1946). For one thing, they were busy seeking retribution from accused Vichy collaborators: from men such as Pétain; Bouthillier; Joseph Darnand, leader of the Milice; and, of course, Bernard Faÿ; and from the enthusiastically pro-German ultras, or Paris collaborationists, including Laval, Fernand de Brinon, and Robert Brasillach, all three of whom were shot to death during the postwar purge. In this politically charged atmosphere, characterized by the central urge "to rebuild a nation and restore its dignity," the Pétainism of an American expatriate like Gertrude Stein would have been dismissed as an anomaly or at the most subsumed by the larger fact of Stein's evident personal vulnerability during the war.[28]

Things might have been different had Stein's intention to promote Pétain and his National Revolution been more publicly successful. In correspondence during the second year of the Vichy regime, as we shall see, Stein referred to herself as a propagandist for France, but ultimately there was little to show for her efforts. With Faÿ, Stein had planned a second lecture tour of America in the fall of 1939 in order to "be of use to France" (and, it appears, to replenish her dwindling savings).[29] This trip was never executed. In early 1941, Stein announced plans to write a book on Vichy for an American audience; this project never took place.[30] At the same time, Stein embarked on her now infamous project to publish the speeches of Petain in English, alongside a glowing introduction; this project was never published. Later in 1941, Stein did manage to publish a pro-Pétainist piece, "La langue française," in the Vichy journal *Patrie*. In addition to the pro-Pétainist essay "The Winner Loses," "La langue française" appears to be the only extant piece of Vichy propaganda Stein actually saw to press during the war.[31]

Of course, all of these "failures" to support Petain's regime raise the question of the strength of Stein's commitments. Was Stein, like many who lived through the nightmare of the Nazi occupation, simply hedging her bets by trying to make herself as quietly agreeable as possible to the authorities? Was Stein a committed propagandist for Vichy—or a shrewd survivor? Announcing her intentions to be an American propagandist for Pétain was one thing; following through with these intentions was another. In between professed desire and act lay a series of delays, deferrals, and postponements. Plans were changed, rescheduled, "forgotten" in the midst of the privations of everyday life; the war and its likely outcome shifted; and by 1943–1944 the Vichy regime was effectively history. At that point, although her personal vulnerability may in fact have increased, Stein's effort to be helpful to Vichy would have been irrelevant. What would have mattered—and did—was careful camouflage by supportive friends in the local community around her.

Nevertheless, it appears that for the first two and a half years of the Vichy regime, Stein's efforts to lend her support to Pétain were both heartfelt and dogged. From 1940 until well into 1943, she continued to write, think about, and give voice to a Pétainist worldview. Even after this point, with *Wars I Have Seen*, she remained a staunch defender of "her hero."[32] Her commitment may be expressed best in an undated draft of a letter "to the Maréchal" from the Gertrude Stein archives at Yale University. It reads: "To his Verdun, where all shared, with great feeling, his effort and victory. To the even more difficult victory of today, and to his complete success—in admiration and with heartfelt feeling."[33]

This letter should not surprise us. After all, for many years before the war Gertrude Stein, with the help and influence of Bernard Faÿ, had been sharpening and hardening her critique of the very things Pétain would himself denounce: democratic, liberal, and parliamentary society and the "weak vices" of a decadent modernity. She had agreed with the assessment of Faÿ and others on the Right that a profound political change in both French and American society was needed, that a return to traditional values would be salutary for everybody, and that the reforms promised by fascist and profascist regimes were better than those of communist ones. And she was even convinced that such a change would lead to aesthetic and literary renewal—a renewal already visible in her own experiments in writing. As she puts it in *Paris France*: "I cannot write too much upon how necessary it is to be completely conservative that is particularly traditional in order to be free" (*PF* 38).

⊡ ⊡ ⊡

With the French-German armistice in June 1940, the Stein-Faÿ collaboration of the 1930s—an intellectual, artistic, and emotional collaboration characterized by genuine affection and mutual political conviction, as well as desire, ambition, and egoism—was transformed into a collaboration of each with the Vichy regime. During this period, Stein and Faÿ had little contact with each other; after the war they would never see each other again. This chapter focuses on the unique wartime experience of Stein, an experience that was spent apart from Faÿ and that would ultimately distance her from Faÿ. Yet this experience was in fact marked by the invisible hand of Bernard Faÿ.

In one of her few letters to Faÿ during the Phoney War, Stein wrote that she was installed safely in her country house at Bilignin and that she was trying to avoid listening to the news, trimming her box hedges, and thinking of ways she could "do something for the good cause."[34] Her book *Paris France*, dedicated "to France and England," was one such effort: Stein described it to Faÿ as written "for London," presumably with the intention of stoking British sympathy for French political maneuvers. Her attempt to return to America for a lecture tour in the fall of 1939 was another such effort, one encouraged by Faÿ. "I went to the Quai d'Orsay," he writes her in October of 1939, "saw the big man [Minister of Foreign Affairs], and was told . . . that you could leave France at any time you wanted without difficulty." Faÿ adds that while "in principle all Americans going back to the U.S.A. are obliged to stay there," Stein could "be given a 'visa' to come back to France as soon as you ask for it."[35] It is clear that neither Faÿ nor Stein seems to have seriously entertained the idea that going to America, and staying there, might in fact be in Stein's best interests. While Faÿ mentions in this letter that "it might be better to take [a cabin] on an American boat" rather than a French one, "as they are less likely to be torpedoed," this seems to be the extent of his worries. Only for a brief moment, just after the fall of France in June 1940, do Stein and Toklas appear to have contemplated a trip to Bordeaux for safe passage back to the United States.[36] But nothing came of it. This, despite the fact that Stein was patently aware of the exodus of her friends from France (Janet Flanner, Gisèle Freund, Virgil Thomson, Man Ray, Balthus), of fearful news from Germany, and of the official warnings by the American ambassador in August 1939 and May 1940 that all American citizens needed to return to the States post haste.[37]

When the armistice was finally signed, Stein writes in "The Winner Loses," she seemed "very pleased" that hostilities had ceased "and a great load was lifted off France."[38] It is important to note that Stein published these words in the *Atlantic Monthly* in November 1940, well into Pétain's regime and well past the point, during the mid-summer of that year, of initial relief at the signing of the armistice. By November 1940, Pétain had shaken Hitler's hand at Montoire, gone on the radio promoting the idea of collaboration with the Nazis, and been subject to a public demonstration in Paris protesting his regime.[39] And he had already, a month earlier, instituted the first "Statut des Juifs": a decree that for the first time in modern French history defined "the Jew" as a discrete legal entity who could be barred from occupying public and professional posts.[40] As Michael Curtis reveals, this decree both preceded and overreached subsequent German anti-Semitic legislation in France: remarkably, "not only can Vichy claim priority in formulating a definition [of 'the Jew'], but also its formula was more extreme and harsher than the German."[41] Nowhere in Stein's writing or correspondence during this period is there any mention of the profound anti-Semitism of Pétain's National Revolution.

By November 1940, indeed, the "great load" that was lifted off France at the armistice had been replaced by the new psychic terror of everyday life under the Vichy regime. Yet as she would do later in *Wars I Have Seen*, Stein in "The Winner Loses" seems almost willfully intent on interpreting the emergence of Vichy as a positive thing and, even more, as the inevitable fulfillment of a prophecy. Stein's original title for "The Winner Loses" was "Sundays and Tuesdays"—a direct reference to the significant days of the prophetic saints who guided her through this period. Throughout "The Winner Loses," Stein acknowledges that she relied heavily on prophetic texts to make sense of the events of 1939–1940, particularly works by the seventh-century Alsatian Saint Odile, as well as by the Curé d'Ars and an English astrologer named Leonardo Blake. Such prophecies "had been an enormous comfort" to her during the uncertainty of the Phoney War and throughout the events of the armistice, Stein writes (*WL* 144). It was the Curé d'Ars, canonized a saint in 1925, who forecast a French war with Germany that would be resolved by German defeat on successive Tuesdays. Or so Stein thought.[42] "The dates the book gave were absolutely the dates the things happened," Stein claims, at the same moment admitting that these things were not exactly indicative of German defeat (*WL* 115). In fact, the prophecies were dead wrong: what was supposed to be German defeat in 1940 turned out to be German victory. But the gap between prediction and reality serves only to emphasize Stein's ultimate will to believe in what the prophecies said. As John Whittier-Ferguson notes, Stein's wartime writings continually return to "the comforting rhythm of what must be."[43] What matters is her "faith" in a given outcome, despite her own often ironic awareness of the limitations of prophecy. As Stein wrote in a letter to Faÿ from the 1930s, "I take a dark view of life but then I have plenty of faith."[44]

In *Wars I Have Seen*, Stein in fact uses the charged term "faith" to describe her reliance on prophecies during the war. Life in 1940 was not a simple thing, she writes, but she "had to have the prophecies of Saint Odile" in order to have "faith."[45] The term "faith" in reference to Saint Odile raises an issue that has so far been ignored even by Stein's best readers and critics: her attraction to the predictions of specifically *Christian* prophets. In her wartime novel *Mrs. Reynolds*, a single line stands out for its incongruity: "The Jews John Ell said are good prophets."[46] This throwaway line, uttered by a marginal character out of the blue, is the only reference to Jewish prophets in all of Stein's writing during the war, writing that elsewhere continually refers to the prophecies of the saints Odile, Godfrey, and the Curé d'Ars. Why this preference for the prophecies of saints? What was it that the Christian saints represented for Stein that she found so comforting during the war?

The answer extends back to Stein's initial attraction to the aesthetics and rituals of Catholic saints and sainthood, discussed in chapter 1. For Stein, saints were extraordinary figures with whom she seems to have felt a deep identification: creative geniuses who simply in their existence brought meaning and significance to the world around them. "Beyond the functions of history, memory, and identity," the saints of Stein's early works, such as *Four Saints in Three Acts*, exist in a kind of pure temporal Now; they are avatars of Steinian modernism and of the immediate and ongoing flux of a continuous present. They are also complex signifiers of a gay or camp sensibility, highly stylized performers who traffic in ecstasy and tragedy. But more than purely aesthetic and performative beings, saints are also inseparable from holiness and religious faith. Again, the religious dimension of saints is not insignificant to Gertrude Stein, and again, we might understand Stein's interest in saints as part of a complex substitution for a repressed Jewish identity unassimilable within her own continuously retold narrative of self. Simply put, saints allowed Stein to articulate through redirection the "faith" that could not be outwardly claimed.

During World War II, Stein's interest in saints resurfaced in surprising ways. "Mrs. Reynolds," she writes in 1941, "liked holiness but only holiness if it is accompanied by predictions. Holiness often is" (*MR* 35). During the war, Stein too liked her "holiness"—her saints—for what they could do for her, for their predictive, miraculous, and palliative powers. This, despite the fact that the validity of their predictions seemed entirely contingent on how one chose to interpret events; or as Stein wryly puts it in *Mrs. Reynolds*, "if the weather was set to be fair all the signs that look like rain do not count and if the weather is set for rain all the signs that look like clearing do not count" (*MR* 80). In short, prophetic outcomes depend upon what one chooses to "count," upon the signs one chooses to read, and this choice itself determines the significance of the prediction. Yet Stein also seems drawn to the psychic necessity of sheer belief in "what must be," a belief inextricable from religious faith. If one has faith, then the words and prophecies of the saints must be believed; there is, reassuringly, no room for skepticism.[47] As she writes in *Mrs. Reynolds*: "she began to believe, for which there is no question and no answer" (*MR* 171). The novel goes on to detail the considerable psychic compensations for unflinching belief: security, collective meaning, purpose, the lessening of fear in the face of arbitrary and unaccountable violence.

As she would often do in her writing, Stein seems to hold in suspension contradictory tendencies—belief and skepticism—in talking about saints during this period. From the beginning of her career as a student in the psychological laboratory of William James, Stein had focused on the likelihood of a "double consciousness" that structured psychic life.[48] Her studies of automatic behavior and distraction convinced her that the self was both an automatic agent and had an "extra" consciousness that observed but did not inhibit automaticity. Some forty years later, Stein seems to be performing precisely this kind of double consciousness. Her writings during the Vichy regime reveal a person at once attempting to believe and watching herself attempt to believe. In a curious passage in *Wars I Have Seen* on science, for example, Stein denies the permanence of ideas of evolution and progress, both of which she associates with that era of decline, "the nineteenth-century."[49] Following on the heels of a discussion of the relevance and rightness of Saint Odile to the twentieth century, this analysis seems to validate the importance in the twentieth century of faith over evolution, prophecy over progress. In an age where "wars are more than ever . . . it is rather ridiculous so much science, so much civilisation" (*W* 40). Yet two paragraphs later, Stein refers to William James—one "of the strongest scientific influences that I had"—to validate a truth-claim based not in belief but in knowledge: "the thing that we know most about is the opposition between the will to live and the will to destroy." Knowing about this opposition seems of a different register from "belief" or "faith"; knowledge here arises from a psychological truth steeped in the "scientific influence" of James, a truth that subsequently allows Stein to explain and affirm the French "will to live" (*W* 41). Taken as a whole, then, this passage is ironic and ambiguous: twentieth-century faith and the words of the prophets win out over the false ideals of nineteenth-century science and "civilisation," but in the end it is science that brings us to the truths "we know most about."

In this and other passages from *Wars I Have Seen*, Stein's will to believe is palpable, yet above and beyond it hovers an uncertainty that such a will may "lack the inner soul of faith's reality," as James himself would put it in *The Will to Believe*.[50] Mixed together in this way, faith becomes something like a gamble, akin to Pascal's wager. It is simply a better bet to believe in God and his saints than not to. Moreover, by willing herself to believe in the prophecies of Christian saints, Stein was also taking out an extra insurance policy against the future. For it was indeed only the Christian saints whose words seemed to "count" at this moment and whose prophecies seemed to hold out the possibility of a cure for the sufferings of herself and those around her. Only the Christian saints, and more specifically the French Christian saints such as Odile, Godfrey, and the Cure d'Ars, seemed justified in predicting the outcome of French defeat in 1940.

In the region of the Bugey, where Stein spent the war years, the miraculous doings of Christian saints were as renowned as they had been when the saints were alive and ministering in this rural locale. Catholic piety and local tradition were still deeply and inextricably rooted in the rolling hills around Belley. Little had changed since the Middle Ages, when saints served to reflect and direct the hopes of their society, existing as "the heavy voice of the group" in heightened situations of anxiety or fear.[51] In "The Winner Loses," Stein emphasizes this connection, noting that the predictions of the nineteenth-century Curé d'Ars—originally a priest from a town close to where Stein was living— were "the ones they talked about most in the country" (*WL* 115). Stein readily adopted the local manner of coping as her own, claiming that she found particular "comfort" in the predictions of the Curé. She even trumped the Catholic faithful in her commitment to the book of prophecies: "and I read the book every night in bed and everybody telephoned to ask what the book said" (*WL* 115). Stein also had frequent and friendly contact, through the intermediary of her friends Bernard Faÿ and Henri Daniel-Rops, with the monks at the beautiful Hautecombe Abbey, ten kilometers to the east of Belley. Through this contact, one local seminarian brought to life for Stein the prophecies of Saint Odile, translating her original Latin text into French. Although Odile was from Alsace, she evidently changed the way Stein thought about the war. For it was Odile who forecast, as Stein put it in *Wars*, "the beginning of the real end of Germany, and it is all true, *as* we all have been cherishing copies of this prophecy ever since 1940."[52] The curious logic of Stein's conjunction "as"—implying that the truth of Odile's prophecies lies in the fact that her text is "cherish[ed]"—again underscores the agency of belief so central to Stein's sense of faith.[53]

The Christian saints and their prophecies did not just offer "comfort" to the rural French community within which Stein found herself in 1940. Belief in their prophecies was also a matter for her of belonging, of social and political fellow feeling, and hence of safety. For amid this piously Catholic environment and its supportive local networks, one group remained largely voiceless: that of a Jewish population increasingly targeted for purges by the Vichy regime. While southeastern France was until 1942 part of the unoccupied zone and thus free from German legislation, it was not free from the homegrown anti-Semitism of the Vichy regime. During the first two years of the war, Vichy enacted two measures designed toward defining, excluding, and limiting the powers of Jews: the Statut des Juifs of October 3, 1940, that established an official "definition" of Jewishness; and, following the establishment of a Vichy anti-Jewish ministry, the more encompassing Statut des Juifs of June 2, 1941, explicitly designed "to fill lacunae in the earlier law."[54] The thrust of the first statute was to define Jews in exclusionary terms; the thrust of the second was

Les actes portant ouverture de crédits en application de l'article 52 du décret du 31 mai 1862, de l'article 39 de la loi du 31 décembre 1907 et de l'article 6 du décret du 25 juin 1934 ;

Les actes portant transfert de crédits pour la réalisation de simples modifications d'ordre.

Art. 2. — Le présent décret sera publié au *Journal officiel* et exécuté comme loi de l'Etat.

Fait à Vichy, le 15 octobre 1940.

PH. PÉTAIN.

Par le Maréchal de France, chef de l'Etat français,

Le ministre secrétaire d'Etat aux finances,

YVES BOUTHILLIER.

LOI portant à 1.500 fr. la limite relative à l'admission de la preuve testimoniale pour les payements de l'Etat, des départements, des communes et des établissements publics.

Nous, Maréchal de France, chef de l'Etat français,

Le conseil des ministres entendu,

Décrétons :

Art. 1er. — Sont portées à 1.500 fr. les limites relatives à l'admission de la preuve testimoniale qui ont été fixées à 500 fr. par l'article 27 de la loi du 27 décembre 1923 et par l'article 322 de la loi du 13 juillet 1925, pour tous les payements à la charge de l'Etat, des départements, des communes et des établissements publics.

Art. 2. — Le présent décret sera publié au *Journal officiel* et exécuté comme loi de l'Etat.

Fait à Vichy, le 16 octobre 1940.

PH. PÉTAIN.

Par le Maréchal de France, chef de l'Etat français,

Le garde des sceaux, ministre secrétaire d'Etat à la justice,

RAPHAEL ALIBERT.

Le ministre secrétaire d'Etat aux finances,

YVES BOUTHILLIER.

LOI portant statut des juifs.

Nous, Maréchal de France, chef de l'Etat français,

Le conseil des ministres entendu,

Décrétons :

Art. 1er. — Est regardé comme juif, pour l'application de la présente loi, toute personne issue de trois grands-parents de race juive ou de deux grands-parents de la même race, si son conjoint lui-même est juif.

Art. 2. — L'accès et l'exercice des fonctions publiques et mandats énumérés ci-après sont interdits aux juifs :

1. Chef de l'Etat, membre du Gouvernement, conseil d'Etat, conseil de l'ordre na-

tional de la Légion d'honneur, cour de cassation, cour des comptes, corps des mines, corps des ponts et chaussées, inspection générale des finances, cours d'appel, tribunaux de première instance, justices de paix, toutes juridictions d'ordre professionnel et toutes assemblées issues de l'élection.

2. Agents relevant du département des affaires étrangères, secrétaires généraux des départements ministériels, directeurs généraux, directeurs des administrations centrales des ministères, préfets, sous-préfets, secrétaires généraux des préfectures, inspecteurs généraux des services administratifs au ministère de l'intérieur, fonctionnaires de tous grades attachés à tous services de police.

3. Résidents généraux, gouverneurs généraux, gouverneurs et secrétaires généraux des colonies, inspecteurs des colonies.

4. Membres des corps enseignants.

5. Officiers des armées de terre, de mer et de l'air.

6. Administrateurs, directeurs, secrétaires généraux dans les entreprises bénéficiaires de concessions ou de subventions accordées par une collectivité publique, postes à la nomination du Gouvernement dans les entreprises d'intérêt général.

Art. 3. — L'accès et l'exercice de toutes les fonctions publiques autres que celles énumérées à l'article 2 ne sont ouverts aux juifs que s'ils peuvent exciper de l'une des conditions suivantes :

a) Etre titulaire de la carte de combattant 1914-1918 ou avoir été cité au cours de la campagne 1914-1918 ;

b) Avoir été cité à l'ordre du jour au cours de la campagne 1939-1940 ;

c) Etre décoré de la Légion d'honneur à titre militaire ou de la médaille militaire.

Art. 4. — L'accès et l'exercice des professions libérales, des professions libres, des fonctions dévolues aux officiers ministériels et à tous auxiliaires de la justice sont permis aux juifs, à moins que des règlements d'administration publique n'aient fixé pour eux une proportion déterminée. Dans ce cas, les mêmes règlements détermineront les conditions dans lesquelles aura lieu l'élimination des juifs en surnombre.

Art. 5. — Les juifs ne pourront, sans condition ni réserve, exercer l'une quelconque des professions suivantes :

Directeurs, gérants, rédacteurs de journaux, revues, agences ou périodiques, à l'exception de publications de caractère strictement scientifique.

Directeurs, administrateurs, gérants d'entreprises ayant pour objet la fabrication, l'impression, la distribution, la présentation de films cinématographiques ; metteurs en scène et directeurs de prises de vues, compositeurs de scénarios, directeurs, administrateurs, gérants de salles de théâtres ou de cinématographe, entrepreneurs de spectacles, directeurs, administrateurs, gérants de toutes entreprises se rapportant à la radiodiffusion.

Des règlements d'administration publique fixeront, pour chaque catégorie, les conditions dans lesquelles les autorités publiques

pourront s'assurer du respect, par les intéressés, des interdictions prononcées au présent article, ainsi que les sanctions attachées à ces interdictions.

Art. 6. — En aucun cas, les juifs ne peuvent faire partie des organismes chargés de représenter les professions visées aux articles 4 et 5 de la présente loi ou d'en assurer la discipline.

Art. 7. — Les fonctionnaires juifs visés aux articles 2 et 3 cesseront d'exercer leurs fonctions dans les deux mois qui suivront la promulgation de la présente loi. Ils seront admis à faire valoir leurs droits à la retraite s'ils remplissent les conditions de durée de service ; à une retraite proportionnelle s'ils ont au moins quinze ans de service ; ceux ne pouvant exciper d'aucune de ces conditions recevront leur traitement pendant une durée qui sera fixée, pour chaque catégorie, par un règlement d'administration publique.

Art. 8. — Par décret individuel pris en conseil d'Etat et dûment motivé, les juifs qui, dans les domaines littéraire, scientifique, artistique, ont rendu des services exceptionnels à l'Etat français, pourront être relevés des interdictions prévues par la présente loi.

Ces décrets et les motifs qui les justifient seront publiés au *Journal officiel.*

Art. 9. — La présente loi est applicable à l'Algérie, aux colonies, pays de protectorat et territoires sous mandat.

Art. 10. — Le présent acte sera publié au *Journal officiel* et exécuté comme loi de l'Etat.

Fait à Vichy, le 3 octobre 1940.

PH. PÉTAIN.

Par le Maréchal de France, chef de l'Etat français :

Le vice-président du conseil,

PIERRE LAVAL.

Le garde des sceaux, ministre secrétaire d'Etat à la justice,

RAPHAEL ALIBERT.

Le ministre secrétaire d'Etat à l'intérieur,

MARCEL PEYROUTON.

Le ministre secrétaire d'Etat aux affaires étrangères,

PAUL BAUDOUIN.

Le ministre secrétaire d'Etat à la guerre,

G' HUNTZIGER.

Le ministre secrétaire d'Etat aux finances,

YVES BOUTHILLIER.

Le ministre secrétaire d'Etat à la marine,

A' DARLAN.

Le ministre secrétaire d'Etat à la production industrielle et au travail,

RENÉ BELIN.

Le ministre secrétaire d'Etat à l'agriculture,

PIERRE CAZIOT.

FIGURE 4.2 The 1940 Statut des Juifs (from *Journal Officiel de la République française*).

Nº 2393. — LOI du 2 juin 1941 prescrivant le recensement des juifs.

Nous, Maréchal de France, chef de l'État français,

Le conseil des ministres entendu,

Décrétons :

Art. 1er. — Toutes personnes qui sont juives au regard de la loi du 2 juin 1941 portant statut des juifs doivent, dans le délai d'un mois à compter de la publication de la présente loi, remettre au préfet du département ou au sous-préfet de l'arrondissement dans lequel elles ont leur domicile ou leur résidence, une déclaration écrite indiquant qu'elles sont juives au regard de la loi, et mentionnant leur état civil, leur situation de famille, leur profession et l'état de leurs biens.

La déclaration est faite par le mari pour la femme, et par le représentant légal pour le mineur ou l'interdit.

Art. 2. — Toute infraction aux dispositions de l'article 1er est punie d'un emprisonnement de un mois à un an et d'une amende de 100 à 10.000 fr., ou de l'une de ces deux peines seulement, sans préjudice du droit pour le préfet de prononcer l'internement dans un camp spécial, même si l'intéressé est Français.

Art. 3. — Des dispositions particulières fixeront les conditions dans lesquelles la présente loi sera appliquée en Algérie, dans les colonies, dans les pays de protectorat, en Syrie et au Liban.

Art. 4. — Le présent décret sera publié au Journal officiel et exécuté comme loi de l'État.

Fait à Vichy, le 2 juin 1941.

PH. PÉTAIN.

Par le Maréchal de France, chef de l'État français :

L'amiral de la flotte, vice-président du conseil, ministre secrétaire d'État à l'intérieur,

Aˡ DARLAN.

FIGURE 4.3 The 1941 Statut des Juifs, announcing census of Jews in unoccupied zone (from *Journal Officiel de l'Etat français*).

effectively to bar Jews from economic and civic involvement in French life. Deportations to French and eventually German concentration camps, first of foreign and then of French Jews, followed within the space of months. Exemptions were few. In the words of historians Michael R. Marrus and Robert O. Paxton, Vichy "measured exemptions out with an eyedropper."[55]

Mysteriously, neither Toklas nor Stein ever appeared on any official Vichy census of the Jews, including the census of the "free" or unoccupied zone of

July 1941. "No Jew was dispensed from the obligation to declare himself—not even those exempt from other laws" write Marrus and Paxton of this remarkably thorough census.[56] Yet Stein and Toklas remained unaccounted for. Their official invisibility seems to suggest that at least during the first years of the Vichy regime—until the Germans occupied the free zone in November 1942—it is possible, even likely, that Stein was deliberately protected from persecution.[57] A story she recounts in *Wars I Have Seen* is telling in this regard. In the fall of 1942, Stein contemplated a lawsuit against her landlord, a captain in the French army, after learning that she would be forced to move out of her beloved eighteenth-century chateau at Bilignin.[58] The substitute house Stein found in early 1943 in the nearby town of Culoz, "quite wonderful even though modern" (*W* 31), appears to have changed her mind. The account of this story in *Wars* remains bizarre to this day. What gave Stein the sense of assurance in late 1942 that a lawsuit against her landlord in this charged environment would have no consequences? Was it really the luck of finding equally "wonderful" quarters that made her drop the lawsuit scheme in early 1943? On the next page of *Wars*, Stein details another, more chilling encounter with her lawyer, who warned her that he had spoken to a Vichy official and that she and Toklas would soon be targeted for deportation to a concentration camp. Stein refused to leave ("here we are and here we stay," she commented [*W* 32]), but the move to Culoz seems more than coincidental. What *Wars* never acknowledges is what presumably took place between late 1942 and early 1943, when Stein was made aware, possibly by Faÿ himself, that dropping the lawsuit scheme and moving to Culoz would be personally expedient.[59] By late 1942, the Vichy state could no longer assure Stein and Toklas of protection. Within several months, they were warned by the local subprefect, Maurice Sivan, to flee to Switzerland or risk deportation (*W* 32). These two elderly Jewish women were now to be at the terrible mercy of the Nazis or of those individuals who took on the risk to protect them.

In many ways, the final two years of the war were likely the most precarious for Stein. After the Nazis invaded all of France in November 1942, they grew increasingly frustrated with Vichy's failure to expedite the deportation of Jews. During this period, as the Vichy regime crumbled, all pretense of favoritism dropped away, and German demands for Jewish deportations became relentless. The surrendering of the Italian zone in September 1943, where Jews had been relatively safe, meant increased persecution for those hiding in the southeastern region of France, including Stein. After April 1944, the Nazi occupiers in Paris declared "that all Jews, whatever their nationality, were to go." During the last eight months of 1944, 14,833 Jews were deported

FIGURE 4.4 Stein's home at Culoz, France.

from France, including a caravan of 232 children on one of the last convoys to leave for Auschwitz, on July 31, 1944. None of the children survived, a fate that also met the forty-four Jewish children hiding in the tiny village of Izieu, some thirty miles to the south of where Stein was living at the time. Seized and deported to Auschwitz in April 1944, all forty-four children and six of their seven minders were executed.[60]

According to Stein herself, it was the local community that protected and ultimately saved her during the war. In an evocative phrase, Stein refers to herself and Toklas as "rather favoured strangers" in their community (*W* 74).[61] After the Liberation in August 1944, Stein told the journalist Eric Sevareid that it was the mayor, the subprefect, and the townspeople who chose to look the other way when official anti-Jewish legislation trickled down to the villages of Bilignin and Culoz. Sevareid reports that it was indeed the mayor of Culoz, Justin Hey, who kept Stein from signing the register of Jews in the town.[62] This claim might make sense in the period from 1943 to 1944, when the Bugey region became a stronghold of the French Resistance. Stein clearly manifests support for the Resistance in the latter part of *Wars I Have Seen* and makes much of this in her postwar writings. Before mid-1943, however, Stein was likely spared by a decision of someone in the Vichy regime—a fact she may not have wanted Sevareid to know. Nevertheless, even in Culoz at the end of the war, as Stein herself wrote in *Wars I Have Seen*, "everybody knowing that everything is coming to an end every neighbor is denouncing every neighbor, for black traffic, for theft, for this and that, and there are so many being put in prison" (*W* 23). This acknowledgment adds yet another twist to the mystery around Stein's survival. Why was Stein somehow exempt from this category of "everybody"? Even if it is true that Stein spent the last part of the war being protected by the locals, the question remains: what was it that these French people saw in their neighbor Gertrude Stein? Why would they have been willing to risk their lives to save her?

The answer to this question may lie in Stein's unusual position as insider-outsider. Stein was from Paris and was well connected to the local Bugey elite: both signifiers of status in provincial France. She was a famous author, something she seems to associate with her wartime survival in *Wars I Have Seen*.[63] She was friendly and endearing to neighbors, sharing an affective bond with her community during her famous walks through town that may have helped her weather the denunciations of "everybody." But she was also, as her interest in Christian saints suggests, a believer. Someone who attempted to belong, in the deepest sense of *sharing* and *witnessing*. Someone who shared with her neighbors a belief in the power of the Christian saints to protect and guide their flock through a terrifyingly uncertain future, and who witnessed with the group the miraculous outcomes of saintly predictions. This neighborliness is recounted in detail in *Wars I Have Seen* as well as in letters Stein wrote to her friend W. G. Rogers, where she specifically notes that the religious predictions were a conduit for social interaction.[64] Combined with a manner cultivated since youth to avoid any outward identification with Jewishness, believing in the Christian saints prevented Stein from being seen as the stereotype of the Jewish "foreigner" disseminated by anti-Semitic propaganda. With her enthusiastic, outspoken efforts to "pass" as a Christian believer, Stein created a bubble of protection around her that spared her, in most instances, the shaming and ostracizing label of "Jew."

Had Stein refused to accept the shame attached to this label or had she had less complex and uncertain feelings about Jewishness, her fate might well have been different. By aligning herself with the saints, however, Stein moved squarely into the circle of her local community. And given that her Jewishness was the chief thing she needed to hide, Stein's ability to pass as a Christian believer—however ambiguous, ironic, or layered it may seem in her writing—may well have contributed to her long-term survival.

▣ ▣ ▣

While the region in southeastern France where Stein lived during the war had been immortalized by Brillat-Savarin as pristine and beautiful, it had yet another, more dubious distinction. In his great early nineteenth-century novel *The Red and the Black*, Stendhal had described this region as the very embodiment of provincial life, as reactionary and deeply traditionalist, as a place where the "tyranny of opinion" held sway.[65] In the Bugey in 1940, there was particularly strong support for Philippe Pétain's National Revolution; at the outset of the Vichy regime, the region was a bastion of Pétainism. For the farmers and small villagers living in and around Belley, Pétain was "one of us"—a simple man from a rural, farming background who had never lost touch with his roots. Pétainist propaganda that emphasized the value of manual labor, traditional family structures, and faith in the power of authority figures was hugely successful in this region. Support for his regime was stoked in the pages of the local press, including the moderately right-wing *Le Bugiste*, which interviewed Stein about her Pétainism in 1942.[66] There Stein reiterated an argument that she had made several times before, including the previous year in the pro-Vichy journal *Patrie (Fatherland)*: that Pétain was a savior because he had brought peace and "daily living" back to France, a country that was "always in strict contact with the earth" and for whom rural life represented the "essence" of vitality.

Stein would go even further in the propaganda she wrote for *Patrie*, making an implicit connection between French rural life and a sense of language steeped in the "eighteenth-century"—always a code phrase, as suggested in chapter 2, for a political and aesthetic ideal as yet uncorrupted by the decadence of "nineteenth-century" modernity. In the *Patrie* piece, Stein suggests that only French peasants speak a "true and pure language," a language not "denuded of reality." She uses as an example the phrase of a farmer referring to the end of the day as "the hour when the poets work" and notes that only in rural France could writing be seen as a form of "labor." The continuity between farm labor and written labor, the emphasis on production rather than consumption, the timeless, vital language of the peasantry, the idea that only people "in contact with the earth" can speak "purely"—Stein's aesthetic-agrarian utopia here blends seamlessly with a Pétainist ideology of return, reaction, and renewal. Toward the end of this cryptic piece of Vichy propaganda, she writes that rural speech does not confuse itself with formal, written language. Yet in times of war, it appears, formal language prevails over the "purity" of rural speech, because "violent and heroic action creates written language." In other words, peace encourages an earthbound, vital language to flourish; violent action requires artificial, stilted expression. Finally, the subtext of this essay becomes clear. By restoring "peace" to France with the armistice, Pétain is doing more than simply healing a defeated country. He is also allowing the French language to be led away from abstract formalism—*la langue écrite*—and back to its spoken, "eighteenth-century" vitality. Pétain's armistice and his National Revolution are salutary not just for the lives of French people but also for the health of the French language.[67]

Stein's argument in the *Patrie* piece is profoundly reactionary, the essence of reactionary modernism. It recalls the subtext of Stein's commentary on her own writing during the 1930s. There, Stein often frames her own experimental writing in terms of a similar aesthetic "return" to a language obscured by more than a century of corrupt usage. She uses a retrogressive chronology to describe her "twentieth-century" writing as an aesthetic form that bypasses "nineteenth-century" modes of writing in favor of "eighteenth-century" ideals. In her 1934 lecture "The Gradual Making of *The Making of Americans*," for example, Stein explains how her "twentieth-century" interest in *paragraphs* allows her to rediscover an "eighteenth-century" focus on *sentences*: "I have explained that the twentieth century was the century not of sentences as was the eighteenth not of phrases as was the nineteenth but of paragraphs," she writes, suggesting at first a distinction between the writing of her own and previous epochs. But in the passage immediately following such a distinction breaks down: "In fact inevitably I made my sentences and my paragraphs do the same thing, made them be one and the same thing. This was inevitably because the nineteenth century having lived by phrases really had lost the feeling of sentences."[68] Making the twentieth century (the period of paragraphs) and the eighteenth century (the period of sentences) "be one and the same thing," at least in writing, allows for the "losses" of the nineteenth century to be overcome. Elsewhere, Stein writes that "You had to recognize that words had lost their value in the Nineteenth Century, particularly towards the end, they had lost much of their variety, and I felt that I could not go on, that I had to recapture the value of the individual word, find out what it meant and act within it."[69] Recapturing the "value" of words lost to the depredations of the nineteenth century was a way, Stein writes, to make her writing "exact, as exact as mathematics." Only by returning to the essence or "value" of a word could this "eighteenth-century" exactitude be achieved.[70]

Stein reiterates this calculus of century-identity when she provides a gloss on her famous phrase "a rose is a rose is a rose": "I think that in that line the rose is red for the first time in English poetry for a hundred years."[71]

Eighteenth-century roses were red: their essence remained the same across time and context. Nineteenth-century roses, functioning within the force field of modernity and the imperatives of realism, had become empty clichés. The rose in the twentieth century, the rose in the hands of Gertrude Stein, brings us back to what she would call the "value" of the word itself. As we saw in chapter 2, Stein's invidious distinction between these loosely defined periods of the eighteenth, nineteenth, and twentieth centuries was in the 1930s as yet relatively inchoate. The *Patrie* piece shows how the emergence of Vichy and its reactionary Pétainist "Revolution" gave Stein a new way to link her nostalgia for the eighteenth century to a political blueprint for social change. Now in 1941, Stein envisions a productive continuity between the political and cultural project of Pétain's National Revolution, her own experimental writing, and an eighteenth-century linguistic ideal lost to the corruptions of nineteenth-century modernity yet still visible in the primitive, vital language of the French provincial "folk."

Equally importantly, Pétain's National Revolution also allows Stein an alternative political vision to that of contemporary, Roosevelt-era America. It was, after all, the "eighteenth-century passion for freedom" that Stein found so deplorably absent in the America she visited during her lecture tour of 1934–1935. In the 1930s, she repeatedly laments the decline of the American agrarian ideal embodied in the worldview of the founding fathers and places the blame firmly on the liberal and mass-oriented "reform movements" of the monstrous Roosevelt administration, which had "enslaved" a pioneering people through "organization." "Organization," Stein writes in 1936, "is a failure and everywhere the world over everybody has to begin again . . . perhaps they will begin looking for liberty again and individually amusing themselves again and old-fashioned or dirt farming."[72] What better model for this renewed society than Pétain's France? In the introduction to the speeches of Maréchal Pétain that Stein wrote late in 1941, she indeed forges a surprising connection between American agrarianism, the founding fathers, and Pétain's National Revolution. There, as we shall see, Stein figures Pétain as the living embodiment of an eighteenth-century American ideal hidden beneath what she called the "catastrophe" of FDR's administration.[73] And she chides Americans for not "sympathiz[ing]" with Pétain's regime, thus losing the opportunity to appreciate Pétain's leadership in a way that might see them through their own trauma after Pearl Harbor.

Through an intricate combination of critique, idealism, nostalgia, and Franco-American doubling, Stein makes her case for why Pétain's speeches should appeal as much to the Americans as to the French. A vote for Pétain, she argues, would be a vote for America: not for the "corrupt" America of FDR but for a renewed, revitalized, pioneering, individualistic America long buried beneath the degenerate, robotic frenzy of modern life.

▣ ▣ ▣

Stein reports that her Belley friends were "all Croix de Feu"—members, informally or not, of one of the most influential French leagues of the extreme Right in the 1930s. These friends may be the individuals whom Stein is referring to when she writes in *Everybody's Autobiography*, "we liked the fascists."[74] Like their predecessors from the 1920s, the Faisceau, the Croix de Feu "actively advocated the overthrow of the Third Republic in order to install a new regime"; many of their members would assume roles in the coming Pétain administration.[75] Stein makes reference to these friends as early as 1936 in the series she wrote for the *Saturday Evening Post*. Comparing the spendthrift American Congress under FDR to the Chamber of Deputies in Third Republic France, Stein writes:

> In France the chamber has been doing the same thing spending too much money and so everybody voted for the communists hoping that the communists would stop them. Now everybody thinks that the chamber under the communists will just go on spending the money and so a great many frenchmen are thinking of getting back a king, and that the king will stop the french parliament from spending money.[76]

The "great many frenchmen" Stein refers to are never identified, but according to historians few modern French people saw the return of the monarchy as a viable political alternative, even at the end of the Third Republic.[77] Stein's claim is thus clearly an exaggeration, yet what is interesting is her familiarity with the monarchist critique. According to Samuel M. Steward, Stein even argued that "I think it takes a monarchy, needs a monarchy, to produce really good writers, really I do, at least in France."[78] It is likely that Stein's familiarity with this critique arose both from her conversations with Bernard Faÿ and from the locale where she was living at the outbreak of war.

At least some of those in Stein's orbit would surely have been involved in a nearby institution located directly south of her home in Belley: the leadership school at Uriage. Nestled in a chateau on a dramatic cliff outside the city of Grenoble, Uriage was one of the ideological centers of Pétain's National Revolution. It was at Uriage that a group of youthful, idealistic, visionary men, all staunch supporters of Pétain, all highly critical of the French Third Republic, met and founded a school that would "create the guidelines of, and the leaders for, a post-liberal and post-Republican society."[79] Among their ranks were the founder of *Le Monde*, Hubert Beuve-Méry, and the militiaman Paul Touvier, infamous for his Vichy-era persecution of the Jews.

In his fascinating study of the leadership school at Uriage, the historian John Hellman has traced the lines of convergence between the idealism of these "shock troops" of the Vichy regime and their counterparts in Hitler's Germany. Hellman argues that Uriage represents a genuine, homegrown example of French fascism, one that saw itself running on a track parallel to Nazism. With their antidemocratic, antiparliamentary stance, their outrage at France's perceived military and moral weakness, and their elitism, the men of Uriage shared a conservative revolutionary ideology with the Nazis. Like the Hitler Youth, the Uriage men adhered to a doctrine of physical toughness, moral probity, and aggressive patriotism: authoritarianism and strict mental and physical discipline were their guides. In their monastic setting almost completely devoid of women, the men of Uriage imagined themselves as "knight-monks of Vichy France," thus differing in one significant respect from the Hitler Youth: they were piously, fervently, and above all politically Catholic. Emerging out of the polarized atmosphere of the 1930s, their role models were the militant revolutionaries of the Faisceau movement of the 1920s; the intellectual radicals of Action Française, who traced the spiritual decadence of modern France to the decline of the Church after 1789; and the Catholic "personalist" philosophers of the early 1930s, with their calls for a "reform of the spirit." Their moment arrived with the advent of the Vichy regime in 1940, whose core conservative Catholic ideology informed and reflected the vision of Uriage. "To live in a community in the spirit of the National Revolution" became the "official objective" of the school, which continued its mission until the Germans occupied the south of France in late 1942. After this point—in a transition typical of other such "gray zones" in Vichy France—a good number of Uriage members stepped up to join the French Resistance.[80]

While Stein had no explicit connection to Uriage other than geographical proximity, she had indirect ties, notably through her close friendship with a French personalist philosopher named Henri Daniel-Rops. Still known today for his best-selling religious writings, including a multivolume *History of the Church* and many accounts of the lives of saints, Daniel-Rops was active during the 1930s in the French movement that sought to merge personalist philosophy with a political "third way" between Soviet-style communism and American-style capitalism. His work on behalf of a group called Ordre Nouveau (New Order) produced among other pieces an infamous 1933 essay, "Letter to

Hitler," in which he and his colleague Alexandre Marc set out the blueprint for a specifically French national socialism that would in part derive from Hitler's own. Their credo was unsparingly national socialist: "We believe that at the spiritual origin, if not in the tactical evolution, of the national socialist movement, is to be found the seeds of a new and necessary revolutionary position."[81] Such a "necessary revolutionary position" was to be grounded in an elite corps of chivalric men who would be trained to embody and propagate this national socialist ideal. Seven years later, the training school at Uriage came into being, a living embodiment of the unholy alliance between French personalist philosophy and German-inspired National Socialism.

Not surprisingly, Daniel-Rops was a regular lecturer and guest at the school of Uriage during the war.[82] He was also a frequent guest of his neighbor Gertrude Stein, whom he probably met at the home of their mutual friends, the Pierlots. Throughout the war, Stein and Toklas seem to have spent much time in the company of the endearingly odd person they called "Rops" and his wife Madeleine, referring to them as "the nicest french couple we have ever known."[83] Stein would also make flattering remarks about Daniel-Rops in *Paris France* and in letters to friends, where he was invariably portrayed as a picturesque intellectual and sympathetic neighbor, if hardly himself an example of the virile, strenuous masculinity he championed in his Ordre Nouveau writings.[84]

But Daniel-Rops's political connections were also not without interest to Stein. Along with another neighbor, Paul Genin, Daniel-Rops appears to have been instrumental in facilitating Stein's efforts to produce propaganda on behalf of the Vichy regime. In the Stein archives at Yale University, there is an undated document written in the distinctive hand of Daniel-Rops: a letter to the prefect of the region outlining a rationale for granting Stein a driving permit. Presenting Stein as a "writer and journalist," Daniel-Rops argues for the necessity for Stein herself to see "all the magnificent efforts that are currently being accomplished" in order " for America to know exactly [about] the new France." He notes that Stein has been asked "by the American press" to write a series of articles on "the reconstruction of France." And he claims that Stein's work is supported by "considerable French writers," of which "one name only" need be cited, that of Bernard Faÿ. Daniel-Rops adds that Faÿ "would give information on the work and the importance of [Stein's] influence on public opinion in the United States."[85]

The idiom of this letter, and the substantive corrections to it in the hand of Alice Toklas, suggest that it was composed directly by Daniel-Rops. Yet it is also likely that if Daniel-Rops was not directly translating, he was mostly facilitating an initiative begun by Stein herself. In the same archival box reside two earlier letters to the prefect asking for driving privileges, all written by Stein herself. In the first of these, dating from April 1941, Stein announces that she has "been asked urgently to prepare a book on France for the United States."[86] Ten days later, Stein impatiently makes her position clearer: "Mister the prefet [*sic*], You accorded me certain privileges as an American writer working for French propaganda in America and now the book I wrote about France at war is now out in America and is having a great success, I am now asked to continue [during] France's last defense, this is of great importance for French propaganda in America."[87] Stein's insistence on her role as Vichy propagandist and reference to the "great success" of *Paris France* apparently fell on deaf ears; none of her special requests seems to have been granted, as she notes in successive letters. In the face of this frustration, Stein must have asked Daniel-Rops to assist her in writing to the prefect on her behalf.

This sequence of letters of early 1941 tells us much about how Stein perceived her position in World War II France. In her public self-presentation, in her appeal for help to Daniel-Rops and other Pétainist neighbors in the region, and in her official invocation of the name of Bernard Faÿ, Stein shows no qualms about presenting herself as sympathetic to the regime. While we might want to assume that Stein was attempting to manipulate a system she secretly reviled, the archival evidence gives us no way to validate that assumption. On the contrary, Stein's own words portray her as a "propagandist" for the "new France." Her letters ask for privileges, but they do so in the name of commitment to and belief in the maréchal. Her letters also make it clear that Stein had already received privileges "as an American writer working for French propaganda in America." Much of this would become obvious once Stein took on the project of translating Pétain's speeches into English in December 1941 and of introducing his National Revolution favorably to an American audience. But with the Daniel-Rops episode many months earlier, we are able to see Stein already fully, and apparently willingly, participating in the Vichy propaganda machine.

Another document found in the same archival folder as the Daniel-Rops letter adds yet one more tantalizing insight into Stein's support for Vichy during early 1941. Dated May 2, 1941, it is a letter from a General Benoît Fornel de La Laurencie to Admiral Darlan, commander of the French Armed Forces under Vichy. Written in French, the letter details La Laurencie's dismay at having been dismissed from the National Council by Darlan for having shown positive leanings toward Britain and America. La Laurencie freely admits to "anglophilia" and to his desire for an Anglo-American victory over a German one. But he argues that he has never wavered in his support for Maréchal Pétain and has "always rigorously abstained from the risk . . . of compromising the authority of the government." The letter ends with La Laurencie's bitter hope that his actions in support of both Vichy and the Anglo-American alliance—actions that have undermined his career—may ultimately one day be proven justified.[88]

What was this letter doing in Gertrude Stein's possession? What could this internal Vichy affair possibly mean to Stein? This letter can only have been given to Stein by the same person who arranged for the Pétain translation project in December of 1941: Bernard Faÿ. La Laurencie was fervently anti-Masonic and moved in the same collaborationist circles as Faÿ.[89] He had also been instrumental in disrupting the career of one of Faÿ's chief Vichy rivals, Marcel Déat.[90] In the tight-knit world of Vichy, La Laurencie and Faÿ were natural allies. But what would he have meant to Stein? What was she meant to do with his letter?

Obviously, there are similarities between the attitudes of La Laurencie and Stein herself. La Laurencie was what one critic has called a "Vichysto-resistant": pro-Vichy but suspicious of the Germans.[91] Adept at negotiating tense but not untenable relationships, he pledged loyalty at once to Pétain and to the Anglo-American cause.[92] In fact, La Laurencie, rather than de Gaulle, had long been favored by the American ambassador William Leahy as the man to bring France back into the war against the Nazis. He had been instrumental in the December 1940 coup against Pierre Laval and had been blackballed by the Germans as a result. Yet he was also a Pétainist and a key player in the inner circle of Vichy politics. Perhaps, then, La Laurencie's letter was meant to reassure Stein that a pro-Pétain/pro-American stance was both feasible and desirable. Perhaps it was also meant to stoke her investment in Vichy-American relations. But in this case it is likely that the letter was given to her by Faÿ for instrumental purposes—for her to translate or somehow disseminate as propaganda to an American public increasingly skeptical of Vichy's aims and integrity. This, of course, would be the point of Stein's Faÿ-initiated project to translate Pétain's speeches into English some months later: convincing the American public that Pétain's National Revolution was a cause worthy of both support and emulation.

Was Stein aware that there was a more sinister side to Général de La Laurencie? For it appears that he was not only anti-Masonic but also anti-Semitic—or at least an enthusiastic supporter of Vichy racial policy. In 1940, in the wake of the first official German anti-Jewish decrees, it was Général de La Laurencie, as Vichy delegate to the Nazi occupied zone, who would

FIGURE 4.5 Général Benoît Fornel de La Laurencie (1939–1940).

urge local prefects to go beyond the letter of the law in collaborating with the required census of Jewish enterprises. He writes in a memo to prefects that they must "use . . . all means of information at your disposal toward a supervision designed to assure you that the census has no omission." The général especially urged prefects to be aware of "the importance of the task incumbent upon them to accomplish." The zeal of the général's demand was seen in his threat to impose "grave sanctions" on administrators who failed to follow through on the anti-Semitic measures.[93]

Most likely Stein knew nothing of La Laurencie other than what is contained in his letter to Darlan. Yet his anti-Semitic activities emphasize yet again the danger of the political world that Stein was trying to negotiate in 1941. It was precisely the zealotry of a man like La Laurencie that would undermine Stein's careful efforts to avoid being defined, first and foremost, as a "Jew." However strong her support for Pétain, however supported and protected by Vichy insiders and Belley Pétainists, Stein was still an outsider to his regime, an uneasy exception to the rule: a "good Jew." And however much she thought herself capable of controlling her fate as a willing propagandist, Stein's position was still deeply insecure at best. Yet despite all of these dangers and uncertainties, and even after Vichy had ceased to be a viable political entity, Stein remained its unlikely collaborator.

▣ ▣ ▣

At the end of 1941, Stein undertook a project to translate the speeches by Philippe Pétain that had been collected in a book edited and introduced by Gabriel-Louis Jaray, a friend of Bernard Faÿ.[94] It was no small endeavor. For the next year and a half, Stein translated some thirty-two of Pétain's speeches into English, including those that announced Vichy policy barring Jews and other "foreign elements" from positions of power in the public sphere and those that called for a "hopeful" reconciliation with Nazi forces. The last of Pétain's speeches that Stein translated was from August 1941, but Stein did not cease working on the project until January 1943—several months after the Germans had occupied the whole of France in November 1942 and long after the United States had entered the war against the fascist forces that Stein was promoting to her fellow Americans.

The Pétain translations to this day remain unpublished, tucked away in the Stein archives at Yale University: several manuscript notebooks, a few typed pages, and the typescript of the introduction that Stein wrote to accompany the translations. The first speech translated is Pétain's address of 1936, delivered at the inauguration of a monument to the veterans of Capoulet-Junac; the last, Pétain's 1940 Christmas address. Stein followed the erratic chronology of the original text, *Paroles aux français, messages et écrits 1934–1941*, translating approximately the first half of the fifty speeches published. Still, she leaves some speeches untranslated, and it is interesting to speculate as to why. Speeches discussing the education of French youth, regional administration, and French legionnaires may have been deemed irrelevant to the kind of popular American audience that Stein was ostensibly trying to court, but Stein also leaves untranslated a speech on Franco-Canadian relations that argues for cross-cultural understanding and a speech announcing Pétain's desire to form a Supreme Court "as is found in the United States." Whether or not these omissions were deliberate, they raise a central question: was Stein herself involved in the selection of these translations, or was she a mouthpiece for someone else's directives?

Stein's notoriously bad handwriting is especially pronounced on these pages, and the manifold corrections in the hand of Alice Toklas only exacerbate the difficulty of reading. But what is most striking about the text is its almost stupefyingly literal rendering of the French original. Translating word by word, Stein completely ignores questions of idiom or style: "Telle est, aujourd'hui, Français, la tâche à laquelle je vous convie" becomes "This is today french people the task to which I urge you." An idiomatic phrase such as "Le 17 juin 1940, il y a aujourd'hui une année" becomes "On the seventeenth of June 1940 it is a year today." "Ils se méprendront les uns et les autres"—a speech denouncing Pétain's critics—is translated "But they are mistaken the ones and the others." Syntax is distorted: a speech describing the refugees from Lorraine notes the abandonment of "le cimetière où dorment leurs ancêtres"; Stein translates this as "their cemeteries where sleep their ancestors." Even the term "speech" is avoided: "Discours du 8 juillet" becomes "Discourse of the 8 July."

Stein told W. G. Rogers that she hoped to interest the *Atlantic Monthly* in this translation project, presumably imagining it as a further extension of the pro-Pétainist line she had put forth in the 1940 *Atlantic Monthly* essay "The Winner Loses."[95] But if Stein's goal was to familiarize an American audience with Pétain's words, these translations seem incongruous, even inept. They are arguably the work of a writer with little or no real familiarity toward the foreign language being translated. Alice Toklas's corrections—more copious and directive than in other of Stein's texts she copyedited—affirm this assessment of Stein as a bungling student reaching beyond her linguistic depth. Yet the weakness of the translations seems to belie Stein's fluency as a reader and relative fluency as a writer of French at this point in her life.[96] Not only had Stein long been a reader of French—her early reading of Flaubert's *Trois Contes* had famously informed her experimental text *Three Lives*—but she had recently finished an original composition in French (*Picasso*, 1938). More than a decade before the Pétain translation project, moreover, she had felt confident enough to embark on a translation into English of a text that would even stretch the skills of a Francophone: the poem cycle *Enfances* by the French surrealist poet Georges Hugnet. This translation would ultimately appear as one of Stein's most hermetic published works, *Stanzas in Meditation*.[97]

Hence the striking literalism of Stein's Pétain translations seem to point to a deeper issue than linguistic ineptitude. It suggests that something profound has happened to a writer whose most experimental work, like *Stanzas in Meditation*, interrogates, and ultimately celebrates, the shifting, unstable relationship between words and meanings, signifiers and signifieds. In the Pétain translations, Stein's attempt to render the French original into English through a one-to-one correspondence between signs seems to be conceding authority, interpretation, and interrogation to the voice of Pétain. This compositional submissiveness suggests a subject in thrall to the aura of a great man: the savior on a white horse, as Stein describes Pétain in her introduction to his speeches. In an interview with her local paper *Le Bugiste* in 1942, Stein is in fact described in a curious state of ravishment: "she abandons herself to her subject, to her hero, she admires the importance of his words and the significance of the symbol."[98] To invoke Susan Sontag: Stein appears "fixated" or "fascinated" by Pétain, mesmerized and rendered passive by an almost masochistic desire for the figure of the authoritarian dictator.[99]

While these conclusions must necessarily remain speculative, such speculation also frees us to think about the complexity of Stein's character and the difficulty of her position during the war. By the time that Stein agreed to take on the Pétain translation project, in December 1941, she was fully inhabiting her role as propagandist for the Vichy regime. For several years before that point, as we have seen, she had been informally but outspokenly developing and refining her critique of the French Third Republic and its "weak vices," of the Roosevelt administration and the welfare state, and of the Jews, "the masses," and what she called the fallacious nineteenth-century ideologies of "progress and understanding." Her idealization of the French peasantry, grafted onto a nostalgic vision of a long-forsaken American pioneering ethos, made her particularly receptive to the reactionary ideas percolating around her, not least those of her friend Bernard Faÿ. The rise to power of Philippe Pétain and the terms of his National Revolution, especially his vision of a return to traditional values of family, manual work, and national pride, appealed greatly to Gertrude Stein. In the wake of the armistice, Pétain's commitment to "peace," his promises to return France to "itself," and his amicable overtures to the United States, were also seen by Stein as a salutary development. With her newfound awareness of the power of celebrity and her sense that only radical social and political change could reform the two countries about which she felt the deepest patriotism—France and America—Stein seemed to see in Pétain a political "genius" not dissimilar to herself.

Yet I have also stressed the sheer vulnerability of Stein's existence in France during World War II, a vulnerability that even Stein herself at her most blinkered could not have failed to recognize. The Pétain translation project allows us to think about this vulnerability in a way that no other texts that Stein composed during this period do. Indeed, if we see the project as less inept than *submissive*, as the concrete manifestation in language of vulnerability deferring to protection, then other aspects of Stein's experience begin to fall into place. Given Stein's lifelong identification with the figure of the child, such an interpretation is hardly unfounded. Despite the enormous authority with which she wrote and presented her writing to the world, despite her own claims to genius and her identification with other larger-than-life individuals (generals, heroes, saints, celebrities, dictators, and prophets), Stein throughout her life had a complex need for dependency and protection of her own. On the one hand, Stein valued performing the role of a child for the creative and social freedoms it offered her and evidently had no trouble projecting herself as a "baby" even as an adult.[100] Yet playing the child (or even infant) had its darker sides for Stein as well, particularly in its association with submissiveness, vulnerability, and passivity. In an infamous account, Ernest Hemingway recalled the profound sexual masochism of Stein's relationship to Alice Toklas, and the thematics of masochism can be seen throughout Stein's writing, from her earliest stories to love notes to Toklas to her more experimental poetry to—as we shall see—some of the other texts Stein composed during World War II.[101] As Stein suggests in *Wars I Have Seen*, war more vividly than other human experiences evoked in her this feeling of child-likeness.[102]

In light of her own claims to genius and in the wake of her own experience of American celebrity in the 1930s, Stein on the one hand seems to have identified with Pétain to the extent that she imagined—for example, in the *Patrie* piece—a continuity between her own experimental writing and the cultural project of his National Revolution, both of which, she suggests, might recover the vitality of the premodern age. Yet the Pétain translation project shows as well another side of Gertrude Stein that complicates this idea of identification. In the translations themselves, as in the introduction she wrote to accompany them, Stein manifests a deference to the dictator's leadership that suggests both childlike vulnerability *and* masochistic submission to the protector who may in fact be the persecutor.

In the introduction to Pétain's speeches—described by Wanda van Dusen as "fetishistic"—Stein's representation of the dictator emphasizes the charismatic performance of heroism over any more objective rendering or critique.[103] Pétain the "hero" functions here both metaphorically—as a signifier of traditional France—and metonymically—in a chain of association with other iconic and redemptive figures from politics and religion, notably George Washington and a saint. These figures link Pétain anachronistically to a premodern nationalist mythos uncoupled from any of present-day Vichy's less savory aspects, including its collaboration with Nazi Germany. Stein does not avoid making cryptic mention of "all the people who helped to ruin France" in this propaganda piece, but her major thrust here is to shed light on Pétain's heroism.[104] By locating him in the transcendent pantheon of American founding fathers and saints, Stein idealizes her subject and elevates his regime to a political religion—a move that deftly forecloses critique, judgment, and any form of dissension.

Like Washington, Pétain is "first in war first in peace and first in the hearts of his countrymen"—a phrase Stein lifted from the "George Washington" chapter of *Four in America*, which itself borrows verbatim from General Henry Lee's famous "Funeral Oration on the Death of George Washington" (1799). In chapter 2, we examined the way Stein evokes Washington in the early 1930s in order to begin framing her "historical" critique of present-day America: Washington, described often as seated on horseback, functions as a kind of Ur-American, in marked contrast to the un-American Roosevelt. By December 1941, in the wake of both the French armistice and the attack on Pearl Harbor, Stein's reading of history has expanded to include Pétain on his white horse. The composite figure of Washington-Pétain serves as a kind of living icon of American possibility, fully visible to Americans only after the tragedy of Pearl Harbor. Before this event, Stein writes, Americans had been "spoiled children": a phrase that suggests both the cocksure refusal of Americans to sympathize with France's defeat in June 1940 and their status as dependent New Deal–era takers who have lost the courage and independence of their forefathers. But Pearl Harbor has given Americans a wonderful opportunity to become good rather than "spoiled" children. It has allowed them not only to sympathize with France but to "have faith" in a figure like the maréchal, the very embodiment of an American founding father. Like Ezra Pound, who in *Jefferson and/or Mussolini* credited Italian fascism with bringing back "Jeffersonian" economic and agrarian values to the modern world, Stein seems to be arguing that Pétain and his National Revolution could recall a (degenerate) American society to its own lost eighteenth-century potential. Hence the rationale for undertaking the Pétain translation project in the first place: not just to provide propaganda on behalf of Vichy but to present Americans with a model of leadership to emulate in their own moment of crisis.

There is another equally crucial image of Pétain in this introduction: that of a saint. The French "have all come to have faith" in Pétain, Stein notes, adding—in a phrase that she would reiterate notoriously after the war—"His defense of the armistice has been a miracle."[105] For Stein, the "miracle" of

Pétain's armistice is not unlike the miracles foreseen by the saints Odile, Godfrey, and the Curé d'Ars. Predicated upon unwavering belief and a refusal to brook skepticism, miracles give shape and meaning to society and function as a kind of reward for participation in a larger community of believers. As she frames it in an enormous sentence at the end of the introduction, "faith" in Pétain and in the "miracle" of Vichy has become a national imperative, an index of national belonging:

> And so we in France having seen France governed, having seen everybody pretty well fed having seen everybody slowly regain their health and strength, felt every one gradually recovering their liberty and their activity, and having seen every time that all being lost actually everything was being held together, I must say little by little the most critical and the most violent of us have come gradually to do what the Maréchal asks all french people to do, to have faith in him and in the fact that France will live.[106]

Spoken to Americans in the wake of the bombing of Pearl Harbor, Stein's message is clear. Submission to and faith in the authoritarian leader supersedes "critique" and "violence." What matters is attending to the voice of this leader as it soothes and guides the faithful. Only this voice, transmitted as literally as possible through the passive medium of the translator, can achieve the miracle of peace.

▣ ▣ ▣

There is little doubt that Stein's support for Pétain was authentic, as shown by her continued postwar defense of the man. Had the Vichy regime not fallen to pieces, it is likely that Stein would have continued to be its champion. While some critics have truly bent over backward to argue otherwise, most have felt that the complex story of Stein's wartime support for an authoritarian regime cannot be simply explained away.[107] Stein believed in what she was doing and knew exactly why she was doing it. She was committed to Pétain and to his vision for national renewal for all the reasons discussed in this chapter. In every way, this commitment seems to have preceded, informed, and overshadowed all other motivations for writing propaganda in support of Vichy. This is not to deny that Stein was also opportunistic, aware that such support might have salutary radiating effects on the vulnerable personal situation of herself and Alice Toklas. Yet on balance, Stein's Vichy activity was less about opportunism than about loyalty to a cause.

Of course, it is altogether probable that despite being its willing propagandist Stein felt real, if hidden or unconscious, unease with aspects of Pétain's National Revolution. This is one way, again, of understanding the paralysis of imagination that seems to inform the literalism of her Pétain translations. It is likely that there were other wrenching moments in Stein's work and activity during this time as she collaborated with an authoritarian regime. Some of this discomfort can be felt in three remarkable and almost unknown short children's plays Stein wrote during 1943: "In a Garden A Tragedy," "Three Sisters Who Are Not Sisters A Melodrama," and "Look and Long."[108] Situating her child protagonists in a dark world of arbitrary and inexplicable violence, Stein's plays are haunting and uncanny: veritable scripts of unconscious anxiety. Her wartime novel about prophecy, *Mrs. Reynolds*, also describes a shadowy landscape dominated by two dictators—thinly veiled versions of Hitler and Stalin—and marked by ominous and often terrifying events. Both the plays and *Mrs. Reynolds* seem imbued, like the translation project, with a masochistic sensibility. They seem to be putting on display the tensions of a subject who has passively chosen to submit to the dominating and potentially dangerous presence of the authoritarian dictator. In the case of *Mrs. Reynolds*, as Phoebe Stein Davis has argued, the highly repetitive narrative form foregrounds "the tedium, terror, and uncertainty" of what Stein ostensibly valued above all else, even under dictatorship: "peaceful" everyday life.[109]

These literary texts clearly run counter to the pro-Pétainist tendencies we see in Stein's more overtly political writings and comments, and they shed light on the complexity of Stein's affiliations at this time as well as the gray zone of her collaboration. The autobiography that Stein finished at the end of the war and that presents itself as the definitive account of her experience, *Wars I Have Seen*, also dances through this gray zone. As we have seen, Stein in *Wars* remains an unrepentant supporter of Pétain ("he was right to make the armistice. . . . To me it remained a miracle" [*W* 57]), and her political views throughout the text remain largely reactionary, if increasingly anti-German and pro-American.[110] Yet the text, which otherwise affects an informal conversational tone, is utterly silent about the Pétain translation project—most likely out of fear of judgment and retribution, possibly also out of remorse or uncertainty. At war's end, Stein writes:

I began to have what you might call a posthumous fear. I was quite frightened. All the time the Germans were here we were so busy trying to live through each day that except once in a while when something happened you did not know about being frightened, but now somehow with the American soldiers questions and hearing what had been happening to others, of course one knew it but now one had time to feel it and so I was quite frightened.

(W 168)

"Posthumous fear" is a suggestive way to describe the feeling of posttraumatic stress or even survivor's guilt; it vividly expresses the way in which a situation like war can numb or "deaden" us to the fear of death, a fear that returns after war is over and "one had time to feel it." In her reference to "hearing what had been happening to others," Stein—as in several other veiled moments in *Wars*—touches lightly but poignantly on her own vulnerability as a Jewish woman and suggests her post facto awareness of the sheer riskiness of having chosen to remain in France during the war. "Posthumous fear" is perhaps the closest Stein gets to admitting that riskiness, and its recognition contributes to our sense that the Stein of *Wars* is not without doubt toward her wartime choices.

Yet none of this doubt or uncertainty appears in Stein's actual Vichy propaganda. In fact, the approval of Pétain's regime evident in "The Winner Loses," "La langue française," and the "fetishistic" introduction to his speeches, throws her actions into stark relief. Especially at a moment when many other writers in France at the time were choosing either to write clandestinely or simply to be silent, Stein's vocal Pétainism is notable. Having decided to stay in France during the war, Stein might have kept a low profile; she might have chosen not to write or publish at all. But, instead, she chose to commit her writing and her name to the service of the Vichy regime. She chose it out of conviction and out of hope. To see her actions otherwise denies our ability to fully grasp Stein's wartime experience as an authentic, lived dilemma.

Still, the story of Stein's wartime experience cannot be put to rest without returning to the role of Bernard Faÿ in Stein's survival. During this period of limited travel even for Vichy insiders, Faÿ had little direct contact with Stein, except for a handful of quick visits on his way to or from one of the many lectures he was giving for the regime on the ills of Freemasonry. He did arrange for Stein to receive perks such as bread tickets, was helpful in securing her certain publishing privileges, and possibly intervened when Stein's name appeared on the third and final installment of the Nazi's list of banned books (the Liste Otto) in May 1943.[111] Faÿ was also a crucial mediator and protector when the Nazis showed up at Stein's apartment in Paris to seize her art collection.[112] But Faÿ's contact with Stein was infrequent and—compared to the conversations they enjoyed before the war—full of what could not be said.[113] In other ways, however, Faÿ's influence deeply marked Stein's existence and sphere of activity for as long as the Vichy administration remained viable. As we have seen in this book, Stein's political and even aesthetic convictions of the 1930s—the convictions that led her to support the Vichy regime—were encouraged, stimulated, and in some respects borrowed from Faÿ himself. The propaganda Stein wrote during the war showed her putting these convictions into practice. And while Stein had a network of Pétainist friends supporting her during this period, it was presumably Faÿ who in the end made possible the production of Stein's Vichy propaganda.

In their admirably thorough and careful essay on this period in Stein's life, the scholars Edward M. Burns and Ulla E. Dydo describe Faÿ as possibly Stein's "single most important French friend of the last fifteen years" before the war.[114] They note that it is "possible" that Faÿ proposed that Stein take on the Pétain translation project and detail how Faÿ discussed and vetted this project with the maréchal himself. Their analysis of Faÿ's varying motivations is astute: "Faÿ not only hoped that Stein's name would add to American support of Pétain but also expected that a translation by a distinguished writer and long-time resident in France might for Americans add luster to the marshall's [sic] book and personality. No doubt Faÿ hoped in turn it would help to assure Stein's safety in wartime France."[115] This enriches the account given by Faÿ himself in his retrospective essay on Stein and the war published in Les précieux (1966). There, Faÿ presents himself as having been purely Stein's guardian angel: "my duty," he writes, "was to keep [Stein] protected in the shadows" (LP 162). In an account that has never been verified, Faÿ claims that he prevailed upon the maréchal directly to see that Stein was protected and provided with the goods necessary for survival, resulting in Pétain making a personal written appeal to the subprefect of Belley, Maurice Sivan, to secure Stein's safety. No trace of this letter exists in the archives, but if the story is true, we can assume that it was this personal involvement of both Faÿ and the maréchal that presumably kept Stein off the Jewish census list.[116] At no point in his retrospective account, however, does Faÿ ever mention Stein undertaking the Pétain translation project.

Yet the importance of this undertaking to both Stein and Faÿ is eminently clear from the historical record. It is clear from the Stein-Faÿ correspondence upon which Burns and Dydo base their analysis, where Stein and Faÿ freely discuss "the translation." And it is clear from the archives, particularly the Bernard Faÿ archives in Paris, where in the preparation file for Faÿ's 1946 trial for collaboration one can find a copy of Stein's introduction to Pétain's speeches. On it the name "Ménétrel" is written by hand, referring to Bernard Ménétrel, Pétain's personal doctor and secretary during the war.[117] Ménétrel, Pétain's "intimate confidant," was perceived by many as the power behind

Pétain's throne: "one didn't see the chief of State without passing by him."[118] According to the Paris prefecture of police, Ménétrel was one of five figures in the inner circle around Pétain, the one most involved with Vichy propaganda; another of the five was Bernard Faÿ.[119] Why did Ménétrel's name appear on Stein's introduction? Did Faÿ give or plan to give a copy of Stein's introduction to Ménétrel? Did Ménétrel himself broker Stein's translation project rather than Pétain, as he did so many of Pétain's other directives? Faÿ wrote to Stein in 1941 that Pétain approved of the translation project "in general" but this may have been the extent of the eighty-five-year-old maréchal's involvement.[120] As Faÿ confided to his friend Denise Aimé Azam about the Ménétrel-Pétain nexus: "if I went there [to Vichy] the Maréchal would have listened to me, then he would have listened to Ménétrel, and finally he would have forgotten everything."[121] Other correspondence between Faÿ and Ménétrel during this period is characterized by high-level behind-the-scenes machinations, revealing the considerable power wielded by both over Vichy deliberations.[122]

If the notoriously anti-Semitic Ménétrel was involved in Stein's translation project, then this adds a new twist to the story that Pétain himself was personally involved in Stein's safety and was somehow moved enough by Faÿ's account of her hardship during the war to secure her special privileges. Presumably any favors that the Vichy regime offered Stein—as for a mere handful of other Jews—were part of an exacting exchange agreement, one that Ménétrel and Faÿ could have worked out in a typical behind-the-scenes Vichy maneuver.[123] In such a scenario, the terms of Stein's protection—including the speeches Stein was to translate, the nature of her introduction, possibly other propaganda Stein actually did write or was planning to write, and the larger propagandistic plan for Franco-American relations that these projects foreshadowed—would presumably be hammered out between Faÿ and Ménétrel without any more than the cursory involvement of Pétain.

Ménétrel's involvement in the Pétain translation project cannot be verified, but the likelihood that he was the recipient of its drafting and his centrality to Pétain's decision making points strongly in that direction. What is undeniable is Stein's real eagerness to follow through with "the translation" and to have it approved by Pétain. One can see this in Stein's *Le Bugiste* interview; in Stein's discussions with the French translator of her introduction, Paul Genin; as well as in Faÿ's letters to Stein during this period.[124] Twice Faÿ appears to be holding back, keeping Stein at bay "until I've spoken to the Maréchal." Meanwhile, it may have been Ménétrel with whom Faÿ was deliberating over Stein's fate. No letter from Stein suggests that she knew anything about this latter possibility; it was not the kind of thing either would put into print. In Stein's willful naïveté about the propaganda she wrote, and in Faÿ's secrecy about his own activities, we can perceive once again the dilemmas of their world—as well as the complex web of double dealing and backstage machinations within which both individuals were trapped.

FAŸ'S WAR

WINNERS AND LOSERS (1940-1946)

CHAPTER FIVE

I N HER recently published novel *Suite Française*, Irène
Némirovsky paints a vivid picture of France in 1940, on the
eve of its capitulation to the Germans:

You could smell the suffering in the air, in the silence. Even people who
were normally calm and controlled were overwhelmed by anxiety and
fear. Everyone looked at their house and thought, "Tomorrow it will
be in ruins, tomorrow I'll have nothing left. We haven't hurt anyone.
Why?" Then a wave of indifference washed over their souls: "What's
the difference! It's only stone, wood—nothing living! What matters is
survival!" Who cared about the tragedy of their country?[1]

Survival: the last hope for a people numbed by too much uncertainty, too much war, too much ruin. The drive that alone could sur-
pass even the tragedy of a broken nation. In the first weeks of June
1940, as Parisians packed their precious belongings into cars, trucks,
and wheelbarrows, joining long, barely moving lines of refugees heading south and west away from the city, desperation filled the air. The
French had been in this situation only two decades before; the wounds
of World War I were still fresh. During the 1920s and 1930s, their public lives had been marked by chaos: governments that rose and fell, an
entrenched economic depression, street demonstrations and riots, the
constant threat of Hitler's Germany on the borders. The only response,

now that a new war seemed inevitable, was to flee. "People leave like rats, without noise," wrote a volunteer for the French Red Cross named William Gueydan de Roussel, "It's a real panic. . . . No one knows where he's going."[2]

In an empty Paris, only a few remained behind, among them Gueydan's superior officer, fellow Red Cross volunteer, and possible lover Bernard Faÿ, at home in his Left Bank apartment on the rue Saint-Guillaume. There, holding a makeshift salon of sorts, Faÿ and a handful of associates felt themselves alone in their concern about "the tragedy of their country." Faÿ lamented "the panic of the government, of the administration, of the so-called elites, of all the people fleeing toward the south."[3] His friend Pierre Ordioni (soon, like Faÿ, to take a post in the Vichy administration), despaired over the weakness of the Reynaud administration, which had disappeared along with the refugees. Both railed against the forces that had led France to its imminent military defeat: "political institutions, the pre-war press, the Jews, the head of state and his courtiers, the freemasons." Other guests called for a *revanchist* solution to the impasse of the moment. In the confusion and despair of the times, only one thing seemed clear to this group of conservative *salonniers* clustered in Bernard Faÿ's apartment on the eve of the armistice: the future of France lay in their hands. Turning to his friends, Faÿ urged them not to abandon their country, to go abroad or to hide from the Germans. Rather, he said, we must take advantage of the opportunity this rupture offered: "to occupy official posts and there work toward the 'Intellectual and Moral Reform of France.'"[4]

True to these words, Faÿ would spend the next four years living and working at the red-hot center of the Vichy regime. When Pétain's representatives signed the armistice with Germany on June 22, 1940, Faÿ lost no time in making his services available to Vichy. In the next several weeks, according to Faÿ's own account, he would be felt out for several top-level Vichy administrative posts, culminating in the offer to head the Bibliothèque Nationale (BN), France's national library.[5] Faÿ initially hesitated to accept, then decided he owed it to "the books": "I couldn't abandon them on the day when they appealed to me, when I knew they were in danger, when they could disappear in the storm."[6] Faÿ would frequently reiterate this theme in defending his actions for posterity, making much of his role as savior of France's literary riches. But what strikes us today is how insufficient this empathy with books seems as a justification for the great ethical problem of Faÿ's wartime activities.

Faÿ was appointed general administrator of the BN by official decree (*arrête*) on August 6, 1940. It was a hugely prestigious honor. Even today, the BN in Paris is more than a public library: a repository of all that has been published in France, it is also the very symbol of France's cultural heritage. As

FIGURE 5.1 Portrait of Bernard Faÿ (early 1940s).

the seat of France's cultural and intellectual patrimony, its holdings are vast and priceless. To be appointed its director is to be given the responsibility and the means to preserve and expand this patrimony. Under the exigencies of an extreme situation like the Nazi occupation of France, this responsibility would be heightened; to a certain extent, therefore, Bernard Faÿ held one of the most culturally influential positions in Paris during this time. "The mission that was given to me," Faÿ wrote in the annual report of the BN in 1943, "had for its principal object . . . to effect, during a period of great national trial, a profound reform."[7] In a September 1941 letter to Stein, Faÿ was giddier: "I am spending 200 millions to house your future books and to build a musical library, a business library and a geographical library. I have a great fun [*sic*] in doing all that."[8]

Faÿ's appointment as general administrator corresponded with the dismissal of the BN's prewar administrator, Julien Cain. This was the first and one of the most unsavory ways in which Faÿ profited from the discriminatory politics of Vichy. The Jewish Cain, who had worked with Faÿ on an exhibit at the BN on George Washington in 1937,[9] was "released" from his duties as administrator on July 23, 1940. Arrested in February 1941, he was eventually deported to Buchenwald in January 1944.[10] Although Faÿ writes in his memoirs that he tried to help Cain flee Paris in 1941, during the war he officially cast aspersions on his predecessor, a fact that would seem to contradict his later assertions.[11] Yet what is undeniable is that Faÿ's rise to power coincided with the downturn in the fortunes of Cain.

It also coincided with an important political initiative instigated by the Vichy administration in the first flush of its power. On August 13, 1940, just four days after Faÿ was named head of the BN, a law was announced in the *Journal Officiel* dissolving all "Secret Societies." The force of this edict would be felt primarily by Freemasons, whose lodges, financial holdings, and archives would henceforth become the property of the state. While Bernard Faÿ appears not to have been directly involved in molding this law, he would immediately become central to prosecuting it.[12] His first action was to require all civil servants to sign a document attesting that they were not, and had never been, Freemasons or members of any secret society; if they had been, there was a special document to sign renouncing any such affiliation. Within four months, Faÿ would be placed in charge of the classification and inventory of archives and objects found in all the Masonic lodges in France. By the summer of 1941, he would be publishing these secret archives, along with the names of living Freemasons that he had collected from the signed attestations as well as secret files, in an official Vichy journal, *Les Documents Maçonniques*. All of these activities would require direct negotiations with the Nazis.

After the war, Faÿ would defend his actions in contradictory ways, claiming to have been variously a heroic savior of archives that might otherwise have fallen into the hands of the Germans or to have been a servant of Pétain, simply following orders. But all sources agree on one thing about Bernard Faÿ: his scholarly interest in Freemasonry had, under the Vichy regime, turned into an "obsessional delirium."[13] The extent of this obsession was clear in a deposition given to the American army after the war, when an unrepentant Faÿ linked the "harm" of French Freemasonry to the failure of "all the efforts to build a big French army, avoid foreign interferences, and clean the administration."[14] If Petain had blamed the French defeat in 1940 on "too few allies, too few weapons, too few babies," for Faÿ, both defeat and its disappointing aftermath were attributable to a single agent: French Freemasonry.

In fact, Faÿ would find a ready ally for his obsessions in Pétain himself, who enjoyed Faÿ's frequent company at private Vichy dinners and remained unfazed even by Faÿ's more bizarre claims, for instance, that there were Freemasons among the French bishopry.[15] It was indeed at a dinner in December 1942 that Pétain turned to Faÿ and uttered the following famous words: "Freemasonry is the main thing responsible for our present-day troubles; it is that which has taught the French lying, and it is lying that has led us to where we are."[16]

⊞ ⊞ ⊟

Faÿ's rapid rise within the Vichy regime came as little surprise to his friends and acquaintances, many of whom were themselves "masters of the moment," to borrow Philippe Burrin's phrase.[17] Since the mid-1930s, Faÿ had been aligned with right-wing forces working to assure the demise of the Third Republic and to bring forth a new reactionary platform to combat France's ills. Indeed, Faÿ had been instrumental in theorizing and legitimating this platform: in his lectures at the Collège de France; in scholarly works such as *Revolution and Freemasonry*, which cloaked its anti-Masonic rhetoric in a wrapper of historical objectivity; and in his contributions to a cross-section of polemical publications during this unsettled period, from the doctrinal Action Française journal *La Revue Universelle* to the profascist and anti-Semitic *Je Suis Partout* to the vehemently anti-Masonic *La Bataille et L'Action Antimaçonnique* to the protocollaborationist *Cahiers franco-allemands*. Traveling widely, from Canada to Spain to Germany, Faÿ became an active lecturer and participant in an international underground network of antidemocratic critics and planners for the future. What resonates across his writings and lectures during the period from 1935 to 1940 is not only critique but energy and a sense of possibility. Like others on the Right, Faÿ seems to have found his voice and vision as the 1930s proceeded; at last, history seemed to be on his side. His hopes for the future lay in particular with two forces on the political horizon.

First, like many of his compatriots, Faÿ was strongly drawn to the idea of a National Revolution that seemed to be taking shape around the figure of Philippe Pétain. Conspiracy theories aside, Pétain had spent the years before the war honing a platform that would provide an ideological model for the Vichy regime to come. Though he could not foresee the defeat of France, he had already developed a *revanchist* attitude toward his country: one based in revenge, reassessment, and rerighting a system gone awry. Throughout the middle and late 1930s, as minister of war (1934) and ambassador to Spain (1939), Pétain played a central role in the futuristic visions of the French Right as the person most favored to lead a "firm regime" unhampered by "parlia-mentarianism."[18] Suspicious of the Popular Front and intensely opposed to any kind of communist organization in France, Pétain was a figurehead who uni-fied—at least for a time—groups as disparate as the paramilitary profascist leagues of the Croix de Feu and the Cagoule and the more nationalist, royalist, and Germanophobic Action Française. With his broad popularity as the "Vic-tor of Verdun," Pétain also forged deep alliances across political lines, even appealing to democratic and left-wing forces imagining him above factional interest.[19] Yet the core support for Pétain in the late 1930s came from those most concerned with the issue of the decadence of the French Republic—an idea that stretched back to predecessors like the Faisceau in the 1920s, the anti-Dreyfusards of the turn of the century, and even to the counterrevolutionaries of 1789.[20] For those, like Bernard Faÿ, who spent the last years before the war railing against democracy, communism, and Freemasonry, Pétain's National Revolution seemed to offer "a new era of creation and of veritable grandeur."[21]

Pétain's prewar message would be disseminated by one of the groups of which Bernard Faÿ was a director: the Committee for National Unity for the Reconstruction of France (Rassemblement National pour la Reconstruction de la France), a shadowy right-wing organization founded in 1936 that would become prominently profascist in its second incarnation during the war.[22] With the slogan "Penser pour agir"—"to think in order to act"—the group saw itself as providing an intellectual foundation for the national revolution to come. Faÿ himself wrote to a friend at the time that the group could have a "profound effect" on the decadence of the era.[23] Alongside figures like Max-ime Weygand, René Gillouin, and Abel Bonnard—all three to become central players in the Vichy regime—Faÿ wrote articles directed against the menace of communism, which had "possessed" France under the guise of the Popular Front, as well as monthly brochures against "Freemasonry, the Jews, the Popu-lar Front, and the 'Crusade of Democracies.'"[24] In a period in which parlia-mentary democratic institutions in France were under attack from all corners of the Right, Faÿ and his cohorts felt emboldened.[25] They were committing themselves to a new kind of crusade, one increasingly directed toward not just a new France but a new Europe, and perhaps a new European "World Order."

This "crusade" was the second force with which Faÿ identified in the late 1930s: the emerging movement to create a federal Europe joined together through "the binding force of an idea and tradition with which Europe is irre-vocably linked."[26] While the federalist movement was indebted to the efforts of Aristide Briand and others to forge international "friendship pacts" during the preceding decade, it was distinctly more ideological than its predecessor.[27]

The New Europe to which Faÿ and his contemporaries on the Right referred in the late 1930s had transformed the Briandist vision of nationalist alliances into the *idea* of a European federation united under the banner of Christianity, a shared past, and the defense of Western civilization.[28] This was a vision of Europe in full rejection of parliamentary democracy and of "the two empires of decadent materialist ideology, the capitalist USA and communist Russia."[29] A Europe, in the words of the Italian fascist philosopher and anti-Masonic ideologue Julius Evola, sharing "a communal spiritual identity and sense of direction," in "revolt against the modern world in favor of what is nobler, higher, more truly human."[30]

There were, of course, pragmatic concerns driving the New Europe movement in France throughout the 1930s. As the historian Bernard Bruneteau has argued in his book *"L'Europe nouvelle" de Hitler: Une illusion des intellectuals de la France de Vichy*, the movement revealed a crosshatching of French interests: a desire for radical social change in the wake of social instability, anxiety about what to do with German economic and military power, and a residual Briandism that would also play into the later stance of appeasement. Those drawn to the "illusion" of a German-led New Europe had shared with their compatriots in the 1930s deep uncertainty about how to respond to various signs of foreign expansionist aggression that undermined both the League of Nations and France's diplomatic leadership, from Japan's invasion of Manchuria in 1931 to the Italian invasion of Abyssinia in 1935 to Germany's Rhineland coup of 1936 and annexation of Czechoslovakia in 1938. "Appeasement"—the diplomatic posture that was ultimately taken to seal the Munich Pact of 1938, granting German control over the Sudetenland—embodied this uncertainty, as French and British politicians sought to answer German domination with "a mixture of conciliation and firmness."[31] The French New Europe movement was formed in the same crucible, reflecting in part the pragmatic desire for European rapprochement in uncertain times: avoiding war while also retaining France's political autonomy and replenishing its economic and social reserves through a diplomatic partnership with Germany. This eagerness for rapprochement would in turn nourish the beginnings of the Vichy regime, "the grand illusion of 1940."[32]

Yet seemingly more than any other motive, the federalist "New Europe" movement of the late 1930s was driven by a deep commitment to the idea of Europe as a shared spiritual entity. It was Italians like Evola who offered the most pungent descriptions of European "spiritual identity"; indeed, the Italian fascists would be at the forefront of efforts to create what they called in 1942 a "European regime of federal union."[33] But in France as well, the New

Europe movement was devoted to the vision of a common European identity that had heretofore been quashed by the forces of "non-European attitudes and lifestyles" as well as by the false "rational nationalism" embodied in the French Revolution.[34] Particularly in its French right-wing incarnation, the movement was indebted to the Francophone nonconformist movement of the early 1930s, which imagined itself transcending "right" and "left" divisions in order to bring about a European "Third Way" orientation that would be "militantly anticapitalist" and "radically federalist" in nature.[35] Alexandre Marc, the founder of the group Ordre Nouveau and one of the chief figures in the European federalist movement in the early 1930s, joined his contemporaries in the *Jeune Europe* movements in Belgium and Switzerland to champion "a federated, integrated Europe, with a common army, no customs barriers, peace and prosperity for all member countries."[36] At the heart of their project was the belief in what Marc in 1933 called "a New Order at the service of *l'homme intégral*"[37]—a rather vague phrase that nevertheless spoke directly to the dreams and aspirations of many European youth.

Integral man—*l'homme intégral*—was a code phrase for spiritual renewal and a communitarian ethos in the face of modern individualistic and capitalist anomie. It was as much a rejection of the establishment Right as of the communist Left; *l'homme intégral* could only emerge through the transcendence of regimes and systems. As we saw in chapter 4, Marc, alongside his fellow ON colleague Henri Daniel-Rops, felt that German National Socialism alone "knew how to comprehend, and make understood, that to americano-bolschevik gregariousness, to democratico-capitalist individualism, one must oppose the feeling of the organic collectivity, rich in fraternity and love."[38] Nazism offered the most promising ground for the emergence of this *l'homme intégral*—even while both Marc and Daniel-Rops clearly had their doubts about Hitler. Their stance has led some historians, including Zeev Sternhell, to argue controversially that the French nonconformist movement had much more in common with Nazism than has previously been thought.[39] What is indisputable is that the nonconformists, in their vision of a New European Order based on "spiritual union," offered key terms for the French Right to appropriate as the 1930s drew to a close.

Indeed, inevitably, the French federalist movement of the 1930s would play directly into the hands of the Nazis and their goal of a *German*-dominated European Order—and perhaps World Order. All too eager to embody the "European spirit," the Nazis presented themselves as fulfilling Germany's historical mission to "function as the hyphen between the peoples of Europe and to guide them toward a new European order."[40] Masterful propagandists, Nazi ideologues did not rely on force alone to consolidate power; often, their ideas were disseminated by German "emissaries" to groups such as Ordre Nouveau, which attracted youth from all sides of the political spectrum hungry for change (the careers of Karl Epting and Otto Abetz, from Franco-German youth organizers to Nazi administrators in Paris during the Vichy regime, are instructive case studies of this phenomenon).[41] By the late 1930s, "European federalism" suggested to many a confederation of weaker nations under the protection of the Nazis, all committed to "victory over the forces of liberal decadence and the Jewish-Communist menace."[42] The French collaborationist Pierre Drieu la Rochelle, in his book *Le Français d'Europe* (*The European Frenchman*), saw that only "a new confederation of nations under the Third Reich" could arrest France's creeping decline.[43] As Admiral François Darlan, Pétain's minister of the navy, put it somewhat cryptically: "Germany, whose design is to reconstitute Europe, dominates its victory in order to allow us to dominate our defeat."[44]

Given Bernard Faÿ's scholarly interest in eighteenth-century federalism, discussed in chapter 2, it is not surprising to see him gravitating toward the discussion of "New Europe" in the late 1930s. Nor is it a surprise to learn that Faÿ, always associated with the Catholic and royalist Right, also had direct ties to the nonconformist movement that was envisioning this new federalist structure.[45] For Faÿ, federalism in its most noble incarnation—as in the American eighteenth century—was perforce a system in which "harmonious unity" between separate interests could coexist with authoritarian leadership vested in a benign elite. Such a federalist system encouraged commonality through a delicate balance of compromise and deferral to the "principle of authority, conferred upon one leader, who alone should discern what is useful." Yet by the 1930s, Faÿ had grown wary of America, and his sacred vision of what he called a "salutary" and "logical" federalism began to shift its locus toward the New Europe movement. Faÿ now looked to Europe as the potential site of a similar state of governance, albeit one faithful to Catholic, elitist, and hierarchical values. This shift can be seen in a variety of Faÿ's writings and activities during this period preceding the outbreak of war.

In October 1935, Faÿ was one of sixty-four signers of a document entitled "Manifesto of French Intellectuals for the Defense of the West," which protested League of Nations sanctions against Italy in the wake of its Abyssinian invasion. Joining Robert Brasillach, Charles Maurras, Fernand de Brinon, Pierre Drieu la Rochelle, and others, Faÿ denounced the League of Nation's attack on the "civilizing spirit" of Europe that lay behind the Italian invasion. The League's sanctions against the Italian action, they wrote, sprang from a "false juridical universalism which puts on an equal footing superior and inferior, civilized and barbarian." The "democratic" impulse that equates African peoples and Europeans risks "putting the security of our world at the mercy of certain savage tribes." Punishing Italy for its legitimate colonial mission represents "an incontrovertible attack against the civilisation of the West, that is, against the only valid future that, now and in the past, would be open to the human race."[46]

This manifesto written explicitly in defense of Western imperialism makes no effort to hide its elitism and ethnocentrism. Sanctions against Italy, it notes, "would not only be a crime against peace" but more seriously a "suicide" for Europe and its glorious humanist tradition. For Faÿ and his co-signers, the Italian-Ethiopian crisis represents a clash between civilization and barbarism, between light and darkness. What matters in this crisis is the survival of a notion of natural cultural "superiority" that terms like "democracy" and "universalism" risk crushing underfoot. Moreover, to condemn Italy for its "legitimate" colonizing mission was to cast aspersions on France's own colonial prerogatives. Tellingly, the appearance of this manifesto at the beginning of October 1935 was timed to influence the decision of the French government as it prepared to take an official stance on the Ethiopian conflict; it was meant, according to its editor Henri Massis, "to make known to the government the opinion of elites."[47]

Two years later, in a 1937 "Manifesto to Spanish Intellectuals" published in the aptly named journal *Occident*, Faÿ again joined a group of prominent intellectuals on the Right calling for a defense of Francisco Franco's Nationalist cause in the name of a common "race, tradition, and culture":

> We cannot do otherwise than wish for the triumph, in Spain, of that which now represents civilization against barbarism, order and justice against violence, tradition against destruction. . . . We thus salute those men who, in their terrible hour of adversity, represent so nobly the intelligence and the culture of their country. We reach out to them and affirm our solidarity with them. . . . Our goal is to show to peoples and to governments that the true France and the true Spain are and remain united.

Here, elitism—"intelligence and culture"—functions as a common currency uniting and distinguishing the "true" European nations from the rest of the barbaric world.[48]

In 1937, Faÿ made a significant visit to Salamanca, Spain, then a strategic stronghold of Franco's right-wing nationalist rebels. The fervently anti-Masonic

Franco apparently thought enough of Faÿ and his positions to grant him a personal interview.[49] In a memoir written about his experience, Faÿ reiterates this common bond of tradition and culture that unites France and Spain, "that which joins France to Spain, those forces and those joys which have produced centuries of intelligent Christianity, subtle civilization, and modest pride." Romanticizing Spain's "soil, blood, and God," Faÿ adopts increasingly fascist terms to describe the nature of European belonging. Spaniards, he writes, are "content to live, to cultivate their land, to believe in their race, and to pray to their God." They are insistently contrasted with those countries willing "to let their spirit be mutilated every day in order to save a little of their material existence."[50] Their "will to renew and continue the most ancient traditions of Spain, leads [them] necessarily . . . to refuse to follow the great Anglo-Saxon capitalist and democratic states."[51] Faÿ's choice is stark: on the one side, a Europe defined by national differences but a common respect for tradition, hierarchy, and "blood"; on the other side, a soulless, modern, Anglo-Americanized world of mass rule and crass materialism.[52]

As what Faÿ had once called the "American experiment" came increasingly to seem to him like the American nightmare, his rejection of the country he had admired became inseparable from his fantasy of Europe's imminent rebirth. It is telling that one of Faÿ's most virulent critiques of America was delivered in 1937 in Berlin, in front of the Academy of the Rights of Nations, a pro-Nazi federalist organization. Entitled "Communism and Democracy," Faÿ's lecture stressed the twin evils of democracy and "brutal . . . industrialism" in America, whose failures had paved the way for communism to gain a strong foothold "in the high schools, in churches, among the leading journalists and within the American intelligentsia."[53] Several months later, this viewpoint would find its fullest expression in the lead article written for the pro-Nazi *Deutsch-Französische Monatshefte / Cahiers franco-allemands.* Entitled "Europa ist eine Wirklichkeit" ("Europe Is a Reality"), Faÿ's essay frames a critique of America in terms of an opportunity for Europe. For Faÿ, America's "formula for industrial production, for great economic planning, and for material growth . . . also includes horrendous, terribly distorted conditions and a kind of yawning inner emptiness." Most troubling, the multiplicity and variety of American life conceals the fact that "there is no possibility for hierarchical differentiation" among peoples; in America, everyone is part of the "manipulable masses." Modern American "federalism" is thus an empty political system that purports to value difference but that obscures the essential inner conformity of so-called American individuality. By contrast, Europe, with its "different standpoints" and "different changing textures," is a world where people and things know their place, whether they be elites or peasants, French aristocrats or German soldiers. It is this true sense of distinction and difference within hierarchy that distinguishes Europe from America and that differentiates the new European federalism in its right-wing manifestation from American political federalism.[54]

"Europe Is a Reality" represents an important turning point in Faÿ's intellectual reconciliation with the forces of fascism. At the same time, Faÿ is careful in these polemical writings of the late 1930s never to argue—as did his friend Drieu la Rochelle—that the New Europe would at bottom "serve a German Europe."[55] Anti-German by background and by faith, Faÿ remained always somewhat circumspect in his public rhetoric about Nazi Germany. His allegiance was always closer to that of Philippe Pétain, who in a speech in October 1940 called for "Honorable collaboration, within the framework of constructive activity of the new European order" ("Collaboration dans l'honneur, dans le cadre d'une activité constructive du nouvel ordre européen").[56]

Still, Faÿ's shift in allegiance from American to European federalism in the late 1930s, combined with his enormous personal and political ambition, could only lead him in a single direction. In the space of several years, Faÿ would become one of the few establishment French intellectuals to work openly in collaboration with the Nazis. This fact did not go unnoticed by Faÿ's contemporaries on either side of the Atlantic. At the start of the Vichy regime, the Massachusetts Historical Society expelled Faÿ, as a corresponding member, for his "political sins."[57] At the same time, the American Library Association referred to Faÿ as "the well-known Royalist and pro-Nazi writer."[58] In 1942, *Life* magazine published Faÿ's name on a "Black List" of "Frenchmen condemned by the Underground for collaborating with Germans."[59] Meanwhile, in France Faÿ was denounced by the left-leaning journal *La Lumière* as "*persona grata in the Third Reich*" after publicly attacking the French Revolution during a sesquicentennial anniversary celebration in 1939. Others criticized Faÿ for publishing in *Deutsch-Französische Monatshefte / Cahiers franco-allemands*, a journal started and maintained by Otto Abetz and financed by Joachim von Ribbentrop, the future foreign minister of the Third Reich.[60] Among the distinguished individuals associated with the journal in 1937 were Alfonse de Chateaubriant, director of the Groupe Collaboration under Vichy and head of the Nazi-sponsored French newspaper *La Gerbe*; Henri Jamet, a friend of Abetz, director of the collaborationist bookstore Rive Gauche, and husband of Annie Jamet, Robert Brasillach's lover;[61] Georges Duhamel, author of the anti-American screed "Scènes de la vie future"; Alfred Rosenberg, one of the main authors of Nazi racial ideology and head of the anti-Freemasonry office under Hitler; and Hermann Göring, second in command to Hitler during the Third Reich. Writing for the *Cahiers franco-allemands* in 1937, for the *Cahiers du Rassemblement National pour la Reconstruction de la France* in 1938, and for *Je Suis Partout* from 1934 on, Bernard Faÿ had found the ideal circle in which to begin his Vichy career.

In 1940, the center of occupied Paris was the Hotel Majestic, near the Champs-Elysées: this was the operations hub for the German military administration (MBF). Less than five kilometers away was the Bibliothèque Nationale, just north of the Louvre and close to the financial center of the city. It was there where Bernard Faÿ set up one of two offices that would serve as his base of operations during the war.

Housed during Faÿ's time in an impressive nineteenth-century building on the rue de Richelieu, the BN to this day holds some of the most valuable treasures in France: Western and Eastern manuscripts, medals, coins, maps,

FIGURE 5.2 Bernard Faÿ at his desk (early 1940s).

SOURCE: COPYRIGHT COLLECTION KEYSTONE/GAMMA-RAPHO

antiques, and books dating from the beginning of print. In August 1939, many of these treasures had already been transferred to two provincial chateaux (Castelnau and Ussé), where—despite Faÿ's effort to get them returned to Paris—they remained under the surveillance of mutually suspicious French and German authorities for the course of the war. The collections removed, there was still much to take care of at the Paris library. From the moment of his arrival, Faÿ found himself tasked with several official duties: retaining and cultivating a functioning staff, maintaining a normal schedule of operating hours for the general public, and working in conjunction with the Nazi service for the protection of libraries, under the leadership of Hugo Kruss, then director-general of the Berlin Library, and his colleague Hermann Fuchs.

Faÿ's relationship with Kruss and Fuchs was amicable if wary. Initiatives were set in place almost immediately for the BN to open to the public, of which a vast majority of users were Nazi officials.[62] Faÿ agreed to "normalize" the workings of the library as much as possible in this way and even supported a special office in the library for Nazi librarians to pursue inventories and special bibliographic projects. In general, he remained deferential toward the German users of the library, whose presence was ostensibly one of research but also of taking stock of the archival documents and treasures housed at the library. Despite his claim after the war that his major effort as BN director was to save the archives from Nazi looting, Faÿ apparently tried to facilitate German demands that the treasures of Ussé be brought back to Paris.[63] But deference would come at a price. As elsewhere in Europe, the Nazi "inventory" of libraries meant that more than a million volumes of stolen books and manuscripts would eventually end up in Germany, where they remain to this day.[64] While Faÿ claimed in retrospect that "I could do nothing to prevent this theft," his actions—and the accounts of others who witnessed them—suggest little resistance to, and even grudging support of, this German appropriation of French library holdings.[65]

After the war, in defending his actions, Faÿ would emphasize his stewardship of a "policy of firm and steady resistance" at the BN.[66] This assessment radically simplifies the complexity of his actions from 1940 to 1944. Like so many other French collaborators, Faÿ found himself playing a complicated double game with the occupiers. At once solicitous and secretive, helpful and intractable, charming and ruthless, Faÿ in his official capacity at the BN did whatever he could to achieve his personal and political aims without alienating the Nazi authorities. A Vichy ideologue at heart, Faÿ was nonetheless not particularly pro-Nazi. This seeming paradox makes sense only within the gray zone of life under the occupation. Committed to the Vichy program and tolerant of the Nazi presence—especially, as we shall see, when it facilitated the attack on Freemasonry—Faÿ's collaboration was of a different order from that of his colleagues such as Robert Brasillach or Marcel Déat, who enthusiastically pursued Franco-German relations even after the total occupation of France in 1942. Rather, Faÿ's actions between 1940 and 1944 fall under the category of what might be called "collaboration d'état" (governmental or administrative collaboration)—a mode of engagement with the Nazis that was pragmatic rather than programmatic, based on supposed common interests of state and on the realization of shared political and social goals.

Still, lack of overt enthusiasm for the Nazi presence in France did not keep Faÿ away from compromising positions. Indeed, wartime sources show that Faÿ repeatedly engaged in a heightened degree of cooperation with the Germans at the BN on most matters. From the start of the occupation, the German military officials announced their intention to remove anti-German propaganda from the BN's holdings. They also constructed a specific list of banned books that were neither to be sold, translated, or circulated in France: the Liste Otto (on which Stein's name would appear in 1943).[67] Faÿ was a willing participant in both of these censoring activities, placing offensive propaganda in sealed and inaccessible containers and enclosing books on the Liste Otto in protective wrappers, which could only be removed in the library with his permission. Faÿ also consolidated his power with the authorities through callous symbolic gestures—for example, cordoning off a certain section of the reading room for Jews—as well as through lavish receptions and concerts hosted by the BN and attended by numerous high-ranking Gestapo officials and Paris collaborationists. Nor did Faÿ—like many more wary French intellectuals—try to limit his participation in German-sponsored events. In fact, Faÿ was at the head of a delegation of French librarians on an all-expenses-paid trip to Salzburg in September 1942 for a conference with the German Society for Documentation.[68] In an official report, Faÿ wrote fawningly of this trip, noting the "perfection" of German documentation methods and the "perfect courtesy and kindnesses" shown him throughout the trip.[69]

Even after the Nazis had occupied all of France in November 1942, revealing Petain's rule to be a sham, Faÿ continued to work with the occupying authorities. This can be seen in two particularly damning incidents. One concerns a list of books that Faÿ requested from the Reich Security Headquarters in February 1943. This list—detailing a "Foundational Library of National Socialism"— represented a cross-section of publications of Nazi thought, history, economics, and racial ideology, including works by Hitler, Goebbels, Göring, Rosenberg, and Werner Daitz. Not a single Jewish name is to be found among the list of authors; indeed, many of the books deal with the so-called Jewish question and with the "German race" and the issue of "German Europe."[70] The scandal of this document is that it shows Faÿ explicitly working to supplement the BN's collections with what might be called the "Nazi canon": an effort that clearly went above and beyond the call of duty for a Vichy official. Faÿ would later emphasize in his defense that he tried to keep the BN free from Nazi ideology; the request for a "Foundational Library" of Nazism proves the contrary.

Even worse was the so-called Pithiviers affair. On September 24, 1942, just as Faÿ was leaving for the library conference in Salzburg, eleven employees of the BN were arrested and deported to the Pithiviers concentration camp, fifty kilometers south of Paris. An interoffice memo from the BN on September 18 shows Faÿ writing to the Ministry of Education about a "communist conspiracy" at the library and urging that the agitators be removed. Several weeks later, Faÿ wrote the ministry praising them for "the rapid and complete cleaning-up operation" that they had just achieved with the help of the Gestapo. Faÿ's culpability in this matter seems undeniable, as it does in his documented denunciation of faculty members at the Sorbonne and the Collège de France.[71] Although none of these denunciations resulted in deaths, the negative effect of Faÿ's actions can be seen in the fate of the eleven Pithiviers deportees. Most were released from the camp after three months for lack of evidence, and several were reintegrated into the BN in "irrelevant" positions, but one, a caretaker named Jules Primitif, was held at Pithiviers for over twenty months. Given the conditions at this so-called work camp and the frequent deportations from it to Auschwitz between 1942 and 1944, life at Pithiviers could only be described as terrifying. In this instance, Faÿ showed himself fully capable of doing harm to his fellow Frenchmen in the name of "cleaning-up operations." More to the point, Faÿ used the power of his position—and his close contacts with French collaborationist and Nazi officials—to follow through on these efforts.

Yet while his German superior Dr. Fuchs would report in 1940 that Bernard Faÿ was "completely loyal"[72] to the collaborationist cause, other secret documents from the MBF, especially those dated later in the war, express concern that Faÿ wasn't *enough* of a collabo. "From the point of view of politics, the attitude of Monsieur Faÿ is rather complex," notes one anonymous document in German: "His relations with the German librarians are stamped with courtesy, and he pays public homage to the services that they render to the French librarians. Nevertheless, it is worth noting that, with regard to essential issues, he does everything to preclude their accomplishment." Particularly frustrating to this writer is the fact that Faÿ seems to resist the idea of a true "intellectual collaboration" with the Nazis.[73] Outside from the request for the Foundational

Library of Nazism, in fact, Faÿ seemed less absorbed with fostering Franco-German collaboration at the BN than with making the library the centerpiece of Vichy's National Revolution. Faÿ writes in 1943 that his primary effort at the BN was to restore it to its ancien régime glory, before the "materialism" and "parlimentarianism" of the French Revolution had broken apart France, undermined the authority of the state, and crippled its central library system.[74] As for the Germans, their usefulness was clear: to "permit us with courtesy and a sense of professionalism, toward which we render them sincere thanks, to protect our collections against all the dangers and bad effects of the war."

Faÿ's BN position offers a fascinating portrait of the complexity of French NB collaboration under the Nazi occupation. Yet ultimately, the thrust of Bernard Faÿ's activity during the war was not to be found in his position at the Bibliothèque Nationale. There, as Martine Poulain points out, Faÿ never managed "to raise his power to the level that he thought ought to be attained."[75] Although the BN position gave Faÿ enormous cultural capital—enough, indeed, to make him the president of the Conseil du Livre Français in 1941, the chief censoring body of the regime—his actual effect on the world of letters in war-torn France was slim. And after the spring of 1942, in the wake of Petain and the regime's growing impotence, Faÿ's star would quickly diminish.

Several city blocks north of the BN, however, Faÿ occupied a different office and pursued a very different kind of agenda, one that was even more important to him than his work at the library. And it was at this second office, at the Grand Orient of France, where Faÿ was able to exercise his power—and to collaborate with the Nazis—in a much more significant and ultimately √ damaging way.

⊞ ⊞ ⊞

Located only a stone's throw away from the BN, the Grand Orient is still the largest Masonic lodge in France and the oldest in continental Europe. Its mysteriously unmarked building at 16, rue Cadet is long gone; today, in its place, stands a showy, ultramodern structure that visually dominates this small street and proclaims the importance and vitality of its brotherhood. Clearly, the anti-Masonic repression of the Vichy years did little to dispel this vitality: today, the lodge's membership is nearly twice what it was in 1939.[76] Yet in August 1940, when the Grand Orient was officially disbanded and its holdings given over to the French state, the fate of the order looked grim.[77] Its sealed doors and the guards patrolling the gate proclaimed death to any unofficial person who entered the premises. Its members were forced to take multiple oaths renouncing

FIGURE 5.3 Grand Orient de France during German Occupation.

all affiliation with Freemasonry.[78] And a series of laws immediately went into effect that served to obliterate all past activity of the lodges, strip them of their valuables, and—most insidiously—consolidate the names of all living Masons into an official file system, or *fichier*.[79]

Without a doubt, Bernard Faÿ was the most senior French official involved in the takeover of Masonic lodges, including the Grand Orient, and in the transfer of their wealth—archives, sacred objects, and furniture—to the BN. On November 22, 1940, he was officially named "delegate of the French government for the liquidation of Masonic lodges" and was specifically tasked with the "composition of a list of French freemasons, appraisal of books, documents, and furniture of French Masonic lodges, [and] preparation of a Masonic museum."[80] Installed in an office at the rue Cadet, Faÿ turned the Grand Orient into a hub of activity: reading, sorting, and classifying the materials

FIGURE 5.4 Advertisement for Vichy propaganda film *Les Forces Occultes* (1943).

found there and in other lodges throughout France. In many ways, this work resembled scholarship, but its goal was far from academic. Faÿ would describe his anti-Masonic activities during this time as bringing "light" into the realm of Freemasonry in order to destroy it—an ironic twist on the presumed association of Masonry and the Enlightenment.[81] Over the course of the next several years, Faÿ would have his finger in almost every affair that dealt with anti-Masonic repression: seizure of lodges throughout France; publications of names and secret archives; anti-Masonic propaganda in the form of conferences, lectures, and expositions; and, of course, denunciations. And he would use the prestige of his position at the BN and as a Collège de France professor to bring a certain gravitas to this sinister effort.

Based on the finds discovered at the Grand Orient and elsewhere, Faÿ and his team were instrumental in launching several propaganda exercises. There

was a film entitled *Les Forces Occultes*, which announced "the mysteries of freemasonry unveiled for the first time on the screen." And there was one of the first major spectacles of the Vichy government, an anti-Masonic exhibition with the title "Freemasonry Unveiled" ("La Franc-Maçonnerie dévoilée").[82] Housed in the Petit Palais during October and November 1940, the exposition drew a crowd of over a million people who entered free of charge in order to view ritualistic objects, furniture, books, and even the reconstruction of a scene of Masonic initiation, complete with a skeleton. Swastikas and streams of anti-Masonic propaganda were plastered across the entrance and walls: "Frenchmen! Visit this exhibition. Here you find out about your real enemies, the cause of your misfortunes and calamities. The names of the persons who caused the downfall of your country."[83] The catalog for the event, written by Jean Marques-Rivière (who would co-edit the Vichy journal *Les Documents Maçonniques* with Faÿ) was even more blunt: "Freemasonry has to disappear. It has no more place in the country that it has bloodied."[84]

In his memoirs, Faÿ claimed that his involvement in this exposition extended only to the point of protecting the objects on display from being surreptitiously "acquired" by the Nazi authorities helping to organize the event.[85] Whatever the truth of this claim, Faÿ had good reason to be suspicious of the Nazi Sicherheitsdienst (Security Service) involved in the repression of Freemasonry, a group headed at the top by Alfred Rosenberg but in its day-to-day matters by Helmut Knochen, senior commander of the Sicherheitsdienst (SD) and Sicherheitspolizei (SP) in Paris until 1942, and by his thuggish assistant Lieutenant August Moritz, nicknamed "the boxer."[86] More than at the BN, where Faÿ's dealings with German librarians tended to be formal and somewhat distant, his relations with the Nazi SD were close, petty, and distrustful. Divergent motives characterized either side. Convinced of the worldwide danger of Masonic "cults," especially as safe havens for Jews, the Nazis had banned Masonic lodges as early as 1935. Yet the Nazis in Paris shared little of the religious zealotry of Faÿ's crusade and indeed remained suspicious and increasingly critical of what they described as Faÿ's "clericalism" regarding Masonry.[87] Their motives were directed variously toward the wealth hidden in buildings such as the Grand Orient, toward finding and arresting Jews and communists named on the lists of Masonic members, and toward stockpiling the archives for use in future anti-French propaganda. Happy to assist Faÿ in plundering the Grand Orient (only Faÿ and the Nazi SD had a set of keys to the building), the Germans were not averse to requisitioning any items they found.[88]

In the event, Faÿ found himself—as he claimed in his memoirs—attempting to monitor and circumscribe all Nazi activity related to Masonic holdings, even when the outcome was highly unethical. Putting Masonic objects on display in the Exposition Anti-Maçonnique in order to publicly "claim" them as French was one example of this strategy. In another instance, Faÿ came to realize that the German authorities had stolen key archives from the Grand Orient when they occupied the building on June 23, 1940, several weeks before the arrival of the French anti-Masonic team.[89] In September of that year, Faÿ secretly pressured the Vichy government to allow for a crucial swap: in exchange for the return of the seized archives, the Vichy authorities, through the intermediary of Faÿ, would allow the Nazis to infiltrate the unoccupied zone of France and arrest suspected Freemasons. In a note Faÿ tried to destroy at the end of the war, he urged Rene Gillouin, a fellow member of the Rassemblement National who became one of Pétain's chief speechwriters, that it would be "pleasing and important" to accept this deal.[90]

A less destructive but more personally revealing action was Faÿ's effort to shield from the eyes of the occupiers the very items he himself wished to expose to public view. At the end of the war, Liberation officials discovered as many as three hundred volumes belonging to the Grand Orient hoarded in Faÿ's country home at Luceau.[91] Faÿ would later claim that he hid the volumes in order to save them from Nazi seizure; at his trial, he even brought forward evidence from a French Freemason thanking Faÿ for having "done excellent work" in saving Masonic archives from the occupying forces.[92] But it is also interesting to speculate about other motives driving Faÿ—this historian of Freemasonry turned ideologue and inquisitor—to hoard Masonic archives in his private home.

Stepping outside of history for a moment, we could say that Faÿ's fascination with the Masonic archives—what one critic called his pronounced "taste for the archives"—exemplify what the philosopher Jacques Derrida has suggestively called "archive fever."[93] Derrida has coined this phrase to describe the compulsive "sickness" that strikes any archivist, or for that matter any knowledge seeker, in search of some hidden meaning or truth that the archive purportedly lays bare. The archive promises authority and interiority, knowledge and meaning; the Greek term from which "archive" derives refers to power and the ability to command or control.[94] Hence the archive is also political, because it "is associated with legal administration, with the beginning of things (government, police, magistracy), and with the rule system of the law."[95] Meaning or truth adheres to the one who controls the archive, the one who controls its interpretation.[96] Yet, in fact, the meaning in (or of) the archive remains elusive, because "archives are always already stories: they produce speech and especially speech effects, of which history is but one."[97] In the end, Derrida posits, archives ironically both solicit *and* work against stable or positivistic knowledge or historical meaning. They are the source of meaning *and* the origin of a repetition compulsion that continually seeks meaning anew. In the case of Bernard Faÿ, this point is particularly suggestive, as "archive fever" seems to describe at once his will to knowledge about Freemasonry—a will described as an obsessional delirium—and his will to put an end to this knowledge through the exposure and eventual annihilation of Freemasonry.

For Bernard Faÿ, the Masonic archives were indeed the source of historical meaning, the cause of all the decadent twists and turns of French history since 1789. They were also the catalyst for his Vichy crusade, the proof that justified his Vichy activities. Only by appropriating and exposing the "Masonic menace" that lay in the archives could France be set back on its rightful course. Hence these archives needed to be studied, reread, reinterpreted for a naïve public as well as preserved as a warning for posterity; their presence was both *essential* and *generative* to Faÿ's entire cause. At the same time, however, the annihilating power of Faÿ's Vichy crusade—the crusade justified by the archives—would also be the very thing that would destroy those same archives, or render them irrelevant, or remove them permanently, at the hands of the Nazis, from the French historian's grasp. Vichy would represent both the culmination and the end of Faÿ's "historical" study. Hence the uncanniness represented by the Masonic archives Faÿ had carefully hoarded away in his country home: the signifiers of his life's work that he could never fully bring to light, never fully let go of.

As Derrida suggests, archive fever cannot be cured: "The archive always works . . . against itself."[98] And as someone who staked his entire career on archival knowledge, Bernard Faÿ also succumbed to the fever that would work against this knowledge, leading his career down ever more paranoid and delusional paths.

⊞ ⊞ ⊞

However suspicious and distrustful of the Germans, Bernard Faÿ was enough of an insider to the occupying forces to become, as early as 1940, an official Gestapo agent with the "matricule" or serial number VM FR1 (*Vertrauensmann Französisch*, or "Trustworthy Frenchman" #1).[99] For most of the war, despite whatever qualms or hesitations he might have felt, Faÿ was an important liaison with the Germans. In the preparation file for his treason trial in 1946, many documents attest to the duties of VM FR1: the engagement on all bureaucratic levels with the persecution of Freemasons; the stewardship of anti-Masonic propaganda and especially an anti-Masonic journal, *Les Documents Maçonniques*; and the seizure and publication of Masonic archives. According to Helmut Knochen, Faÿ was "for him a useful agent, having brought him much precious information."[100] Accompanied by his former Red Cross assistant William Gueydan de Roussel[101]—also known as Vertrauensmann Französisch #3—Faÿ was given passage during October, November, and December 1940 to traverse the unoccupied zone seizing archives and transporting them into the occupied zone where they could be assessed— under the watchful eyes of the Gestapo.[102] These trips show Faÿ brazenly breaching the line between the two zones of France in order to collaborate with the Nazis. Even a pro-Nazi insider such as Pierre Pucheu, Vichy's minister of the interior, protested against these overtly collaborationist actions of Faÿ, who nevertheless remained free to transfer Masonic files from Vichy to Paris undisturbed by either the French or the German security forces.[103]

Most of the material that Faÿ and his cohorts seized from Masonic lodges would end up in a newly formed department at the BN: the "Centre d'histoire contemporaine."[104] More than 14,000 seized objects would be put on display in a "Masonic museum" at rue Cadet.[105] And the rest of this material would end up as evidence in the pages of *Les Documents Maçonniques*, a monthly journal edited by Faÿ that ran from October 1941 to almost the end of the war, June 1944.[106] Part propaganda, part exposé of Masonic rituals, the journal was an exercise in bilious anti-French Republicanism and was widely distributed throughout France in schools, civic centers, and even in French POW camps in Germany. With the star of David gracing its cover, the journal also emphasized the solidarity between the Jews and the Freemasons. Faÿ, who had first envisioned the journal "if the occupying authorities permit it,"[107] wrote the lead article for every issue except the last two, and his topics were unambiguous: "Freemasonry and the Corruption of Morals," "Freemasonry Against the State," "The Masonic Lie." He would recycle this material in the lectures he gave in Paris and throughout France between 1941 and 1943, most of them under the aegis of *Les Documents Maçonniques* or the German-financed journal *La Gerbe*.

Behind closed doors, meanwhile, Faÿ worked closely with German and Vichy authorities at consolidating anti-Masonic repression into a single organizational entity. In April 1941—some nine months after he first installed himself at the Grand Orient—Faÿ was given funds from Pétain to create a Service des Sociétés Secrètes (SSS): a secret service devoted to the investigation of secret societies.[108] The SSS, which Faÿ directed from May 1941 to April 1942, would mark both the nadir of his paranoid crusade and the pinnacle of his power within the two spheres governing France: the Pétainist Vichy regime and Nazi-occupied Paris.

The SSS was among the largest official French information services established during the occupation.[109] It had many and varying functions over the course of the war: from an initial period of organization, requisition, and classification of archives (1940–1941); to a second period of increased bureaucratization organized around subsections (classification of archives, research and census taking, police, provincial affairs, propaganda) (1941–1942); to a third and final period of relative bureaucratic stability characterized by an enlarged scope of repression, with "secret societies" now defined as not just Freemasons but any group "opposed to the politics of collaboration" (1942–Liberation).[110] Its most notorious effort was the compilation of a *fichier* of the names of Freemasons, a task that had already begun when Faÿ moved to the rue Cadet in 1940. While the names of some members of the Grand Orient had been spirited away to Bordeaux by the Masons themselves at the start of the occupation, by March 1941 Faÿ was able to declare to Petain's chief military adviser that "the files concerning the names of members of the Grand Orient (about 29,000) are finished, and we can attest that on this account we have arrived at a more or less perfect result."[111] During this same period, all Masons were required by law to declare themselves to authorities. "Faux-déclarants" were punished with fines and sometimes jail sentences. In all, more than 170,000 names were included in the *fichier*, which served as both a hidden threat and a public weapon with which to target living and clandestine Masons during the occupation.[112]

The effects of the *fichier* were initially professional. While random lists of Freemasons had been published in the Vichyite press since the beginning of the regime,[113] between August 14 and October 22, 1941, the names of some 14,600 Masonic "dignitaries" were published in the *Journal Officiel*.[114] According to a decree of August 11, 1941, anyone appearing on the list would henceforth be prohibited from partaking in the public professions of law, the civil service, and the military. As a result, some three thousand Freemasons lost their jobs. Significantly, this anti-Masonic legislation would be modeled on the second discriminatory Statut des Juifs of June 2, 1941, which removed Jews from industry and the professions. The August 1941 list of Masons would be followed by periodic updates in the *Journal Officiel*. Faÿ would also be part of a special commission set up to hear requests for exemption from the August 11 decree—a commission that notoriously rejected almost all petitioners. By the end of the war, the price of the *fichier* would be evident. According to information presented at Faÿ's 1946 trial, six thousand Freemasons were directly questioned or placed under surveillance over the course of the war, 989 were deported to concentration camps, and 549 were killed, either by firing squad or through deportation.[115] Other sources rank these figures even higher.[116]

No document exists that directly links Faÿ to these deportations or killings; whatever involvement he had in the system that facilitated these actions was steps removed from their terrible final outcome. Nevertheless, while Faÿ claimed in the deposition before his trial, "I protest that I did not assume any responsibility for the file collection and did not say I had. I obeyed governmental instructions requiring me to maintain the file collection," such deference hardly seems characteristic of Faÿ's attitude toward the so-called Masonic problem.[117] Indeed, documents from the Paris Prefecture of Police suggest that Faÿ was actively involved in both the compilation and the publication of the *fichier*.[118] His guilt by association—through both organizational zeal and nefarious intent—would extend not only to the Freemasons he helped hunt down but also to others linked in the popular imagination with Masonry: communists, secularists, and above all, the Jews.

Of particular interest to our study is, of course, the question of how much Faÿ's guilt goes beyond the repression of Freemasons to the repression of the Jews—a question that has indeed been the subject of some debate in recent assessments of his life.[119] In the view of both the Nazis and the men of Vichy, Jews were perceived widely as Masonic fellow travelers; as foundational adversaries of traditional, Catholic France; and as archenemies of Pétain's National Revolution. So inevitable was the linkage of anti-Semitic and anti-Masonic propaganda in Vichy propaganda that it even produced an ugly neologism: "Judeo-Masonic." At his trial and in his later autobiography, Faÿ claimed that he was not and had never been an anti-Semite: a claim that would appear to be contradicted by certain of his writings, including statements in *Je Suis Partout* and nationalist pamphlets to which he signed his name during the late 1930s.[120] His editorship of *Les Documents Maçonniques*, a journal that often indulged in the specter of "Judeo-Masonry," is also damning. On the other hand, Faÿ had enough Jewish friends before and during the war—including, of course, Gertrude Stein—to lead one suspicious Nazi colleague to comment on Faÿ's "goût pour les milieux enjuivés" ("taste for Jewish milieus").[121] The list of Faÿ's Jewish supporters at his trial reinforces this claim, as do attestations by even the most critical of his colleagues.[122] One Jewish friend, Denise Aimé Azam, was vocal enough in her support of Faÿ to call him her protector during the war; it later turned out that she had converted to Catholicism before the war with Faÿ's help.[123] Stein herself, who had hardly seen Faÿ after 1943, agreed to write a letter in his support for his postwar trial—a fact that Faÿ makes much of even many years later, in his memoirs. Still, it is difficult to ascertain whether it was in fact Stein's Jewishness, rather than her fame, that mattered to Faÿ in this instance.

What remains undeniable is that Faÿ's position as chief Vichyite in charge of anti-Masonic propaganda was indissolubly tied to institutional and legal anti-Semitism in the regime. Even if Faÿ's official anti-Semitism in the pages of *Je Suis Partout* was purely opportunistic, it did not cease with the onset of the Vichy regime in 1940. Nor did this fact go unnoticed by the Nazi occupiers, who early in 1941 put Faÿ's name on a list of "Frenchmen worthy of confidence" to serve on an advisory committee for Jewish affairs.[124] This in turn led Faÿ to be suggested as a possible writer for a never-realized monthly anti-Semitic review, *La Question Juive*.[125] And while Faÿ's defense lawyer stressed his efforts to protect a number of Jewish individuals during the war, including Gertrude Stein, the fact remains that Faÿ made no effort to hide the identities of Freemasons who were also Jews in the *fichier* given to the Nazis. At the same time, many Vichy-era officials were virulent and outspoken anti-Semites; Faÿ was clearly not. His position falls again into a gray zone, one perhaps best summarized in this way: beyond a few chosen exceptions, the Jews and their unhappy fate mattered little to Bernard Faÿ. They were casualties of the "cleaning-up operations" required to purge France of a century and a half of democratic decadence.

▣ ▣ ▣

Despite postwar claims to the contrary, the SSS was a home-grown Vichy operation, funded by the secret coffers of Pétain and supported by one branch of the French police, in conjunction with the Nazis.[126] If the French Revolution, the Dreyfus affair, and the Vichy regime all laid bare the ongoing conflict between the "two Frances," the SSS represented the very epitome of the French against the French. And Bernard Faÿ, in the words of his trial prosecutors, was the driving force behind this activity, "the great animator of the French antimasonic organization, of which he commanded the centers of Paris and of Vichy."[127]

Faÿ in fact took pride in being one of the few political figures between 1940 and 1942 who was capable of managing the tensions that coursed between the Pétainists residing in Vichy, where Faÿ was a frequent visitor, and the more overt Germanophiles residing in Paris, where Faÿ lived and worked alongside the Gestapo. One former colleague tried to capture Faÿ's demeanor at the height of the Vichy regime: "At the same time as he was a man of Vichy, Mr. Bernard Faÿ was a man of the Germans: ostentatiously so. During the first months of the regime he did not say "Abetz told me . . ." but rather "My friend Abetz told me. . . ."[128] Other acquaintances described the "oily" way in which Faÿ insinuated himself as a friend to both French collaborators and the Germans, a supporter of both the National Revolution of Pétain and the cleaning-up operations of the Nazis. In his capacity as figurehead of the SSS, Faÿ spent much of 1941 and the first part of 1942 traveling the country, not only requisitioning archives and other Masonic treasures but also running interference between a large and fractious bureaucracy staffed by Germans and French collaborators of differing degrees of intensity. The vicissitudes of his personal dealings during the first years of the war provide an insider's look into the ardent ambitions, grand plans, and supreme pettiness of the men most involved in the running of Occupied France.[129] While Faÿ shared these traits, he was also charged with the difficult task of keeping them in check in others. With understatement, Faÿ wrote to Stein in early 1942: "My responsibilities are growing and will grow steadily in the coming months. It's not dull."[130]

But like many of those who flourished in the first two years of the Vichy regime, Faÿ would find his moment of glory to be short lived. Never stable— there were four interior ministers and five education ministers during the course of the regime—Vichy was also inseparably joined to the fate and fury of the Nazi occupiers. After the disastrous Nazi invasion of the USSR in June 1941, which precipitated new and more brutal dealings with the French, Pétain's regime became increasingly weakened; after the total Nazi invasion of France in November 1942, it became isolated and ineffectual. This had direct repercussions on the repressive programs of the National Revolution, including those directed at Freemasons. In the event, a figure like Bernard Faÿ— whose influence ultimately rested with Pétain rather than with the Nazis— found himself increasingly pushed aside in the shuffle.

When Pierre Laval was returned to power as Vichy prime minister in April 1942—after having been removed from the government by Pétain in December 1940—the harshest measures against Freemasons were revoked. Laval made sure that a new administrative shakeup of the SSS removed Faÿ from some of the day-to-day workings of the organization, leaving Faÿ licking his wounds.[131] Indeed, almost overnight Faÿ found himself on the defensive, particularly toward those in the newly reorganized administration who favored closer collaboration with the Nazis over Pétainist loyalty and who saw the persecution of Freemasons as "obsessive." Many of these administrators were themselves Freemasons.[132] He had a formidable antagonist less in Laval—toward whom

Faÿ remained respectful to the end—than in the person of Marcel Déat, an *ultra* (archcollaborationist) and former Third Republic leftist who edited an influential pro-Nazi newspaper during the war, *L'Oeuvre*, and whose political fortunes were closely tied to the rise and fall (and rise again) of Pierre Laval. For Déat, Faÿ represented the most reactionary and clerical tendencies of the men around Pétain, the exemplar of the "great clerical enterprise" of Vichy. Faÿ had his own take on Déat, referring to him as an opportunistic collaborator whose affiliations with Freemasons, like those of Laval, were rather too close for comfort. Their animosity, fueled by the Nazi policy of "divide and conquer," became a nasty public affair in the fall of 1941. Faÿ wrote a public letter to Déat rebuking him for "the number of Masons who surround you . . . who have followed the lectures that you have given in lodges." Déat published the letter in the pages of *L'Oeuvre* beside a broadside against Faÿ, describing him as a "Grand Inquisitor" and "a Jesuit disguised as a librarian." Two months later, Déat made the deliberately outrageous charge that Faÿ's chair at the Collège de France had been funded by American Freemasons.[133] Their exchange reached a low point—shocking even to the Nazis—when Déat suggested that Faÿ retreat "to the dust of his archives with his letter pinned to his ass, awaiting the imprint of my foot."[134] For Déat, this exchange would spell the end of Faÿ's power; in his memoirs, he claims that his public denunciations gave Faÿ "a thrashing from which he never recovered."[135] Faÿ refused to award Déat that credit, but his own memoirs recount the Déat affair as significant in the sidelining of his career. Faÿ's memoirs also portray him as the victim of one who firmly refused to recognize the work he had done to "save" France from "its huge troubles."[136]

Yet however much Faÿ's influence as a key player in the regime may have faded by the summer of 1942, it did not disappear. While Philippe Pétain became increasingly marginal to both the Germans and the Paris collaborationists around Laval, especially after the Nazis occupied the whole of France in November 1942, he still had enough popular support to shape the political landscape of his embattled country and to strategize around his prime minister. As one of Pétain's few remaining trusted friends, Bernard Faÿ became an essential ally in this strategic effort. A secret file from the Paris Prefecture de la Police on Faÿ's activities during the war details how after 1943 "he alone has become the true guardian of the thought of the Maréchal. . . . Every week he goes to Vichy, leaving the impression of giving life to the Maréchal with each of his visits."[137] Faÿ gave his own twist on this association in a September 1941 letter to Stein: "I spend a week every month in Vichy to call on the Marshal and advise him how to run his business. He is very nice, and says 'yes, yes'— and I go home feeling great. We do it every month."[138]

The real test of Faÿ's influence—and indeed the most overt example of his collaboration—came in September of 1943, long after Pétain's power had seemingly been ceded to Laval. In a last-ditch effort to topple his political adversary, and in the face of a rapidly weakening Germany, Pétain announced that he would be using the power vested in him by the National Assembly in July 1940 to create a new constitution, one whose effect would neutralize Laval's power. Faÿ's role in this plot was significant. Alongside Yves Bouthillier (Pétain's minister of finance) and Gabriel Auphan (minister of the navy), Faÿ declared himself "ready to constitute" a new government for Pétain.[139] It was Faÿ who then approached a faction within the German camp to try to sidestep Laval and gain support for Pétain's constitutional upheaval. As Pétain's official envoy, Faÿ spent the months of September and October 1943 meeting with Heinrich Himmler and his SS cohort to discuss the change in political orientation in France—one, perhaps, that might also involve a pact with the Americans.[140] Despite Himmler's doubts over the ninety-year-old Pétain's abilities to broker a deal, Faÿ successfully laid the groundwork for top-secret negotiations between Pétain and the Nazis.

Yet all would ultimately be lost when Laval caught wind of the plot. With Pétain's capitulation to Laval and his German allies in December 1943, Faÿ's influence ceased to count for anything. At this point, during the endgame of the war, Faÿ would find the tables turned on him. No longer profiting from his closeness to the maréchal, Faÿ would find himself suddenly the object of universal suspicion and dislike. In March of 1944, Laval personally intervened to try to have Faÿ fired from the BN.[141] He would be placed under surveillance not only by Germans and the Americans from afar but by a group installed in the apartment across the street from his home: Paris Freemasons with plans for future retaliation.[142] Most importantly, his intellectual and "spiritual" commitments to a renovated France and to a federal Europe dissolved into the ether. "The Great Imprudence," he wrote retrospectively in 1946, "was to remain in France from 1940 to 1944, to dream of its regeneration, to consecrate all my forces to it, to risk my life for it, and to believe in it."[143]

By the time Liberation officials came to arrest him on August 19, 1944, there was no doubt the game was up: Faÿ was in the process of burning documents at his desk.[144] He was suspended from his duties at the BN a day later. Writing secretly to his brother Jacques from the detention center at Drancy, Faÿ tried to arrange for the destruction of other documents in his country home at Luceau that, he warned, would "implicate many people." His letter was apprehended and would become evidence of his duplicity at his trial two years later, at the end of 1946.[145] One by one, the rewards of Faÿ's distinguished prewar career would be revoked. First, his honorary lifetime membership in the Faculty of Letters at the University of Clermont-Ferrand, where he had held his first academic position. Then, his chair at the Collège de France.[146] His name, which had supported a considerable reputation throughout the interwar period and the first years of the Vichy regime, would appear on the infamous 1944 *liste noire* (blacklist) of collaborationist writers by the Conseil National des Écrivains.[147] By the time of his trial, where he would be found guilty of "collaboration with the enemy," Bernard Faÿ would be known chiefly and widely as the Frenchman who had helped the Germans persecute Freemasons. All the erudition, commitment, and judgment—and all the fear, disdain, resentment, and ultimate ambition that characterized Faÿ's trajectory to the heights of Vichy power—would boil down to a single assessment: collaborator.

❑ ❑ ❑

At the Liberation, France would finally confront its "culture of defeat" by scapegoating the scapegoaters. In the press and among much public opinion, the thirst for justice was acute, the need for retribution keen. In the absence of a unified wartime experience, French people in the immediate aftermath of the war clung to what Henry Rousso has called "the Resistencialist myth": "that all the French had stood united in the (Gaullist) Resistance and had fought together against the foreign enemy, who had only a handful of collaborators."[148] In hindsight, the installation of the Vichy regime was deemed the aberration of a few power-hungry individuals bent on reversing the great ideals of Republican France, its legitimacy a mere sham. The embarrassing fact of widespread support for Pétain in 1940 was quickly repressed and as quickly displaced onto the real enemies, the overt collaborators. Out of this moment was born the idea of a "purge," in which the prosecution of traitors would give rise to a new and renovated national feeling. Special courts of justice, including a High Court of Justice for prominent collaborators, became the official organs through which this purge was to be enacted; juries composed of former members of the Resistance and victims of Vichy presided.[149] And enacted the purge was: between 1944 and 1949, more than three hundred thousand cases of collaboration were investigated, with 6,783 individuals ultimately sentenced to death. In the face of successive amnesties, that number was reduced to around 1,600, yet it was still significantly greater than the two to three hundred Nazis who were tried and executed in the German court system immediately after the war.

All things considered, the fifty-three-year-old Bernard Faÿ was lucky. Interned at Drancy for over a year, Faÿ almost escaped prosecution due to the disorganization of the commission in charge of Vichy internments.[150] On September 3, 1945, he was moved to Fresnes prison, outside of Paris, where he joined such notorious collaborators as Robert Brasillach, Fernand de Brinon, and Jacques Benoist-Méchin. In the journal he kept during his fifteen-month stay at Fresnes awaiting trial, Faÿ remained certain that he would be put to death: "we await the trial, and death," he writes on August 19, 1946. "My lawyer has hardly hidden it from me."[151] Remarking that his "juge d'instruction"—the French magistrate in charge of assembling the facts of the case—was an "Israelite and a Freemason," Faÿ assumed that the negative outcome of his trial was a fait accompli.[152] Yet by November 30, the opening day of his trial, the mood in France had shifted. The emotion that led to the early executions of such notorious collaborators as Brasillach (February 1945), Pierre Laval, and Joseph Darnand (both October 1945) had lessened a year or so later. Faÿ's was hardly a show trial, an exercise in vengeance: great care was taken in handling the facts of the case by both the state prosecutor and Faÿ's able lawyer, Georges Chrestiel. However damning these facts, the outcome of the trial was by no means inevitable. While Faÿ's collaboration with the enemy was as serious and involved as that of his friend Brasillach—arguably more so, if we consider the effects of the *fichier* that Faÿ willingly compiled—his punishment was hardly equivalent. After two weeks of testimony, on December 6, 1946, Bernard Faÿ was sentenced to hard labor for life by the Court of Justice of the Seine, one of eight other Vichy officials to receive this sentence. This sentence would be commuted two years later to twenty years of forced labor. Alongside the five other chief French administrators of the SSS, Faÿ was also charged with "dégradation nationale"— the loss of the key rights of citizenship, such as voting, holding public office, and practicing certain professions. This was a fate especially galling for one of Faÿ's background and ambition.[153] Nonetheless, it was not a death sentence.

Faÿ's life was spared, but almost against his own wishes. Aloof and even disdainful at his own trial, Faÿ spent his time as a defendant in court reading and dozing. Sporting "an ironic and slightly vain smile at the corner of his lips" and using an arch vocabulary when called upon to speak, Faÿ won over few spectators in the room. When accused of having ties to General Karl Oberg, Himmler's representative and the so-called Butcher of Paris, Faÿ merely shrugged his shoulders.[154] Most importantly, he remained resolutely unrepentant about any of his Vichyite activities—as he would for the rest of his life. In fact, perhaps the most striking aspect of his trial was the unwillingness of prosecutors to argue with Faÿ about the political opinions he still freely expressed, as when he stated to the court that "for many numbers of years, I have considered

Masonry as a dangerous institution, and on this point for some twenty years I have changed neither opinion nor language. The presence of the Germans had no effect on my ideas."[155]

By 1946, such were the bitter, proud, and resigned words of a man confronted with the failure of his career and the darkened horizon of his future. They contrast sharply with the account of Faÿ just five years earlier, at the height of his career, flushed with power and with the pleasure of his own oratory. Speaking to a standing-room audience only, lecturing on "Freemasonry Against French Intelligence," Faÿ was described in glowing terms by an anonymous member of the audience: "He expresses himself in a familiar tone of voice, lightly ironic and superior with a constant tendency toward historical digressions on the margin of his subject, but careful to develop a literary quality and a witty turn of phrase appreciated by his worldly audience."[156] History, literature, and wit were Faÿ's stock in trade; discoursing on ideas was his métier. What the German occupation of France in 1940 meant for Faÿ was that at last his *ideas* about the "dangerous institution" of Freemasonry could be put into *practice*. And to this end he remained faithful for as long as he had any power to wield.

FIGURE 5.5 Bernard Faÿ giving an anti-Masonic lecture at the Salle Wagram in Paris (1941).

Among the members of this "worldly audience" in one of Faÿ's lectures in the fall of 1941 was Gertrude Stein, and she too remarked on Faÿ's rhetorical skill as she had so many years before in the early 1930s: "We enjoyed your lecture, it works up awfully well, the *mis en scene* [*sic*] that you create is completely convincing," she writes, with an enthusiasm reminiscent of their earlier exchanges.[157] Yet however "convinced" Stein was by Faÿ's comments on Freemasonry in 1941, she was soon enough to change her mind. The last time Stein saw Faÿ alive was in the autumn of 1943, when he spent two nights in Culoz; a year later he was already in prison. Stein agreed to write a testimony in support of him in March 1946 for his upcoming trial, but the document is lukewarm at best: it acknowledges Faÿ's work to save Stein's art collection and his "patriotism" but ultimately falls far short of an enthusiastic defense.[158] Her only other postwar remarks on the matter of her relationship with Faÿ are revealing for the distance they create between the two friends. In a letter she wrote after the war to their mutual acquaintance Francis Rose, Stein claims that Faÿ "certainly did certain things he should not have done, but that he ever denounced anybody, no, that I do not believe, in fact I know he did not, he was a monarchist he was a church man, but he was a passionate patriot always, about that there is no doubt, really not."[159]

Stein is right about one thing here: Faÿ was "a monarchist . . . a church man . . . [and] a passionate patriot," and it was precisely this combination of qualities that lay behind his belief in "France for the French," in a nation purged of democrats, communists, and Freemasons. But Stein is also wrong: Faÿ did in fact denounce many French people during the war, including Masons, communists, academicians at the Sorbonne, and eleven of his junior colleagues at the Bibliothèque Nationale.[160] That Stein is wrong about this despite claiming certain "knowledge" of Faÿ's innocence accords with her other, more peremptory statement: that Faÿ "certainly did certain things he should not have done"—that is, collaborating with the Nazis. In her letter to Rose, Stein lays claim to an authority about Faÿ's actions that is not only disingenuous but ultimately seems designed to emphasize her own moral superiority. In this final accounting, indeed, Stein emerges as the unsuspecting yet generous witness while Faÿ appears as the benighted acolyte who went sadly astray.

Early in her career, in a short story called "The Good Anna," Stein wrote a sentence that remains revealing to this day: "In friendship, power always has its downward curve."[161] No words could better describe the shifting dynamic between Stein and Faÿ over the course of their twenty-five-year friendship. From an initial period that saw Faÿ eager to win Stein's favor and ascend into her inner circle of disciples, to an equalization of their friendship based on mutual attraction and ambition, to a strange new negotiation steeped in the dilemmas and dangers of Vichy, the arc of their relationship would always remain inextricable from a calculus of power. After the Liberation, this calculus would shift yet again: Bernard Faÿ was now the social pariah awaiting whatever meager defense Stein could offer him, while Stein for the first time in almost ten years became a newfound celebrity both in France and abroad.

Indeed, the "downward curve" of Faÿ's power in his friendship with Stein would seem to be definitive: Stein was to die in July 1946, five months before Faÿ was tried and found guilty for collaboration with the Nazis. Yet after their long collaboration, and after the moment of Vichy had faded, it was Bernard Faÿ who would in fact have the last word in his relationship with Gertrude Stein.

EPILOGUE

VICHY-SUR-LÉMAN

T HE ROAD to Bernard Faÿ's house in Luceau winds straight through the middle of the Loire valley in west-central France—a place of flat, lush farmland and large skies, of meandering vineyards and provincial towns. Known for its wines, its chateaux, and its cathedrals, the Loire is a region steeped in history. France's most famous cathedral, Chartres, is just to the north, hauntingly beautiful as it rises out of the flat misty plains. Nearby are the famous chateaux of Blois, Chambord, Chenonceau, Chinon—fairy-tale castles of the French Middle Ages and Renaissance, visible reminders of the glory of the French aristocracy. Joan of Arc led the defeat of the English at the Loire town of Orleans in 1429; some five hundred years later, in 1940, Philippe Pétain shook the hand of Adolf Hitler in a notorious collaboration ceremony at the eastern Loire town of Montoire.

Luceau, a tiny hamlet outside the provincial center of Chateau-du-Loir, in the département of the Sarthe, was the spot Faÿ chose when he went searching for a country house in the late 1930s. With his deep sense of connectedness to prerevolutionary France, Faÿ was naturally drawn to the Loire valley. In Luceau he found his dream house—an elegant stone priory connected to a small twelfth-century church, which he purchased for 35,000 French francs on September 18, 1939.[1] To the end of his life, Faÿ found solace and peace in this place. It was to Luceau that he retired during the war when the pressures of Vichy became too much to handle. And it was along the tree-lined road to Luceau that Gertrude Stein traveled for a summer vacation in 1946 at the invitation of Faÿ, who was still sitting in the prison at Fresnes, awaiting his trial for collaboration with the Nazis.

Stein only stayed at Luceau for a few days. Suddenly crippled with the abdominal pain that had been bothering her for months, she was rushed to the American Hospital in the Paris suburb of Neuilly, where she succumbed on July 27, 1946, at 7 p.m. to uterine cancer.[2] Her death at the age of seventy-two came as a shock to the many friends, acquaintances, and admirers who had never perceived Stein as anything but enormously vital. As an American friend wrote to Alice Toklas: "There seemed to be a permanence in Gertrude that belongs to no one else I have ever known."[3] For her own part, Toklas, bereft, referred to the moment Stein died as the beginning of "the empty years," the twenty-one years she would live on alone without Gertrude.[4] "Now she is gone and there can never be any happiness again," she wrote.[5]

Shocked by the loss, Bernard Faÿ too wondered how he would soldier on. "I lost more and better than a friend," he mused. "I lost a woman who helped me to love life."[6] Writing to Toklas, he returned to what had always seemed so strong in Stein, her joie de vivre:

> She has been one of the few authentic experiences of my life—there are so few real human men and women—so few people really alive amongst the living ones, and so few of them are continuously alive as Gertrude was. Everything was alive in her, her soul, her mind, her heart, her senses. And that life that was in her was at the same time so spontaneous and so voluntary. It is a most shocking thing to think of her as deprived of life.[7]

Years later, Faÿ remembered feeling glad that Stein had spent the end of her life at Luceau, where "all the objects spoke to her of me, and the walls, decorated with her books, recalled for her our friendship." And he remembered as well the central lesson she had taught him: "to love the rich tissue of existence" without feeling "disgust" and "anger."[8] "The most useful knowledge is what Gertrude taught me with her easy ways, her broadmindedness, and her gay understanding of people," he wrote Toklas in 1947.[9] Struggling within his postwar "prisons"—literal and psychological, moral and spiritual—Faÿ attributed any moments of serenity to this remembered influence of Gertrude Stein.

For the next five years, Faÿ would indeed know nothing but life in prison. After his trial and sentencing in December 1946, suffering from cardiac trouble, he was sent to the prison hospital on the Île de Ré, an island off the west coast of France. He remained there from January 1947 to August 1950, when he was transferred to Fontevrault, a prison that, with an average of two deaths per week, was widely considered one of the harshest in France. At Fontevrault, his health seems to have rapidly deteriorated, causing him to be transferred to the nearby hospital at Angers. It was there where Faÿ would plan, and successfully carry out, his escape to Switzerland.[10]

Toklas, supported "for life" by Stein's will, spent several relatively secure years in Paris after the war, first as the grieving widow and then as an emerging writer in her own right ("As for Alice, she is now running the whole show and seems to be thriving. Talks just as though she were the original Stein," wrote Sylvia Beach to Richard Wright in 1947).[11] Yet Toklas was eventually robbed of most of her livelihood by legal maneuvers among Stein's relatives. The story of how Stein's increasingly valuable art collection was literally spirited away from her apartment while Toklas was taking a health cure in Italy is the stuff of legend. Her subsequent destitution was, according to all who saw her, heart-breaking. Nevertheless, in part thanks to Bernard Faÿ, Toklas too would even-tually be "saved" by a late-life conversion to Christianity.

Only Gertrude Stein would triumph after the war, her death arriving at a moment of renewed celebrity and long before the depredations of old age could diminish her capabilities. Rediscovered at the Liberation by American GIs and journalists, Stein immediately became a symbol of survival and for-titude for Americans at home and abroad. With her broad smile, homespun aura, and patriotic fervor, Stein embodied the image of healthy, uncomplicated American values triumphing over European decay and despair. Returning to Paris with Toklas in December 1944, Stein found herself again hosting a regu-lar salon, this time made up of a mix of old acquaintances and freshly minted American GIs. Back in the United States, Stein enjoyed a resurgence of the media attention she had experienced ten years earlier. The publication of *Wars I Have Seen* in 1945 put Stein on the covers of *Publishers Weekly* and the *Satur-day Review of Literature*. But her biggest coup was a multipage *Life* magazine spread on August 6, 1945, featuring photos of Stein and GIs touring postwar Germany, accompanied by a text written by Stein, "Off We All Went to See Germany."[12] In a telling example of their divergent fates, this celebratory article appeared almost three years to the day after Bernard Faÿ had been named in *Life* on a "Black List" of French collaborationist writers.

Reading this article today—knowing what we do about Stein and the Vichy regime—may well cause some discomfort. The jaunty humor and blithe tone of Stein's text is jarring in relation to the sober subject at hand. "One would suppose that every ruined town would look like any other ruined town but

FIGURE 6.1 Gertrude Stein and American GIs at Berchtesgaden.

it does not," Stein quips in this piece, as though comparing types of break-fast cereal. "Roofs are in a way the most important thing in a house . . . and here was a whole spread out city without a roof," she wonders with faux-naïve amazement about the bombed-out city of Cologne. A photo of Stein among a group of soldiers performing the Hitler salute at his bunker in Berchtesgaden seems at once sophomoric and chilling, given Stein's attraction to authoritari-anism in the 1930s and 1940s. In one of the few serious passages of the text, Stein criticizes the American soldiers for believing in the duplicitous "flattery" of Germans, yet her entire piece in turn both flatters and belittles her Ameri-can cohorts, who are at once endearing young men and "big babies." Through-out this article, indeed, Stein seems to want both to celebrate and to mock the American liberation, preventing us from grasping the supposedly "critical, satirical edge" that one critic has noticed in Stein's visual and written position in this piece.[13]

No doubt some contemporaries were also made uncomfortable by the *Life* article, with its disconnect between tone and subject, affect and focus. In fact, there were a few people, such as Bennett Cerf and Saxe Commins at Random

House, who acknowledged outright that they found Stein's postwar stance disturbing. Commins referred to her political views in *Wars* as "at best reactionary and at worst reprehensible."[14] Cerf, who had received the proposal for Stein's introduction to the speeches of Pétain, was already well aware of what he called her "disgusting" views—an opinion he freely shared with her.[15] Yet the *Life* article was clearly meant to capitalize on Stein's previous celebrity and on the quirky character she had personified so successfully in *The Autobiography of Alice B. Toklas* and her American lecture tour of 1934–1935, now somewhat disconcertingly transplanted into the apocalyptic wasteland of postwar Germany. In other postwar media events, Stein began to be referred to as "Gerty," a long-lost friend and patriotic mother-figure for GIs abroad. She seemed only too happy to play this role in her postwar appearances and writing, even collaborating with Virgil Thomson on a highly autobiographical new opera, "The Mother of Us All," which portrays the suffragette Susan B. Anthony orienting her nation within a progressive narrative of freedom and empowerment.[16]

Two of the several texts Stein wrote at the end of her life suggest the complexity of her postwar stance. In the narrative play *Brewsie and Willie*, Stein uses her characters as a platform to put forward an uneasy mix of patriotism and reactionary criticism. Brewsie and Willie are both American GIs located within an indeterminate postwar landscape of possibility and despair. Their dialogue centers on the future of America, and the scenarios put forth by Brewsie in particular are far from reassuring. While both Brewsie and Willie are thoughtful and curious figures—the best of American men, Stein would say—both are also dire national prophets. Their comments about the double standards facing black American soldiers are particularly prescient and reveal Stein's newfound attention to American racism. Yet, in other ways, the book shows Stein rehearsing familiar political views about the United States, including the line from the 1930s that Left politics will only rob America of its wealth and essential independent spirit. Stein has Brewsie utter this line, and it is clear that she shares his views when, in the book's epilogue, she directly addresses her audience:

> To Americans . . . We are there where we have to fight a spiritual pioneer fight or we will go poor as England and other industrial countries have gone poor, and dont [*sic*] think that communism or socialism will save you, you just have to find a new way, you have to find out how you can go ahead without running away with yourselves, you have to learn to produce without exhausting your country's wealth, you have to learn to be individual and not just mass

job workers, you have to get courage enough to know what you feel and not just all be yes or no men.[17]

The specter of a mass of overworked yes-men enslaved to the ideology of production seems as potent in this address to the reader from 1945 as it did in Stein's political comments from the 1930s. Even at this late date, Gertrude Stein continued to see "communism" or "socialism"—identified always in her mind, as her 1935 articles on money make clear, with the "organization" of Franklin D. Roosevelt—as the greatest threat to the American spirit.

Brewsie and Willie is a strange and unprocessed mix of reaction and enlightenment, patriotism and critique. Yet in a less well-known play written immediately after, and about, the war—*In Savoy; or, Yes Is for a Very Young Man*—we see another side of the postwar Gertrude Stein emerge. Unlike *Wars I Have Seen* or "The Mother of Us All," Stein in this late play avoids featuring herself in a narrative of uplift and triumph. Unlike *Brewsie and Willie*, Stein doesn't use the text as a platform to announce her fears about American decline. Rather, *Yes Is for a Very Young Man* stands as a unique text in Stein's oeuvre. Stein uses the characters within this play to foreground multiple and often contradictory perspectives, putting on display the "gray zone" of life during wartime. There is Denise, the Pétainiste and fervent anticommunist who believes in taking sides and laments the demise of the "dear marshal."[18] There is Ferdinand, the young Resistance fighter and "silly boy" who stands for love and "disobedience." And finally there is the Constance, the intelligent but complacent American who watches in dismay as her lover Ferdinand takes his leave from her to join the "organization" of the Resistance. All of these figures are tied together in a morally ambiguous landscape where executions, bloody revenge, and the rending apart of families characterize everyday life. Learning how to say "yes" to this life despite its despair is the only moral of this story, one that perhaps speaks to Stein's own mature awareness of the difficulty *and* inevitability of moral judgment during wartime.

On another level, *Yes Is for a Very Young Man* questions the idea of war as meaningful, something from which we can take away a lesson to be applied in other contexts. It makes a strong case for the importance of sheer survival in the midst of chaos. And this may be the most useful knowledge Gertrude Stein offers us out of her experience with World War II and its aftermath. It is a lesson to heed when we find ourselves wanting to be assured that Stein emerged from the war with her prewar views and leanings clearly changed. Yet Stein's postwar stance offers us no such assurance. In fact, it brings us little closure on the problem of how to understand the relationship between her experimental aesthetics and her reactionary politics. Like her fellow modernists

drawn before the war to the political Right—Ezra Pound or T. S. Eliot, Louis-
Ferdinand Céline or William Butler Yeats, to name just a few—Stein was taken
by the promises of political authoritarianism, always complexly tied to her
sense of her own genius and of the "free creative spirit . . . without limits" that
coursed through her aesthetic. Yet while the war turned Pound and Céline into
hardcore fascists, while Eliot retreated into the largely religious meditations
of *Four Quartets* (1943), and while Yeats was spared the whole ordeal, Stein's
experience during the war seems not to have changed her mind about much.
Neither rabid nor resigned, Stein survived World War II—and emerged from it
with her views on America, on Pétain, and on the overriding value of tradition,
peace, and everyday life more or less intact.

In *Yes Is for a Very Young Man* Stein demonstrates why this might be so.
Neither hastily patriotic nor bitterly vengeful, *Yes* presents a vision of war as
"pretty bad" and then "over": an event outside the range of discussion and
argument. No decision that is made during this period is a good one; no argument is justifiable. "Peace" is achieved not through well-meaning compromise
or pacifist commitments but through an arbitrary end to senseless violence.
But its achievement is reason enough for continuing on. In the end, *Yes* suggests, there is simply the fact of survival and the affirmation of vitality that this
fact brings with it: "Yes."

The stark image of Stein stricken by the cancer that would kill her while visiting Faÿ's empty country house in 1946 seems somehow representative of the
endgame of their relationship. With Stein's death, this twenty-year relationship
came to its natural end, yet in fact the end had been foreshadowed for several
years. Shared interests had brought Stein and Faÿ together—the entwined his-
tories of America and France, modernist writing and art, reactionary politics,
homosexuality, and a simple love of talk—and for many years the two had
enjoyed one of the closest collaborations of their lives. Yet the separate and
mutual collaboration of each with Philippe Pétain's Vichy regime would end
up weakening this bond, and it would never again be the same as it was before
the war. One of the points of this book has been to show how deeply fascist
and profascist politics divided and severed human beings from one another,
creating invidious, dehumanizing racial, national, and religious distinctions
that would eventually result in the "death world" of World War II. The story of
Stein and Faÿ's friendship is a compelling personal story, but it also captures in
microcosm the shape of this era.

Still, if there is any reckoning to be made about the friendship between Gertrude Stein and Bernard Faÿ, we might point to the fact that after Stein's death Faÿ seemed to retreat into an ever more isolated, dogmatic, and reactionary worldview. This is apparent during the years Faÿ spent in exile in Switzerland and for the rest of his life after his official pardon in 1959. As Antoine Compagnon has written perceptively:

> This man, whose intellectual and worldly career had been extraordinarily successful between the two world wars—his existence very full despite his infirmity—had lived at an intense pace between 1919 and 1940 . . . ; he had [now] become a recluse after seven years of prison, a discreet decade in Catholic Switzerland, and a bitter retirement in his house in the Sarthe region, with no more Gertrude Stein to distract him from his traditionalism and to enlighten his conservatism.[19]

The implication that Stein, while she was alive, saved Faÿ from extremism in his thinking and writing brings a new twist to their relationship. It suggests that however much their political views ran parallel during the interwar period, their collaboration was also kept in check by countervailing tendencies, especially on the part of Stein, toward democratic, liberal, and "enlightened" ways of thinking. At the very least, her sheer presence—Jewish, homosexual, and American, identity markers with increasing visibility from the start of the war on—would have been a reminder to Faÿ of earlier affinities and attractions that had not yet been rejected or incorporated into an extremist worldview. And while their shared dialogue during the interwar period propelled both into the troubled midst of the Vichy moment, only Stein seemed capable of reassessing after the war—however tentatively—her wartime actions and views. For Faÿ, it is clear, there was no going back.

After the war, and after Stein's death, Faÿ's stance toward the world around him became one of ever greater animosity. Most importantly, his *aesthetic* connection to the world of art and letters—embodied in his relationship with Stein—was increasingly given over to a *religious* worldview dominated by clear divisions between saints and sinners, virtue and vice, redemption and corruption. This is an important point that goes to the heart of Stein and Faÿ's collaboration. As this book has attempted to show, Stein and Faÿ were drawn to each other through a shared political and historical vision, one steeped in an eighteenth-century ethos at odds with the industrialized, technocratic era of modernity. Both also saw themselves as future-oriented in rejecting the "communist" orientation of France and American and in anticipating the radical political vision of Philippe Pétain's National Revolution. Their attraction to each other revolved around this playful vacillation between conservatism and revolution. In their sense of a shared mission the two friends allowed each other to have it both ways. But Stein and Faÿ also had an aesthetic bond that coursed through and beyond politics. For Faÿ in particular, there was the sheer pleasure—the "joy"— that Stein's extraordinary linguistic experimentation offered him, her devoted reader and translator during the 1920s and 30s. Her writing was for him not just political but also intellectual, emotional, erotic, and instinctually vital. For such an ambitiously political individual, Faÿ's response to Stein's writing as brilliant, profound, and joyous seems, in hindsight, at once anomalous and fascinating—a sign of aesthetic openness that was lacking in other facets of his life.

In an important way, then, Stein's death paralleled the death, for Faÿ, of this aesthetic openness. From the Vichy regime onward, Faÿ became increasingly rigid, increasingly self-righteous. Indeed, as his trial for collaboration made evident, Faÿ seems never to have felt any remorse for his Vichy-era activities. Even in his private prison diary, with its discourse of expiation, Faÿ consistently justified his actions by arguing that his single goal was to save France from the decadent elements in its midst as well as from rampaging occupiers. The latter seemed always to justify the former; protecting France also meant cleaning it up. Resolutely unrepentant, a Pétainst to the end, Faÿ after the war found himself allied with a new and ever more rigid group of interlocutors. Many of these were ex-Vichy ideologues who looked to the rise of Pétain's movement—rather than its downfall—as evidence that a new form of political organization *could* take root in France. Some of these figures had been colleagues of Faÿ in the prewar European federalist movement, a movement that after the war ceded its ground to the more progressive movement to create an economic Council of Europe. The postwar environment forced these men to take their politics underground, but it seems not to have dissuaded them from adhering to their positions.[20] And even from their postwar prisons, the prewar Right found a ready network of international interlocutors and publishing ventures that would help them broadcast their views. One of these interlocutors was a man with whom Faÿ had had a close correspondence in the late 1930s, a man who shared with Faÿ both a deep sense of history and a Catholic and authoritarian worldview: Gonzague de Reynold, the eminent professor of French literature at the University of Fribourg, Switzerland.

One of the most renowned and eloquent proponents of Swiss nationalism during the interwar period, de Reynold advocated in the 1930s a "third way" between liberalism and communism centered on aristocratic and Catholic values. With his noble particule and eighteenth-century dress, de Reynold seemed to live a life where "time had stood still," and his values were inherently attractive to Bernard Faÿ.[21] As with Faÿ, de Reynold's opposition to the French Revolution and the Catholic traditionalism he had inherited from his family would define him; alongside Faÿ, de Reynold would take part in such activities as an annual commemoration of soldiers killed protecting the French monarchy in 1792.[22] And again like Faÿ, de Reynold's ultratraditionalism would inevitably be co-opted by the Nazis, especially by intellectuals and ideologues who had no trouble manipulating the slippage between Catholic authoritarianism and fascist totalitarianism. Although de Reynold had been intrigued by the idea of a Catholic and Latin "federation" of dictatorships as an alternative to modern liberalism, this idea also would play right into the decidedly secular plans of the Nazis. One Nazi intellectual, the German jurist Hans Keller, was likely the figure who introduced Faÿ and de Reynold. It was Keller who had himself first published in Switzerland a work entitled *The Third Europe*, devoted to the idea of an "ideal" national socialism of independent nations connected through "supranational peace." Predictably, Keller argued for the sanctity of national "identity" and "cultural values" under the protection of a German-dominated Europe. Keller's organization, the Academy of the Rights of Nations, had solicited the views of both Faÿ and de Reynold, even bringing Faÿ to Berlin in March 1937 to give a speech on the subject of the looming threat of communism in the United States.[23] Two years later, Faÿ and de Reynold would appear together in a book edited by Keller, *Der Kampf um die Völkerordnung* (The Battle for a People's Order) as academy representatives in their respective countries.[24] They had already worked together in 1938 to nominate Charles Maurras for the Nobel Peace Prize, and by the start of the war they had a voluminous shared correspondence.[25]

Gonzague de Reynold appears to be the friend who moved into the vacuum created in Faÿ's life by the loss of Stein. He would prove to be essential to Faÿ's postwar activities, providing a sounding board for his ideas and the intellectual and institutional cover to keep his enemies at bay, at least for a time. But Faÿ's actual route to exile in Switzerland, starting with his dramatic escape from prison, would be made possible by the combined efforts of a small circle of friends and fellow postwar reactionaries. And once in Switzerland, Faÿ would feel right at home in the atmosphere of familiar faces in the cities clustered around Lac Léman (Lake Geneva), a place so full of ex-collaborators that after the war it earned the unhappy title of "Vichy-sur-Léman."

Fay, Nazi Collaborator, Escapes French Custody

Bernard Fay
The New York Times

Special to THE NEW YORK TIMES.

PARIS, Oct. 2—Bernard Fay, former librarian of the French Bibliotheque Nationale and chief investigator of Freemasonry for the Vichy Government, today escaped from a hospital in Angers.

M. Fay, who before the war was well known as a historian, was sentenced to life at hard labor by a court of justice in 1944 as a collaborator with the Nazis. He had been placed in a hospital a few months ago where he was recovering from a serious illness.

It was during a religious mass in the hospital chapel that M. Fay escaped. These services being public, certain persons from the outside can attend them and it is thought that M. Fay escaped in an automobile of one of those who had been admitted to hear the services.

Prior to the war M. Fay was well known in the United States for historical and other writings and in France he had the reputation of being one of the chief authorities on the United States.

FIGURE 6.2 *New York Times* announcement of Faÿ's escape from prison (1951).

▣ ▣ ▣

In his memoirs, Faÿ writes that sometime during the course of 1951, during his stay at the Fontevrault prison, his health took a sudden turn for the worse. He was rushed to the municipal hospital in the nearby town of Angers. "Death was coming along slowly, and then more rapidly," he writes. "When I felt it approaching, I decided to escape."[26] However the dying Faÿ mustered the strength to flee across France for Switzerland, he was apparently aided in his efforts by the financial support of Alice Toklas.[27] Her help served him well. Crossing the border in disguise on the morning of October 1, 1951, Faÿ found a brand new life awaiting him in exile. Not only would he survive his escape, but he would live on for almost three more decades, to the ripe old age of eighty-five. He would date each passing year after this event in terms of his Christ-like resurrection ("Resurrectionae meae Anno I, II, III," etc.).

The story of Faÿ's escape from prison is a dramatic one. According to his own account in his memoirs, as well as to the official police report from Angers, events began unfolding on September 29, 1951. During that day, an unusual young woman was spotted in an alleyway underneath Faÿ's hospital window, dressed in an alpine-style pointed hat and blue cape with the insignia of the Red Cross. The following day, a Sunday, the same woman appeared at the hospital Mass, which Faÿ too attended, under the watch of his guard Francis Meignan. Leaving Mass together, Faÿ "accidentally" jostled the young woman—earning a rebuke from Meignan and creating enough confusion to slip the woman a note. Returning to his room, he asked Meignan if he could use the bathroom, which was located down a dark hallway. Meignan, knowing Faÿ suffered from a heart condition and "walked shufflingly and only with great effort," agreed to let Faÿ go alone. Fifteen minutes later, Meignan found the bathroom empty and realized that Faÿ had disappeared. An intern of the hospital later reported seeing a young blonde woman in a navy cape leading an elderly man through the side gates of the building. By the time the police in Angers were alerted, at four that afternoon, Faÿ and his companion were already halfway across the country.[28]

Slipping across the border dressed in a cassock, Faÿ entered Switzerland early on the morning of October 1. His anonymous French benefactress—probably a young woman named Jeanne Marie Therese Bigot—handed Faÿ over to the warm embrace of reactionary Swiss friends and fellow French collaborators.[29] The anti-Semitic writer Paul Morand, the Pétainist intellectuals René Gillouin and Alfred Fabre-Luce, Abetz's friend Jacques Benoist-Méchin, and Henri Jamet, the director of the collaborationist Paris bookstore Rive

Gauche were just a few of the Vichy allies who surrounded Faÿ in Switzerland. Other friends came from the wealthy elite of right-wing French-speaking Switzerland. One of Faÿ's first stops after his arrival in Switzerland was at the home of Lucien Cramer, a lawyer, journalist, and historian who wrote on the Swiss nobility, including his own family. His sumptuous villa in the eastern suburbs of Geneva was also the meeting place for an international organization devoted to fighting the spread of communism. It was at the Cramer villa where Faÿ would receive his mail, addressed to him under his Swiss pseudonym: Pierre Conan.[30]

Henry Rousso has eloquently described this postwar Swiss setting as a "provisional crucible" of ex-collaborators who lived, wrote, and "discoursed at length about a more-than-uncertain future while awaiting better days."[31] The holding pattern of these "exiles"—as Faÿ called himself, to avoid the unpleasantries associated with being a fugitive—was marked by a shared bitterness toward the course of present-day history and an increasingly black-and-white sense of the future. Writing about his "liberation" onto the streets of Geneva in October 1951, Faÿ nevertheless turned his mind to darker thoughts: "I realized that . . . up to my death, I would be, like everyone else, captive to madness, to violence, and to hatred over which no-one would triumph until the birth of a new and divine wisdom."[32] Faÿ equated the birth of this new day with two events: the moment when he would be pardoned by France and allowed to return home to his native country and the time when bolshevism, communism, and/or leftism would finally cede to a "rebirth" of traditional "wisdom."[33] This would be the vision to which he devoted himself with increasing religious fervor until the end of his life.

Aside from a brief stint teaching in Madrid from October 1952 to May 1953, Faÿ would call the French-speaking cantons of Switzerland home for the next decade. There he would be aided by the Catholic intelligentsia as well as by certain high-ranking authorities in the Swiss federal administration and police force who were favorably inclined toward his political position. Already known as a *refuge brun* ("brown refuge," after the color of the Nazi uniforms) for its covert willingness to aid fugitive Nazis, Switzerland after the war accepted an array of French ex-collaborators ranging from high-ranking ministers to more radical collaborationists. According to Luc van Dongen in his recent book on Switzerland as a "transitional zone" for ex-Nazis and their collaborators, one has to take seriously the possibility that certain elements within Switzerland welcomed these figures as refugees "out of respect for their fundamental principles."[34] Such would be the case with Faÿ's former assistant William Gueydan de Roussel, who, despite having been identified to the Swiss authorities as a

Gestapo agent in early 1945, was still able to find work in the Swiss federal government before the war had even ended.[35] This political bias—or willful blindness—on the part of certain Swiss authorities may explain the ease with which Faÿ was able to travel and work within a matter of months after arriving in Switzerland. It also explains why Faÿ was granted refugee status by the Swiss state as early as 1953.[36]

Arriving in the small Swiss town of Fribourg in December 1951, Faÿ at last found a place where he could settle, a profoundly Catholic environment where he could finally enjoy the Christian holidays of Christmas and Lent. He was soon surrounded by aristocratic friends—Philippe de Weck, the former head of the Swiss bank UBS; Viscount Georges de Plinval, a right-wing dean at the University of Fribourg;[37] Count Raoul de Diesbach and his son Frédéric, the editor of *La Revue Anticommuniste*; and the equally anticommunist Swiss diplomat Carl Jacob Burckhardt. Doctor Walter Michel, the head of the Mouvement National Suisse, a fascist group active in Switzerland during World War II, was a faithful ally to Faÿ, just as he had been to Faÿ's former assistant Gueydan de Roussel.[38]

But most important to Faÿ's well-being in Fribourg was Gonzague de Reynold, a man who seems to have replaced Stein in Faÿ's affections after the war. Correspondents since before the war, Faÿ and de Reynold became intimate friends after it. Manifesting the same combination of hard-headed political critique and demonstrative banter, the correspondence between the two intellectuals of the Right recalls the Stein-Faÿ correspondence from the 1930s. As with Stein, Faÿ flattered the elder de Reynold, praising him for the gift of his friendship and for his stimulating companionship during an otherwise bleak moment of history.[39] As with Stein, Faÿ seems to have appreciated the "virility" of his friend, referring to de Reynold as a salutary counterforce to the "feminine" twentieth century.[40] In turn, de Reynold, like Stein, praised Faÿ for being a cultural intermediary between France and his own native country. Both pairs of friends laced their correspondence with sharp observations about the decadence of their times and the menace of communism.

But there are several telling differences between the two sets of correspondence. Above all, Faÿ appealed to de Reynold on the grounds of a shared religious faith, even implicitly comparing the latter to Christ.[41] Where Stein's Jewishness remained at times a point of difference between herself and Faÿ, there was no such sensitivity regarding de Reynold. Likewise, Faÿ felt no compunction about disparaging what he called "Judeo-American" politics with de Reynold. And Faÿ's rhetoric becomes even sharper in the hearing of de Reynold: describing a trip to Solesmes Abbey in France, Faÿ registers

FIGURE 6.3 Gonzague de Reynold, in eighteenth-century breeches (1940).

disgust at the unholy juxtaposition between the ancient monastery and the heterogeneous racial and cultural mix of the French tourists around him.[42] In this and other letters, the two aging reactionaries solidified their postwar bond by means of a vocabulary that was at once pious, bitter, and uncomprehending—far different from the energetic right-wing critique shared by Stein and Faÿ in the 1930s.

Gonzague de Reynold, a figure who as a boy had been coached by his aristocratic mother to publicly snub the bourgeoisie, would facilitate Faÿ's entry into Fribourg high society.[43] Although Faÿ himself had bourgeois origins, his much-published defense of the aristocracy and his Catholic piety effectively gave him a free pass into the Fribourg nobility. It was also de Reynold who would help Faÿ secure teaching positions at various institutions around town.[44] With its strong reputation for hosting the foreign-study programs of American institutions including Georgetown, La Salle College, and Rosary College, Fribourg was the perfect place for Faÿ to not only survive but thrive. The modest family income on which he had been living was soon supplemented by work. Because of his scholarly background and teaching experience, Faÿ found himself a regularly employed adjunct professor in both Fribourg and at a high school in Lausanne. Eventually, in 1957, he became a *chargé de cours* (lecturer) at the Institute of French Language at the University of Fribourg. It was a far cry from the Collège de France but certainly better than Fontevrault prison. Gradually, through his contacts with de Reynold and others, Faÿ developed a circle of sorts: Fribourg nobility, fellow French "exiles," and a gaggle of students who knew nothing of his past but who enjoyed his elegant social teas, held every week at five o'clock at his house on the Grand Rue.[45]

But even more it was Gonzague de Reynold, again, who helped Faÿ develop an association with the religious conservatives centered in Fribourg. A town of some thirty thousand inhabitants, of whom the majority are Catholic, Fribourg has long been known as "a small island of traditionalism."[46] As its "spiritual head" during the 1950s and 1960s, de Reynold shared with many of his neighbors a deeply conservative understanding of Catholicism.[47] A central tenet was the belief in a strict interpretation of the faith based in the traditional Tridentine Latin mass. Tied to this belief was an equally strong sense that the Catholic faith had lost its moorings and that the Church of Rome was increasingly moving toward a troubling reconciliation with contemporary values. The modernizing and secularizing reforms of Vatican II (1962–1965) were imminent. Sensing this, de Reynold and other members of the Fribourg Catholic elite felt themselves to be the last bastion of standards keeping the church from sliding into modern decadence. Their discontent would prove enormously attractive to Bernard Faÿ, who over the course of his time in Fribourg transferred his bitterness about the turn of events of his life, and of history, into a new commitment to anti–Vatican II Catholicism.

Among the close friendships Faÿ developed in Fribourg through de Reynold was with the man known as the "rebel archbishop" in Rome, Marcel Lefebvre. Deeply opposed to what he called the "adulterous union of the church with the [French] Revolution," Lefebvre eventually broke with Rome over the reforms of Vatican II. [48] Activist and archconservative, Lefebvre was aligned not just with traditionalist forces within the church but with right-wing elements outside it. His friendship with Bernard Faÿ was founded on this seamless union of reactionary religious and political worldviews. For Lefebvre, the critique of Vatican II was inseparable from the critique of the French Revolution's "Masonic and anti-Catholic principles."[49] Faÿ would soon provide the moral support—and initial physical space—for Lefebvre to plan a breakaway seminary espousing his ideas, originally to be based in Fribourg but eventually established at Ecône, Switzerland.[50] Lefebvre's seminary was called the Fraternité Sacerdotale de Pie X, named after the resolutely antimodern pope Saint Pius X. The organization continues to be active today and is known as a breeding ground for reactionary political ideas, including Holocaust denial.[51]

Faÿ was a key player in helping Lefebvre set up the Ecône seminary. In the 1970s, he gave frequent lectures there, most of them centered around forces in history that had sought to topple the church, including humanism, the French Revolution, and the inevitable Freemasonry.[52] Meanwhile, ever prodigious in his writing, Faÿ began publishing work that reflected this increasingly dogmatic religious orientation. On the one hand, he continued to produce scorching critiques of modernity, democracy, and liberalism in books such as *Naissance d'un monstre: L'opinion publique* (1965) and *Louis XVI, ou la fin d'un monde* (1966). He wrote a hagiographic treatment of Philippe Pétain in 1952, finally published in 2000 under the title *Philippe Pétain, portrait d'un paysan avec paysages*. But other tracts Faÿ wrote after the war confronted more directly the liberalism of the modern Catholic church. In *L'église de Judas?* (1970), for example, Faÿ attempts to trace the insidious lines of influence between the contemporary church and Marxism, Freemasonry, and science. All had contributed to the process of "ruining, everywhere they could, traditional faith."[53] It was not enough that Marxists had "infiltrat[ed] the seminaries" during the Popular Front or that certain Jesuits had attempted to "make a bridge between theories of evolution and the Catholic faith."[54] More dangerous still was the way in which modernity itself had led people to "want to bend their God to their tastes, and take their habits as more important than the dogmas of their faith."[55] Turning inevitably to politics, Faÿ even suggests in this book that in the long run Hitler was less destructive to France than Otto Abetz. If Hitler—"incapable of commanding his victory"—had caused havoc in France, he nevertheless had waged an "indifferent war against the church." Abetz, on the other hand, had encouraged the forces of anticlericalism, socialism, and republicanism to flourish during the occupation and thus had a more lasting and detrimental effect on the Catholic church in particular and France in general.[56]

d. 1978

Vilifying science, progress, liberalism, democracy, "laicité," and above all modernity, *L'église de Judas* is Faÿ's darkest screed, a cry of outrage from a man no longer able to contain his loathing for a world that, by 1970, seemed utterly foreign to him. When he died eight years later, on December 31, 1978, Faÿ was described by *Le Monde* as a "'Man of the ancien régime' as one doesn't find them anymore—and as one didn't during the high point of the regime." He remained always "faithful to himself almost to the point of rigidity."[57] In an era that had weathered the 1960s and remained gripped by the specter of nuclear war, Bernard Faÿ in the 1970s had become somewhat of a caricature, existing in a fantasy land of monarchs, nobles, and popes. The urbane Collège de France professor, the lover of all things American, the connoisseur of experimental modernist literature—all these real-life roles seemed to have vanished. So too had a reputation that before the war extended across the Atlantic and that had made him, for a time, the "'unofficial ambassador' of France to the New World."[58] At his death the *New York Times*, a newspaper that had mentioned Faÿ by name over 150 times between 1923 and 1944, did not even publish an obituary. Bernard Faÿ had been largely erased from history.

But some remembered. Archbishop Lefebvre, who had heard Faÿ deliver a lecture at Ecône only two months before his death, gave a powerful eulogy at his funeral mass in the archtraditionalist Church of Saint Nicolas de Chardonnet in Paris. He spoke there of Faÿ's "courageous battles and sufferings which he endured for his Faith."[59] And the postwar journal of Action Française, *Aspects de la France*—still churning out Maurrassian propaganda in 1979—eulogized Faÿ in the terms that would have mattered to him: "Faithful to himself, to his King, to his God."[60]

▣ ▣ ▣

Religion would increasingly take center stage in Faÿ's postwar years. But religion would also prove to be a source of disappointment and frustration for the elderly Faÿ. When he was finally pardoned by French President René Coty in January 1959, an act that restored to him his civil rights and pension and allowed him to travel freely in France, the celebration was short lived. Within months, Faÿ would find himself at the center of a new controversy concerning his Vichy past.

 pardon 1959

On the eve of the 1960s, Switzerland was just beginning to assess its own actions during the recent world war. In a controversy that pitted Swiss youth against their elders and Catholics against Freemasons, Faÿ became the point man for this debate. His profile raised by having been asked, for the first time, to teach a course on the fraught subject of "French culture and civilization" at the University of Fribourg in 1959, Faÿ soon found himself on the hot seat. Student groups, catching wind of the rumor that they were about to be taught about France by an ex-Vichy official, notified the media of their unease. Immediately articles in the *National Zeitung* of Basel, a liberal German-language newspaper, and in the French-Swiss newspaper *La Gruyère* questioned why a man accused of "anti-Semitic and anti-Masonic activities" by the French government had been "given the contract to make Fribourg students familiar with French civilization."[61] Faÿ's defenders quickly mobilized, announcing publicly that *La Gruyère* was the organ of disgruntled Freemasons and rehearsing the familiar line that Faÿ's Vichy activities had been directed toward saving the Masonic archives rather than destroying them. Moreover, by this date Faÿ had already been pardoned by the French government and was no longer a fugitive. Nevertheless, the damage was done, less in alienating Faÿ from Swiss Freemasons than in sticking him with the public charge that he was an anti-Semite. This charge had been rather marginal in Faÿ's 1946 trial for collaboration, but by 1959, it was fatal. Within months the image of Faÿ as a Vichy-era persecutor of Jews working freely in Switzerland would become the latest *scandale* in a country that was just coming to terms with its postwar past as a "brown refuge."

While Faÿ conferred with a lawyer, the *Affaire Faÿ* exploded. Almost a year after the first newspaper attacks, in early 1960, the Jewish Student Union of Switzerland, a group composed of students in Basel and Zurich, with a small satellite group in Fribourg, issued the following statement: "The association of Jewish students in Switzerland . . . supports the Fribourg Student Association in its position that the professorship of Herr Faÿ is incompatible with the principles of freedom and dignity of man."[62] Newspapers across Switzerland jumped on the story. A Swiss judge was asked by the cantonal government of Fribourg to investigate the charges. He found Faÿ "innocent of anti-Semitism." Nevertheless, at the end of November 1960, Faÿ—who had remained largely silent about the affair—asked the University of Fribourg to discharge him from his duties. Perhaps fearing further disclosures, Faÿ chose to close the door on his past and retreat. The tides of history and society had definitively turned against him. One Fribourg acquaintance who saw him after his resignation recalls that Faÿ had an air of negativity and sadness about him and rarely smiled.[63] Teaching occasional courses for foreign-study students in Fribourg, traveling back and forth from Switzerland to Luceau to his brother Jacques' home in Paris, Bernard Faÿ spent the last two decades of his life writing, ruminating, and dreaming of a Catholic life unmarred by the catastrophe of modernity.

FIGURE 6.4 Bernard Faÿ in Fribourg, Switzerland (1960s).

▣ ▣ ▣

But Faÿ did publish one short response to his Swiss critics. In a letter to the Geneva newspaper *La Suisse*, in June 1960, Faÿ disputed the "tendentious and false" claims against him, announcing that he had "always been opposed to Nazism and detested its agents." In fact, Faÿ writes, he had "protected or saved" Jews throughout the war, including "Gertrude Stein and Alice Toklas during the entire Occupation."[64] Ironically enough, this official line—first uttered by Faÿ and repeated uncritically by every single one of Stein's subsequent biographers—would remain the most memorable utterance Faÿ ever made. It would be the one assertion that would keep Faÿ's name in print as Stein's star continued to rise in the last two decades of the twentieth century and as biographers began to assess her life. The complexities of Stein's own actions during the Vichy years and the shifting influence of Faÿ over his fractious Vichy colleagues would be turned into a potted narrative. Bernard Faÿ was now a "Vichy official" with a soft spot for an old friend; Stein and Toklas simply "persecuted Jews."

Inevitably, the charge of anti-Semitism against the elderly Faÿ has also become, for recent critics, the single most important mystery surrounding his relationship with Gertrude Stein. However much Stein, who shared some of Faÿ's attraction to Catholicism, may have felt conflicted about the issue of Jewishness during her lifetime, and however much their relationship may have been founded on a variety of other interests, passions, and political and aesthetic affiliations, recent critics have fixated their attention upon the unlikelihood of a friendship between "the anti-Semite" and "the Jew."[65] Allowing their story to remain on this reductive but moralistic terrain distracts us from the reality of their actions and convictions. It also keeps us from grasping the real dilemmas of their time—most importantly, the seemingly improbable attraction of modernist writers and thinkers to right-wing or reactionary politics.

It was Stein's greatest defender, the Jewish-born Alice Toklas, who would, at the end of her own life, bring Stein and Faÿ back together again. In 1957, with the help of Faÿ and his friend Denise Azam—herself a Jewish-born Catholic convert—Toklas was initiated into the Catholic church. Her conversion was made "most of all," according to her biographer Linda Simon, "for the conception of a populated heaven where she would find Gertrude."[66] Rejecting the Jewish background that she had never really acknowledged, Toklas made Catholicism into an expedient means toward an end. For the next decade of her life, until her death on March 7, 1967, Toklas continued to look forward to this final and ultimate reunion with Stein. And to the end of her life she praised Faÿ for giving her faith and for making this dream seem possible.[67] "You were her dearest friend during her life and now you have given her that eternal life," she wrote to him in a poignant letter.[68]

For his part, Bernard Faÿ remained skeptical. He had converted Toklas and Denise Azam, but Gertrude was somewhere in limbo, the place of unbaptized souls. As he said to a family member, the greatest regret of his life with Stein was in fact his inability to convert her to Christianity: "Avec Gertrude, j'ai raté" ("With Gertrude, I failed").[69] Faÿ had ultimately failed to bring Stein around to his worldview, and because of this neither he nor Toklas would ever meet her again. The death of Stein was a loss of both his power and his love. Never fully able to separate one from the other, Faÿ could only regret, as he would do so often in his life, being misaligned with a fallen world.

NOTES

1. ENDINGS AND BEGINNINGS (1918-1930)

1. Gertrude Stein, "I Have No Title to Be Successful," in *Painted Lace and Other Pieces, 1914–1937* (New Haven, Conn.: Yale University Press, 1955), 23.
2. Gertrude Stein, *The Autobiography of Alice B. Toklas* (New York: Harcourt, Brace, 1933), 207 (hereafter cited in the text as *ABT*).
3. Stein received the Medaille de la Reconnaissance on September 15, 1920.
4. Donald Roy Allen notes that while the regiments were meant to march "in alphabetical order according to the official name of their countries . . . an exception was made, however, for General Pershing's regiment to march under 'America' rather than the 'United States,' thus permitting the Americans to lead off the victory parade." *French Views of America in the 1930s* (New York: Garland, 1979), vii–viii.
5. Bernard Faÿ, "Harvard 1920," *The Harvard Graduate's Magazine* 28 (June 1920): 587–588 (hereafter cited in the text as H). See also Bernard Faÿ, *Les précieux* (Paris: Perrin, 1966), 39 (hereafter cited in the text as *LP*).
6. Bernard Faÿ, "The Course of French-American Friendship," *The Yale Review* 18 (Spring 1929): 443 (hereafter cited in the text as FAF); "La joie et les plaisirs aux Etats-Unis," *Revue de Paris* (July 1, 1925): 155 (hereafter cited in the text as JP).
7. In *Pétain et les français, 1940–1951* (Paris: Perrin, 2002), Michèle Cointet disputes the myth of Pétain as "the savior of Verdun," arguing that in fact General Joseph Joffre was the "strategist of genius" at Verdun (who himself attributed the French victory to General Robert Nivelle) (39–40).
8. Faÿ: "Il respectait la souffrance et ne croyait pas que le chef eût le droit de verser le sang quand il pouvait l'éviter" ("He respected suffering and did not believe that the one in charge had the right to spill blood when he could avoid doing so") (*LP* 38).
9. Bernard Faÿ, *L'homme mesure de l'histoire* (Paris: Labergerie, 1939), 72.

10. Gertrude Stein, *Paris France* (New York: Liveright, 1970), 17 (hereafter cited in the text as *PF*).

11. Gertrude Stein, "The Winner Loses: A Picture of Occupied France," in *How Writing Is Written: Volume II of The Previously Uncollected Writings of Gertrude Stein*, ed. Robert Bartlett Haas (Los Angeles: Black Sparrow Press, 1974), 131 (hereafter cited in the text as *WL*).

12. Gertrude Stein, "Introduction to the Speeches of Maréchal Pétain," *Modernism/modernity* 3, no. 3 (September 1996): 95.

13. Mark Mazower, *Dark Continent: Europe's Twentieth Century* (New York: Knopf, 1999), 3.

14. Ibid., x.

15. Marc Ferro, *The Great War, 1914–1918* (London: Routledge, 1973), 247.

16. Georges Duhamel, *America: The Menace; Scenes from the Life of the Future* (Boston: Houghton Mifflin, 1931).

17. "U.S. Is Held in Danger of Going Communist: Professor Bernard Faÿ of Paris Tells Germans America Faces an Economic Catastrophe," *New York Times* (March 12, 1937): L13.

18. William Pfaff, *The Bullet's Song: Romantic Violence and Utopia* (New York: Simon & Schuster, 2004), 26.

19. See Stein's nomination of Hitler for the Nobel Peace Prize (chapter 3).

20. Gertrude Stein, "A Political Series," in *Painted Lace and Other Pieces, 1914–1937* (New Haven, Conn.: Yale University Press, 1955), 72; Gertrude Stein, *Wars I Have Seen* (London: Batsford, 1945), 4 (hereafter cited in the text as *W*).

21. Stein, "A Political Series," 73.

22. Gertrude Stein, *Brewsie and Willie*, in *Gertrude Stein: Writings 1932–1946* (New York: The Library of America, 1998), 778 (hereafter cited in the text as *BW*).

23. Gertrude Stein, "Money," "More About Money," "Still More About Money," "All About Money," and "My Last About Money," in *How Writing Is Written: Volume II of the Previously Uncollected Writings of Gertrude Stein*, ed. Robert Bartlett Haas (Los Angeles: Black Sparrow Press, 1974), 106–112.

24. Gertrude Stein, *Everybody's Autobiography* (New York: Vintage, 1973), 310–311 (hereafter cited in the text as *EA*).

25. Charles Maurras, quoted in David Carroll, *French Literary Fascism* (Princeton, N.J.: Princeton University Press, 1995), 74. But Eugen Weber, in his chapter on decadence in *The Hollow Years: France in the 1930s* (New York: Norton, 1994), 111–112, argues that this period only *seemed* more decadent than other periods because of its effect on a populace already exhausted and demoralized by the Great War.

26. Maurras's definition is discussed in Achille Segard, *Charles Maurras et les idées royalistes* (Paris: Fayard, 1919), 172.

27. In a letter from Faÿ to a Monsieur de Vaux of the Action Française, dated November 26, 1926, Faÿ reports on the likelihood that the organization could play a role in the United States. Fonds Charles Maurras, Paris Archives Nationales AN 576/AP/73.

28. Stein, "Still More About Money" and "My Last About Money," 109, 111.

29. James R. Mellow describes *Wars* as "an amazingly shrewd, warm, and humane account" (*Charmed Circle: Gertrude Stein and Company* [Boston: Houghton Mifflin, 1974], 449), while Janet Hobhouse writes that "*Wars I Have Seen* is an extraordinary account

of Gertrude's day-to-day cheerfulness during a long and exhausting war. At the age of seventy she was not only a survivor, but one who took profound joy in all the challenges to that survival. As a document of the artist's ability to make a pleasure of hell's despite, *Wars I Have Seen* is unique, and uniquely moving." *Everybody Who Was Anybody: A Biography of Gertrude Stein* (New York: Doubleday, 1975), 204. Phoebe Stein Davis, who acknowledges the Pétainism of *Wars*, nevertheless argues that "the personal anecdotes Stein recounts reflect her acute awareness of the danger she and other Jews faced during World War II." " 'Even Cake Gets to Have Another Meaning: History, Narrative, and 'Daily Living' in Gertrude Stein's World War II Writings," *Modern Fiction Studies* 44, no. 3 (1998): 597. And Dana Cairns Watson, who foregrounds the discussion of the French Resistance in *Wars*, uses the text as a springboard to suggest that "a case can be made for the likelihood that Stein and Toklas participated energetically in the French Resistance." *Gertrude Stein and the Essence of What Happens* (Nashville, Tenn.: Vanderbilt University Press, 2005), 163.

30. Wanda Van Dusen, "Portrait of a National Fetish: Gertrude Stein's Introduction to the Speeches of Maréchal Pétain (1942)," *Modernism/modernity* 3, no. 3 (1996): 69–92. Van Dusen was not the first to mention the Pétain translation project: Stein's early biographer, Richard Bridgman, made brief mention of it in *Gertrude Stein in Pieces* (New York: Oxford University Press, 1970), 316–318, as did Janet Hobhouse, in her 1974 biography *Everybody Who Was Anybody* (202). Yet Van Dusen's exposé, written in the wake of the Paul de Man scandal, was the first to explore the project in detail and in light of renewed academic attention to the modernism-fascism nexus. See also "Appendix IX," in Edward M. Burns and Ulla E. Dydo with William Rice, *The Letters of Gertrude Stein and Thornton Wilder* (New Haven, Conn.: Yale University Press, 1996), 401–421.

31. Alice B. Toklas, *Staying on Alone: Letters of Alice B. Toklas* (New York: Liveright, 1973), 383. Stein herself would refer to Bernard Faÿ as "one of the four permanent friendships of Gertrude Stein's life" (*ABT* 305).

32. Our knowledge of Bernard Faÿ's life and actions has been considerably enriched of late thanks to Compagnon's biography, *Le cas Bernard Faÿ: du Collège de France à l'indignité nationale* (Paris: Gallimard, 2009), and to chapters in two other French-language works: Jean-Marie Goulemot, *L'amour des bibliothèques* (Paris: Ed. du Seuil, 2006); and Martine Poulain, *Livres pillés, lectures surveillées. Les bibliothèques françaises sous l'Occupation* (Paris: Gallimard, 2008). Also see the insightful essays on Faÿ by John L. Harvey, "Conservative Crossings: Bernard Faÿ and the Rise of American Studies in Third-Republic France," *Historical Reflections/Réflexions historiques* 36 (2010): 95–124; "Bernard Faÿ," in *French Historians, 1900–2000: New Historical Writing in Twentieth-Century France*, ed. Philip Daileader and Philip Whalen (West Sussex: Wiley-Blackwell, 2010), 202–217.

33. As Matei Calinescu perceptively notes, "Clearly good politics . . . does not necessarily result in good art, nor bad politics in bad art." "Modernism and Ideology," in *Modernism: Challenges and Perspectives.*, ed. Monique Chefdor, Ricardo Quinones, and Albert Wachtel (Urbana: University of Illinois Press, 1986), 89. For the charge against Stein on the Internet, see, for example, American Poems.com (http://www.americanpoems.com/poets/Gertrude-Stein).

34. Among the significant works in the Stein critical tradition are a "first generation" of groundbreaking books on Stein, including Marianne DeKoven, *A Different Language:*

Gertrude Stein's Experimental Writing (Madison: University of Wisconsin Press, 1983); Harriet Chessman, *The Public Is Invited to Dance: Representation, the Body, and Dialogue in Gertrude Stein* (Stanford, Calif.: Stanford University Press, 1989); Ellen Berry, *Curved Thought and Textual Wandering: Gertrude Stein's Postmodernism* (Ann Arbor: University of Michigan Press, 1992); and the articles by Catharine Stimpson: "The Mind, the Body, and Gertrude Stein," *Critical Inquiry* 3, no. 3 (Spring 1977): 489–506; "Gertrude Stein: Humanism and Its Freaks," *Boundary 2* 12, no. 3 (Spring 1984): 301–319; "Reading Gertrude Stein," *Tulsa Studies in Women's Literature* 4, no. 2 (Fall 1985): 265–271. A newer generation of books on Stein that have attempted to engage more directly with her politics in the wake of the Van Dusen article are Watson, *Gertrude Stein*; Karin Cope, *Passionate Collaborations: Learning to Live with Gertrude Stein* (Victoria, B.C.: ELS, 2005); and Janet Malcolm, *Two Lives: Gertrude and Alice* (New Haven: Yale University Press, 2007). The two best essays on Stein's wartime writing that also engage directly with the Van Dusen article are Phoebe Stein Davis, "'Even Cake"; and John Whittier-Ferguson, "Stein in Time: History, Manuscripts, Memory," *Modernism/modernity* 6, no. 1 (1999): 115–151. See also Liesl M. Olson, "Gertrude Stein, William James, and Habit in the Shadow of War," *Twentieth-Century Literature* 49, no. 3 (Fall 2003): 328–359.

35. See, for example, two recent books on Stein: Georgia Johnson, *The Formation of Twentieth-Century Queer Autobiography: Reading Vita Sackville-West, Virginia Woolf, Hilda Doolittle, and Gertrude Stein* (New York: Palgrave Macmillan, 2007); and Karin Cope, *Passionate Collaborations*.

36. Linda Wagner-Martin offers a particularly developed argument along these lines in *"Favored Strangers": Gertrude Stein and Her Family* (New Brunswick, N.J.: Rutgers University Press, 1995).

37. Burns and Dydo, quoted in Janet Malcolm, *Two Lives*, 53. Malcolm refers to Stein's "perverse project" to translate Pétain's speeches on 52.

38. Barbara Will, *Gertrude Stein, Modernism, and the Problem of "Genius"* (Edinburgh: Edinburgh University Press, 2000).

39. Roland Barthes, "The Death of the Author," in *Image, Music, Text* (New York: Hill and Wang, 1977), 142–148. Barthes writes: "The reader is the space on which all the quotations that make up a writing are inscribed without any of them being lost; a text's unity lies not in its origin but in its destination . . . we know that to give writing its future, it is necessary to overthrow the myth: the birth of the reader must be at the cost of the death of the Author" (148).

40. Ibid., 147. In "Stein in Time," John Whittier-Ferguson has recently made the case for seeing Stein's writing as essentially "empty," as deliberately and radically open-ended, imbued with "the power of forgetting . . . the capacity of feeling unhistorically." Such writing, he argues, demands an audience situated "outside of time," an audience that refuses "to seek out references and make narratives" but revels in the absolute presence and ultimate unaccountability of the textual process (140).

41. In her recent book *Gertrude Stein and the Essence of What Happens*, Dana Cairns Watson argues along these lines, suggesting that by making the reader "feel in great doubt about meaning," Stein "forces us to look carefully at what we thought we already knew." In so doing, "Stein points out her readers' psychic blindness as she simultaneously offers

a reading experience that acts as a therapeutic cure." This, in turn, has the capacity to make us "better thinkers" and more enlightened citizens (47, 55, 52).

42. The attraction of modernist writers to fascist politics has been richly explored in the last twenty-five years. Significant contributions to the field include the work by Alice Kaplan, Andrew Hewitt, Richard Golsan, Charles Ferrall, Roger Griffin, Lawrence Rainey, Alastair Hamilton, and Fredric Jameson. Founded in 1994, the journal *Modernism/modernity* has also been on the cutting edge of this discussion; see, for example, its special issue on fascism, vol. 15, no. 1 (January 2008). For the particular debates surrounding female modernists and fascism, see Erin G. Carlson, *Thinking Fascism: Sapphic Modernism and Fascist Modernity* (Stanford, Calif.: Stanford University Press, 1998); Marie-Luise Gättens, *Women Writers and Fascism: Reconstructing History* (Gainesville: University Press of Florida, 1995); Elke P. Frederiksen and Martha Kaarsberg Wallach, eds., *Facing Fascism and Confronting the Past: German Women Writers from Weimar to the Present* (Albany, N.Y.: SUNY Press, 2000). The case of Leni Riefenstahl, Hitler's propagandist, has generated particularly charged responses: see Susan Tegel, "Leni Riefenstahl: Art and Politics," *Quarterly Review of Film and Video* 23, no. 3 (May 2006): 185–200; and Ray Müller's 1994 film *The Wonderful, Horrible Life of Leni Riefenstahl.* Also see note 45.

43. In 1987, four years after his death, more than two hundred articles that Paul de Man wrote for a pro-Nazi Belgian newspaper during World War II were unearthed. See "Yale Scholar Wrote for Pro-Nazi Newspaper," *New York Times* (December 1, 1987). The revelation of de Man's wartime activity occasioned a series of articles by friends and colleagues, including Jacques Derrida, Shoshana Feldman, and J. Hillis Miller. See Jacques Derrida, "Like the Sound of the Sea Deep Within a Shell: Paul de Man's War," *Critical Inquiry* 14 (Spring 1988): 590–565; Shoshana Felman, "Paul de Man's Silence," *Critical Inquiry* 15, no. 4 (Summer 1989): 704–744; J. Hillis Miller, "Paul de Man's Wartime Writings," *Times Literary Supplement* (June 17–23, 1988).

44. Andrew Hewitt, *Fascist Modernism: Aesthetics, Politics, and the Avant-garde* (Stanford, Calif.: Stanford University Press, 1993), 4.

45. The debate over the relationship between modernism and fascism takes many forms, from skepticism (Matei Calinescu: "The fact is that in Europe, with the exception of Mussolini's Italy . . . few writers whom we could call modernist favored the extreme right-wing movements that swept the continent in the 1920s and 1930s" ("Modernism and Ideology," 83) to outright identification (as in Paul Virilio, *Art and Fear* [New York: Continuum, 2006], which links the avant-garde to terrorism and rejects outright the validity of modernist "autonomy" by arguing that modernism's aesthetic break with mimesis, as in Futurism, "led directly . . . to the shower block of Auschwitz-Birkenau" [16]). Early concerns among the Frankfurt School include Georg Lukács's contention in 1934 that modernist "abstraction" as an "emotive yet empty declamatory manifesto" could be easily appropriated by fascism, as opposed to older forms of realism and naturalism, which were inherently incompatible with fascism (Georg Lukács, "Expressionism: Its Significance and Decline," in *Essays on Realism*, ed. Rodney Livingstone [London: Lawrence and Wishart, 1980], 76–113); as well as Walter Benjamin's by now classic definition of fascism as the "aestheticization of politics," which has produced an entire critical industry in its wake. See Russell A. Berman, "The Aestheticization of Politics:

Walter Benjamin on Fascism and the Avant-garde," *Stanford Italian Review*, 8, nos. 1–2 (1990): 35–52). Benjamin argues that with its emphasis upon performance and packaging and its appeal to the emotional or intuitive responses of an audience, fascism renders politics into an experience of "submission and spectacle." The audience at a fascist rally or in the presence of the charismatic authoritarian leader feels at once the thrill of belonging and the masochistic pleasure of submission. In his most original insight, Benjamin links this fascist experience to that of spectators in front of a modernist work of art or literature. Like the modernist work, the fascist state offers itself to its public as pure form, "autonomous" and independent of judgment and even critique. See Walter Benjamin, "The Work of Art in the Age of Mechanical Reproduction," in *Illuminations: Essays and Reflections*, ed. Hannah Arendt (New York: Schocken, 1969), 217–251. See also Fredric Jameson, *Fables of Aggression: Wyndham Lewis, the Modernist as Fascist* (Berkeley: University of California Press, 1979), which stresses "the affinities between protofascism and Western modernism" (18).

46. Jeffrey Herf, *Reactionary Modernism: Technology, Culture, and Politics in Weimar and the Third Reich* (Cambridge: Cambridge University Press, 1984), 12.

47. Ibid., 12. Charles Ferrall, in *Modernist Writing and Reactionary Politics* (Cambridge: Cambridge University Press, 2001), views this movement through a primarily Anglo-American lens: "the reactionary modernists expressed their hostility towards what was variously called 'liberalism,' 'democracy,' 'industrialism,' and 'progress' in terms of a nostalgia for the cultures of premodernity while at the same time feeling compelled, in Pound's famous phrase, 'to make it new'" (2).

48. Roger Griffin, *Modernism and Fascism: The Sense of a Beginning Under Mussolini and Hitler* (Basingstoke: Palgrave Macmillan, 2007), 53. Or as Russell A. Berman writes: "Art becomes the means through which the discontents in contemporary civilization are to be answered—or stifled" ("The Aestheticization of Politics," 41).

49. Griffin, *Modernism and Fascism*, 9.

50. "Appel de 25 juin 1940 de Philippe Pétain," quoted in Robert Paxton, "Vichy a gagné la guerre de la mémoire," *L'Histoire* 352 (April 2010): 95. For "jouissance," read "frivolity."

51. Herf, *Reactionary Modernism*, 18.

52. Gerald Steig, quoted in Scott McLemee, "Sex and the Single Genius" [review of new edition of Otto Weininger, *Sex and Character*], *Inside Higher Ed* (March 15, 2005). http://www.insidehighered.com/views/mclemee/mclemee13.

53. Barbara Hyams, "Weininger and Nazi Ideology," in *Jews and Gender: Responses to Otto Weininger*, ed. Nancy Anne Harrowitz and Barbara Hyams (Philadelphia: Temple University Press, 1995), 155.

54. Hitler apparently reported this phrase, attributed to his mentor Dietrich Eckart, to Henry Picker in 1941: "Dietrich Eckart once told me that he had made the acquaintance of only one decent Jew, Otto Weininger, who took his life when he realized that the Jew lives from the destruction of other peoples" (quoted in ibid., 160).

55. Toklas comments from personal correspondence of author with Leon Katz.

56. I develop this connection more substantially in my book *Gertrude Stein, Modernism, and the Problem of "Genius,"* 63. See also Leon Katz: "The whole encrustation of Stein's ideas and feelings in her writing from 1908 to the end of her life emanate from

Weininger's envisioning of the highest 'type' of human being." Leon Katz, "Weininger and *The Making of Americans*," *Twentieth-Century Literature* 24, no. 1 (Spring 1978): 16.

57. Griffin describes his own book as "a radical process of 'revision' . . . a process which must obviously be carried out in a way that avoids 'revisionism,' by refusing to mitigate, or to simply elide from discussion, the crimes against humanity committed by fascism with which intellectual or artistic fellow-travelers colluded in their quest for transcendence." But he adds that this is not to "postulate any *direct* lineage between cultural modernism and those crimes [of fascism]" nor to argue, for example, that "even the most ecstatic 'proto-fascist' prose of Filippo Marinetti or Ernst Jünger can be blamed for Fascism or Nazism." Griffin, *Modernism and Fascism*, 359–360.

58. I discuss Weininger's definition of genius as both a type *and* the transcendence of type in *Gertrude Stein, Modernism, and the Problem of "Genius,"* 64–66.

59. In one of the notes she wrote during *The Making of Americans*, Stein writes of wanting to make "the reality of the object count, what I might call the actual earthyness of the object the object for the object's sake." Gertrude Stein, notebooks to *The Making of Americans* (unpublished), NB, B-1, Gertrude Stein and Alice B. Toklas Papers, Yale Collection of American Literature, Beinecke Rare Book and Manuscript Library.

60. This is not, however, to deny that Stein was also attracted to Pétain as a child to an authority figure; especially after the war began, as we shall see in chapter 4, Stein not only seemed to identify with but also idealize the dictator.

61. Stein quoted in Steven Meyer, introduction to Gertrude Stein, *The Making of Americans: Being a History of a Family's Progress* (Normal, Ill.: Dalkey Archive Press, 1995), xiii (hereafter cited in the text as *MOA*). The text defines itself as a record: "anyhow reader, bear it in your mind—will there be for me ever any such a creature,—what I have said always before to you, that this that I write down a little each day here on my scraps of paper for you is not just an ordinary kind of novel with a plot and conversations to amuse you, but a record of a decent family progress" (33).

62. *The Making of Americans* runs 925 pages; by the end of the first third of the text, the conventional narrative of "a decent family progress" has been abandoned, and the text now almost exclusively proceeds to concern itself with the possibility of "a complete history of each one who ever is or was or will be living" (335).

63. Stein, notebooks to *The Making of Americans*, NB, I-12.

64. Stein, notebooks to *The Making of Americans* NB, MA-32; *MOA* 708. In the early sections of the novel, the narrator more directly frames her project as a critique of bourgeois limitations: "To a bourgeois mind that has within it a little of the fervor for diversity, there can be nothing more attractive than a strain of singularity that yet keeps well within the limits of conventional respectability, a singularity that is, so to speak, well dressed and well set up. . . . Brother Singulars, we are misplaced in a generation that knows not Joseph. We flee before the disapproval of our cousins, the courageous condescension of our friends who gallantly sometimes agree to walk the streets with us, from all them who never any way can understand why such ways and not the others are so dear to us" (*MOA* 21).

65. See, for another example, of this idea of modernism as radical break, Virginia Woolf's famous statement from "Mr. Bennett and Mrs. Brown" (1924): "On or about December 1910 human character changed. I am not saying that one went out, as one might into a

garden, and there saw that a rose had flowered, or that a hen had laid an egg. The change was not sudden and definite like that. But a change there was, nevertheless; and, since one must be arbitrary, let us date it about the year 1910." Woolf's periodization is playfully ironic in acknowledging its own arbitrariness; nevertheless, she seems unambiguous enough in asserting "a change there was." Virginia Woolf, "Mr. Bennett and Mrs. Brown," in *The Captain's Death Bed and Other Essays* (New York: Harcourt, 1978), 94–119.

66. Matei Calinescu, in "Modernism and Ideology," traces the idea that "art in and of itself is a *revolutionary* force" from the romantics to the modernists (80).

67. See Herf, *Reactionary Modernism*, 12.

68. For a particularly acute rendering of the relationship in modernism between artistic and political breakthrough, see Thomas Mann, *Doctor Faustus* (New York: Knopf, 1948), esp. 299–309.

69. The striking exception is the *Je Suis Partout* feature article on Stein by Bernard Faÿ, discussed in chapter 3.

70. Pablo Picasso, quoted in James Lord, *Six Exceptional Women: Further Memoirs* (New York: Farrar, Straus, Giroux, 1994), 15.

71. Zeev Sternhell, *Neither Right nor Left: Fascist Ideology in France* (Berkeley: University California Press, 1986), 315n37.

72. Ibid., 45.

73. Ibid., 303.

74. Samuel Kalman, "Reconsidering Fascist Anti-Semitism and Xenophobia in 1920s France: The Doctrinal Contribution of Georges Valois and the Faisceau," *French History* 16, no. 3 (2002): 347.

75. Valois, quoted in Allen Douglas, *From Fascism to Libertarian Communism: Georges Valois Against the Third Republic* (Berkeley: University of California Press, 1992), 27.

76. Stein's comments about "washing" in the early sections of *The Making of Americans* create a historical and linguistic pun around the cleanliness of newly assimilated immigrants and the founding father of the nation, George Washington. For example, in her discussion of George Dehning, the namesake of Washington, Stein writes: "The boy George bade fair to do credit to his christening. George Dehning now about fourteen was strong in sport and washing. He was not foreign in his washing. Oh, no, he was really an american" (*MOA* 15). Here, washing is a sign of national belonging and of the suppression of foreignness, comparable to the "americanizing" of the Jewish names in successive drafts of the text. See also chapter 2, note 56.

77. Gertrude Stein, "The Modern Jew Who Has Given Up the Faith of His Fathers Can Reasonably and Consistently Believe in Isolation," *PMLA* 116, no. 2 (March 2001): 426. In her excellent introduction to this article, Amy Feinstein draws out the public/private distinction (420n10).

78. Bridgman, *Gertrude Stein in Pieces*, 161.

79. Linda Wagner-Martin, "Gertrude Stein (1874–1946)," in *Jewish American Women Writers: A Bio-Bibliographical and Critical Sourcebook*, ed. Ann Shapiro (London: Greenday Press, 1994), 436.

80. Priscilla Wald, *Constituting Americans: Cultural Anxiety and Narrative Form* (Durham, N.C.: Duke University Press, 1995), 242.

81. Ibid., 239.

82. Otto Weininger, *Sex and Character* (London: Heinemann, 1906), 320.

83. See Leon Katz's unpublished dissertation, "The First Making of *The Making of Americans*: A Study Based on Gertrude Stein's Notebooks and Early Versions of Her Novel (1902–1908)," Columbia University, 1963. Katz discusses how Stein distinguished herself from Weininger while making use of his conceptual apparatus. Stein saw Weininger as having "suffered from what Stein thought of as the inevitable failure of Jews: that they 'run themselves by their minds'" (282). Hence Weininger could never be a "genius," in his own sense, since his intelligence was purely cognitive (rather than affective, creative, and relational, as Stein considered hers to be).

84. Gertrude Stein, "Melanctha," in *Three Lives* (New York: Penguin, 1990). This argument is developed further in chapter 1 of my book *Gertrude Stein, Modernism, and the Problem of "Genius,"* 37–43 (reprinted as "Race and Jewishness," in *Three Lives and Q.E.D.*, ed. Marianne DeKoven [New York: Norton, 2005], 503–513).

85. Toklas, quoted in Janet Malcolm, "Strangers in Paradise: How Gertrude Stein and Alice B. Toklas Got to Heaven," *New Yorker* (November 13, 2006).

86. For more on the importance in general of erotic role playing to Stein's creativity, see Kay Turner, "This Very Beautiful Form of Literature," introduction to *Baby Precious Always Shines: Selected Love Notes Between Gertrude Stein and Alice B. Toklas*, ed. Kay Turner (New York: St. Martin's Press, 1999), 2–40.

87. Gertrude Stein, "The Reverie of the Zionist," in *Painted Lace and Other Pieces, 1914–1937* (New Haven, Conn.: Yale University Press, 1955), 94.

88. Michael R. Marrus and Robert O. Paxton, *Vichy France and the Jews* (New York: Basic Books, 1981), 41, 43.

89. Bravig Imbs, *Confessions of Another Young Man* (New York: Henkle-Yewdale, 1936), 177, 205.

90. Hemingway letter to F. Scott Fitzgerald, quoted in Ulla E. Dydo, *Gertrude Stein: The Language That Rises, 1923–1934* (Evanston: Northwestern University Press, 2003), 385.

91. According to Steven Watson, Hemingway also saw the "decline" of Stein's salon, as well as her literary judgment, to be inseparable from her new "patriotism" about homosexuality. He also suggested that all of these events had a biological dimension and could be traced to "the onset of menopause." Steven Watson, *Prepare for Saints: Gertrude Stein, Virgil Thomson, and the Mainstreaming of American Modernism* (New York: Random House, 1998), 39.

92. Imbs, *Confessions*, 177.

93. Van Vechten, quoted in Dydo, *Gertrude Stein: The Language That Rises*, 61.

94. Wagner-Martin, *"Favored Strangers,"* 189. See also Ulla Dydo's sympathetic portrait of Stein's salon in the late 1920s, in *The Language That Rises*, 221–222.

95. Wagner-Martin, *"Favored Strangers,"* 154.

96. *LP* 139–140; Bernard Faÿ, *Civilisation américaine* (Paris: Sagittaire, 1939), 249–250.

97. The phrase is Virgil Thomson's, who in his memoirs describes Faÿ's family as "a tribe of bankers and solicitors, ultra-bourgeois by financial position and ultra-Catholic through their mother (née Rivière), one of whose brothers was an archbishop (at Aix-en-Provence) and the other (later bishop of Monaco) then pastor of the stylish Saint-Thomas-d'Aquin." Virgil Thomson, *Virgil Thomson* (New York: Alfred Knopf, 1966), 66.

98. According to a note signed by Bernard Faÿ's lawyer M. Chrestiel in the preparation file for his 1946 trial for collaboration, Faÿ undertook regular "electrical treatments" and something called "mécanothérapie" (machine therapy) for his polio throughout much of his life. These treatments were apparently unavailable to him during his years in prison and contributed to his declining health. See the unpublished *Dossier d'instruction for Bernard Faÿ*, in the Cour de justice du département de la Seine, Archives Nationales, Paris AN Z/6/288–292 (hereafter cited in the text as *D d'I*, followed by the call number).

99. Faÿ gave the Harris Lectures at Northwestern in 1927 and the Bergen Lectures at Yale in 1936; he also received an honorary degree from Northwestern in 1933.

100. Faÿ's connection to *Les Six* and discussion of his artist brother in Thomson, *Virgil Thomson*, 55, 66–67; his connection to Proust and Gide is discussed in Compagnon, *Le cas Bernard Faÿ*, 13–29.

101. Bernard Faÿ, *Revolution and Freemasonry, 1680–1800* (Boston: Little, Brown and Co., 1935), 123. Hereafter cited in the text as *RF*.

102. "Parasite monstrueux, la Franc-Maçonnerie a grandi de notre abaissement." Bernard Faÿ, quoted in http://www.fm-fr.org/Anti-Maçonnerie.

103. Bernard Faÿ, *The Revolutionary Spirit in France and America* (New York: Harcourt, Brace and Co., 1927), 418, 151. Hereafter cited in the text as *RSFA*.

104. Faÿ is referring to the perception of America by French revolutionaries in this statement. But it is clear from his later attacks on the French Revolution that he himself held similar views, contrasting the "violen[ce]" of the French experience to the "ideal and Arcadian republic" (472) to which the American Revolution was committed.

105. The soldier to whom Faÿ refers was Avery Claflin, who would become his co-editor of the 1929 volume *The American Experiment*. See chapter 2.

106. Bernard Faÿ, "Protestant America," *Living Age* 334 (January–August 1928), 1199.

107. F. Scott Fitzgerald, *The Great Gatsby* (New York: Scribner, 1995), 6.

108. Thomson, *Virgil Thomson*, 89.

109. Bernard Faÿ to Gertrude Stein (January 8, 1930). From the unpublished correspondence, Gertrude Stein and Alice B. Toklas Papers, Yale Collection of American Literature, Beinecke Rare Book and Manuscript Library.

110. Bernard Faÿ, "A Rose Is a Rose," *Saturday Review of Literature* 10, no. 7 (September 2, 1933): 77.

111. *GSP* 164; Dydo, *The Language That Rises*, 61n11. Linda Wagner-Martin writes that Stein had actually been interested in saints since her undergraduate years at Radcliffe, when she took a course on religion with George Santayana. Wagner-Martin, *"Favored Strangers,"* 32.

112. Melissa R. Jones, in her unpublished dissertation "Modernist Hagiography: Saints in the Writings of Joyce, Stein, Eliot, and H. D." (Kent State, May 2004), also discusses the way Stein "freely reconstitute[s] the religious icon of the saint into the secular symbol of the modern artist" (105).

113. Stein, "Talks to Saints or Stories of Saint Remy," in *Painted Lace and Other Pieces, 1914–1937* (New Haven, Conn.: Yale University Press, 1955), 111.

114. Corinne E. Blackmer, "The Ecstasies of Saint Teresa: The Saint as Queer Diva from Crashaw to *Four Saints in Three Acts*," in *En Travesti: Women, Gender Subversion, Opera*,

ed. Corinne E. Blackmer and Patricia Juliana Smith (New York: Columbia University Press, 1995), 333.

115. Jones, "Modernist Hagiography," 105.

116. Gertrude Stein, *Four Saints in Three Acts*, in *Gertrude Stein: Writings 1903–1932*, (New York: The Library of America, 1998), 633.

117. Gertrude Stein, quoted in Samuel M. Steward, *Dear Sammy: Letters from Gertrude Stein and Alice B. Toklas* (Boston: Houghton Mifflin, 1977), 13.

118. Gertrude Stein, "Melanctha," in *Three Lives*, ed. Linda Wagner-Martin (Boston: Bedford/St. Martin's, 2000), 147.

119   Georges Sorel, quoted in *NLNR* 73.

120. See Wagner-Martin, *"Favored Strangers,"* esp. 184–185, for another viewpoint on Stein's response to anti-Semitism during this period.

121. Steward, *Dear Sammy*, 12.

122. Imbs, *Confessions of Another Young Man*, 277, 222–223.

123. In his memoirs, Thomson attests that it was he who introduced Faÿ to Stein (Thomson, *Virgil Thomson*, 181), a claim partially confirmed by Alice Toklas, who writes that it was René Crevel who first brought Faÿ to Stein and Toklas's attention but that "Virgil Thomson one day took us to meet him, and that was the beginning of our long friendship with Bernard Faÿ." Alice B. Toklas, *What Is Remembered* (New York: Holt, Rinehart, 1963), 128. Still, there is some controversy about this account. A letter from Faÿ to Stein written on May 25, 1926, introduces himself and invites her to tea, making no mention of the Thomson connection. Bernard Faÿ letter to Gertrude Stein (May 25, 1926), in *The Flowers of Friendship: Letters Written to Gertrude Stein*, ed. Donald Gallup (New York: Alfred Knopf, 1953), 193.

124. The characterization is Brenda Wineapple's, in *Sister Brother: Gertrude and Leo Stein* (New York: Putnam's, 1996), 72.

125. William Lundell, "Gertrude Stein: A Radio Interview" [1934], *Paris Review* 32 (1990), 90.

126. Gertrude Stein letter to Bernard Faÿ, n.d. From the unpublished correspondence of Gertrude Stein and Bernard Faÿ, Vincent Faÿ collection.

127. Stein quoted in Dydo, *The Language That Rises*, 350.

128. Gertrude Stein, "Bernard Faÿ," in *Portraits and Prayers* (New York: Random House, 1934), 42.

129. Ibid., 44. The "noun debate" between Stein and Faÿ is discussed in Dydo, *The Language That Rises*, 351–352.

130. Stein, "Bernard Faÿ," 45.

2. TRANSATLANTIC CROSSINGS, TRANSLATIONAL POLITICS (1930–1935)

1. Marc Ferro, *The Great War, 1914–1918* (London: Routledge, 1973), 250.

2. Robert H. Ferrell, *Peace in Their Time: The Origins of the Kellogg-Briand Pact* (New Haven, Conn.: Yale University Press, 1952), 265.

3. Carl Schmitt, *The Concept of the Political*, trans. George Schwab (Chicago: University of Chicago Press, 1996).

4. Valentine Thomson, *Briand: Man of Peace* (New York: Covici-Friede, 1930), 301.

5. See Philippe Roger, *The American Enemy: A Story of French Anti-Americanism* (Chicago: University of Chicago Press, 2005). Bernard Faÿ, writing in *Harper's* magazine in 1931, commented that "It would be useless to conceal that there exists in France to-day a considerable number of people who look upon the United States as the symbol of a hateful future and the agent of an atrocious universal metamorphosis." Bernard Faÿ, "The French Mind and the American: An Interpretation in Time of Discord," *Harper's Monthly Magazine* 163, no. 978 (November 1931): 712.

6. Bernard Faÿ, FAF, 439–440.

7. In a remarkable feat of logic, Faÿ even argues that Franco-American tensions over war debts are of little lasting import, because American economic growth, expansion, and technological innovation produces "more profits for everybody" (FAF 443–444).

8. Bernard Faÿ, with Avery Claflin, *The American Experiment* (New York: Harcourt Brace, 1929) (hereafter cited in the text as *AE*). Claflin (1898–1979), an American composer and president of the French American Banking Corporation, met Faÿ while he was serving in the Norton Harliss Ambulance Corps during World War I. Their friendship, which may have been intimate, continued into the 1920s and 1930s and had a significant effect on both men. It was Faÿ who converted Claflin to Catholicism. And according to Robert Dundas, of Florida International University, it was Claflin who introduced Virgil Thomson to Faÿ at Harvard. Dundas is completing a monograph on Claflin and his operas.

9. In a scathing account of Faÿ's lectures at the Collège de France, Harry Levin recalls the "dynastic note" Faÿ would sound to describe American presidents, as though America were to be viewed "as a repetition of the feudal past" rather than "an adumbration of the democratic future." Harry Levin, "*France-Amérique*: The Transatlantic Refraction," in *Comparative Literature: Matter and Method*, ed. A. Owen Aldridge (Urbana: University of Illinois Press, 1969, 277. Levin also notes that he saw Gertrude Stein at Faÿ's Collège de France lectures (277).

10. On the nonconformists, see John Hellman, *The Communitarian Third Way: Alexandre Marc's Ordre Nouveau, 1930–2000* (Montreal: McGill-Queen's University Press, 2002); and chapter 5.

11. "Banish the myth of the omnicompetent voter and the omniscient majority," Faÿ writes (*AE* 260).

12. Drieu, quoted in Roger Griffin, "Europe for the Europeans: Fascist Myths of the New Order, 1922–1992," in *A Fascist Century* (New York: Palgrave Macmillan, 2008), 151.

13. In *Hitler's Empire* (London: Penguin, 2008), Mark Mazower points out how crucial the idea of empire was to the discussion of European-American relations in the interwar period. Europe saw its own empires disintegrating and looked to America as a new model of an empire, possibly one without colonies—an empire of ideas and values that might dominate the world. See in particular, chapter 18, "The New Order in World History."

14. See Roger, *The American Enemy*, 293.

15. "La Manille aux Enchères," in Bernard Faÿ, *Faites vos jeux* (Paris: Grasset, 1927) (hereafter cited in the text as *FVJ*). *La manille aux enchères* is a French card game that proceeds through the raising of stakes.

16. Faÿ: "The Anglo-Saxon American is the legitimate or voluntary descendant of the Puritans. From them he received his stature, his strength, and that handsome refinement and simplicity which bespeak the traditions of an ancient civilization. . . . His carriage bears evidence of a free and glorious destiny; and even among the humblest of his kind, one notices a natural pride and distinction" (*AE* 209).

17. In *The Autobiography of Alice B. Toklas*, Stein recounts the following scene at her atelier: "Gertrude Stein who has an explosive temper, came in another evening and there were her brother, Alfy [Alfred Maurer, a friend] and a stranger. She did not like the stranger's looks. Who is that, said she to Alfy. I didn't bring him, said Alfy. He looks like a Jew, said Gertrude Stein, he is worse than that, said Alfy" (*ABT* 13). Samuel M. Steward, however, writes that Stein identified with Jewishness ("I never make any bones about it") but was adept at manipulating the genteel anti-Semitism of her contemporaries. Samuel M. Steward, *Dear Sammy: Letters from Gertrude Stein and Alice B. Toklas* (Boston: Houghton Mifflin, 1977), 9.

18. Gertrude Stein, "What Is English Literature," in Gertrude Stein, *Look at Me Now and Here I Am: Writings and Lectures 1909–45* (London: Penguin, 1971), 42.

19. Gertrude Stein, "My Last About Money," in *How Writing Is Written: Volume II of the Previously Uncollected Writings of Gertrude Stein*, ed. Robert Bartlett Haas (Los Angeles: Black Sparrow Press, 1974), 111.

20. As Jefferson himself put it: farmers "are the chosen people of God, if ever He had a chosen people, whose breasts he has made his peculiar deposit for substantial and genuine virtue." Cited in Richard A. Levins, *Willard Cochrane and the Family Farm* (Lincoln: University of Nebraska Press, 2000), 1.

21. The story of Thomas Jefferson's revival by twentieth-century intellectuals—particularly in relation to a wide-ranging critique of modernity from both the Left and the Right—remains as yet untold. Stein and the following cohorts are just a handful among many. The Jeffersonianism of Williams was nurtured through his friendship with Ezra Pound, alongside a strong critique of modern capitalism and a belief in the alternative economic system of "Social Credit"; unlike Pound, however, Williams "despised the fascist dictators of Germany and Italy." Hugh Witemeyer, "Introduction to Part III," in *Pound/Williams: Selected Letters of Ezra Pound and William Carlos Williams*, ed. Hugh Witemeyer (New York: New Directions, 1996), 124. The most developed study of this relation is Alec Marsh, *Money and Modernity: Pound, Williams, and the Spirit of Jefferson* (Tuscaloosa: University of Alabama Press, 1998). Dos Passos, who wrote a biography of Thomas Jefferson (*The Head and Heart of Thomas Jefferson* [Garden City, N.Y.: Doubleday & Co., 1954]), was a Communist fellow traveler for much of his youth but turned against the movement over the course of the 1930s and in the wake of disillusionment over the Spanish Civil War and the politics of Franklin D. Roosevelt. While never a fascist sympathizer, Dos Passos's politics during World War II became increasingly isolationist; afterward, like his fellow Jeffersonian Ayn Rand, Dos Passos identified with a primarily libertarian political agenda that sought to return America to a lost ethic of individualism. Edgar Lee Masters felt that Jefferson was at "the foundation for many things" in his famous *Spoon River Anthology*; he also concurred with Stein and others that "the democratic ideal that originated with Jefferson" was destroyed in the nineteenth century and particularly by the Civil War, which "allowed materialistic

and repressive forces to dominate the country. In short, America degenerated from primal innocence." Masters, quoted in Herbert K. Russell, *Edgar Lee Masters: A Biography* (Urbana: University of Illinois Press, 2005), 97–98. John Dewey saw Jefferson as a "model both for an understanding of democracy and for personal emulation." Daniel F. Rice, *Reinhold Niebuhr and John Dewey: An American Odyssey* (Albany, N.Y.: SUNY Press, 1993), 334n15. In an essay on Jefferson, Dewey advocated returning to this model, arguing that "defense of democracy against the attacks to which it is subjected . . . depend[s] upon taking once more the position Jefferson took about its moral basis and purpose. . . . A renewal of faith in common human nature, in its potentialities in general and in its power in particular to respond to reason and truth, is a surer bulwark against totalitarianism than is demonstration of material success or devout worship of special legal and political forms." John Dewey, "Presenting Thomas Jefferson," in *John Dewey, The Later Works, 1925–1953*, ed. Jo Ann Boydston (Carbondale: Southern Illinois University Press, 1988), 220.

22. Ezra Pound, "The Jefferson-Adams Letters as a Shrine and a Monument," in *Ezra Pound: Selected Prose, 1909–1965* (New York: New Directions, 1973), 147. For Pound's use of Jefferson, see Marsh, *Money and Modernity*, and Gregory Eiselein, "Jefferson in the Thirties: Pound's Use of Historical Documents in Eleven New *Cantos*," *Clio* 19 (Fall 1989), 31–40. For an account of the intellectual roots of Pound's attraction to fascism, see Leon Surette, *Pound in Purgatory: From Economic Radicalism to Anti-Semitism* (Urbana: University of Illinois Press, 1999).

23. See Marsh, *Money and Modernity*, 7.

24. Alec Marsh writes: "The myth of the American farmer freeholder that is the legacy of Jefferson can descend very easily into a shrill nativism, because a 'Jeffersonian' distrust of finance capitalism can readily become a septic anti-Semitism." Ibid., 6.

25. Stein, "My Last About Money," 111; *EA* 63–64.

26. In *Wars I Have Seen*, Stein makes an observation about social class that attributes "life in the nineteenth century" to the petit bourgeoisie: "and that is what the lower middle class is and it is they that make the last there is of life in the nineteenth century because they have no hope and no adventure" (*W* 17).

27. Stein, "What Is English Literature," 47.

28. Steven Ungar, *Scandal and Aftereffect: Blanchot and France Since 1930* (Minneapolis: University of Minnesota Press, 1995), 3.

29. Benedict Anderson, *Imagined Communities: Reflections on the Origin and Spread of Nationalism* (London: Verso, 1983). Wolfgang Sauer argues that "fascism can be defined as a revolt of those who lost—directly or indirectly, temporarily or permanently—by industrialization." Wolfgang Sauer, "National Socialism: Totalitarianism or Fascism?" *American Historical Review* 73, no. 2 (December 1967), 417. While Sauer's focus is on Germany, his argument helps explain Pétain's profound appeal to the French "déclassé" and to veterans groups on the grounds of "turn[ing] against technological progress and economic growth" and "return[ing] to the earlier, 'natural' ways of life" (417).

30. The term "democratic decadence" was first used in Jean de Fabrègue's young Right manifesto in *Reaction pour l'Ordre*, a journal for which Bernard Faÿ also wrote. See John Hellman, *The Communitarian Third Way*, 24.

31. *BW* 778. Stein begins these observations during the mid-1930s, referring to America as an old century because it started "twentieth-century writing" before anyone else: "the United States had the first instance of what I call Twentieth Century writing. You see it first in Walt Whitman." Gertrude Stein, "How Writing Is Written," in *How Writing Is Written: Volume II of the Previously Uncollected Writings of Gertrude Stein*, ed. Robert Bartlett Haas (Los Angeles: Black Sparrow Press, 1974), 153. See also "Why I Do Not Live in America": America "is the mother of modern civilisation. . . . A country this is the oldest and therefore the most important country in the world quite naturally produces the creators, and so naturally it is I an American who was and is thinking in writing was born in America and live in Paris" (51).

32. Stein quote from interview in "Yank—The Army Weekly" magazine (1945), in *Gertrude Stein's America*, ed. Gilbert A. Harrison (New York: Liveright, 1996), 82.

33. For Stein as Benjamin Franklin, see Pierre Ordioni, *Tout commence à Alger 40/44* (Paris: Stock, 1972), 60.

34. Note from Gertrude Stein to Bernard Faÿ, n.d. Unpublished correspondence, Gertrude Stein and Alice B. Toklas Papers, Yale Collection of American Literature, Beinecke Rare Book and Manuscript Library. Stein writes, possibly in reference to the 1930 publication of her text "Lucy Church Amiably": "For Bernard Faÿ, Lucy Church Amiably all about the Bugey the nice country where we so contentedly cemented our friendship, Gertrude Stein."

35. Jean Anthelme Brillat-Savarin, *The Physiology of Taste; Or, Meditations on Transcendental Gastronomy*, trans. M. F. K. Fisher (New York: The Heritage Press, 1949), 9n.

36. Stein's friend Elliot Paul, who gave a colorful and unreliable account of the leasing episode in *Understanding the French* (New York: Random House, 1954), 21–22, offers another version of this mythification of French provincial life when he writes about a Bugey harvest festival: "Hosanna! The glow of the embers at twilight is reconciled with the tinted clouds of sunset, and the smell of roast meats, pungents and charred grass and the gleam of the Rhone and the sky and the Alps, around the French, leave an impression of cosmic unity and universal harmony which, because of its theoretical structure beneath the transient light and sound waves, endures, world without end" (23–24).

37. *ABT* 281; Alice B. Toklas, *The Alice B. Toklas Cook Book* (New York: Harper & Row, 1982), 94.

38. Ulla E. Dydo, *Gertrude Stein: The Language That Rises, 1923–1934* (Evanston, Ill.: Northwestern University Press, 2003), 329; Bernard Faÿ, "Gertrude Stein, Poète de l'Amérique," *Revue de Paris* 42, no. 22 (November 15, 1935): 295.

39. Gertrude Stein letter to Bernard Faÿ, n.d. From the unpublished correspondence of Gertrude Stein and Bernard Faÿ, Vincent Faÿ collection.

40. Toklas's comment appears in an undated note following an undated letter to Georges Maratier in the Papers of Gertrude Stein and her Circle, Special Collections, University of Maryland Libraries. The letter begins: "Here is the information about our brave lieutenant." For Stein's sense of guilt about the Bonhomme affair, see the cryptic passages in Stein's 1930 text *History or Messages from History* (Copenhagen: Green Integer, 1997): "A lieutenant is not a captain in which way he finishes. I never like to think of anybody" (19); and "There will be an emigration. They will have satisfaction. Hours of

their opportunities and they do not like to think about them. In this way they are self-ish" (20).

41. Cited in an undated letter to Georges Maratier in the Papers of Gertrude Stein and Her Circle, Special Collections, University of Maryland Libraries.

42. Gertrude Stein note to Bernard Faÿ, n.d.. From the unpublished correspondence of Gertrude Stein and Bernard Faÿ, Vincent Faÿ collection.

43. Stein's "megalomania" has been a recurring charge in criticism of her work and life, fueled in large part by Stein's own pronouncements during the 1930s that she was a genius (a term whose use by Stein, as I explain in my book *Gertrude Stein, Modernism, and the Problem of "Genius"* [Edinburgh: Edinburgh University Press, 2000], was in fact highly overdetermined). See, for example, the attack on Stein by Tristan Tzara in "Testimony against Gertrude Stein": "I cannot believe it necessary for me to insist on the presence of a clinical case of megalomania." Georges Braque et al., "Testimony Against Gertrude Stein," *transition* 23 (February 1935), 13. Indeed, "megalomania" has remained the favored term to describe Stein during this particular period, with John Herbert Gill, for one, describing the Bilignin episode as "an especially outrageous instance of the cold amorality of megalomania." John Herbert Gill, *Detecting Gertrude Stein and Other Suspects on the Shadow Side of Modernism* (New York: Democritus Books, 2003), 130. In her defense, Ulla Dydo (*The Language That Rises*, 411) argues that "Stein's so-called megalomania is a compensatory mechanism for her real frustration about publication and reception of her work," as though by inflating her own importance and influence over others Stein could make up for her lack of public recognition in the "dry spell" before the publication of *The Autobiography of Alice B. Toklas*. My own sense is that "megalomania" is an inadequate term to describe Stein's self-identity, particularly because of its problematic association with delusion.

44. Bernard Faÿ wrote several articles in English and French on Gertrude Stein in the 1930s, including the piece in *Je Suis Partout* discussed in chapter 3. See also "Portrait de Gertrude Stein," *La Revue Européenne*, reprinted in Victor Llona, Bernard Faÿ, et al., *Les romanciers américains* (Paris: Denoël and Steele, 1931), 371–378, which also includes Faÿ and Grace-Ives de Longevialle's translation of "Melanctha"; "A Rose Is a Rose," *The Saturday Review of Literature* 10, no. 7 (September 2, 1933): 77–79; "Gertrude Stein et ses souvenirs," *Le Figaro* no. 300 (October 27, 1934): 6; and "Gertrude Stein: Poète de l'Amérique," *La Revue de Paris* 42, no. 22 (November 15, 1935): 294–312. He also wrote the preface to the abridged edition of *The Making of Americans*, published as *The Making of Americans: The Hersland Family* (New York: Harcourt Brace, 1934). *The Making of Americans* was translated in 1932 by Faÿ and Renée Seillière and published as *Américains d'Amérique: Histoire d'une famille américaine* (Paris: Librairie Stock, 1933); and *The Autobiography of Alice B. Toklas* was translated by Faÿ and published as *Autobiographie d'Alice Toklas* (Paris: Gallimard, 1934).

45. Bradley, cited in Dydo, *The Language That Rises*, 570.

46. Gertrude Stein letter to Bernard Faÿ, n.d. From the unpublished correspondence of Gertrude Stein and Bernard Faÿ, Vincent Faÿ collection.

47. Faÿ, "Portrait de Gertrude Stein", 2; "Préface" to *Américains d'Amerique*, 11.

48. See my essay "Lost in Translation: Stein's Vichy Collaboration," *Modernism/modernity* 11, no. 4 (November, 2004): 651–668, which discusses the Hugnet affair at length.

49. Ulla Dydo, who mentions that during the early 1930s "American leaders were . . . topics of conversation with Faÿ" (*The Language That Rises*, 577), does not go further than this observation.

50. Gertrude Stein letter to Bernard Faÿ, n.d. From the unpublished correspondence of Gertrude Stein and Bernard Faÿ, Vincent Faÿ collection.

51. Bernard Faÿ, *George Washington: Republican Aristocrat* (Boston: Houghton Mifflin, 1931) (hereafter cited in the text as *GW*). Gertrude Stein letter to Bernard Faÿ, n.d. From the unpublished correspondence of Gertrude Stein and Bernard Faÿ, Vincent Faÿ collection. Another letter by Stein to Faÿ in the Vincent Faÿ collection is full of praise for his "address to the Academy": "In that you did really create your space. Compared to that the space in the Washington was only described but in this the space and all its consequences are really created." Stein never identifies the academy where she heard Faÿ lecturing.

52. Bernard Faÿ letter to Frank Monaghan, October 3, 1931. Division of Rare and Manuscript Collections, Carl A. Kroch Library, Cornell University.

53. Faÿ's ideological representation of Washington's aristocratic stance has been curiously overlooked by contemporary readers, who continue to cite Faÿ's biography as an example of objective scholarship. See for example, Jeremy Engels, "Reading the Riot Act: Rhetoric, Psychology, and Counter-Revolutionary Discourse in Shays' Rebellion, 1786–1787," *Quarterly Journal of Speech* 91, no. 1 (February, 2005): 85n17.

54. Dydo writes that "the basic idea of *Four In America*" was "that American genius is inevitably expressed and is not restricted to one calling," an idea that supported Stein's investigation of the four figures "for what they might have become had they not become what they did." Dydo, *The Language That Rises*, 580, 578.

55. Gertrude Stein, "Finally George: A Vocabulary of Thinking," in *How to Write* (New York: Dover, 1975), 278.

56. See Stein's undated letter to Faÿ from the early 1930s: "I like writing to you from here because it was here that our friendship really began and it is a nice friendship and I am very pleased with it and I was awfully moved by your note and I love you very much and it will be nice seeing you this summer and it is lovely here . . . and we are all clean and peaceful." From the unpublished correspondence of Gertrude Stein and Bernard Faÿ, Vincent Faÿ collection. See also my discussion of washing and ethnicity, chapter 1.

57. See Ulla Dydo's discussion of this in *The Language That Rises*, 591.

58. Gertrude Stein, *Four in America* (New Haven, Conn.: Yale University Press, 1947), 169 (hereafter cited in the text as *FIA*).

59. There is also a tantalizing suggestion that Faÿ himself may have served as a model for her "George Washington." Sometime in 1930, Stein writes Faÿ a note while helping to edit his *George Washington*: "I am looking forward to having the rest of the Washington, I like doing it, and I also want very much to know how it goes on and how it finished, I am not without meditation about you and a novel." Gertrude Stein letter to Bernard Faÿ, n.d. From the unpublished correspondence of Gertrude Stein and Bernard Faÿ, Vincent Faÿ collection.

60. "As Gertrude Stein Reviews a Book on President Roosevelt," *Kansas City Star* (January 20, 1934): 5.

61. "Theodore and Franklin Roosevelt like Napoleon and Louis Napoleon even though they belonged to the country to which they belonged were foreign to it." Gertrude

Stein, *The Geographical History of America or the Relation of Human Nature to the Human Mind* (Baltimore, Md.: The Johns Hopkins University Press, 1995), 127 (hereafter cited in the text as *GHA*). Gertrude Stein, "A Political Series," in *Painted Lace and Other Pieces (1914–1937)* (New Haven, Conn.: Yale University Press, 1955), 73.

62. Gertrude Stein letter to Bernard Faÿ, marked 1932 in margins. From the unpublished correspondence of Gertrude Stein and Bernard Faÿ, Vincent Faÿ collection.

63. John L. Harvey, "Conservative Crossings: Bernard Faÿ and the Rise of American Studies in Third-Republic France," *Historical Reflections/Réflexions historiques* 36 (2010): 105.

64. Bernard Faÿ, "An Invitation to American Historians," *Harper's Monthly Magazine* 166 (1932): 20–31.

65. Stein, *History or Messages from History*, 37.

66. Gertrude Stein letter to Bernard Faÿ, n.d. From the unpublished correspondence of Gertrude Stein and Bernard Faÿ, Vincent Faÿ collection.

67. Faÿ's success was reported in the weekly Parisian newspaper *L'Illustration*. Elisabeth Clevenot, "Une chaire d'histoire des Etats-Unis au Collège de France," *L'Illustration* 4642 (February 20, 1932): 232.

68. Marguerite Bistis, "Managing Bergson's Crowd: Professionalism and the *Mondain* at the Collège de France," *Historical Reflections/Réflexions historiques* 22, no. 2 (1996): 391.

69. Roger, *The American Enemy*, 271, 203.

70. André Siegfried, *America Comes of Age* (New York: Harcourt, Brace, 1927), 347, 350.

71. Faÿ had reviewed Tardieu's *France and America: Some Experiences in Cooperation* and Siegfried's *America Comes of Age* in the *New York Herald Tribune* (May 1, 1927), referring to the latter as "a French Protestant, endowed with very strong control," whose writing "does not always flow easily," while Tardieu in comparison was "a proud soul, an original mind and a powerful will": "a man" rather than "a professional writer."

72. Eugen Weber, *The Hollow Years: France in the 1930s* (New York: Norton, 1994), 163.

73. Bernard Oudin, *Aristide Briand* (Paris: Perrin, 2004), 526.

74. André Tardieu, *France and America: Some Experiences in Cooperation* (Boston: Houghton Mifflin, 1927), 5.

75. "[B]ourgeoisie, parliamentarism, democracy are as hollow as nobility, royalty, Estates General were 150 years ago." Tardieu, quoted in Weber, *The Hollow Years*, 117. Faÿ adds his own interpretation of Tardieu's allegiance with the Right in a note to Gertrude Stein: "The Briand defeat [by Tardieu] is good for me. Briand fell before my friends, I daresay." Bernard Faÿ letter to Gertrude Stein, May 17, 1931. From the unpublished correspondence of Gertrude Stein and Bernard Faÿ, Vincent Faÿ collection.

76. Bernard Faÿ letter to Gertrude Stein, November 18, 1931. From the unpublished correspondence of Gertrude Stein and Bernard Faÿ, Vincent Faÿ collection.

77. Dydo, *The Language That Rises*, 578n44.

78. Ibid., 462.

79. Bernard Faÿ letter to Gertrude Stein, April 3, 1930. From the unpublished correspondence, Gertrude Stein and Alice B. Toklas Papers, Yale Collection of American Literature. Beinecke Rare Book and Manuscript Library. Gertrude Stein letter to Bernard Faÿ, n.d. From the unpublished correspondence of Gertrude Stein and Bernard Faÿ, Vincent Faÿ collection.

80. Gertrude Stein letter to Bernard Faÿ, n.d. From the unpublished correspondence of Gertrude Stein and Bernard Faÿ, Vincent Faÿ collection. Stein voices her disagreements over the merits of Siegfried with a local Belley neighbor, Mademoiselle de Canisey. It is interesting to note the revisionism that emanated from Siegfried's side as well concerning the 1932 Collège appointment. In a 1960 *Hommage à André Siegfried*, an administrator at the Collège de France, Marcel Bataillon, wrote that despite Siegfried's failure to win the chair in American civilization, his success at winning a chair in economic and political geography in 1933 (which he held until 1946) was better suited to his interests, allowing him to "extend . . . his gifts as an observer of a world in transformation" into many different arenas. *Hommage à André Siegfried*, par L'Association André Siegfried (Paris: L'Imprimerie R. Foulon, 1961).

81. Stein quoted in Dydo, *The Language That Rises*, 468.

82. Gertrude Stein letter to Bernard Faÿ, n.d. From the unpublished correspondence of Gertrude Stein and Bernard Faÿ, Vincent Faÿ collection. In this letter, Stein discusses trying to get a visa for two new, presumably reliable, Swiss servants, Marius Piguet and his wife, since "I, a femme de lettre [*sic*], have been interrupted all summer by scenes with drunken domestics."

83. Gertrude Stein, quoted in *LP* 154.

84. Gertrude Stein letter to Bernard Faÿ, n.d. From the unpublished correspondence of Gertrude Stein and Bernard Faÿ, Vincent Faÿ collection.

85. Bernard Faÿ letter to Gertrude Stein, February 18, 1930. From the unpublished correspondence of Gertrude Stein and Bernard Faÿ, Vincent Faÿ collection.

86. This commitment is exemplified by a famous story about the French writer Paul Valéry. During World War II, Valéry was approached at the door to the Collège by a German officer who demanded to know what was being taught inside. Valéry answered, "It's a place where speech is free." Valéry quoted in Christophe Charle, "Le Collège de France," in Pierre Nora, ed., *Les lieux de mémoire: La nation* (Gallimard, 1986), vol. 2, part 3:422. It is of course ironic that Bernard Faÿ, working in the service of the Germans during World War II, was also allowed to practice free speech at the Collège, only losing his chair after the war was over, in 1946.

87. James Laughlin, "About Gertrude Stein," *The Yale Review* 77 (October 1988): 535.

88. See the analysis of "talking and listening" in chapter 3 of my book, *Gertrude Stein, Modernism, and the Problem of "Genius,"* 79–107.

89. Gertrude Stein, *Lectures in America* (London: Virago, 1988), acknowledgments page.

90. Stein, quoted in Dydo, *The Language That Rises*, 573.

91. Interestingly, Faÿ was one of the first people to whom Stein showed the manuscript of *Q.E.D.*, after having "completely forgot about it for many years" (*ABT* 104).

92. Gertrude Stein, *Fernhurst, Q.E.D. and Other Early Writings* (New York: W. W. Norton, 1996), 60.

93. Laughlin, "About Gertrude Stein," 535.

94. Gertrude Stein letter to Bernard Faÿ, n.d. From the unpublished correspondence of Gertrude Stein and Bernard Faÿ, Vincent Faÿ collection. The reference to René Crevel in this letter shows that it was written before Crevel's death on June 18, 1935.

3. MOVING RIGHTWARD (1935-1940)

1. Gertrude Stein, "Gertrude Stein Views Life and Politics: Interview with Lansing Warren," *New York Times Magazine* (May 6, 1934): 9.

2. See Edward M. Burns and Ulla E. Dydo with William Rice, *The Letters of Gertrude Stein and Thornton Wilder* (New Haven, Conn.: Yale University Press, 1996), 414; also Brenda Wineapple, "The Politics of Politics; or, How the Atomic Bomb Didn't Interest Gertrude Stein and Emily Dickinson," *South Central Review* 23, no. 3 (Fall 2006): 37–45.

3. Helen Buchalter, "Gertrude Stein Doesn't 'Take From' Causes, She Tells an Ardent Reformist," *Washington Daily News* (December 31, 1934): 14.

4. Gertrude Stein, notebooks to *The Making of Americans* (unpublished), NB, 14–7. Gertrude Stein and Alice B. Toklas Papers, Yale Collection of American Literature. Beinecke Rare Book and Manuscript Library.

5. Jolas, quoted in Georges Braque et al., "Testimony Against Gertrude Stein," *transition* 23 (February 1935): 11.

6. Gertrude Stein, "I Came and Here I Am," in *How Writing Is Written: Volume II of the Previously Uncollected Writings of Gertrude Stein*, ed. Robert Bartlett Haas (Los Angeles: Black Sparrow Press, 1974), 68.

7. In an interview with Stein for *Vogue* conducted in 1941, Thérèse Bonney notes that Stein "stayed because she has found in Billignen [*sic*] the calm and peace that are necessary to her work." "Gertrude Stein in France," *Vogue* (July 1, 1942): 61.

8. Adolf Hitler, quoted in Neil Gregor, *How to Read Hitler* (New York: W. W. Norton, 2005), 61.

9. Stein's self-Orientalizing gesture in *Everybody's Autobiography* is far from coherent or simple, as shown by her anxious effort to describe herself as "Oriental" rather than "Jewish."

10. Gertrude Stein, "Off We All Went to See Germany," *Life* (August 6, 1945): 58.

11. Alice Kaplan, *The Collaborator: The Trial and Execution of Robert Brasillach* (Chicago: University of Chicago Press, 2000), x.

12. Eugen Weber, *Action Française: Royalism and Reaction in Twentieth-Century France* (Stanford: Stanford University Press, 1962), 506.

13. Kaplan, *The Collaborator*, 23.

14. Ibid, 32.

15. Bernard Faÿ, "Salzbourg d'été," *Je Suis Partout* (September 15, 1934); "L'apothéose de Gertrude Stein," *Je Suis Partout* (January 19, 1935).

16. "Gertrude Stein: Poète de l'Amérique," *La Revue de Paris* 42, no. 22 (November 15, 1935): 294–312.

17. David Carroll, *French Literary Fascism: Nationalism, Anti-Semitism, and the Ideology of Culture* (Princeton: Princeton University Press, 1995), 104–105.

18. Ibid., 106, 107.

19. Bernard Faÿ, *Civilisation américaine* (Paris: Sagittaire, 1939), 252.

20. Eugen Weber, *The Hollow Years: France in the 1930s* (New York: Norton, 1994), 111.

21. Ibid., 113.

22. Weber, *Action Française*, 15.

23. Faÿ received an honorary degree in literature from Northwestern University on June 3, 1933.

24. Dudley Andrew and Steven Ungar, *Popular Front Paris and the Poetics of Culture* (Cambridge, Mass.: Harvard University Press, 2005), 16.

25. Bernard Faÿ letter to Fanny Butcher, May 31, 1934. Gertrude Stein collection, Harry Ransom Humanities Research Center, The University of Texas at Austin.

26. See Paul F. Jankowski, *Stavisky: A Confidence Man in the Republic of Virtue* (Ithaca, N.Y.: Cornell University Press, 2002). In a 1937 letter to W. G. Rogers, Stein writes: "You see in the old days the government changed all the time there were so many parties, but Stavisky was a real boss and he organized the Radical Socialists to stay and that machinery is still functioning though the real majority are tired of it." Stein, quoted in W. G. Rogers, *When This You See Remember Me: Gertrude Stein in Person* (New York: Rinehart and Co., 1948), 216. In fact, the Radical party had been largely in power in France since the first ministry of Camille Chautemps in 1930.

27. *Action Française*, quoted in Carmen Calil, *Bad Faith: A Forgotten History of Family and Fatherland* (London: Jonathan Cape, 2006), 108. As Jacques Bariéty has noted, the events of early 1934 arose out of complex and overdetermined sources from the outside as well as the inside. While the Stavisky affair made visible the antagonism of the two Frances, it also revealed public discontent over French foreign affairs, especially the pacifist stance that had accompanied Hitler's rise to power. "Les partisans français de l'entente franco-allemande et la 'prise du pouvoir' par Hitler, Avril 1932–Avril 1934," in *La France et L'Allemagne entre les deux guerres mondiales*, ed. Bariéty et al. (Nancy: Presses universitaires de Nancy, 1987), 29.

28. Bernard Faÿ, "Le bilan de l'action maçonnique en France," April 18, 1942, lecture given at the Grand Orient de France, rue Cadet, Paris. Cited in Bernard Faÿ dossier (Renseignements Generaux), Archives de la Prefecture de la Police, Paris.

29. In the wake of Dan Brown's bestselling novel *The Lost Symbol* (New York: Doubleday, 2009), which deals with a shadowy Masonic organization just steps away from the White House, this benign assessment may be changing.

30. Jasper Ridley notes that in 1998 the number of American Freemasons was over 2,200,000; in France today, the number is 84,000. *The Freemasons: A History of the World's Most Powerful Secret Society* (New York: Arcade, 2001), 275.

31. For more on Freemasonry in France, see Pierre Chevallier, *Histoire de la franc-maçonnerie française*, 3 volumes (Paris: Fayard, 1974); Lucien Botrel, *Histoire de la francmaçonnerie française sous l'occupation* (Paris: Ed. Detrad, 1987); Dominique Rossignol, *Vichy et les franc-maçons. La liquidation des sociétés secrètes, 1940–1944* (Paris: J-C Lattès, 1981); and the special issue on French Freemasonry and anti-Freemasonry in *Sciences et Avenir* (February 2003): 38–59.

32. Lacan, summarized in Bran Nicol, "Reading Paranoia: Paranoia, Epistemophilia, and the Postmodern Crisis of Interpretation," *Literature and Psychology* 45, nos. 1–2 (1999): 46.

33. Cynthia Hendershot discusses the link between paranoia and totalization in "Paranoia and the Delusion of the Total System," *American Imago* 54, no. 1 (1997): 15–37.

34. See Bernard Faÿ, *Franklin, the Apostle of Modern Times* (Boston: Little, Brown, 1929); *George Washington, Republican Aristocrat; The Two Franklins: Fathers of American*

Democracy (Boston: Little, Brown, 1933); *Roosevelt and His America* (Boston: Little, Brown, 1933).

35. This blurring of boundaries between Freemasons and other perceived adversaries is evident in the nineteenth century as well, but in the first decades of the twentieth century it took on a new intensity, as when the notorious tract *The Protocols of the Elders of Zion* (first published in 1903) claims that Freemasons were in the service of the "Elders of Zion." From David Bankier, "Freemasons," in *Encyclopedia of the Holocaust*, ed. Israel Gutman (1990), 2:531.

36. See Lucien Sabah, *Journal de Gueydan "de" Roussel* (Paris: Klincksieck, 2000), 288–290 (hereafter cited in the text as *JGR*). Sabah reproduces a Vichy-era "Report on Monsieur Philippe Poirson" written by Faÿ in 1943 wherein he details his prewar familiarity with Poirson through an anti-Masonic group called the Committee for National Unity for the Reconstruction of France (*Rassemblement National pour la Reconstruction de la France*): "Ce groupe . . . était etabli rue Duphot et avait comme secretaire le commandant Souchon. Nous publiions des brochures mensuelles contre la Maçonnerie, les Juifs, le Front Populaire, et la 'Croisade des Democraties'" ("This group . . . was established on rue Duphot and had as Secretary Commander Souchon. We published monthly brochures against Freemasonry, the Jews, the Popular Front, and the 'Crusade of Democracies'"). For more on this group, see chapter 5. In the same report, Faÿ also refers to having been to reunions of the RISS (Revue Internationale des Sociétés Secrètes), which had an "antimasonic and antidemocratic" bent.

37. See, among others, the following articles by Faÿ: "L'Espagne et son destin," *La Revue Universelle* 16 (November 15, 1937): 385–398; "Un siècle et demi de République démocratique aux Etats-Unis," *La Revue Universelle* 9 (August 1, 1939): 256–267; "Instruction et enseignement en France," *Courrier Royal* 26 (December 28, 1935): 1; "Europa ist eine Wirklichkeit," *Deutsch-Französische Monatshefte / Cahiers franco-allemands* 7–8 (1937): 217–220.

38. See the following articles by Faÿ: "Le français en face de lui-meme," *La Gerbe* (July 18, 1940): 1; and "Du courage," *La Gerbe* (August 1, 1940): 1.

39. The Interparliamentary Group of Action is discussed in Charles Grant Hamilton, "Freemasonry, A Prisoner of War," *The New Age* 57, no. 3 (March 1949): 149.

40. Pierre Gaxotte, "La franc-maçonnerie [review of *La franc-maçonnerie et la révolution intellectuelle du XVIIIe siècle* by Bernard Faÿ]," *Je Suis Partout* 240 (June 29, 1935): 1.

41. Pascal Ory, *Les Collaborateurs* (Paris: Editions du Seuil, 1976), 148.

42. The most positive American review of Faÿ's book comes from Cuthbert Wright, "Freemasonry and Revolutions," *New York Times* (January 26, 1936), which appreciates the "charm" of Faÿ's writing and the significance of his argument to the French Catholic context.

43. Henry Steele Commager, "Free Masonry, the Key to the XVIII Century [Review of *Revolution and Freemasonry, 1680–1800*]," *New York Herald Tribune Books* (December 8, 1935), VII:3. Other contemporary critics have been equally skeptical about Faÿ's claims. See, in particular, Neil L. York, "Freemasons and the American Revolution," *The Historian* 55 (1993): 315–330.

44. Vincent Scramuzza, "*Revolution and Freemasonry, 1680–1800* by Bernard Faÿ [review]," *American Sociologial Review* 1, no. 2 (April 1936): 337.

45. Bernard Faÿ, "American Civilization Assayed: Bernard Faÿ believes that Europe needs to examine the American Way to see if it does not contain, despite mistakes, principles that are of definite value to the whole world," *New York Times Magazine* (February 28, 1932), SM18.

46. *The Franco-American Review*, published in France as the *Revue Franco-Américaine*, was the brainchild of Faÿ and Frank Monaghan, professor of History at Yale University. It published five issues, appearing between 1936 and 1938.

47. Bernard Faÿ letter to Gertrude Stein, March 22, 1935. From the unpublished correspondence of Gertrude Stein and Bernard Faÿ, Vincent Faÿ collection.

48. Deposition of Bertrand de Lagger [March 7, 1946] *D d'I*, AN Z/6/290.

49. Bernard Faÿ, "Les origines et l'esprit de la franc-maçonnerie," *La Revue Universelle* 66, no. 8 (July 15, 1936): 174.

50. Bernard Faÿ letter to Lt. August Moritz, July 17, 1942. *D d'I* AN Z/6/290.

51. Bernard Faÿ, *Roosevelt and His America* (Boston: Little Brown, 1933), vi.

52. Bernard Faÿ's phrase about Roosevelt is from "French News from France," *Commonweal* 23 (January 10, 1936): 286.

53. See chapter 2, p. 59.

54. Faÿ, *Roosevelt and His America*, 245.

55. In the French version of his text, Faÿ makes much of this distinction for a presumably unfamiliar (French) audience: "Tandis que Harvard est en Amérique la citadelle de l'Amérique blanche, blonde, anglo-saxonne et puritaine, Columbia est l'un de ces creusets où se forment les idées internationales, où se mêlent les races, et où l'intelligence aiguë des juifs se plaît à briller" ("While Harvard is in America the citadel of white, blond, Anglo-saxon and Puritan America, Columbia is one of those melting pots where international ideas are formed, where the races are blended, and where the sharp intelligence of Jews likes to shine forth"). Bernard Faÿ, *Roosevelt et son Amérique* (Paris: Plon, 1933), 184, 278.

56. "Telle est sa grande force, ou sa faiblesse secrète." Note that this is the final sentence of the French original. Faÿ, *Roosevelt et son Amérique*, 330. The English translation has an "Epilogue" that paints FDR in a much more flattering light.

57. Bernard Faÿ, "Roosevelt Plebiscité: Choses Vues par Bernard Faÿ," *Je Suis Partout* (November 2, 1936): 9.

58. Bernard Faÿ, "De quoi parle-t-on en Amérique?" *Je Suis Partout* (February 27, 1937): 9.

59. Bernard Faÿ, "L'Amérique se retrouve," *Je Suis Partout* (November 20, 1935).

60. Bernard Faÿ, "Le marasme aux Etats-Unis: 'L'Amérique Débraye,'" *Je Suis Partout* (April 8, 1938).

61. Bernard Faÿ, "Où en est la civilisation des U.S.A.?" *Je Suis Partout* (February 10, 1939).

62. Bernard Faÿ, "La civilisation américaine: Le conflit des croyances," *Je Suis Partout* (February 24, 1939).

63. Faÿ, *Civilisation américaine*, 286.

64. Ibid., 287.

65. Ibid., 299.

66. Faÿ, "Où en est la civilisation des U.S.A.?"

67. Stein, "I Came and Here I Am," in *How Writing Is Written*, 72.

68. Stein, "American Food and Houses," "American States and Cities and How They Differ From Each Other," "I Came and Here I Am," in *How Writing Is Written*, 85, 80, 67.

69. Stein, "The Capital and Capitals of the United States of America," in *How Writing Is Written*, 73–76.

70. Stein, "American States and Cities and How They Differ From Each Other," in *How Writing Is Written*, 82.

71. See chapter 2, note 60.

72. Gertrude Stein letter to Bernard Faÿ, n.d. From the unpublished correspondence of Gertrude Stein and Bernard Faÿ, Vincent Faÿ collection.

73. Stein, "American States and Cities and How They Differ From Each Other," in *How Writing Is Written*, 81.

74. *GHA* 72, 105.

75. *EA* 175.

76. Stein, "And Now," in *How Writing Is Written*, 63.

77. Stein, "American States and Cities and How They Differ From Each Other" and "American Food and American Houses," in *How Writing Is Written*, 79, 88.

78. See chapter 1, p. 31–33.

79. Gertrude Stein, "Melanctha," in *Three Lives*; *Ida* (New York: Vintage, 1968).

80. A declassified memorandum dated February 21, 1945, reports the observations of undercover agent William Brandhove about Stein, whom he visited in Paris sometime during 1937: "She did not seem to be a pro-any nationality, but she was anti-Roosevelt" (Document 100-HQ-340145, National Archives and Records Administration, Washington, D.C.).

81. Gertrude Stein, *Painted Lace and Other Pieces (1914–1937)* (New Haven, Conn.: Yale University Press, 1955), 73. Stein's comments about the Democratic party are in an unpublished letter to Faÿ: "Politically I feel that you have justified my feeling about the Democratic party, it is a party of the two Franklins and the riff-raff and the riff-raff is all Irish or if it isn't Irish it is in the hands of the Irish" (Vincent Faÿ correspondence).

82. *EA*, 63–64; Stein, "My Last About Money," in *How Writing Is Written*, 111. Stein repeats this anecdote in *Everybody's Autobiography* and identifies her interlocutor as "a very able young man Donald Vestal" (*EA* 64), a Chicago gallery owner and puppeteer whom Stein met during her American lecture tour.

83. Stein makes a similar statement in "All About Money," in *How Writing Is Written*: "The thing that differentiates man from animals is money" (110). Stein's interest during this period in the hierarchy between humans and animals is developed most thoroughly in *The Geographical History of America*. There, Stein distinguishes the superior functions of "the human mind," similar to what she calls "genius," from "human nature," a state of "connection" that Stein associates with her relationship to her dog. "A dog does not know what the human mind is," Stein writes (59).

84. All quotes from *EA* 41.

85. "Gertrude Stein Sees U.S. Again Individualistic," *New York Herald Tribune* (January 27, 1935): 8. Although most historians do not define Huey Long as a fascist but rather as a populist demagogue, literary thinkers have stressed fascist tendencies in Long's platform and self-presentation. See, for example, Sinclair Lewis, *It Can't Happen Here* (New York: Doubleday Doran, 1935); and Robert Penn Warren, *All the King's Men* (New

York: Harcourt Brace, 1946). Lawrence Dennis, the ultra-right-wing author of *The Coming American Fascism* (1936), defined Long as "the nearest approach to a national fascist leader" (cited in William Ivy Hair, *The Kingfish and his Realm: The Life and Times of Huey P. Long* [Baton Rouge: Louisiana State University Press, 1996], 296).

86. Stein, "Money," in *How Writing Is Written*, 107.

87. Catharine Stimpson, "Comments on Stein's Landscape: Politics, Love, and Art," in "A Play To Be Performed; Excerpts from the Gertrude Stein Symposium at New York University," *Theater* 32, no. 2 (2002): 11.

88. Rogers, *When This You See Remember Me*, 217.

89. Ibid., 217–218.

90. Weber, *The Hollow Years*, 141.

91. Bernard Faÿ letter to Gertrude Stein, December 19, 1936. From the unpublished correspondence of Gertrude Stein and Bernard Faÿ, Vincent Faÿ collection.

92. Fanny Butcher letter (2 pages) to Bernard Faÿ, January 31, 1934 (?). From the unpublished correspondence of Gertrude Stein and Bernard Faÿ, Vincent Faÿ collection. Butcher writes: "First about the degree for Gertrude Stein. I've thought about it a lot, tentatively discussed it with Alice and Bobsy Goodspeed and we all agree that the chances of Bob Hutchins doing it is very slight. There are lots of reasons . . . his precarious position with the faculty as it is, being accused of foisting 'modernity' on a staid institution" (1).

93. Lucille Hecht, "Gertrude Stein's Magnificent Hoax: How a Party in Paris, Where the Wine Flowed Freely, Led to the Most Gigantic Practical Joke Ever Perpetrated on the American Literary Public," *Real America* 6, no. 4 (January 1936): 8.

94. Ibid., 8–11.

95. Bernard Faÿ letter to Gertrude Stein, n.d. From the unpublished correspondence, Gertrude Stein and Alice B. Toklas Papers, Yale Collection of American Literature, Beinecke Rare Book and Manuscript Library.

96. Hecht, "Gertrude Stein's Magnificent Hoax," 8–11.

97. In a letter to Gertrude Stein dated December 27, 1935, Faÿ writes "I sent to the United Press the enclosed statement [missing]. Today I sent it to B. Cerf and to K. Simpson, with instructions to the latter to use legal means to stop Voorhies using my name." Bernard Faÿ letter to Gertrude Stein, December 27, 1935. From the unpublished correspondence, Gertrude Stein and Alice B. Toklas Papers, Yale Collection of American Literature, Beinecke Rare Book and Manuscript Library.

98. Bernard Faÿ letter to Alice B. Toklas, January 13, 1936. From the unpublished correspondence of Gertrude Stein and Bernard Faÿ, Vincent Faÿ collection.

99. "As I never take any notice of personal attacks there is to be no mention of me or of this article insofar as it concerns me in your notice of it. So there is nothing further for us to say about this." Gertrude Stein letter to Bernard Faÿ, n.d. From the unpublished correspondence of Gertrude Stein and Bernard Faÿ, Vincent Faÿ collection.

100. " . . . cela lui fit mieux sentir la valeur de notre intimité et me la rendit plus sensible" (*LP* 160).

101. Bernard Faÿ letter to Gertrude Stein, February 13, 1935. From the unpublished correspondence of Gertrude Stein and Bernard Faÿ, Vincent Faÿ collection.

102. Bernard Faÿ letter to Gertrude Stein, February 13, 1935. From the unpublished correspondence of Gertrude Stein and Bernard Faÿ, Vincent Faÿ collection.

103. Bernard Faÿ note. From the unpublished correspondence of Gertrude Stein and Bernard Faÿ, Vincent Faÿ collection. Vincent Faÿ correspondence.

104. Both Gertrude Stein letters to Bernard Faÿ, n.d. From the unpublished correspondence of Gertrude Stein and Bernard Faÿ, Vincent Faÿ collection.

105. See Stein comments to W. G. Rogers, note 89, above. In the same letter to Rogers, identified by him as written "three years before World War II threw a definitive light on these issues," Stein writes: "When I gave the lecture to the french students they too asked me about proletarian literature and I said one of my troubles was that for me gens [people] were just gens, and really they arouse a different kind of interest if you like one class or another class, like dull or not dull but really otherwise they were just what they were that is people. Every class has a kind of charm and since occupations and distribution and force and brains and personality are bound to be different inevitably there are bound to be classes and each class undoubtedly is what it is and the members of it have that kind of charm" (Rogers, *When This You See Remember Me*, 219).

106. Anonymous Vichy diplomat quoted in letter from Epy Coronio to Gertrude Stein, February 24, 1941. From the unpublished correspondence, Gertrude Stein and Alice B. Toklas Papers, Yale Collection of American Literature, Beinecke Rare Book and Manuscript Library.

107. Bernard Faÿ, "Will There Be An Explosion in Europe?" *New York Times Magazine* (May 29, 1938), 10; Faÿ, "La crise de septembre 1938," *Conference prononcée à l'Institut Canadien, Palais Montcalm, October 21, 1938* (Québec: Le Soleil, 1938), 28; Faÿ, "Le Français en face de lui-même," *La Gerbe* (July 18, 1940): 1.

4. STEIN'S WAR: "HAVING FAITH" IN PÉTAIN (1940-1944)

1. Zeev Sternhell, *Neither Right nor Left: Fascist Ideology in France* (Berkeley: University California Press, 1986), 299. For Pétain and the French in 1940, see Michèle Cointet, *Pétain et les français, 1940–1951* (Paris: Perrin, 2002); Charles Williams, *Pétain* (New York: Palgrave Macmillan, 2005).

2. Mario Rossi, *Roosevelt and the French* (Westport, Conn.: Praeger, 1993), 38. The statistics of lives lost during the May 1940 Battle of France are found in "France 1940—Autopsie d'un Défait," *L'Histoire* 352 (April 2010), 59.

3. Charles Glass, *Americans in Paris: Life and Death Under Nazi Occupation, 1940–1944* (London: Harper Press, 2009), 85.

4. Many of his disciples, referred to as "hagiographers" by Julian Jackson, followed Pétain's own lead. Pierre Taittinger, vintner and founder of the right-wing group Jeunesses patriotes, referred to Pétain as "a new Christ, who has sacrificed himself, to allow the regeneration of defeated France." Julian Jackson, *France: The Dark Years* (Oxford: Oxford University Press, 2001), 280.

5. Wolfgang Schivelbusch, *The Culture of Defeat: On National Trauma, Mourning, and Recovery* (New York: Metropolitan Books, 2003), 128.

6. Gide, quoted in Robert O. Paxton, *Vichy France: Old Guard and New Order, 1940–1944* (New York: Columbia University Press, 1972), 34. Gide reiterates this theme in his journal of July 28, 1940: "Softness, surrender, relaxation in grace and ease, so many charming

qualities that were to lead us, blindfolded, to defeat." André Gide, *Journals*, Urbana: University of Illinois Press, 2000), 4:39.

7. Paxton, *Vichy France*, 21.

8. Postwar assessments of what Marc Bloch perceptively called France's "strange defeat" have radically challenged the Pétainist line. As Jean-Louis Crémieux-Brilhac has argued in a two-volume study, "the major cause of the disaster was essentially military and of an intellectual [rather than moral] order." *Les Français de l'an 40* (Paris: Gallimard, 1990), 2:364.

9. Denis Peschanski et al., eds. *Collaboration and Resistance: Images of Life in Vichy France 1940–1944* (New York: Harry Abrams, 2000), 29.

10. Pétain, quoted in Herbert R. Lottman, *Pétain, Hero or Traitor: The Untold Story* (New York: William Morrow, 1985), 181, 210. Or as Paul Grillet, a Pétainiste who belonged to the leadership school of Uriage, put it: "The challenge was quite simply to create a society other than the one we had known. . . . We had to totally change society. Our priority was to live in another society." Quoted in John Hellman, *The Knight-Monks of Vichy France: Uriage, 1940–1945* (Montreal: McGill-Queen's University Press, 1993), 10.

11. Williams, *Pétain*, 164, 198.

12. Lottman, *Pétain*, 211, 214.

13. Yves Bouthillier, *Le drame de Vichy* (Paris: Librairie Plon, 1950), 8, 11.

14. Pétain cited in Paxton, *Vichy France*, 358.

15. Mario Rossi, *Roosevelt and the French*, 69.

16. Donald A. Reed, *Admiral Leahy at Vichy France* (Chicago: Adams, 1968), 26.

17. Letter from Admiral William Leahy to Franklin D. Roosevelt, July 28, 1941. In William D. Leahy, *I Was There: The Personal Story of the Chief of Staff to Presidents Roosevelt and Truman, Based on His Notes and Diaries Made at the Time* (New York: Whittlesey House, 1950), 47.

18. Letter from Admiral William Leahy to Franklin D. Roosevelt, November 22, 1941. Ibid., 60.

19. Paxton, *Vichy France*, 323.

20. In fact, Roosevelt would remain suspicious of de Gaulle and the supposed "radical and communist elements supporting him" until the Liberation. Rossi, *Roosevelt and the French*, 119. His preference for General Henri Giraud, who became the successor to Admiral Darlan as high commissioner of the government of French North Africa in December 1942, would be shared by Faÿ, himself a friend of Giraud (see chapter 5, note 140). See also Rossi, *Roosevelt and the French*, 105–119.

21. Gaston Henry-Haye, *La grande éclipse franco-américaine* (Paris: Plon, 1972), 181.

22. Julian G. Hurstfield, *America and the French Nation, 1939–1945* (Chapel Hill: University of North Carolina Press, 1986), 98.

23. Henry-Haye, *La grande éclipse franco-américaine*, 10.

24. Ibid., 240, 242, 327, 321, 326, 316.

25. Jean Wahl, "Miss Stein's Battle," *New Republic* (January 19, 1945), 396–398. Wahl's severity continued: "The apparent naïve improfundity of Gertrude Stein's writing does not always hide profundity" (397).

26. Djuna Barnes also found Stein's tone in *Wars* disquieting: "You do not feel that she is ever really worried about the sorrows of the people; her concern at its highest pitch is a

well-fed apprehension." "Matron's Primer [Review of *Wars I Have Seen*]," *Contemporary Jewish Record* (June 8, 1945): 342–343. Other criticisms of *Wars*, when they have been offered, have focused more on style than politics. See, for example, John Malcolm Brinnin, *The Third Rose: Gertrude Stein and Her World* (Reading, Mass.: Addison-Wesley, 1987): "*Wars I Have Seen* is a dull, long-winded and self-indulgent book which does not outlive its topical interest. Naïve, self-justifying mannerisms that had seemed artlessly fresh in the *Autobiography of Alice B. Toklas* now tended to be tiresome and cute" (375). Barnes concurs that she is "thrown off by the 'happy idiot' simplifications, the baby-like repetition" of Stein's style (342).

27. See chapter 1, note 29.

28. Alice Kaplan, *The Collaborator: The Trial and Execution of Robert Brasillach* (Chicago: University of Chicago Press, 2000), 228.

29. Gertrude Stein letter to Bernard Faÿ, n.d. From the unpublished correspondence of Gertrude Stein and Bernard Faÿ, Vincent Faÿ collection. Carl Van Vechten letter to Gertrude Stein, March 19, 1940, where Van Vechten refers to the possibility of Stein "making money" from a lecture tour. In Donald Gallup, ed. *The Flowers of Friendship: Letters Written to Gertrude Stein* (New York: Alfred Knopf, 1953), 349–350.

30. See note 86, below.

31. Gertrude Stein, "La langue française," *Patrie: Revue Mensuelle illustrée de L'Empire* (August 10, 1941): 36–37. In a letter to Carl Van Vechten of May 31, 1941, Stein writes, "I have been asked to do a little thing in french on the french language, for a new review called Patrie, an official thing under the patronage of Marshal Pétain." Gertrude Stein letter to Carl Van Vechten, in *The Letters of Gertrude Stein and Carl Van Vechten, 1913–1946*, ed. Edward Burns (New York: Columbia University Press, 1986): 724–725. Stein's other propaganda plans are discussed below.

32. W. G. Rogers, *When This You See Remember Me: Gertrude Stein in Person* (New York: Rinehart and Co., 1948), 212.

33. Unsigned, undated note "Au Maréchal" ("To the Maréchal"), in the hand of Alice Toklas. Gertrude Stein and Alice B. Toklas Papers, Yale Collection of American Literature, Beinecke Rare Book and Manuscript Library. Note the cryptic grammar (and no diacritical marks) of the original: "Au Maréchal, A son Verdun que tous on partager en toute sympathie son effort et sa victoire. A la victoire d'aujourd'hui encore plus difficile et a son complet reussite. En admiration et en sympathie de tout mon coeur."

34. Gertrude Stein letter to Bernard Faÿ, n.d. From the unpublished correspondence of Gertrude Stein and Bernard Faÿ, Vincent Faÿ collection.

35. Bernard Faÿ letter to Gertrude Stein, October 9, 1939. Gertrude Stein and Alice B. Toklas Papers, Yale Collection of American Literature, Beinecke Rare Book and Manuscript Library.

36. Stein and Toklas's French driving permits, allowing them one-way travel to Bordeaux on June 12, 1940, in response to "consular instructions," are in the Gertrude Stein and Alice B. Toklas Papers, Yale Collection of American Literature, Beinecke Rare Book and Manuscript Library.

37. Linda Wagner-Martin details Stein's response to these events in *"Favored Strangers": Gertrude Stein and Her Family* (New Brunswick, N.J.: Rutgers University Press, 1995), 234–238.

38. *WL* 128.

39. See Ian Ousby's excellent chronology in the back of his book *Occupation: The Ordeal of France, 1940–1944* (New York: Cooper Square Press, 2000), 322–334.

40. The Statut des Juifs of October 3, 1940, defined "Jews" as individuals having three grandparents of the "Jewish race" and established their right or denial of access to certain professions. "Jews were excluded from political office, judicial appointments, diplomatic and prefectorial posts, and the senior branches of public services. They could not be officers or heads of enterprises in which the state was involved. They could not be managers or directors in the press, radio, cinema or theater." A second Statut des Juifs of June 2, 1941, further specified the meaning of "race" to assert that "Jews were now those people who, *irrespective of religion*, had at least three grandparents of Jewish race." Bizarre exceptions were made: for example, "If an individual abandoned the Jewish religion, that person could claim to be non-Jewish if the abandonment occurred before 25 June 1940 and if the person had only two grandparents of 'Jewish race.'" Michael Curtis, *Verdict on Vichy* (London: Weidenfeld and Nicholson, 2002), 112–113. In October 2010, the *New York Times* reported the discovery in France of a document proving that Pétain himself had participated in "harden[ing]" and "toughen[ing]" the language of the first Statut des Juifs. "Far from the enfeebled and senile general manipulated by his peers, as the French have long viewed him, Marshal Philippe Pétain was an unapologetic anti-Semite, said Serge Klarsfeld, one of France's leading Holocaust experts." "Vichy Leader Said to Widen Anti-Jewish Law," *New York Times* (October 5, 2010).

41. Curtis, *Verdict on Vichy*, 113.

42. According to Dominique Saint-Pierre, the Curé d'Ars, also known as Jean-Marie Vianney (1786–1858), never wrote a book of predictions. However, other writers and astrologers published work under his name. *Gertrude Stein, le Bugey, la guerre: d'aout 1924 à décembre 1944* (Bourg-en-Bresse: Musnier-Gilbert, 2009), 205n481.

43. John Whittier-Ferguson, "Stein in Time: History, Manuscripts, Memory," *Modernism/modernity* 6, no. 1 (1999), 14.

44. Gertrude Stein letter to Bernard Faÿ, n.d. From the unpublished correspondence of Gertrude Stein and Bernard Faÿ, Vincent Faÿ collection.

45. In the text, Stein in fact makes a distinction between having faith "simply" and having faith through the intervention of prophecies: the former is the prerogative of believers like a group of French POWs who "took it simply and completely for granted that the Germans were not going to win." In contrast, Stein notes, "Well we the civilian population did not have it [faith] so simply, we had to have the prophecies of Saint Odile but they did help a lot" (*W* 37).

46. Gertrude Stein, *Mrs. Reynolds* (Los Angeles: Sun & Moon Press, 1995), 313 (hereafter cited in the text as *MR*).

47. Here I would take issue with Karen Lawrence's claim that for Stein prophecy is useful because it is a form of "pre-diction," providing a "language that paradoxically prevents foreclosure." Karen Lawrence, "Who Could Have Read the Signs? Politics and Prediction in Gertrude Stein's *Mrs. Reynolds* and Christine Brooke-Rose's *Amalgamemnon*," *Western Humanities Review* 59, no. 2 (Fall 2005): 20. My sense is that Stein, like her character Mrs. Reynolds, is drawn to prophecy precisely because of its dictative power, as a speech-act that can bring into being a given future.

48. See chap. 1 of Will, *Gertrude Stein, Modernism, and the Problem of "Genius,"* (Edinburgh: Edinburgh University Press, 2000).

49. "Naturally if you were born in the nineteenth century when evolution first began to be known, and everything was being understood, really understood everybody knew that if everything was really being and going to be understood, and if everything was understood then there would be progress and if there was going to be progress there would not be any wars, and if there were not any wars then everything could be and would be understood.... That was what the nineteenth century knew to be true, and they wanted it to be like that ... and now everybody knows that although everybody is civilised there is no progress and everybody knows even though anybody flies higher and higher they cannot explain eternity any more than before, and everybody can persecute anybody just as much if not more than ever, it is rather ridiculous so much science, so much civilisation" (*W* 40).

50. William James, "The Will to Believe," in *The Will to Believe and Other Essays in Popular Philosophy* (Mineola, N.Y.: Dover, 1956), 6.

51. Peter Brown, *Society and the Holy in Late Antiquity* (Berkeley: University of California Press, 1982), 330. In his analysis of saints in late antiquity, the eminent historian Brown emphasizes the inextricable ties between saints and their local communities. "It was through the hard business of living his life for twenty-four hours in the day, through catering for the day-to-day needs of his locality, through allowing his person to be charged with the normal hopes and fears of his fellow men, that the holy man gained the power in society" (105). Likewise, the "miracles" worked by saints, as well as their providential powers, spoke to the expectations of a "cure" in the eyes of the suffering society around them. A saint who prophesied a certain outcome to a present uncertainty gave "form, and so the hope of resolution to what is experienced . . . as the nebulous and intractable fact of suffering" (142). Simply through the appropriateness of this form-giving act, the saint produced "an oasis of certainty in the conflicting aims and traditions of the world" (148). After death, saints continued to reflect and direct the hopes of their communities, serving as "the heavy voice of the group" in heightened situations of anxiety or fear (330).

52. *W* 44; italics mine. The possibility that Stein's sentence contains a comma splice (with "as" commencing a new sentence) does not alter its meaning. The entire sentence continues, "as we all have been cherishing copies of this prophecy ever since 1940, and as there is a copy in Latin of the original prophecy in Lyon, which one of the young Seminarists at Belley translated for me into French, there is no doubt about it."

53. A similar instance of grammar underscoring the will to believe in the face of skepticism is apparent in the double negatives at the end of a letter Stein wrote to W. G. Rogers shortly after the fall of France: "Everybody is feeling more hopeful and the prophecies go on, we are all now completely devoted to St. Odile, who says the germans will leave France being impelled thereto by a mal etrange [peculiar sickness], and I am not sure that she is not right" (Rogers, *When This You See Remember Me*, 210).

54. Marrus and Paxton, *Vichy France and the Jews*, 98. See also note 40, above.

55. Ibid., 100.

56. Ibid.

57. There is no evidentiary basis for the contention by Charles Glass, in his recent book *Americans in Paris*, 148, that the Vichy regime did not discriminate against American

Jews "to maintain cordial relations with Washington." As Charles L. Robertson has shown, there were many instances in which both German and Vichy authorities discriminated against Americans, including Jews. Charles L. Robertson, Professor Emeritus of Government, Smith College, chapter 4 of unpublished manuscript "They Stayed: Americans in Paris Under the Nazi Occupation."

58. Her landlord, M. Putz, had leased Stein the house since 1929, when she had displaced the lieutenant who was living there. See chapter 2.

59. According to Stein's friend W. G. Rogers, such a move promised greater safety because Culoz, a railroad town, "was more important than Bilignin to the Germans, whose hand lay less onerously on the population which supplied labor to keep essential trains running" (Rogers, *When This You See Remember Me*, 199). Faÿ's involvement in the issue is obscure, but he notes in *Les précieux* that he kept an eye on them after their move (*LP* 163).

60. Carmen Callil, *Bad Faith: A Forgotten History of Family and Fatherland* (London: Jonathan Cape, 2006), 370.

61. See Saint-Pierre, *Gertrude Stein, le Bugey, la guerre*. Although relying on published sources for his sense of Stein's wartime activities, Saint-Pierre adds much to our knowledge of the friends and neighbors who surrounded her during the war.

62. Eric Sevareid, *Not So Wild a Dream* (New York: Alfred A. Knopf, 1946), 458–459. A story in *Wars I Have Seen* about a French Jewish woman who was protected by an official in the prefecture of Chambéry during the war is provocative but sheds little light on Stein's own situation. As Stein notes at the end of this anecdote: "Most of the French officials were like that really like that" (*W* 160), a statement that leaves ambiguous whether the French officials who did indeed deal with Stein "were like that really like that."

63. Stein recounts a conversation with a French shopkeeper in Aix-les-Bains: "and he said and these gentlemen, that is the way the Germans are always mentioned and these gentlemen do not bother you and I said no we are women and past the age to be bothered and beside I said I am a writer and so the French people take care of me" (*W* 78).

64. "Everybody is feeling more hopeful and the prophecies go on, we are all now completely devoted to St. Odile," Stein writes in one letter to Rogers, and then later, "I have come across lots of new old predictions . . . everybody brings them to me and tells me about them and I like it, and as they all predict the same, not too long away and France victor and it is a comfort" (Rogers, *When This You See Remember Me*, 210).

65. Stendhal, *The Red and the Black*, trans. Burton Raffel (New York: Random House, 2004), 6.

66. This untitled interview is reported in Rogers, *When This You See Remember Me*, 212.

67. Stein, "La langue française," 36–37.

68. Stein, *Lectures in America*, 158–159.

69. Gertrude Stein, "A Transatlantic Interview 1946," in *The Gender of Modernism*, ed. Bonnie Kime Scott (Bloomington: Indiana University Press, 1990), 504.

70. Although it is outside the scope of this study, the notion of "exactitude" plays an important role in Stein's aesthetic, especially in problematizing the idea that this aesthetic is somehow antireferential or indeterminate, unmoored from any conceptual "ground" or logical system. See Jennifer Ashton, " 'Rose is a Rose': Gertrude Stein and the Critique of Indeterminacy," *Modernism/modernity* 9, no. 4 (November 2002): 581–604.

71. Stein, quoted in Thornton Wilder, "Introduction," *FIA*, vi.

72. Stein, "My Last About Money," 112.

73. Gertrude Stein, "A Political Series," in *Painted Lace and Other Pieces, 1914–1937* (New Haven, Conn.: Yale University Press, 1955).

74. Stein, quoted in Rogers, *When This You See Remember Me*, 216; *EA* 309.

75. Samuel Kalman, *The Extreme Right in Interwar France: The Faisceau and the Croix de Feu* (London: Ashgate, 2008), 9.

76. Stein, "More About Money," 108.

77. J. G. Shields, *The Extreme Right in France: From Pétain to Le Pen* (New York: Routledge, 2007). Shields writes that even by the late nineteenth century, "the competing claims of Bourbon, Orléanist, and Bonapartist dynasties made monarchism a complex, and ultimately self-defeating cause" and during the 1930s, the Right "deriv[ed] its ideological impetus less from monarchism than from an authoritarian nationalism" (24).

78. Samuel M. Steward, *Dear Sammy: Letters from Gertrude Stein and Alice B. Toklas* (Boston: Houghton Mifflin, 1977), 61–62.

79. John Hellman, *The Knight-Monks of Vichy France: Uriage, 1940–1945* (Montreal: McGill-Queen's University Press, 1993), 10.

80. Antoine Delestre, *Uriage, une communauté et une école dans la tourmente, 1940–1945* (Nancy: Presses Universitaires de Nancy, 1989), 148.

81. Hellman, *The Communitarian Third Way: Alexandre Marc's Ordre Nouveau, 1930–2000* (Montreal: McGill-Queen's University Press, 2002), 88. See also chapter 5, note 38.

82. See John Hellman, *Emmanuel Mounier and the New Catholic Left 1930–1950* (Toronto: University of Toronto Press, 1981), 176.

83. Gertrude Stein letter to Thornton Wilder, August 25, 1938. In Edward M. Burns and Ulla E. Dydo with William Rice, *The Letters of Gertrude Stein and Thornton Wilder* (New Haven, Conn.: Yale University Press, 1996), 222.

84. According to Samuel Steward, Daniel-Rops "had a congenital defect that kept his eyelids at half-droop, so that he had to tilt his head backward to look at you to talk, and he was thin as a rail." Steward, *Dear Sammy*, 18.

85. Gertrude Stein letter to M. le Prefet in the handwriting of Henri Daniel-Rops, n.d. Gertrude Stein and Alice B. Toklas Papers, Yale Collection of American Literature, Beinecke Rare Book and Manuscript Library. (All of the Prefect letters are to be found in Box 134, folders 2951–2953). The last point about Faÿ is written in the hand of Alice Toklas and then crossed out.

86. "Monsieur le Prefet, On vient de me demander de preparer de toute urgence un ouvrage pour les Etats-Unis sur la France au printemps de 1941. Pour cet ouvrage il faut que je circule en automobile" ("Mr. Prefect, I have just been asked urgently to prepare a book on France for the United States in the spring of 1941. For this book it is necessary that I be able to drive"). Gertrude Stein letter to M. le Prefet, April 17, 1941. In Gertrude Stein and Alice B. Toklas Papers, Yale Collection of American Literature, Beinecke Rare Book and Manuscript Library.

87. Gertrude Stein letter to Mister the Prefet, n.d. Gertrude Stein and Alice B. Toklas Papers, Yale Collection of American Literature, Beinecke Rare Book and Manuscript Library. The letter is in Stein's handwriting, followed by a French translation in the handwriting of Alice Toklas.

88. Le Général de La Laurencie letter to Monsieur l'Amiral de la Flotte Darlan, May 2, 1941. Gertrude Stein and Alice B. Toklas Papers, Yale Collection of American Literature, Beinecke Rare Book and Manuscript Library. A copy of the same letter also exists in the personal file of the général in the Archives of the French Army, Vincennes.

89. Johanna Barasz, "Un vichyste en Résistance, le général de La Laurencie," *Vingtième Siècle* 94 (April–June 2007): 169.

90. Général de La Laurencie was involved in getting Faÿ's nemesis Marcel Déat arrested in December 1940, for which de La Laurencie was himself sacked by the Germans. See Herbert Lottman, *Pétain: Hero or Traitor* (New York: William Morrow, 1985), 226–227.

91. Barasz, "Un vichyste en Résistance," 167.

92. In fact, La Laurencie would be solicited by the Americans (Leahy in particular) to play the role that de Gaulle finally did.

93. Report by Général de La Laurencie on the "General Situation" of the Occupied Zone in France, November 17, 1940, n19. In archival file "Reports of the Prefects of Vichy," Institut d'Histoire du Temps Présent. http://www.ihtp.cnrs.fr/prefets/fr/f171140dgto.html#_ftn19.

94. Le Maréchal Pétain, *Paroles aux français, messages et écrits 1934–1941*, ed. and introduced by Gabriel-Louis Jaray (Lyon: H. Lardanchet, 1941). Gertrude Stein's unpublished introduction and translations to the speeches of Maréchal Pétain, in Gertrude Stein and Alice B. Toklas Papers, Yale Collection of American Literature, Beinecke Rare Book and Manuscript Library. Gabriel Louis-Jaray was a scholar of Freemasonry and the executive director of the Comité France-Amerique and its publishing organ, the Institut des Études Américaines. Founded in 1909 to "inform and alert leaders and public opinion of the importance assumed by the United States in the life of the world" ("L'Historique de France Amérique," http://www.france-ameriques.org), the Comité France-Amerique was also presided over by Pétain during the 1930s until his appointment as ambassador to Spain in 1939. Burns and Dydo, *The Letters of Gertrude Stein and Thornton Wilder*, 405. During the Vichy regime, Jaray would not only edit the speeches of Pétain in French but also "place his *Institut* at the government's disposal as a minor conduit for American diplomacy." John Harvey, "Conservative Crossings: Bernard Faÿ and the Rise of American Studies in Third-Republic France," *Historical Reflections/Réflexions Historiques* 36, no. 1 (Spring 2010): 101. In the only letter from him to Stein housed at the Beinecke Library, dated October 23, 1942, Jaray makes it clear that he has attempted to intervene with "my Vichy friends" about some unnamed matter on her behalf. YCAL Mss 76, Box 107, Folder 2147. In the 1942 article in Stein's local paper, *Le Bugiste*, Jaray is identified as the person who "has made all the arrangements with [Stein]" for the translation of Pétain's speeches. *Le Bugiste* article, quoted in Rogers, *When This You See Remember Me*, 212.

95. Rogers, *When This You See Remember Me*, 213.

96. Bridgman notes that Stein "was far from illiterate in French, even if her errors were often gross" (*Gertrude Stein in Pieces*, 288n).

97. Gertrude Stein, "Stanzas in Meditation," in *Stanzas in Meditation and Other Poems (1929–1933)* (New Haven, Conn.: Yale University Press, 1956), 3–151.

98. *Le Bugiste* interview, reported in Rogers, *When This You See Remember Me*, 212.

99. Susan Sontag, "Fascinating Fascism," in *Under the Sign of Saturn* (New York: Farrar, Straus and Giroux, 1980), 71–105. Sontag's essay underscores the link between fascism and sadomasochism, emphasizing the insistence with which representations of fascism portray its extreme exercise of power and barbaric violence as a form of sadomasochistic erotics. See also Laura Frost, *Sex Drives: Fantasies of Fascism in Literary Modernism* (Ithaca, N.Y.: Cornell University Press, 2002). For a contrasting reading of Stein's representation of Pétain as full of "quiet comedy," see John Whittier-Ferguson, "Stein in Time: History, Manuscripts, Memory," *Modernism/modernity* 6, no. 1 (1999): 24–25.

100. In the opening paragraph of *Wars I Have Seen*, for example, Stein notes "that I was the youngest of the children and as such naturally I had privileges the privilege of petting the privilege of being the youngest one. If that does happen it is not lost all the rest of one's life, there you are you are privileged, nobody can do anything but take care of you, that is the way I was and that is the way I still am" (*W* 1).

101. Hemingway's portrayal of Stein and Toklas in *A Moveable Feast* cannot be separated from his own strained feelings toward Stein in this arena. See Ernest Hemingway, *A Moveable Feast* (New York: Scribner, 2009), 92, as well as Janet Malcolm's mention of this episode and of the "regular repertoire of sadomasochistic games the couple [Stein and Toklas] played. *Two Lives: Gertrude and Alice* (New Haven, Conn.: Yale University Press, 2007), 63. Stein's masochism seems to have been linked to her lifelong obsession with the death of children, arising from a macabre personal calculus in which she attributed her own existence to the fact that she had been conceived to replace an older sibling who died at birth. Throughout her life, Stein would return obsessively to the themes of survival, identity, and nonexistence, often in relation to the number five (the number of children in her own family). See also Stein's college essay "In The Red Deeps" (1895): "When I had a hurt, I would press it til the agony of the pain thrilled me with an exquisite delight. As in the physical so in the mental world did I revel in the joy of suffering." In Gertrude Stein and Alice B. Toklas Papers, Yale Collection of American Literature, Beinecke Rare Book and Manuscript Library. For the masochism in Stein's love notes to Toklas, see "A Command Poem," in *Baby Precious Always Shines: Selected Love Notes Between Gertrude Stein and Alice B. Toklas*, ed. Kay Turner (New York: St. Martin's Press, 1999), 109. See also "Pink Melon Joy" (1915), with its suggestive passage titled "Harnessing on or another. Harnessing another." Gertrude Stein, "Pink Melon Joy," in *A Stein Reader*, ed. Ulla E. Dydo (Evanston, Ill.: Northwestern University Press, 1993), 301.

102. "In time of war you know much more what children feel than in time of peace.... In time of peace what children feel concerns the lives of the children as children but in time of war there is a mingling there is not children's lives and grown up lives there is just lives and so quite naturally you have to know what children feel. And so it being now war and I seeing just incidentally but nevertheless inevitably seeing and knowing of the feeling of children of any age I do not now have to remember about my feeling but just feel the feeling of having been a certain age" (*W* 3).

103. Wanda Van Dusen, "Portrait of a National Fetish: Gertrude Stein's Introduction to the Speeches of Maréchal Pétain (1942)," *Modernism/modernity* 3, no. 3 (1996): 70.

104. Stein has "a Frenchman" utter this phrase in a paragraph that reports the complex points of view of "any one French one." At issue in her reportage is not the fact that people

"helped to ruin France" but that any defeat of France by the English would "bring . . . back into France" these same people (presumably, Third Republic politicians and supporters of de Gaulle). Gertrude Stein, introduction to the speeches of Maréchal Pétain, Gertrude Stein and Alice B. Toklas Papers, Yale Collection of American Literature, Beinecke Rare Book and Manuscript Library.

105. Gertrude Stein, introduction to the speeches of Maréchal Pétain, Gertrude Stein and Alice B. Toklas Papers, Yale Collection of American Literature, Beinecke Rare Book and Manuscript Library; *W* 57.

106. Gertrude Stein, introduction to the speeches of Maréchal Pétain, Gertrude Stein and Alice B. Toklas Papers, Yale Collection of American Literature, Beinecke Rare Book and Manuscript Library. The Stein collection includes her introduction in manuscript, along with a typed transcription of it and a typed copy of a translation of the project by Paul Genin, entitled "Projet d'introduction à un edition américaine des 'Paroles Aux Français.'"

107. For an informed reading of Stein's wartime actions, see Liesl M. Olson, "Gertrude Stein, William James, and Habit in the Shadow of War," *Twentieth-Century Literature* 49, no. 3 (Fall 2003): 328–359. Olson writes that "[Stein's] reaction to the twentieth century's worst crimes illuminates an extremely problematic escapism, cloaked as pacifism and anchored in habit" (350).

108. These plays are collected in a volume entitled *The First Reader and Three Plays* (Boston: Houghton Mifflin, 1948).

109. Phoebe Stein Davis, "'Even Cake Gets to Have Another Meaning: History, Narrative, and 'Daily Living' in Gertrude Stein's World War II Writings," *Modern Fiction Studies* 44, no. 3 (1998): 579.

110. Stein's nationalist rhetoric in *Wars* is surprising, given the disastrous effects of nationalism in the very epoch she chronicles. Perhaps this explains the somewhat defensive tone of the following passage: "Nobody not born in a country or if they are born in another country by accident must be born of parents born in that country, nobody not born in a country has really the ultimate feeling of that country. Let them have all the privileges of residence, of earning their living in that country or of enjoying that country but not of becoming citizens of that country. Citizenship is a right of birth and should remain so . . . after all I am an American, and it always does come back to that I was born there, and one's native land is one's native land you cannot get away from it and only the native sons and daughters should be citizens of the country and that is all there is to it" (*W* 86). Later on, Stein makes a comment that is of a piece with this statement, referring to the distinction between "emigrant families" and "pure American families" (*W* 166).

111. See Burns and Dydo, *The Letters of Gertrude Stein and Thornton Wilder*, 420. Their appendix on Stein's war years also discusses her relationship with the French publisher René Tavernier, who published writings by Stein in his wartime journal *Confluences*, including—somewhat bizarrely—excerpts of *Everybody's Autobiography* in which Stein discusses Faÿ (418–421). Burns and Dydo note that Tavernier was aware of Faÿ's role as Stein's protector, and it is possible that he understood the political expediency of publishing these excerpts in order to underscore the Stein-Faÿ friendship.

112. On July 28, 1944, at the instigation of Picasso, Faÿ wrote to a Monsieur Courtet requesting that he contact the Nazi Service for the Protection of Fine Arts to prohibit the

confiscation of paintings at Stein's rue Christine apartment. On July 31, Faÿ wrote Picasso that he had received assurances that "no one [will] touch the collections of Gertrude." *D d'I*, AN Z/6/291.

113. In an undated letter where Stein refers to wanting to "be of use to France" she notes: "My dear Bernard, We have not said a word to each other but we do know how we feel, sad and glad." Gertrude Stein to Bernard Faÿ, n.d. From the unpublished correspondence of Gertrude Stein and Bernard Faÿ, Vincent Faÿ collection.

114. Burns and Dydo, *The Letters of Gertrude Stein and Thornton Wilder*, 405.

115. Ibid., 408.

116. Saint-Pierre, in *Gertrude Stein, le Bugey, la guerre*, 53n143, notes that "This letter has not been found in the Archives of the Ain, série Z (sous-préfets)." The Ain is the département that includes the Bugey, where Stein was living during the war.

117. *D d'I*, AN Z/6/291.

118. Michèle Cointet, *Pétain et les Français*, 250; Bénédicte Vergez-Chaignon, *Le docteur Ménétrel, eminence grise et confident du Maréchal Pétain* (Paris: Perrin, 2001), 10. In 1944, Pierre Laval remarked about Ménétrel: "I had predicted everything except that France would be governed by a doctor." Laval, quoted in Julian Jackson, *France: The Dark Years, 1940–1944* (Oxford: Oxford University Press, 2001), 145.

119. Bernard Faÿ dossier (Renseignements Generaux), Archives de la Prefecture de la Police, Paris.

120. Bernard Faÿ letter to Gertrude Stein, February 7, 1942. Gertrude Stein and Alice B. Toklas Papers, Yale Collection of American Literature, Beinecke Rare Book and Manuscript Library. Faÿ writes: "Pour la traduction, je n'ai point encore eu l'occasion d'en parler en detail avec le Maréchal, mais en gros, l'idée lui plaît" ("About the translation, I haven't yet had the occasion to speak in detail about it with the Marshal, but in general the idea pleases him"). Burns and Dydo note that Stein received a contract for the book in October 1942 from Gabriel-Louis Jaray, but "no copy of the contract is preserved. Burns and Dydo, *The Letters of Gertrude Stein and Thornton Wilder*, 409.

121. " . . . si j'y étais alle le Maréchal m'aurait écouté, puis il aurait écouté Ménétrel et il aurait finalement tout oublié." From deposition by Denise Aimé Azam (March 7, 1946), in *D d'I*, AN Z/6/290.

122. The Ménétrel file in the Archives Nationales contains several letters from Bernard Faÿ, including one that shows the two men arranging to have Pétain return to Paris in the spring of 1944, an event that Stein also explicitly praises in *Wars I Have Seen* (114). "Bertrand Ménétrel" dossier, AN 2/AG/75.

123. According to the French historian Lucien Sabah, Bernard Faÿ was involved in another such exchange agreement involving his friend Denise Aimé Azam, later to become a friend of Alice B. Toklas (see epilogue). Sabah cites secret documents from the preparation file for the trial against the Secret Societies Department of the Vichy administration ("Service des Sociétés Secrètes") in November-December 1946 (see chap. 5). One of these documents, which Sabah speculates was written by Gueydan de Roussel, quotes from the journal of Denise Azam, who was Jewish by origin but a Christian convert and who is discussing Faÿ's being nominated to the post of Director of the Bibliothèque Nationale in 1940: " 'Sécurité matérielle pour lui, c'est-à-dire tranquillité pour moi.'" De Roussel (?) comments, "Cette phrase a pu signifier que Faÿ a reçu de l'argent de Mme

Azam avant sa nomination" ("This phrase could signify that Faÿ received money from Mrs. Azam before his nomination"). See Lucien Sabah, "Annexe: Au sujet de Faÿ," in *Une police politique de Vichy: le Service des Sociétés Secrètes* (Paris: Klinksieck, 1996), 428.

124. *Le Bugiste* article, in Rogers, *When This You See Remember Me*, 212–213; for Stein's discussions with Genin and Faÿ's letters to her about the translation project, see Burns and Dydo, *The Letters of Gertrude Stein and Thornton Wilder*, 408–410.

5. FAŸ'S WAR: WINNERS AND LOSERS (1940–1946)

1. Irène Némirovsky, *Suite Française*, trans. Sandra Smith (New York: Knopf, 2006), 29.
2. Gueydan de Roussel, journal entry of June 14, 1940. *JGR* 99.
3. Pierre Ordioni, *Tout commence à Alger, 40–44* (Paris: Ed. Stock, 1972), 60. Ordioni shared Faÿ's royalist sympathies and in 1938 published a book with a preface by Faÿ entitled *Vocation monarchique de la France* (Paris: Grasset, 1938).
4. Ordioni, *Tout commence à Alger*, 60. To Gonzague de Reynold Faÿ was equally bracing, describing the crisis of June 1940 as the total overturning of an old world; at such a moment, the need for religious constancy was paramount. Bernard Faÿ to Gonzague to Reynold, June 3, 1940. From the unpublished correspondence of Bernard Faÿ to Gonzague de Reynold, Archives littéraires suisses (ALS), Fonds Gonzague de Reynold.
5. In *JGR* 300, there is a letter from Jean Marques-Rivière to Gueydan de Roussel, dated January 4, 1943, stating that Faÿ was given the BN appointment with the strong support of Docteur Ménétrel. According to Pierre Chevallier, Ménétrel was an avowed anti-Mason and "one of the most fervent supporters of the publication of the list of [Masonic] brothers in the *Journal officiel*." Pierre Chevallier, *Histoire de la franc-maçonnerie francais* (Paris: Fayard, 1974), 3:315.
6. Bernard Faÿ, *La guerre des trois fous: Hitler-Staline-Roosevelt* (Paris: Perrin, 1968), 177 (hereafter cited in the text as *GTF*).
7. "La mission qui m'était confiée avait pour objet principal . . . d'effectuer à une époque de grande épreuve nationale, une reforme profonde." *JGR* 275.
8. Bernard Faÿ letter to Gertrude Stein, September 13, 1941. In Donald Gallup, ed. *The Flowers of Friendship: Letters Written to Gertrude Stein* (New York: Alfred Knopf, 1953), 356. Linda Wagner-Martin comments: "The irony of his using the pronoun *your* when Jewish books were already banned is not acknowledged." *"Favored Strangers": Gertrude Stein and Her Family* (New Brunswick, N.J.: Rutgers University Press, 1995), 246.
9. "George Washington. Exposition organisée pour la commemoration de centcinquantième anniversaire de la Constitution américaine" (Paris: Bibliothèque nationale, 1936).
10. See "Julien Cain," by Thérèse Kleindienst, in *Histoire des bibliothèques françaises* (Paris, 1992), 4:94–95. As well as being Jewish, Cain was also identified with two aggravating factors that influenced his dismissal: he took part in the ill-fated Reynaud administration and followed the government to Bordeaux after France's defeat, and, according to an anonymous letter in the Cain archives at the Centre de Documentation Juive Contemporaine (hereafter referred to in the text as CDJC), Cain was also a "high-ranking Freemason . . . he is considered by the French as one of the chief figures of decay [*décomposition*] in France." It is likely that the author of this letter was Guillaume de

Van, the music librarian at the BN from 1937 on and a close associate of Bernard Faÿ. From Archives of the CDJC, Mémorial de la Shoah, Paris, CXLI-I90.

11. In *GTF* 228, Faÿ describes how he attempted to aid Cain when he was faced with deportation, but in a "Rapport au Ministre de l'Education nationale sur la discipline de la BN" ("Report to the Minister of National Education Concerning the Discipline of the BN"), Faÿ referred to Cain explicitly as an "Israelite" and "a militant member of the Popular Front" who "had introduced a number of unsavory elements" into the BN during his tenure. See *D d'I*, AN Z/6/292.

12. The law against secret societies was crafted by Vichy Minister of the Interior Adrien Marquet and Vichy Minister of Justice Raphaël Alibert. Chevallier, *Histoire de la franc-maçonnerie française*, 3:328.

13. The phrase—"délire obsidional"—belongs to Marc Olivier Baruch, in *Servir l'état français: L'administration en France de 1940 a 1944* (Paris: Fayard, 1997), 435.

14. Bernard Faÿ, "On My Activities from September 1939 to 1944," Ex 0683.698.34, Department of Rare Books and Special Collections, Princeton University Library.

15. See Charles Rist, *Une saison gâtée: Journal de la guerre et de l'occupation (1939–1945)* (Paris: Fayard, 1983), 433–434. Rist, the distinguished French economist, noted that Faÿ "sees Masons everywhere. . . . He is a mean and dishonest man." On Faÿ's frequent appearance as Pétain's dinner guest, see the memoirs of Pétain's chief of staff, Henri du Moulin de Labarthète, *Le temps des illusions: Souvenirs (Juillet 1940–Avril 1942)* (Geneva: Les Eds. du Cheval Ailé, 1946): "Bernard Faÿ was . . . one of the regulars at the Hotel du Parc. He expressed himself with an exasperating courtesy and seemed marked by a sort of lethargy of the heart. His astonishing erudition impressed the Marshal, who too willingly gave him free rein. . . . But we knew him to be gripped by a solid ambition. He wanted in fact to replace [Jèrome] Carcopino at the Ministry of Education" ("Bernard Faÿ était . . . l'un des familiers de l'Hotel du Parc [Pétain's residence in Vichy]. Il s'exprimait avec une courtoisie désespérante et semblait frappé d'une sorte d'atonie du coeur. Son étonnante érudition faisait l'admiration du Maréchal qui lui lâchait trop volontiers la bride. . . . Mais nous le savions mordu d'une solide ambition. Il désirait en fait remplacer Carcopino à l'Éducation nationale") (249–250).

16. "La Franc-Maçonnerie est la principale responsable de nos malheurs actuels, c'est elle qui a appris aux Français le mensonge et c'est le mensonge qui nous a menés où nous sommes." Quoted in André Combes, *La franc-maçonnerie sous l'occupation* (Paris: Ed. du Rocher, 2001), 53.

17. Philippe Burrin, *France Under the Germans: Collaboration and Compromise* (New York: The New Press, 1996), 47.

18. Nicholas Atkin, *Pétain* (New York: Longman, 1998), 58. For a discussion of Pétain's ties to the Rassemblement National as well as his possible involvement in a plot to overthrow the Popular Front, see Jacques Nobécourt, *Le Colonel de la Rocque (1885–1946) ou les pièges du nationalisme chrétien* (Paris; Fayard, 1996), 563, 578, 598.

19. Atkin, *Pétain*, 58.

20. See Peter Davies' excellent overview of right-wing groups in France during the 1930s: *The Extreme Right in France, 1789 to the Present: From de Maistre to Le Pen* (New York: Routledge, 2002), 79–99. Note that Bernard Faÿ had more than a passing connection to the Croix de Feu league: he wrote the "Préface" to a book authored by Maurice

d'Hartoy, founder of the league. Bernard Faÿ, "Préface," in Maurice d'Hartoy, *Histoire du passeport français: Depuis l'antiquité jusqu'à nos jours* (Paris: Librairie Ancienne Honoré Champion, 1936), 5–6.

21. *GTF* 134.

22. A U.S. War Department pamphlet on French profascist groups gives more information about the second incarnation of the Rassemblement National. Known as the Rassemblement National Populaire, it was founded with German backing by Marcel Déat on February 1, 1941. It differed from its predecessor in being less pro-Pétain and more pro-Nazi: in fact, "the group was intended as a countermove against Marshal Pétain's short-lived Rassemblement National and as a protest against the dismissal of Laval in December 1940." "French Pro-fascist Groups," U.S. War Department Pamphlet no. 31–191 (October 5, 1944), 14. Déat's party was in fact the first political party to be founded under the occupation.

23. Bernard Faÿ letter to Gonzague de Reynold, October 7, 1937. From the unpublished correspondence of Bernard Faÿ to Gonzague de Reynold. Archives littéraires suisses (ALS), Fonds Gonzague de Reynold.

24. See chapter 3, note 36.

25. William D. Irvine quotes Republican Federation leader Victor Perret in 1935: "the great majority of all Frenchmen today condemn parliamentarianism" (*French Conservatism in Crisis* [Baton Rouge: Louisiana State UP, 1979]), 101.

26. Julius Evola, "United Europe: The Spiritual Pre-Requisite," *The Scorpion* 9 (1986): 18.

27. Bernard Oudin, *Aristide Briand* (Paris: Perrin, 2004), 534ff.

28. Jeffrey Mehlman, in *Emigré New York: French Intellectuals in Wartime Manhattan, 1940–1944* (Baltimore, Md.: The Johns Hopkins University Press, 2000), writes: "It was one of the ironies of history that Briand's dream of 1930 had now turned into a nightmare. The elements of Briand's vision—a new European union, centered on Franco-German collaboration, resting on an ideological bed of pacifism—had become the elements of Pétain's France" (178).

29. Roger Griffin, "Europe for the Europeans: Fascist Myths of the New Order, 1922–1992," in *A Fascist Century* (New York: Palgrave Macmillan, 2008), 140.

30. Evola, "United Europe: The Spiritual Pre-Requisite," 20.

31. Anthony Adamthwaite, *Grandeur and Misery: France's Bid for Power in Europe, 1914–1940* (London: Arnold, 1995), 221.

32. Bernard Bruneteau, *"L'Europe nouvelle" de Hitler: Une illusion des intellectuels de la France de Vichy* (Monaco: Rocher, 2003), chap. 5.

33. Anthony James Gregor, *The Ideology of Fascism: The Rationale of Totalitarianism* (New York: The Free Press, 1969), 356.

34. Evola, "United Europe: The Spiritual Pre-Requisite," 18; Hans K. E. L. Keller, *La troisième Europe* (Zurich and Paris: Ed. Batschari, 1934), 41.

35. John Hellman, *The Communitarian Third Way: Alexandre Marc's Ordre Nouveau, 1930–2000* (Montreal: McGill-Queen's University Press, 2002), 37. While "New Europe" identified itself as a trans-European movement, it took different forms in different countries. In England, the New Britain/New Europe movement that became "Federal Union" in 1938 was militantly antipacifist and antiappeasement, oriented toward ties between Britain and European countries opposed to Nazi expansion. See Griffin, "Europe for the Europeans," 146–155.

36. Hellman, *The Communitarian Third Way*, 125.

37. Ibid., 127.

38. "Lettre à Hitler," *Ordre Nouveau* 5 (November 1933): 11. John Hellman proves that the letter, although signed only "Ordre nouveau," was in fact composed by Alexandre Marc and Henri Daniel-Rops. Hellman, *The Communitarian Third Way*, 87.

39. Zeev Sternhell, *Neither Right nor Left: Fascist Ideology in France* (Berkeley: University California Press, 1986), 286.

40. The phrase belongs to the nineteenth-century German philosopher Constantin Frantz, who, like Friedrich Nietzsche, provided the Nazis with an intellectual framework for the Third Reich. Lucien de Sainte-Lorette, *L'idée d'union federale européene* (Paris: Librairie Armand Colin, 1955), 105. In fact, as Paul Kluke has argued, "the Nazis, except for purely propagandistic purposes, had no concept of a united Europe, but conceived instead an all-powerful Germany enslaving the rest of the Continent." Kluke, cited in Geoffrey G. Field, "Nordic Racism," *Journal of the History of Ideas* 38, no. 3 (July–September 1977): 533.

41. Hellman discusses this in *The Communitarian Third Way*, 29–50. See also Burrin, *France Under the Germans*, 53.

42. Griffin, "Europe for the Europeans," 151.

43. Drieu, paraphrased in ibid.

44. Darlan, quoted in de Sainte-Lorette, *L'idée d'union fédérale européene*, 106.

45. In 1933, Faÿ wrote a two-part essay that appeared in the nonconformist journal *La Revue du Siècle*, edited by Jean de Fabrègues (a founding member of the Jeune Droite movement who would eventually take an active role in Vichy policy and who, after the war, would remain a player in the European federalist movement). See Bernard Faÿ, "D'un cahier de rêves," *La Revue du Siècle* 2 (May 1933): 21–27. For Faÿ's intellectual ties to Emmanuel Mounier and the Catholic nonconformist movement, see René Remond and Janine Bourdin, *La France et les français en 1938–1939* (Paris: Presses de la fondation nationale des sciences politiques, 1978), 135.

46. "Manifeste d'intellectuels français pour la defense de l'Occident," *Le Temps* (October 4, 1935): 2. This manifesto was signed by sixty-four individuals.

47. Massis, quoted in Jean-François Sirnielli, *Intellectuels et passions françaises* (Paris: Fayard, 1990), 94. This book also contains the complete version of the "Manifeste d'intellectuels français" (92–93).

48. "Manifeste aux intellectuels espagnols," *Occident, le Bimensuel Franco-Espagnol* 4 (December 10, 1937). The manifesto was signed by forty-two individuals.

49. Bernard Faÿ letter to Gonzague de Reynold, October 1, 1937. From the unpublished correspondence of Bernard Faÿ to Gonzague de Reynold, Archives littéraires suisses (ALS), Fonds Gonzague de Reynold. Faÿ writes to de Reynold that he has just returned from Spain, where he saw de Reynold's book *Portugal* in the office of General Franco.

50. Bernard Faÿ, *Les forces de l'Espagne: Voyage à Salamanque* (Paris: S. G. I. E., 1937), 13–14, 48, 45, 49.

51. Bernard Faÿ, "L'Espagne et son destin," *La Revue Universelle* 16 (November 15, 1937), 397.

52. Faÿ would continue these efforts when in June 1938 he presided over the creation of a "French association for the restoration of hospital sanctuaries and orphanages in Spain" This organization, whose motto was "Solidarité d'Occident" ("Solidarity of the West"),

affirmed its commitment "to the Christian spirit and to its traditions which have produced France and the other Western nations." Cited in Gisèle Sapiro, *La guerre des écrivains, 1940–1953* (Paris: Fayard, 1999), 160.

53. "U.S. Is Held in Danger of Going Communist: Professor Bernard Faÿ of Paris Tells Germans America Faces an Economic Catastrophe," *New York Times* (March 12, 1937): L13.

54. Bernard Faÿ, "Europa ist eine Wirklichkeit," *Deutsch-Französische Monatshefte / Cahiers franco-allemands* 7–8 (1937), 217–220. See also note 60, below.

55. Sylvain Schirmann, *Quel ordre européen? De Versailles à la chute du IIIè Reich* (Paris: Armand Colin, 2006), 272.

56. Pétain, quoted in François Darlan, *Lettres et notes de l'amiral Darlan* (Paris: Economica, 1992), 201.

57. The incident is recounted in Arthur M. Schlesinger, *In Retrospect: The History of a Historian* (New York: Harcourt, Brace, 1963), 144. Schlesinger also adds, without elaboration, that he had a "low estimate of Faÿ as a historian."

58. "'Culture-Direction' in Paris," *The Library Association Record* 42 (December 1940): 298.

59. "Black List," *Life* (August 24, 1942): 86.

60. In his article "Le 'couple France-Allemagne' vu par les Nazis: L'idéologie du 'rapprochement franco-allemand' dans les *Deutsch-Französiche Monatshefte / Cahiers franco-allemands* (1934–1939)," in *Entre Locarno et Vichy: Les relations culturelles franco-allemandes dans les années 1930*, ed. Bock, Meyer-Kalkus, and Trebitsch (Paris: CNRS editions, 1993), Michel Grunewald notes that the journal was fundamentally pro-Nazi and sought above all to make its readership "accept the idea that only the politics of Hitler serves the peace, and by consequence constitutes the best foundation for a solid reconciliation between the French and the Germans" (133).

61. For more on the Rive Gauche bookstore and its role in collaborationist Paris, see Alice Kaplan, *The Collaborator: The Trial and Execution of Robert Brasillach* (Chicago: University of Chicago Press, 2000), 44, 155. During the Vichy regime, Henri Jamet would also become the editor of the confiscated publishing house Calmann-Lévy, renamed Editions Balzac.

62. According to a note by Faÿ, more than fifty German officers worked in the library on a daily basis. Cited in Martine Poulain, "La Bibliothèque nationale sous l'occupation: Les 'difficultés' de la collaboration ou comment servir deux maîtres," *Gutenburg-Jahrbuch* (2004): 264.

63. See Jérome Carcopino, *Souvenirs de sept ans: 1937–1944* (Paris: Flammarion, 1953): 457–460.

64. See Michael Sontheimer, "German Libraries Hold Thousands of Looted Volumes," *Der Spiegel* (October 24, 2008). http://www.spiegel.de/international/germany/0,1518,586379,00.html.

65. *GTF* 206.

66. Faÿ, "On My Activities," 3.

67. Three versions of the Liste Otto were published: on September 28, 1940; July 8, 1942; and May 10, 1943.

68. On July 11, 1942, Faÿ wrote to Gueydan de Roussel, asking him to transmit the message to Gestapo Lt. Moritz: "before leaving Paris, I ordered and arranged that six rows on the side be reserved for Jews in the oval room [Reading Room]." *D d'I* AN Z/6/290.

69. Faÿ, quoted in Poulain, "La Bibliothèque nationale sous l'occupation," 264. In his post-war trial, Faÿ defended the Salzburg trip, claiming that he went in order to talk "in person" with Dr. Kruss about keeping the Germans from confiscating French archives. The transcript of Faÿ's trial is in the Paris Archives Nationales, "Le Procès Sociétés Secrètes," AN 334/AP/22 (hereafter cited in the text as *PSS*). A shortened version of the trial transcript has been published as a pamphlet: *Aux ordres de la Gestapo, une entreprise de Vichy: le Service des Sociétés dites "Secrètes." Le procès Bernard Faÿ et Consorts*. Paris: Foyer Philosophique, n.d.

70. Hans Schick (?), "Eine 'Schrifttumsliste' für die Pariser Nationalbibliothek (February 1943)." Sent by the Reich Security Main Office Section VII B5 (Schick) at the initiative of Faÿ to the commander of the security police and the security service in France (Biederbick) on February 27, 1943. According to German scholar Gerd Simon, this document can be found in the Bundesarchiv Koblenz, file B I 493, pp. 216–223. It is unclear who actually compiled this list; Hans Schick drafted the document. Also see http://homepages.uni-tuebingen.de/gerd.simon/FaySchrifttum.pdf.

71. Faÿ's denunciation of members of the Sorbonne and Collège de France is seen in a confidential letter he wrote to Pierre Laval on October 31, 1940. *D d'I* AN Z/6/289.

72. Fuchs quoted in Allan Mitchell, *Nazi Paris: The History of an Occupation, 1940–1944* (New York: Berghahn Books, 2008), 32n27.

73. Unsigned, undated note, translated from the German. *D d'I*, AN Z/6/288.

74. Faÿ's immediate successor at the BN after the war, Jean Laran, would put his vision in slightly more negative terms: "[Faÿ's] work is tendentious, often full of lies, whose principal idea is that our Library only prospered under the ancien régime, that the Republic had been fatal to it and that the very condition for its prosperity and prestige is that it be under the direct authority of the Chief of State" ("C'est une oeuvre tendancieuse, souvent mensongère, dont l'idée directrice est que notre Bibliothèque n'a prospéré que sous l'Ancien régime, que la République lui a été funeste et que la condition de sa prospérité et de son prestige est qu'elle soit sous l'autorité directe du chef de l'Etat"). Jean Laran, "Rapport sur la réunion des bibliothèques nationales pendant les années 1943 et 1944," *Journal Officiel de la République française*, Annexes administratives (July 25, 1946).

75. Poulain, "La Bibliothèque nationale sous l'occupation," 263.

76. In 1940, the Grand Orient had close to 29,000 members; today it has close to 48,000. See Lucien Botrel, *Histoire de la franc-maçonnerie française sous l'occupation 1940–1945* (Paris: Ed. Détrad, n.d. [1986?]), 28.

77. "Decree of August 19, 1940" announcing the "nullité juridique" of the Grand Orient, *Journal Officiel* (August 20, 1940).

78. Mark Mazower notes that "in July 1941, Pétain ordered all civil servants to *repeat* an earlier compulsory denial that they were freemasons, and he followed this with a spate of public oath-taking ceremonies." *Hitler's Empire* (London: Penguin, 2008), 435.

79. Combes, *La franc-maçonnerie sous l'occupation*, 61–62 and passim.

80. The agreement signed by Bernard Faÿ and the Nazi SD is reproduced in Dominique Rossignol, *Vichy et les franc-maçons. La liquidation des sociétés secrètes, 1940–1944* (Paris: J-C Lattès, 1981), 117–118.

81. "Light was necessary to destroy it" ("Pour le detriure, il fallait la lumière"). Bernard Faÿ, "La liquidation de la F. M. en France," *Les Documents Maçonniques* 5 (February 1942): 3.

82. Although Jean Marques-Rivière, author of the early anti-Masonic tract *La trahison spirituelle de la franc-maçonnerie* (Paris: Eds. des Portiques 1931), was the official organizer of this exposition, his help had been solicited by Faÿ, who was himself following orders "by the German authorities to make an anti-Masonic exhibition in Paris." Dominique Rossignol, *Histoire de la propagande en France de 1940 à 1944: L'utopie Pétain* (Paris: PUF, 1991), 251.

83. Quoted in Charles Grant Hamilton, "Freemasonry, A Prisoner of War," *The New Age* 57, no. 3 (March 1949): 150.

84. Cited in Rossignol, *Vichy et les francs-maçons*, 121. Marques-Rivière was also the screenwriter for the anti-Masonic propaganda film *Les Forces Occultes*, which was first shown in Paris on March 9, 1943.

85. *GTF* 170–171.

86. Faÿ describes Moritz as "a type of boxer, always knocked-out, self-enclosed in a hostile silence" ("du genre boxeur toujours K.O. [knocked-out], se renfermait dans un silence hostile"). *GTF* 207. But in the deposition for his trial, Faÿ is confronted with a document he wrote on June 13, 1943, courteously praising Moritz for "our work in common, that we have made in the midst of so many difficulties and with so much effort" ("ce travail en commun, que nous avons fait parmi tant de difficultés et avec tant de peine"). *D d'I* AN Z/6/289.

87. A fascinating document from the Nazi Central Office of Security in Berlin of October 15, 1941, details the growing unease felt by the German embassy in France toward the "clericalism" of the anti-Masonic faction: "The German ambassador is of the advice that a Frenchman, even if he might have previously belonged to a Lodge as a low-grade Freemason ["petit Franc-Maçon"], is always preferable to a Jesuit." Quoted in Lucien Sabah, *Une police politique de Vichy: le Service des Sociétés Secrètes* (Paris: Klinksieck, 1996), 134.

88. See *JGR* 391, which notes an accord between Helmut Knochen (head of the Nazi SP) and Alfred Rosenberg's office in Germany to send to the latter all historical archives relating to Freemasonry.

89. See *JGR* 108n40: German officers confirm this report.

90. Exposé des Faits, *PSS*. Prosecutors at Faÿ's trial argued that after the Liberation he tried to hide from the authorities the letter he wrote to Gillouin.

91. A list of items discovered after the postwar search of Faÿ's home at Luceau is in *D d'I* AN Z/6/289.

92. The complete letter from Monsieur Michel Dumesnil de Gramont, Grand Maître de la Grande Loge de France, can be found in *JGR* 206. Lucien Sabah's commentary suggests that Faÿ, who knew Dumesnil de Gramont before the war, worked hard to convince the latter that he was a savior of the archives ("that which will be moreover his system of defense in front of the tribunal" ["ce qui sera d'ailleurs son système de défense devant le tribunal"], Sabah comments [*JGR* 205]).

93. Faÿ, described by an unnamed journalist in *La Dépeche de Paris* (November 27, 1946). Quoted in Dominique Rossignol, "Antifranc-maçonnerie, anti sociétés secrètes: Iconographie de la France occupée 1940–1944" (unpublished 3ème Cycle Thèse, Paris, 1980), 433. Jacques Derrida, *Archive Fever: A Freudian Impression* (Chicago: University of Chicago Press, 1996).

94. Derrida, *Archive Fever*, 2.

95. Carolyn Steedman, *Dust: The Archive and Cultural History* (New Brunswick, N.J.: Rutgers University Press, 2002), 67.

96. "There is no political power without control of the archive, if not of memory. Effective democratization can always be measured by this essential criterion: the participation in and the access to the archive, its constitution, and its interpretation." Derrida, *Archive Fever*, 4n1.

97. Antoinette Burton, "Introduction: Archive Fever, Archive Stories," in *Archive Stories: Facts, Fictions, and the Writing of History*, ed. Antoinette Burton (Durham, N.C.: Duke University Press, 2005), 20.

98. Derrida, *Archive Fever*, 12.

99. Fay himself vehemently denied that he was a German agent and claimed to have no familiarity with the matricule VM1 in a deposition for his trial (May 31, 1946, *D d'I* AN Z/6/291). Yet several original Gestapo documents in his *Dossier d'Instruction* (Z/6/291) ascertain that Fay was, in fact, VM FR1, including an unsigned document from October 22, 1941 that discusses the disagreement with Pucheu about transferring Masonic files from the unoccupied to the occupied zones (see note 103, below). The argument by his lawyer M. Chresteil that Faÿ's matricule "was only for security purposes, used only by the Germans" is far from a convincing defense (Exposé des Faits, *PSS*). Lucien Sabah even goes so far as to suggest that Faÿ was given "an Information Agent number" as soon as the Nazis arrived in Paris, a fact that would suggest that Faÿ "had already served the Nazis before their arrival in the city," because his loyalty would have needed to be proven before the assignment of a matricule (*JGR* 48).

100. Knochen, quoted in unsigned note, "Bernard Faÿ" (Dossier individuel des Renseignements generaux), Centre des archives contemporaines, Fontainebleau (CAC).

101. William Gueydan "de" Roussel was a Swiss citizen and one of Faÿ's closest confidantes during the first part of the Vichy regime. The author of a 1940 book on the French origins of racism for which Faÿ wrote the preface, *À l'aube du racisme: L'homme, spectateur de l'homme* (Paris: Eds. de Boccard, 1940), Gueydan also wrote a diary during the war that remains one of the most damning accounts of Faÿ's involvement with the Nazis. Sabah notes that Gueydan had a "nostalgia for noble titles" and appended the preposition "de" to his last name in order to pass for a count (*JGR* 29–30). The nature of Faÿ and Gueydan's personal relationship is unclear. According to documents in Faÿ's dossier, the Germans referred to Faÿ as "Nadette" and Gueydan as his "Tante." But in the deposition for his trial (July 3–9, 1945), Faÿ responds to these charges by saying "If you maintain this damning accusation, I will immediately demand witnesses to my morality" ("Si vous maintenez cette accusation infame, je reclamerai immediatement des témoignages sur ma moralité"). *D d'I* AN Z/6/288.

102. In his journal dated November 11, 1940, Gueydan writes: "I am leaving on a mission to the free zone to bring back to Paris the archives of the Masonic lodges. I am leaving with a truck from the Secours national, a driver from the Secours national, and B. F. [Bernard Faÿ]" ("Je pars en mission en zone libre pour ramener les archives des loges maçonniques à Paris. Je pars avec un camion du Secours national, un conducteur du Secours national et B. F."). *JGR* 125.

103. This is seen in an unsigned, classified document of November 22, 1941 (*D d'I* AN Z/6/291): "Concerning—governmental measures against Freemasonry. VM FR1 let it

be known to the person named below in a strictly confidential manner that Minister of the Interior Pucheu, during the course of an interview several days ago, formally forbade him from taking any Masonic document found in the free zone to Paris, where it might fall into the hands of the Germans. VMFRı in no way considers himself obligated by this injunction, because his work as chief of the French anti-Masonic Service is under the immediate direction of the Marshal" ("Conc.—Mesures gouv. Anti-Maçonniques. VM FRı a fait savoir aujourd'hui au soussigné d'une façon strictement confidentielle que le Ministre de l'Interieur Pucheu, au cours d'un entretien il y a quelques jours, lui avait formellement interdit d'amener aucun document franc-maçonnique trouvé en zone libre à Paris, où il tomberait entre les mains des allemands. VMFRı ne se considere nullement obligé par cette injonction, car dans son travail, comme chef du Service français anti-maçonnique, il est sous la direction immediate du Maréchal").

104. In his official annual "Report on the Bibliothèque Nationale," written in 1943, Faÿ announced the rationale behind the formation of the Centre: "The librairies and archives seized from the French people stripped of their nationality, or because of political associations declared dissolved, present in effect collections of extraordinary richness and of particular interest." Faÿ's unpublished "Rapport sur la Bibliothèque Nationale" is reproduced in *JGR* 277.

105. Combes, *La franc-maçonnerie sous l'occupation*, 79.

106. Faÿ edited every issue of this journal except for the last two.

107. Bernard Faÿ, "Rapport à M. Du Moulin de la Barthète" (March 31, 1941). In *D d'I* AN Z/6/289.

108. The Service des Sociétés Secrètes in the occupied zone, of which Faÿ was the director, was located in Paris at the Grand Orient; it was the "central service" of anti-Masonic activity. For the unoccupied zone, the central service was located at Vichy, under the direction of Robert Labat. In April or May 1942, Labat left the service and was replaced by Jean de Verchère. Faÿ, who in 1942 was moved over to the "historical section" of the SSS, was replaced by J. Sens-Olive. *D d'I* Z/6/289.

109. Rossignol, *Histoire de la propagande*, 244.

110. *PSS*. The later activities of the SSS are described by de Verchère in an undated memo sent to his SSS delegates: "the regional delegates should enter into close liaison with the Legion [la Legion Française des Combattants, the Veterans Affairs organization], the Milice [the Collaborationist citizens army], and the Jewish Affairs service" ("le délégués regional doit entrer en liaison intime avec la Legion, la Milice et les Affaires Juives"). *D d'I* AN Z/6/288.

111. "Les fiches concernant les noms des membres du Grand Orient (environ 29,000) sont terminées, et l'on peut dire que sur ce terrain, nous sommes arrivés à un résultat à peu près parfait." Bernard Faÿ, "Rapport à M. Du Moulin de la Barthète" (March 31, 1941). In *D d'I* AN Z6/289.

112. Combes, *La franc-maconnerie sous l'occupation*, 80.

113. In August 1940, the journal *Gringoire* named ministers from the defunct Third Republic who had belonged to lodges, while in November 1940 *Au Pilori* published the names of men who occupied the highest grades in the order, alongside an announcement: "Frenchmen! See here the murderers of France and their names! The list begins today. It will be long. Keep it. We're going to need it" ("Français! Voilà les meurtriers de la

France et leurs noms! La liste commence aujourd'hui. Elle sera longue. Gardez-la. Nous en aurons besoin"). Henri Amouroux, *La grande histoire des français sous l'occupation* (Paris: Robert Laffont, 1976), 1:687. Published denunciations proliferated, including an anonymous Vichy publication, *La Franc-Maçonnerie démasquée: Listes de F . . . M . . . appartenant au Parlement, à la presse, au barreau et les dirigeants de la secte* (Paris: Eds Anti-Maçonniques, n.d.).

114. André Combes points out that the Vichy definition of "dignitaries" was much more far reaching than might be thought, including both those who had achieved a high degree within the organization and those who were apprentices in the lodges. *La franc-maçonnerie sous l'occupation*, 84.

115. *PSS.* According to Dominique Rossignol, names on the *fichier* were annotated not in terms of identity but in terms of intended police investigation: "to be placed under surveillance, to be eliminated, to be interned, dangerous, very dangerous, to be dismissed, escapee, sought by the Gestapo, Gaullist, listens to British radio, etc." ("à surveiller, à eliminer, à interner, dangereux, très dangereux, à revoquer, en fuite, recherché par la Gestapo, Gaulliste, écoute la radio anglaise, etc."). Rossignol, *Vichy et les franc-maçons*, 157.

116. See Combes, "Annexe" to *La franc-maconnerie sous l'occupation*, 386–404, which provides a list of Freemasons killed during the Nazi occupation. Combes notes that the official estimate of persecuted individuals (as of 2001) "is not definitive. It does not include those who died in prison camps. . . . It is missing, notably, the names of those who were in combat in the Free French Forces" (386). Combes does not identify which Freemasons who died at the hands of the Nazi or Vichy authorities were persecuted for other affiliations. Many Freemasons were Jews, politically on the Left, or involved in the Resistance, all affiliations that could have contributed to their persecution.

117. "Je proteste que je n'ai point assumé la responsabilité du fichier et ne l'ai pas dit. J'ai obei à des instructions gouvernementales me prescrivant de recompléter le fichier." "Procès-Verbal" of Bernard Faÿ, conducted by René le Pottevin, Commissaire de Police Judiciaire (July 3–9, 1945), in *D d'I* AN Z/6/289.

118. In a typed report of June 29, 1946, an unsigned document notes that Faÿ put at the disposal of the Germans "a file of 'Masons' that he had compiled. Also the Gaullist activity of 'Masons' was mentioned in the files" ("un fichier de 'maçons' qu'il avait constitué. Or, l'acitivité gaulliste des 'maçons' était mentionée sur les fichiers"). The same document notes that among the names of those who died as a result of this file given to the Germans was Pierre Brossolette, the journalist and Gaullist, who committed suicide in 1943, a "martyr" who was much celebrated after the war. Cited in Bernard Faÿ dossier (Renseignements Generaux), Archives de la Prefecture de la Police, Paris.

119. Janet Malcolm claims outright that Faÿ was a "Royalist anti-Semite" (*Two Lives: Gertrude and Alice* [New Haven, Conn.: Yale University Press, 2007], 74), but Antoine Compagnon offers a more measured assessment, suggesting that "Faÿ, despite his recourse to [certain anti-Semitic] clichés of the period, seems to have never given proof of a spiteful or systematic anti-Semitism." *Le cas Bernard Faÿ: du Collège de France à l'indignité nationale* (Paris: Gallimard, 2009), 90.

120. At his trial, Faÿ claimed any references he made to Jews as "usurers" were "more literary than political," arising out of his familiarity with Shakespeare's play "The Merchant of Venice" (*PSS*).

121. This comment appears in the same unsigned letter discussed above in note 73.

122. Jean Laran, "Rapport à la commission d'épuration des bibliothèques, 5 décembre 1944" ("Report on the Commission for the Purge of Libraries, December 5, 1944"), in *JGR* 283. At his trial, Faÿ's lawyer gave a series of testaments in his favor by Jewish friends of Faÿ, including the claim that Faÿ had procured a certificate of "Aryanism" for one of his Jewish colleagues in the library's Department of Prints and Engravings. Faÿ also pointed out that he had been personally denounced by the archcollaborationist Marcel Déat as a "judeophile" (*PSS*).

123. For more on Denise Aimé Azam, see chapter 4, note 123, and chapter 6.

124. Dr. Kurt Ihlefeld, Notiz für Herrn Botschafter, March 1, 1941. AN Wiii 212.2 no. 46[17]. The "Botschafter" (ambassador) is never identified, but is presumably Otto Abetz. The other names on the list with Faÿ were Leon de Poncins, Georges Batault, Claude Vacher de la Pouge, and the notorious anti-Semites Louis Darquier, George Montandon, Serpeille de Gobineau, and Louis-Ferdinand Céline. The office was founded in March 1941 under the name "Commissariat-General for Jewish Affairs" and was directed by Xavier Vallat until March 1942; after that, by Louis Darquier.

125. "Projet, non daté, de revue mensuelle 'La Question Juive' de Gabriel Malglaive" ("Undated Project Proposal for a Monthly Review, *La Question Juive*, by Gabriel Malglaive"), Fonds CGQJ, Archives of the CDJC, Mémorial de la Shoah, Paris, CXCV-III-001.

126. The SSS was supported secretly until June 1942 by "fonds speciaux" (secret funds) of the Cabinet Civil of Philippe Pétain. After June 1942, the SSS was given an official budget (*PSS*).

127. *PSS*.

128. Laran, "Rapport à la commission d'épuration des bibliothèques," 284.

129. According to the Commissaire du Gouvernment's statement at Bernard Faÿ's trial in 1946 (*PSS*), Faÿ sought assurance from Pétain early in the war that he would be the chief liaison between French and German anti-Masonic activity. Nevertheless, his power would be challenged on many fronts. Lieutenant August Moritz was the German officer most directly involved in coordinating the SSS with Faÿ; he also was keeping Faÿ under surveillance and reporting his findings back to his Nazi superiors. Robert Labat, a naval commander, was the man that Pétain assigned to coordinate the SSS in the unoccupied zone and the effective director of operations throughout France; administratively beneath Faÿ, his power often eclipsed Faÿ's. In the occupied zone, at the end of 1941, a second Service des Rechèrches et de Renseignments (Research and Information Service) oriented toward the investigation of Freemasons in the north was established and placed under the control of Faÿ's old friend Jean Marques-Rivière. This service would vie for power with the Ministry of the Interior under the direction of Pierre Pucheu, who was already at odds with Faÿ over the transfer of Masonic archives from the south (unoccupied) to the north (occupied) zones. In 1942, after the arrival of Pierre Laval, the police service of the SSS officially ceased to persecute; however, the information-gathering process continued in both zones.

130. Bernard Faÿ letter to Gertrude Stein, May 1, 1943. In Gallup, ed., *The Flowers of Friendship*, 363.

131. In a letter to Madame Jacqueline Aubry of Buenos Aires, dated July 31, 1942, Faÿ writes: "Mr. Laval has relieved me from the whole practical side of the Freemason question,

finding me too harsh! For myself, I am happy because it was difficult, tiring, ungrati-
fying, and dangerous work to do. . . . For the country, I believe frankly that this is an
error" ("M. Laval m'a dessaisi de tout le coté pratique de la question F. M. me trouvant
trop dur! Pour moi je m'en réjouis car c'était une besogne difficile, fatiguante, ingrate et
dangereuse à faire. . . . Pour le pays, je crois franchement que c'est une erreur"). "Bernard
Faÿ" (Dossier individuel des Renseignements generaux), Centre des archives contemporaines, Fontainebleau (CAC).

132. Mazower, in *Hitler's Empire*, makes a strong case for the idea that Vichy France ran as
well as it did by ensuring a seamless continuity of administrators from the pre- to the
post-1940 period. Because—as Faÿ himself so often pointed out—Freemasons made up
a large percentage of the ranks of the French civil service, Faÿ's anti-Masonic crusade
invariably faced resistance and ultimately suppression by both Germans and French
who recognized that "administration was the essence of a military occupation" (432).
The continuity and docility of French administration is also the central point of Marc-
Olivier Baruch's book *Servir l'état français: L'administration en France de 1940 à 1944*
(Paris: Librairie Arthème Fayard, 1997).

133. Marcel Déat, "Réponse à un jésuite déguisé en bibliothécaire," *L'Oeuvre* (October 9,
1941). See Lucien Sabah, *Une police politique de Vichy*, where in a letter to Déat dated
December 26, 1941, Faÿ refutes Déat's charge of December 24 and notes that the chair
was created "after a vote of the Collège de France and of Parliament . . . without the
participation of any French or foreign donor" (488).

134. Cited in Compagnon, *Le cas Bernard Faÿ*, 170. The German response to the Faÿ-Déat
spat is interesting. A secret "Situation Report" of the German Embassy in Paris (October 29, 1941) emphasizes the need for supporting Déat in his battle with Faÿ while continuing to struggle against the "Freemason problem" in France. Yet in a document dated
April 16, 1942, entitled "Attaque de Déat contre Faÿ dans *l'Oeuvre*," the German Ober-
sturmführer de SS (Knochen) notes the importance of "prohibiting new publications
concerning this affair" because of the need to work closely with Faÿ. "Situation Report"
in Archives of the CDJC, Mémorial de la Shoah, Paris, LXXV-217. "Attaque de Déat"
in *D d'I* AN Z/6/290.

135. Marcel Déat, *Mémoires politiques* (Paris: Denoël, 1989), 618.

136. *GTF* 263.

137. Bernard Faÿ dossier (Renseignements Generaux), Prefecture de la Police, Paris. The
unsigned document also notes that Faÿ replaced Jean Baudry in Pétain's inner circle.
Baudry was a member of Pétain's civil cabinet until 1943 and one of the editors of *Les
Documents Maçonniques*; he had moved in the same right-wing circles as Faÿ before the
war.

138. Bernard Faÿ letter to Gertrude Stein, September 13, 1941. In Gallup, ed., *The Flowers of
Friendship*, 356–357.

139. Jacques Bardoux, *La délivrance de Paris: Séances secrètes et négociations clandestines*
(Paris: Fayard, 1958), 61.

140. The Himmler affair is recounted in Michèle Cointet, *Le Conseil National de Vichy: Vie
politique et réforme de l'état en régime autoritaire (1940–1944)* (Paris: Aux Amateurs de
Livres, 1989), 328–332; as well as in *GTF* 332–335. Faÿ may have been chosen as intermediary in this instance because of his friendship with General Henri Giraud, the

Americans' choice during this period to lead the French Resistance. In *La guerre des trois fous*, Giraud makes an appearance as a guest at one of the salons Faÿ frequented before the war (47–53). Elsewhere, he is described as an "intimate friend" of Faÿ (*D d'I* AN Z/6/289).

141. Unsigned document in German from the "Einsatzstab FR" (French Special Staff), March 21, 1944. In the same document, it is reported that Pétain is resisting firing Faÿ. Archives of the CDJC, Mémorial de la Shoah, Paris, CXLI-194.

142. Botrel, *Histoire de la franc-maçonnerie francaise sous l'occupation 1940–1945*, 154. A declassified, unsigned U.S. State Department document from January 25, 1944, reveals that Faÿ was the object of American surveillance: it concerns "a list of names culled from our French Files which fall into a miscellaneous category of *Suspects*, those who by virtue of their office or connections in private life have been reported as questionable." "Bernard Faÿ" file, National Archives and Records Administration, Washington D.C.

143. Bernard Faÿ, *De la prison de ce monde: Journal, prières, et pensées 1944–1952* (Paris: Plon, 1974), 95.

144. On August 22, 1944, a letter signed by L. Villard, elected secretary of the Conseil de l'Ordre (Council of Order), noted that Faÿ had burned most of his papers at the rue Cadet office as well. Cited in Rossignol, *Vichy et les franc-maçons*, 39.

145. *D d'I*, AN Z/6/290.

146. Faÿ's honorary membership at the University of Clermont-Ferrand was revoked February 2, 1945; his chair at the Collège de France was revoked March 30, 1946.

147. Cited in Henry Coston, dir., *Partis, journaux et hommes politiques d'hier et d'aujourd'hui* (Paris: Lectures français, 1960), 19.

148. Rousso, paraphrased in Megan Koreman, *The Expectation of Justice: France 1944–1946* (Durham, N.C.: Duke University Press, 1999), 3. Koreman's book effectively shows how difficult the ideological "unification" of France was in the years immediately following the war, given the range of local experiences of the occupation.

149. In *Vichy en prison: Les épurés à Fresnes après la Libération* (Paris: Gallimard, 2006), a study of the postwar purge, the imprisonment of collaborators, and their trials, Bénédicte Vergez-Chaignon states the obvious: "the [purge] juries were obviously not neutral, whatever the high conscientiousness with which they accomplished their task" (75).

150. See ibid., 40.

151. Faÿ, *De la prison de ce monde*, 101.

152. Faÿ, quoted in Vergez-Chaignon, *Vichy en prison*, 281.

153. At the time, the journalist Janet Flanner had described "dégradation nationale" as "being deprived of nearly everything the French consider nice." Flanner, quoted in Tony Judt, *Postwar: A History of Europe Since 1945* (New York: Penguin, 2005), 46.

154. Reports of Faÿ's demeanor at his trial are described in Rossignol, *Vichy et les franc-maçons*, 216–217. Faÿ's shrug at the mention of Oberg is reported by an eyewitness at the trial, in Bernard Faÿ dossier (Renseignements Generaux), Prefecture de la Police, Paris.

155. "[D]e très nombreuses années, je considère la maçonnerie comme une institution dangereuse, et...sur ce point depuis une vingtaine d'années, je n'ai changé ni d'opinion ni de langage. La presence des allemands n'a pas eu d'action sur mes idées." "Procès-Verbal" of Bernard Faÿ, June 9, 1945, *D d'I* AN Z/6/289.

156. Anonymous, undated note from "Bernard Faÿ" (Dossier individuel des Renseignements generaux), Centre des archives contemporaines, Fontainebleau (CAC).

157. Gertrude Stein letter to Bernard Faÿ, n.d. From the unpublished correspondence of Gertrude Stein and Bernard Faÿ, Vincent Faÿ collection. Confined to the region of her country home in the Ain, Stein presumably attended the lecture in the nearby town of either Aix-les-Bains or Chambéry, ten or twenty kilometers south of Belley. It would be the only such public lecture she would attend during the war.

158. A copy of the letter Stein wrote to Maître Chresteil, Faÿ's attorney, can be seen in the Gertrude Stein and Alice B. Toklas Papers, Yale Collection of American Literature, Beinecke Rare Book and Manuscript Library. As Burns and Dydo write, "It is not a powerful testimony." Edward M. Burns and Ulla E. Dydo with William Rice, *The Letters of Gertrude Stein and Thornton Wilder* (New Haven, Conn.: Yale University Press, 1996), 412.

159. Gertrude Stein letter to Francis Rose, n.d. Gertrude Stein collection, Harry Ransom Humanities Research Center, The University of Texas at Austin.

160. For Faÿ's denunciation of Masons, communists, and BN colleagues, see above. Faÿ's denunciation of colleagues at the Sorbonne appears in a letter written to Pierre Laval on October 31, 1940 (in *D d'I* AN Z/6/290). Faÿ's language is particularly harsh in this instance: "The damned soul of the anglophile resistance is Mr. Maurice Guyot, General Secretary of the University and Academy of Paris at the Sorbonne. . . . He is supported by a series of people, who are identified on the attached list. It is these whom it would be urgent to make disappear, and to replace." The fate of Guyot, who was removed from his post at the Sorbonne on November 15, 1940, and of the three colleagues whom Faÿ identifies (Professors Maurin, Baudouin, and Faral), is not known.

161. Gertrude Stein, "The Good Anna," in *Three Lives* (New York: Penguin, 1990), 35.

6. VICHY-SUR-LÉMAN

1. Copy of deed of purchase, from Registry of Public Civil Acts, Office of Château-du-Loire. Archives Dèpartementales, Château-du-Loire, 3 Q 3821.

2. The exact cause of Stein's death was ascertained through a document filed with the American Foreign Service, "Report of the Death of an American Citizen," August 12, 1946, 351.113, National Archives and Records Administration, Washington, D.C. It states that Stein died of "carcinoma of the uterus according to doctor's statement." It has often been erroneously reported that she died of stomach cancer.

3. Thomas Whittemore, cited in Linda Wagner-Martin, *"Favored Strangers": Gertrude Stein and Her Family* (New Brunswick, N.J.: Rutgers University Press, 1995), 267.

4. The letters Toklas wrote after Stein died are collected in a volume entitled *Staying on Alone: Letters of Alice B. Toklas*, edited by Edward Burns (New York: Liveright, 1973).

5. Alice Toklas letter to Saxe Commins, August 22, 1946, in *Staying on Alone*, 12.

6. *LP* 169.

7. Bernard Faÿ letter to Alice Toklas, August 1, 1946, in *The Flowers of Friendship: Letters Written to Gertrude Stein*, ed. Donald Gallup (New York: Alfred Knopf, 1953), 402.

8. *LP* 168–169.

9. Bernard Faÿ letter to Alice Toklas, March 10, 1947. Gertrude Stein and Alice B. Toklas Papers, Yale Collection of American Literature, Beinecke Rare Book and Manuscript Library.

10. According to Virgil Thomson, in his autobiography, Faÿ was helped in his effort to be transferred to the prison hospital in Angers by the intervention of Suzanne Blum, a Jewish lawyer. Virgil Thomson, *Virgil Thomson* (New York: Alfred Knopf, 1966), 388. The Blum-Thomson correspondence at Yale University, however, gives no indication of this intervention. If anything, Blum insists to Thomson that she cannot help with the case of Faÿ: "I don't envision the possibility—morally speaking—to do anything for him" ("je ne vois pas la possibilité—moralement—de faire quelque chose pour lui"). Suzanne Blum letter to Virgil Thomson, January 18, 1947. Virgil Thomson Papers, Irving S. Gilmore Music Library, Yale University.

11. Sylvia Beach letter to Richard Wright, May 26, 1947. Richard Wright Papers, Yale Collection of American Literature, Beinecke Rare Book and Manuscript Library.

12. Gertrude Stein, "Off We All Went to See Germany," *Life* (August 6, 1945): 54, 56–58.

13. John Whittier-Ferguson, "The Liberation of Gertrude Stein," *Modernism/modernity* 8, no. 3 (2001): 421. Although I not persuaded by Whittier-Ferguson's reading of the tone of "Off We All Went to See Germany," I am in agreement with his sense that Stein's post–World War II writings are much more ambiguous and uncertain about the war than one might think from the contemporary American press accounts (417).

14. Cited in Wagner-Martin, *"Favored Strangers,"* 261.

15. Burns and Dydo describe an unusual chain of events that led to Cerf receiving Stein's proposal for the Pétain translation project after the war had ended, in February 1946. Cerf immediately sent an angry rejection letter to Stein, to which she responded in a short telegram that again reveals an evolution in her thinking: "Keep Your Shirt On Bennett Dear Letter Re Petain Was Written In 1941." Edward M. Burns and Ulla E. Dydo with William Rice, *The Letters of Gertrude Stein and Thornton Wilder* (New Haven, Conn.: Yale University Press, 1996), 414.

16. Sarah Bay-Cheng argues that "The Mother of Us All" is "a deeply personal, perhaps even narcissistic work in comparison with every other play Stein wrote." *Mama Dada: Gertrude Stein's Avant-Garde Theater* (New York: Routledge, 2004), 109.

17. Gertrude Stein, "Brewsie and Willie," in *Gertrude Stein: Writings, 1932–1946*, ed. Catharine R. Stimpson and Harriet Chessman (New York: The Library of America, 1998), 778.

18. Gertrude Stein, *In Savoy; or, Yes Is for a Very Young Man* (London: The Pushkin Press, 1946), 57.

19. Antoine Compagnon, *Le cas Bernard Faÿ: du Collège de France à l'indignité nationale* (Paris: Gallimard, 2009), 125.

20. Many of these postwar interlocutors are present in a volume dedicated posthumously to Robert Brasillach and published on the key date of February 6, 1965: "Hommages à Robert Brasillach" (*Cahiers des amis de Robert Brasillach* 11–12 [*février 1965*]). In his "hommage" to Brasillach, Faÿ writes bitterly: "As it is just to be punished for having served a blind people, he and I found ourselves together at Fresnes [prison]" ("Comme il est juste d'être puni pour avoir servi un peuple aveugle, lui et moi nous retrouvâmes à Fresnes") (153).

21. See Aram Mattioli, *Gonzague de Reynold: Idéologue d'une Suisse autoritaire* (Fribourg: Editions Universitaires, 1997), 26. In describing de Reynolds's family, Mattioli writes: "They abhorred the upheavals introduced by the French Revolution, the origin of everything bad in their eyes, that had deprived patrician families of their privileges, of their titles, of their material goods. . . . [They] took the democratic governmental system as a vulgar and populist concession to the detestable spirit of the times" (26–27).

22. Faÿ describes this event in a letter to de Reynold, July 17, 1939. From the unpublished correspondence of Bernard Faÿ to Gonzague de Reynold. Archives littéraires suisses (ALS). Fonds Gonzague de Reynold.

23. See chapter 5, note 53.

24. Hans K. E. L. Keller, ed., under the sponsorship of Akademie für die Rechte der Völker, *Der Kampf um die Völkerordnung* (Berlin: Franz Vahlen, 1939).

25. Compagnon, *Le cas Bernard Faÿ*, 195.

26. *GTF* 402.

27. According to Edward Burns, the executor of the Alice B. Toklas estate, Toklas helped Faÿ financially by funneling money to him through the intermediaries of Virginia Knapik and Denise Aimé Azam. In order to raise this money, Toklas sold two works by Picasso, a drawing and a gouache. Personal correspondence between Edward Burns and the author, July 2010.

28. The account of Faÿ's escape is described in "Bernard Faÿ" (Dossier individuel des Renseignements generaux), Centre des archives contemporaines, Fontainebleau (CAC); and by Faÿ himself in *GTF* 403–407.

29. Three people were arrested and charged with aiding Faÿ in his escape from the hospital at Angers: Jeanne Marie Thérèse Bigot (born March 8, 1925), a nursing student who was sentenced to fifteen days in prison for "trafic de correspondances" (illegal transport); Nicole de la Chaise (born January 15, 1898), sentenced to two months in prison for "trafic de correspondances"; and Paul Bureau (born August 4, 1917), sentenced to two years in prison for "complicité d'évasion" (helping an escape). From "Bernard Faÿ" (Dossier individuel des Renseignements generaux), Centre des archives contemporaines, Fontainebleau (CAC).

30. In a letter to de Reynold of October 18, 1951 Faÿ asks him to direct all correspondence to him using this pseudonym. From the unpublished correspondence of Bernard Faÿ to Gonzague de Reynold. Archives littéraires suisses (ALS). Fonds Gonzague de Reynold.

31. Henry Rousso, "Préface," in Luc Van Dongen, *Un purgatoire très discret: La transition "helvétique" d'anciens nazis, fascistes et collaborateurs après 1945* (Paris: Eds. Perrin, 2008), iv.

32. *GTF* 407.

33. Bernard Faÿ letter to Gonzague de Reynold, July 10, 1952. From the unpublished correspondence of Bernard Faÿ to Gonzague de Reynold. Archives littéraires suisses (ALS). Fonds Gonzague de Reynold.

34. Van Dongen, *Un purgatoire très discret*, 278.

35. Ibid., 171–172.

36. From Kathy Casey interview with Professor Francis Python, University of Fribourg, June 20, 2008. Van Dongen implies that the French may have actually been in favor of Faÿ receiving shelter in Switzerland. *Un purgatoire très discret*, 314.

37. Sylvie Couchepin, *La correspondence de Gonzague de Reynold et de Bernard Faÿ: Regard de deux intellectuels de droite sur un XXe siècle en mutation*, unpublished master's thesis (Mémoire de Masters), Faculty of Letters, University of Fribourg, Switzerland (2009), 26n61.

38. Van Dongen, *Un purgatoire très discret*, 488n18.

39. Bernard Faÿ letter to Gonzague de Reynold, January 3, 1955. From the unpublished correspondence of Bernard Faÿ to Gonzague de Reynold. Archives littéraires suisses (ALS). Fonds Gonzague de Reynold.

40. Bernard Faÿ letter to Gonzague de Reynold, July 18, 1955. From the unpublished correspondence of Bernard Faÿ to Gonzague de Reynold. Archives littéraires suisses (ALS). Fonds Gonzague de Reynold.

41. Bernard Faÿ letter to Gonzague de Reynold, July 10, 1952. From the unpublished correspondence of Bernard Faÿ to Gonzague de Reynold. Archives littéraires suisses (ALS). Fonds Gonzague de Reynold.

42. Bernard Faÿ letter to Gonzague de Reynold, September 21, 1957. From the unpublished correspondence of Bernard Faÿ to Gonzague de Reynold. Archives littéraires suisses (ALS). Fonds Gonzague de Reynold.

43. Mattioli, *Gonzague de Reynold*, 25.

44. de Reynold collaborated in helping Faÿ find jobs with José Python, the director of cantonal education, and Professor Cherix. From Kathy Casey interview with Professor Francis Python, University of Fribourg, June 20, 2008.

45. Kathy Casey, a Rosary College student who studied with Faÿ in Fribourg in 1964–1965, describes the atmosphere at his social teas: "the guests included one female student from his literature classes at the Villa des Fougères who acted as his hostess and poured the tea and a contingent of young men from the German fraternity at the University. Faÿ was a charming host and a mesmerizing conversationalist who spoke with ease, self confidence, and good humor . . . [but] there was a sad sense of mystery about him." From personal correspondence with author.

46. Mattioli, *Gonzague de Reynold*, 14.

47. Ibid., 14.

48. W. D. Dinges, "Marcel Lefebvre," in *New Catholic Encyclopedia* (Detroit: Thomson Gale, 2003), 8:448.

49. Marcel Lefebvre, *Open Letter to Confused Catholics* (Angelus Press, 2007).

50. Ecône was established in 1970. According to Jean-Marie Savioz, before founding Ecône, Lefebvre also created a *maison d'étude* (study center) in Fribourg at the initiative of Faÿ. Jean-Marie Savioz, "Essai historique sur la fondation de la Fraternité sacerdotale Saint Pie X par Mgr Lefebvre et sur l'installation de son séminaire à Ecône en Valais (1969–1972)," unpublished undergraduate thesis (Mémoire de Licence) in Theology, Fribourg (1995), 35.

51. Rachel Donadio, "Healing Schism, Pope Risks Another," *New York Times* (January 26, 2009).

52. Bernard Tissier de Mallerais, *Marcel Lefebvre, The Biography* (Arlington, Va.: Angelus Press, 2004), 445.

53. Bernard Faÿ, *L'église de Judas?* (Paris: Plon, 1970), 26, 39.

54. Ibid., 26, 32–33.

55. Ibid., 42.

56. Ibid., 28.

57. Alain Clément, "Bernard Faÿ est mort," *Le Monde* (January 4, 1979): 30.

58. Editor's preface to "As Gertrude Stein Reviews a Book on President Roosevelt," *Kansas City Star* (January 20, 1934): 5.

59. Archbishop Lefebvre, cited in Angelus (Information Bulletin for Ecône). Available online at: http://www.angelusonline.org/modules.php?op=modload&name=News&file=article&sid=3275&mode=thread&order=0&thold=0. The Church of Saint Nicolas de Chardonnet is the seat of the Society of Saint Pius X in Paris; as recently as 2009 it celebrated a requiem mass on the anniversary of the death of Louis XVI.

60. Georges Narcy [pseudonym of René Rancoeur], "Bernard Faÿ," *Aspects de la France* (January 25, 1979).

61. D. I., "Bernard Faÿ Wieder Aufgetaucht," *National-Zeitung* 308 (July 7, 1959); Gérard Glasson, "Présences suspectes," *La Gruyère* 54 (May 14, 1959); and "Paladin de la franc-maçonnerie?" *La Gruyère* 59 (May 26, 1959).

62. Union des Etudiants Juifs en Suisse, "Resolution," May 30, 1960. Unpublished draft found in IB JUNA-Archiv, Dossier 561, Archiv für Zeitgeschichte, Zürich.

63. Kathy Casey, interview with Alex Erik Pfingsttag, Fribourg, June 24, 2008.

64 Bernard Faÿ, "Mise au point," *La Suisse* 168 (June 16, 1960): 9.

65. See Janet Malcolm, *Two Lives: Gertrude and Alice* (New Haven, Conn.: Yale University Press, 2007), 74.

66. Linda Simon, *The Biography of Alice B. Toklas* (Lincoln: University of Nebraska Press, 1991), 293.

67. Toklas writes Faÿ on March 10, 1958: "When you come to Paris I shall ask you to tell me how we can pray for her [Stein]—for my father confessor gives me no such hope. It would be a great comfort to be able to include her in a mass and Denise Azam says I can pray for her—but is that not catholic as well as Catholic? You will tell me when you get here." From the unpublished correspondence of Gertrude Stein and Bernard Faÿ, Vincent Faÿ collection.

68. Alice Toklas letter to Bernard Faÿ, June 1960 (?), in *Staying on Alone*, 383.

69. Author interview with Vincent Faÿ, Paris, July 21, 2002.

INDEX

GENDER AND CULTURE

A Series of Columbia University Press

Nancy K. Miller and Victoria Rosner, Series Editors

Carolyn G. Heilbrun (1926–2003) and Nancy K. Miller, Founding Editors

Paris, France 1940
Wars I Have Seen

Barbara Will 2000
See Benjamin re Mechanical Reproduction
free masonry - google

Wars I Have Seen
transition feb 1935, 11
76 Whitman (google)
Order Will's first book on Stein
Feb '34 debut of Four Saints in Three Acts 90
1940 Atlantic Monthly The Winner Loses
See Sontag Under the Sign of Saturn
71-105 "Fascinating Fascism"
get Hemingway - Bas